# BEYOND THE MALE MYTH

# BEYOND THE MALE MYTH

## What Women Want to Know about Men's Sexuality

### A Nationwide Survey

## Anthony Pietropinto, M.D. and Jacqueline Simenauer

NYT
Times
BOOKS

Manufactured in the United States of America. Published
simultaneously in Canada by Optimum Publishing Company Limited, Montreal.

Designed by Beth Tondreau

**Library of Congress Cataloging in Publication Data**

Pietropinto, Anthony.
  Beyond the male myth.

  Includes index.
  1. Men—United States—Sexual behavior.
  2. Men—United States—Attitudes. I. Simenauer,
Jacqueline, joint author. II. Title.
HQ28.P54 1977   301.41′76′320973   77–79036
ISBN 0–8129–0726–4

To our spouses,

Joy Ann Pietropinto
and
Peter Simenauer,

whose understanding, patience, and help sustained us through the writing of this book.

# Acknowledgments

In undertaking a survey of this scope, we were immeasurably aided by many of our friends, colleagues, and loved ones, and we would like to express our appreciation for their contributions.

We would like to thank first Elaine Piller Congress, M.S.W., for her professional assistance in planning the survey, her input throughout the course of the work, and especially for her conscientious and capable handling of additional responsibilities as clinic coordinator of the Lutheran Medical Center Mental Health Program during the periodic absences of the medical director that this book required.

We are deeply indebted as well to clinical psychologists Evelyn Sanchez, John C. Fitzpatrick, and Giuseppe Costantino, Ph.D., and to Janet Walsh, R.N., for their expertise in the development of our questionnaire. Our thanks also to mental health workers Jill Hansen, Gail Perez Rogers, Carmen Roman, and Linda Trotman for guiding us in our determination of what women wanted to know about male sexuality.

We would like to express our appreciation to the members of the Union Center for Women, Brooklyn, New York, and particularly to Donna DeQuattro, coordinator, and Marilyn Tsilimparis, chairperson of the mental health task force, for their help in our preliminary survey of women's greatest concerns about men.

We are grateful to Cornelius A. Szabo for the time he spent in sharing his expert knowledge of computer technology and his guidance in our initial approach to the survey.

A special note of thanks goes to Peggy McGarry and Dr. Leonard Learner at Crossley Surveys for their invaluable help in planning and executing the survey.

Also an acknowledgment of appreciation to Doris Walfield, Helena DePaola and Bert Himelstein for their assistance and time.

Our gratitude is extended to our editor, Roger Jellinek, for his perceptive criticisms and ongoing cooperation in the transformation of a survey into a book—and for supporting our attempts to bring something creative and original to a scientific study.

A loving thank you goes to Rita Diana Pietropinto for cooperation, patience, and sacrifice beyond the demands usually placed on a six-year-old.

We would like to include a special remembrance of Tillie and Harry Himelstein and express the depth of our gratitude for the inspirational legacy of love they left behind.

And, finally, we want to give thanks to the 4,066 men who participated in our survey; we shall never see their faces or hear their names, but we have nevertheless come to know them. Without them, this book would not have been possible.

ANTHONY PIETROPINTO, M.D.
JACQUELINE SIMENAUER

# Contents

# BEYOND THE MALE MYTH

# Introduction:

# In Search of Man

DON JUAN: Your weak side, my diabolic friend, is that you have always been a gull: you take Man at his own valuation. Nothing would flatter him more than your opinion of him. He loves to think of himself as bold and bad. He is neither one nor the other . . .

—GEORGE BERNARD SHAW, *Man and Superman*

Don Juan and the Devil, two of the world's most fascinating male myths, are arguing about Man, the most enigmatic myth of all.

Modern man has been depicted in a variety of ways, most of them unflattering, all of them sketchy and simplistic. The TV situation comedies portray him as an emasculated, uninspired bungler, while the adventure shows cast him as a cold-blooded, violent hunter of men and cynical predator of women. The feminists accuse him of being exploitative, egotistical, and obsessed with indiscriminate sexual gratification. Writers of popular psychology books describe him as uncommunicative, insensitive, and driven by machismo. These generalizations are highly dubious given the effects on men wrought by the sexual revolution and the Women's Liberation Movement.

But myths often contain as much truth as fiction, which is why they persist. In the case of myths about male behavior, women or even men themselves sometimes have a psychological need to view males in a certain way, even if that view is no longer accurate or never was true to begin with. Even if the myths have a certain validity, they often contradict one another, and, as in a Homeric battle between centaurs and demigods, wage war among themselves.

To go beyond the male myth, we must reach the real-life male

3

behind the myth, apprehend him in the midst of his ongoing transitions, and explore his thoughts and feelings in all their complexity.

This book proposes to do precisely that. It is based on a study of more than 4,000 American males encompassing all age groups, geographical areas, and social strata. To avoid the past errors of authors with preconceived prejudices and biased samples, we have based our findings on the words of the men themselves. We have worked, not with typical patients or typical magazine readers, but with typical men. If our readers do not agree with our interpretations or conclusions, they may formulate their own from the data we have presented. We will draw conclusions and give advice and guidance for the reader to take, to leave, or to modify—advice from a male psychiatrist who directs a community mental health clinic that services several thousand individuals from all walks of life with all sorts of problems and from a female journalist who has served as psychiatric editor for a weekly national newspaper and has spent years interviewing top experts on every aspect of psychotherapy and human behavior.

This is a book about male sexuality, but not just about sex. We do not feel that sex can be separated from concepts of love, dependency, marriage, self-image, and life goals; neither, apparently, did the men we surveyed. If we had limited our questions to what men do and how they do it, rather than what they want and how they feel, we would have produced a far different and less valuable book.

Our advice is directed primarily at women; to help them use this new knowledge to enrich their relationships with friends, lovers, and husbands. But we believe that men, too, will profit from sharing the frank views and emotions of their colleagues across the country, and that the experience will encourage them to explore their own feelings more deeply.

This book required the cooperation of thousands of randomly selected men, and we were frankly apprehensive about their willingness to cooperate. Their candid answers demolished the myth of male reticence; many more myths would crumble by the end of our study.


## Modern Man—The Latest Mystery

While femininity was once synonymous with mystery, it is men who are the great mystery today. Women's ability to create new life caused men to regard them with awe, and, in ancient times, they assumed the roles of oracles and temple priestesses, guardians of sacred secrets. As late as the sixteenth-century, an English physician was executed for disguising himself as a woman so that he could witness the birth of a child, an event presided over only by midwives.

Psychoanalysis removed much of the mystery from women, though not in its early stages. Unabashedly chauvinistic, Sigmund Freud regarded women as nothing more than males who lack a penis; he stated: "I cannot escape the notion (though I hesitate to give it expression) that for woman the level of what is ethically normal is different from what it is in men. . . . We must not allow ourselves to be deflected from such conclusions by the denial of feminists, who are anxious to force us to regard the two sexes as completely equal in position and worth." And Harry Stack Sullivan, one of the most noted analysts who followed Freud, is reputed to have limited his treatment to men because he simply could not understand women.

The past decade, however, has witnessed the rending of ancient veils by psychiatrists, feminists, and writers who, in an attempt to understand the changes being wrought in women by the liberation movement and the sexual revolution, proceeded to probe women's past and present sexual and emotional responses with unrelenting thoroughness. Women seemed astonishingly eager to participate in their psychic vivisection, pouring forth reams of data about their orgasms, fantasies, frustrations, hang-ups, dreams, and fears. Thanks to their candor, courage, and exacting self-exploration, we have learned much about women and their role in a rapidly changing society. After literally centuries of reading what men had to say about female sexuality, what woman was all about, what she desired, how she functioned, and why she failed, we finally had woman's own feelings, needs, and responses. Yet it was not enough; we were not much closer toward resolving the gaps in understanding and communication between the sexes. We still lacked half the pieces in the puzzle.

In all of man's obsessive ruminations and scientific hypotheses about female sexuality, he had cleverly avoided writing about himself. Compared with the present literature about women, the data on men is appallingly scarce. Since Kinsey's study of sexual behavior in the human male a generation ago in 1948, no one has taken a long, objective look at the American male. Even the Kinsey report is nothing more than a compilation of sexual chronology, preferences, and deviations that adds little to our understanding of man's intellectual and emotional orientation to his own sexuality.

Why have men been so neglected? Partly, because just as women have been stereotyped as mysterious and unfathomable, men have been categorized as just the opposite—straightforward and uncomplex. It is this attitude that has led to such sweeping and unflattering generalizations as "Men are only after one thing" or "All men are animals." Even animals change their behavior when their environment changes, and the increased availability of sexual partners for men has not been gained without accompanying new problems: increased sophistication in women, pressure to perform well in bed, lack of commitment from women, new definitions of virtue and promiscuity, and reassessment of concepts of masculinity. These new situations have aroused new feelings and attitudes which might be suppressed from consciousness but are available for the asking.

Why hasn't anyone asked? In exploring sexuality, the most bilateral of all phenomena, why have recent investigations been so unilateral? Part of the problem lies in the nature of the researchers. Men would much rather probe women for conflicts and foibles rather than their brethren in a process dangerously akin to self-confrontation. As for female investigators, it has taken women long enough to begin examining themselves instead of accepting what men write about them—they are to be commended for their courage in self-exploration and forbearingly excused if they have not yet had the time to turn the tables completely enough to research their former researchers.

But the main problem in learning more about men lies with the quarry, rather than the pursuers. Most books on human behavior are written by psychiatrists and other psychotherapists who base much of their observations and theories on their experience with patients in clinical situations. While we do not support the generalization that men are totally uncommunicative and afraid to confront their emotions and vulnerabilities, it is true that women turn to therapy more often than men. Women tend to be acutely aware of their sexual anxieties, conflicts, and frustrations, and will spew them in such profusion that the therapist will often feel overwhelmed in attempting to stanch the flow sufficiently to enable his patients to deal with this material in coherent fashion. Men seem less complex only because most of the time nothing is coming out. The therapeutic work is infinitely slower because men are not only reluctant to talk about sex, but actually fail to confront their feelings about it. Many of them regard their genitals as detached objects, independent of their thoughts and emotions, and their sexual partners become the equally detached targets of their genitals. The therapist's task with male patients is generally to awaken them to the inseparable association between sex and psyche.

Our experience in a large psychiatric clinic has made the magnitude of the problem even clearer, for one becomes aware not of dozens of patients, but of thousands. While no single therapist could become acquainted with every patient on the rolls, the opportunity for daily interaction with thirty other therapists soon makes the recurrent, urgent problems apparent. Repeatedly, clinical conferences focused on women, for female patients were thought to have more complex problems; they were given more frequent sessions, kept in therapy longer, and organized into groups, headed by female therapists. And the female therapists came back to the conference table and said, "They talk about men—how mean they are, how unreliable, how frustrating!" The male patients did not agonize over failed relationships; they either got drunk or moved on to the next woman. And slowly a light dawned over the conference table. Maybe women were treated so intensively because only they would cooperate. And while female therapists could share their knowledge of women from their sessions with voluble clients, their readings in *Ms.* and *Cosmopolitan,* and (we suspect) their own varied love-lives, the males could supply nothing but their own subjective experience—which they were not inclined to share.

Women adapt more easily to psychotherapy than do men. Some feminists, such as psychologist Phyllis Chesler, see the preponderance of women receiving various forms of psychiatric treatment as the result of being conditioned by men to regard their natural feelings of frustration as "illness" and they deplore women's acceptance of ersatz "mothering" from therapists in the absence of more genuine sources of emotional gratification. Other therapists, such as Theodore Rubin, praise women for being more self-accepting, more in touch with their feelings, and better able to ask for professional help. Whatever one's analysis of the situation, it is unwise to draw conclusions about men solely from one's clinical experience with male patients, as Dr. Rubin does, since the "average" male does not present himself for therapy to begin with.

We can learn much from male and female patients since their conflicts reflect a variety of familial and cultural influences that exert pressures on their self-images and relationships with the opposite sex; while we may be sure that many nonpatients are confronting the same difficulties, we cannot be sure whether they are managing perfectly well or are too insensitive, unsophisticated, or defensive to seek therapy. But a cardiologist would never write a book about how the average heart functions based entirely on examination of people with cardiac complaints; he would then be likely to conclude that the heart was a very inefficient and impractical organ. Yet, while the cardiologist has the opportunity to examine hundreds of normal hearts, psychotherapists rarely, if ever, discuss feelings and attitudes at length with people who do not have some sort of perceived emotional problem. A psychiatrist's office is no more the proper place to gather information about the average man than an operating room would be to gather information about healthy internal organs.

So, the only feasible way to conduct a study of the average male is to seek him out in his natural habitat. Inviting him to come to you involves another basic error. Suppose a cardiologist offered free physical examinations of the heart—who do you suppose would show up? Most likely, people who felt they had reason to be concerned about the status of their hearts, not the average fellow who does not see his dentist twice a year unless his teeth hurt. Or, suppose a newspaper invited readers to write in their opinions of their city—who would respond? Chiefly people who had grievances to voice, not those who were perfectly happy with their hometown; also, not those who don't read newspapers, who don't like to write letters, who put off nonessential projects indefinitely, or who have more pressing demands on their time. Yet Shere Hite, citing her master's thesis "which involved a critique of the application of scientific method to the social sciences," proceeds to write up studies based on responses from volunteers willing to write lengthy answers to 58-item questionnaires, and applies her conclusions to the overall population. When confronted with the nonrepresentative nature of her sample (only 38 percent of her women married, 21 percent with postgraduate education, etc.), she murmurs vaguely, "My book is a study, not a survey."

We were determined not to fall into the initial error of writing a book about typical men without the benefit of information from typical men. We agreed with Alexander Pope that "the proper study of mankind is man"—not psychiatric patients, organization members, or letter writers. The proper study should be a survey, properly done.

We especially hoped this book would do a lot for women. We wanted it to give them a psychological insight into the workings of men's minds and how they view women, to tell them about the kind of women men look for, and turn away from, the women that make men nervous, and the kind they would want or reject as potential wives. We wanted information that would help women to communicate properly with men, to express feelings in a noncritical way, and to avoid the things that trigger off unconscious threats in men's minds. We wanted to help women attract and hold men, to help their mates give them more pleasure, and to enrich the sex lives of both partners through increased emotional understanding. We also wanted to dispel the many misconceptions about men that often worry a woman needlessly and even impede her relationships by causing her to avoid natural actions that she fears will turn a man off.

We wanted to give men the opportunity to share their experiences and philosophies with one another. Through this book, a man will be able to compare his feelings not only with men in general, but particularly with those in his own age group, occupation, and marital status. We wanted to focus on some of the areas of conflict in men's relationships with women, both the age-old ones and the new ones brought about by the social changes that are sweeping our world.

Since we were addressing ourselves particularly to what women wanted to know about men, it seemed only fitting to find out from women themselves what they most wanted to learn. We obviously did not intend to do one mammoth survey to prepare for another one, but we felt that even a modest sampling of women's opinions would be immensely helpful. And so, we prepared a list of 96 potential questions and presented them to a number of women from various backgrounds, both working women and housewives, and asked them to rate each question on a scale of 0 to 3, giving the highest ratings to the ones which they would most like to have answered by men. Our raters included female therapists from the mental health clinic whom we asked to rate the questions not only in terms of their own preferences, but also as they felt the selection would benefit their female patients seeking to better their understanding of men. These professionals included mental health workers who dealt primarily with unemployed mothers of large families receiving welfare, as well as psychologists and psychiatric social workers who treated women from all social strata. Because of their training and broad experience, we especially valued the opinion of these consultants and felt they could guide us as well as a larger sample of randomly selected women.

The results of this preliminary poll indicated something we had already suspected. Women were as much or more interested in men's feelings about women and sex than they were in what men actually did. Thus, we selected questions about men's ideals, opinions of women, preferences, and turn-offs, instead of questions about how often men were having intercourse or how often they masturbated. The women were given the opportunity to write in other questions which they felt should be included, and, for example, so many mentioned birth control that we added this item to our final questionnaire.

We wanted to survey at least 4,000 men because, according to statistical principles, a sample that large is equivalent to an infinitely greater population. In other words, if we had gone on to survey 10,000 or 100,000, or 4,000,000 men, the percentages who responded in various ways would not be expected to differ significantly from the results obtained from 4,000. This holds true, of course, only if the sample is a truly balanced one, representative of the entire nation. Surveying 4,000 New Yorkers, 4,000 construction workers, or 4,000 graduate students would not give a valid picture of American men in general. Thus, a magazine survey might yield 30,000 responses, but unless it could be shown that those readers were representative of Americans as a whole, the findings would be valid only for a population that resembled the majority of the readership in age, education, occupation, and other variables.

The final questionnaire that was presented to the 4,066 men nationwide consisted of two parts. The first was a 40-item questionnaire of the multiple-choice type, in which the subject could check the answer that most coincided with his feelings. These answers could be readily tabulated and reported as percentages by computer analysis, and would ensure representation of every man who participated. The second part of the survey material comprised a total of 32 questions requiring handwritten answers. Since these answers would tend to be highly subjective and individualized, it would not be possible to tabulate them by computer, and their value would lie in our being exposed to a variety of original responses from which we could draw typical and atypical examples, and identify, if not quantify, trends in male thinking today. We called these our "essay questions," the term used in school for examination questions that required a written answer instead of the simpler check-off response. We did not ask our subjects to attempt to answer all 32 essays, feeling this would tax their patience; if only a small percentage of subjects was willing to complete the questionnaire, the whole study would become meaningless. Therefore we divided the 32 questions into eight forms containing 4 questions each. Every subject received one of these forms, along with the 40-item multiple-choice sheet. Thus, all 4,066 subjects answered the multiple-choice questions, while we had 500 potential responses to each of the "essays." Many of the "essays" elaborated on questions already covered in the multiple-choice section, thus giving us both numerical data on preferences and subjective reasons for these preferences.

The survey questionnaire underwent several revisions before we took it to the men of America, and again we consulted with a panel of mental health professionals, adding male psychologists to the group of female therapists previously involved. Question by question, we laboriously searched for ambiguities and strove to make each item as meaningful and productive as possible. We wanted a final questionnaire that would confront the crucial issues openly, but which would not intimidate a man or otherwise discourage his full cooperation. With the aid of our colleagues, we, as our many subjects would do soon afterward, settled on our choices. Following are the questions we posed.

# Part I—The Multiple-Choice

The following 40 questions were answered by all of the 4,066 men who participated in the study. We are presenting here only the questions, not the 3 to 10 (6 was average) responses from which they could choose. The complete survey results are presented in the Appendix. The first seven questions (household or marital status, section of the United States, age, race, schooling, income, and job) covered basic personal information which allowed the computer to tabulate responses for various age, racial and occupational groups, married men versus single, etc., along with the overall response percentages. The other 33 questions explored men's preferences, practices, and opinions. More than one answer could be selected, although most men chose only one response. The computer was able to report what percentage of men failed to answer a given question: this was generally under 2 percent, exceeded 3 percent in only 4 questions, and reached a high of 8 percent for one question. The answers which were presented as possible responses to each question will be found in the sections of the book that cover that particular question.

The questions in the order presented here (and grouped by the chapters that deal with them) deal initially with men's physical preferences, then their attitudes toward sex and contemporary women, communication with women, mutual orgasms, negative aspects of sex, attitudes toward love and marriage, fidelity and cheating, and the realm of fantasy:

1. What is your current household status?
2. In what section of the United States do you live?
3. What is your age?
4. What is your racial background?
5. What is your total amount of schooling?
6. What was the approximate total income of your household before taxes in 1976?
7. What type of job do you currently hold?

8. What sexual activity gives you the most pleasure during foreplay?
9. What could your partner do to make you more excited?

10. What would you most like to do more often?
11. With what type of partner do you usually engage in sex?
12. Ideally, how often would you want intercourse?

13. How do you feel about sex?

14.   How have your feelings about sex changed over the past five years?

15.   What do you consider the ideal sex life for yourself?

16.   How do you feel about today's women?

17.   How do you feel about having sex with older women?

18.   Do you tell the woman you have sex with what you'd like her to do?

19.   Who should take responsibility for birth control?

20.   Do you deliberately try to delay your orgasm and for how long?

21.   When does a sex act end?

22.   How do you usually feel after climaxing?

23.   What percent of the time does your partner have an orgasm during intercourse?

24.   What percent of the time does the woman you're having sex with have an orgasm either *before* or *after* sexual intercourse?

25.   What type of woman makes you feel most nervous?

26.   What is the most unpleasant aspect of sex for you?

27.   What most irritates you during sex?

28.   When are you likely to be so "turned off" you can't complete a sex act?

29.   How do you feel about having intercourse during partner's period?

30.   How do you feel about stimulating a woman's sexual organs with your mouth?

31.   How do you feel about being in love?

32.   What type of woman would you most want for a long-term relationship?

33.   How do you feel about hugging and kissing without it leading to sexual intercourse?

34.   How would you feel when a love affair ends?

35.   What else besides love would be your main reason for getting married?

36.   What sort of sexual experience would you prefer a wife to have had prior to marriage?

37.   Have you ever cheated on your wife or steady girl friend?

38.   What is your attitude towards cheating on your wife or steady girl friend?

39.   What would be most likely to tempt you to cheat?

40.   What sort of thoughts do you have during intercourse or masturbation?

If you tried to predict as you read these questions what the response of most men would be, we think you're in for a few surprises.

# Part II—The "Essays"

Along with the 40 questions above, which required only a check beside the selected answer, each man received a sheet with four questions requiring a handwritten answer. As presented below, they deal, like the multiple-choice questions, with matters of physical preferences, attitudes towards sex and female partners, areas of communication, orgasms, "turn-offs," love, marriage, cheating, and fantasies:

What turns you on about a woman? What things about her body, her personality, and the way she acts would you find exciting?
What could a woman do to excite you more? What would you prefer her to wear, what kind of atmosphere do you like, and how would you like her to act?
How important is foreplay to you? What do you enjoy doing and what do you do to please your sexual partner?
Do your orgasms differ from time to time, and how? How could your orgasms be improved? How do you feel after an orgasm? Do you try to delay them, and why?

How do you like a woman to act during sex? Do you want her to be passive, or to do various things to you? What would give you the most pleasure?
What makes a woman a good lover? Should she be aggressive, a little shy, tender, eager to try new things? How much experience should she have had?

How do you feel about sex? What does it mean to you? How important is it and how would you compare it with other things in your life?
Have your feelings about sex changed over the years? Do you find it as interesting and important as ever? Are you less inhibited and

more adventurous, or have you become more conservative—and why?

What would be the *ideal* sexual relationship for a man? Would you prefer marriage, steadily dating one woman, having a variety of sexual partners—and why?

How do you feel about today's women? Have they changed for the better or worse, and why? Do they make good wives and mothers and why?

When do you feel most manly—when you are making love to a woman, socializing with other men, competing in sports, on the job? When do you feel least manly?

What do you think makes a man a good lover—understanding women's needs, performing well in bed, making a woman feel secure? What's most important and why?

Do you feel that you communicate well with women? Can you make them understand the way you feel? If not, what do you think the problem is?

What do you find hard to understand about women? What would you like to know about them? Do you understand them well, or are they a mystery to you?

What do you think women want most from men, and why? Do you think they want love, security, children, a home, sex—and which do you think is most important to them?

What do you think women don't understand about men? What advice would you give women to help them understand men better?

How do you think most women feel about sex in general? Do they use it mainly to please men, to get a husband? How interested do you think women really are in sex?

How would you feel if the woman you are having sex with fails to have an orgasm? What would you do to help her have an orgasm?

What things about a woman turn you off? What things about her body, her personality and the way she acts would make you lose interest in her?

What do you think men want most from women—sex, a good home-life, companionship, love? What is most important to men?

How do you feel about being in love? Do you prefer to be in love with your sexual partners, how important is love in your life, and what does love mean to you?

What do you think men look for in choosing a wife? What qualities did you, or would you, look for? What's most important—brains, looks, sincerity, being a good homemaker, a good mother—and why?

Under what circumstances would you like to be hugged and kissed without it leading to intercourse? Do you find hugging childish or unmanly, or is it something you crave at times?

How would you be likely to feel if a love affair of yours broke up? How would it affect your feelings, your work performance, your sex life, and your relationship with women?

How do you feel about marriage? Do most men want it? Is it becoming old-fashioned or is it as important as ever? What do you think are its advantages and disadvantages?

If you are married, would you rather be single, and why? If you are single, would you rather be married, and why?

Do you feel that married sex gets boring and why? If you are single, how do you picture it? If you are married, what's your sex life like —had it become routine or more enjoyable with time and why? Did you enjoy sex before you were married?

Should a woman tell a man about her past sex life? Do you want a woman to be experienced, and what kind of experience should she have? How much experience would you want a wife to have?

What are the qualities that make a good husband—being a good provider, sensitivity, being a good parent, a good lover? What's most important? Are you or would you be a good husband, and why?

Have you ever thought about cheating on your wife or girl friend? Did you, and under what circumstances? What conditions might tempt you to cheat?

What are your favorite sexual fantasies during masturbation? Do you think about famous sex symbols, about far-out sexy things, or about your usual sexual partner? Do you ever fantasize during intercourse, and what about?

Have you ever had a "dream girl"? What is she or what was she like?

While the responses to these questions were too individualized to be tabulated in the manner of the multiple-choice questions, they were really the "heart" of our study, for they put us in touch with the human beings behind the cold computer-generated statistics. We have included the "voices" of our subjects throughout the book so that the reader may share the gratifying experience of learning firsthand the feelings, opinions, and hopes of thousands of men throughout the country.

# Launching the Quest

Having finally decided what we wanted to ask men across the country, the problem now was how to reach them. We decided the only truly reliable way would be through the services of a large and trustworthy research service organization. We selected Crossley Surveys, Incorporated, in New York City, a firm founded over 50 years ago for private marketing research and public opinion polling.

The research firm then set up and printed our questionnaire in a practical form, and after a brief test run in Long Island, New York, to ensure that the questions were comprehensible, the questionnaires were shipped out to testing sites in 18 states and Washington, D.C. In spite of the success of the trial run in Long Island, we were far from confident about the willingness of men across the nation to respond to so intimate a questionnaire. The research firm had never undertaken a study on such a complex and personal subject as male sexuality, and was as much in the dark about the eventual outcome as the designers of the survey. Like everyone, we had been exposed to the generalization that men are uncommunicative, unwilling to admit to feelings, unable to share, and impatient with things that take up their time with no direct and immediate purpose. Having found this to be true to some extent with motivated patients, we feared it would be even more true of "average" men. We shared the assumption that the average man lived with the "machismo" ideal and would never present himself to a complete stranger in any way that would indicate vulnerability; he would boast and lie, even to himself, or, at best, refuse to admit that he had any misgivings or problems regarding his sexuality. Of course, we tried to avoid phrasing any questions in a way that would make him seem weak, ineffectual, or callous. Still, more than once, we silently murmured, "If only this were a study on women!"

We felt from the outset that complete anonymity was critical. This not only meant that no one would know the name of the respondent, but also that the respondent would be assured that his completed questionnaire would not be seen by any of the personnel at the testing site. We gave each subject an envelope into which he would place the completed questionnaire and drop it in a sealed box.

As for motivating subjects to cooperate, we took a cue from Kinsey, who in conducting his classic study of sexual behavior in the human male, published in 1948, said, "The chief appeal has been altruistic —an invitation to contribute to basic scientific research, an opportunity to help others by sharing one's experience." Since we are dealing with a more sexually sophisticated and uninhibited population than Kinsey's, due in a large part to the efforts of Kinsey and other researchers over the past three decades, we were able to use a forthright and honest approach, without melodramatic appeals and exaggerated claims about the study's ultimate importance to mankind. Each respondent was given, along with his questionnaire, the following printed statement:

## Your Opinion Is Important

March 1977

Dear Sir:

This survey is an important and serious professional effort to gather information on current attitudes toward sex. The questions on the survey are what women want to know about men. "Why ask me?" you might say. Your participation is needed so that your anonymous opinion can be included with the opinions of several thousand others across the United States.

You are being asked to take this questionnaire and fill it out in privacy. When you have checked all the answers, place the questionnaire in the envelope and drop it in the sealed box we have provided. Your answers will not be seen by anyone at this location and since you are not asked to sign anything there will be no way to identify the responses with you.

In the past, surveys have been done on this subject but there has never been a survey like this one which will cover several thousand men, across the country, from all walks of life. It is important that you participate so that the final results include men like yourself. It will only take a few minutes of your time. Why not have your opinion counted?

Thank you.

Readily enlisting the cooperation of people approached is extremely important. If only exhibitionistic or very uninhibited persons participate, the findings will reflect the practices and opinions of only the most liberal members of society. Even today, people tend to attack Kinsey's findings by saying, "What kind of a person is going to sit down with a stranger and discuss the intimate details of his sex life.

*I* certainly wouldn't!" When Morton Hunt reported on a nationwide survey of males and females in *Sexual Behavior in the 1970's* (a study that dealt primarily with sexual practices and value judgments, such as "masturbation is wrong"), subjects were randomly contacted by telephone and asked to participate in small, private panel discussions; Hunt states, "About one out of five agreed, a rate considered normal for opinion surveys using this technique." (Hunt's subjects were asked to fill out "anonymous questionnaires" only after they had engaged in extensive group discussion and were "unwilling to walk out on the group"—a somewhat devious way of obtaining a "voluntary" questionnaire.) Our research firm estimated that half of the men approached by the field agents agreed to participate—a phenomenal percentage in view of other studies.

The men were approached primarily in shopping centers and malls, as well as office building complexes, tennis clubs, college campuses, airports, and bus depots. The communities in which the testing sites were located varied in affluence, ensuring that our sample would include ample representation from all income groups. Since people travel to shopping centers and the other sites, we were able to survey men from more localities than if we used sites visited only by a specific community. Since the experienced field agents (we can't call them interviewers, as they didn't interview anyone) could see prospective subjects as they approached, they could select representative numbers of younger and older men and those of different racial backgrounds.

The men were generally willing to take about 20 minutes to answer the questionnaire. Men accompanied by their wives were, understandably, more reluctant to answer the questionnaire. Men seemed equally receptive to approaches by male or female field agents, we learned, although one male agent in Long Island, New York, was bluntly asked by a prospective subject, "Are you some kind of pervert?"

Difficulties encountered in running the study were trivial compared with what Kinsey confronted 30 years ago. Kinsey faced threats of suits for practicing medicine without a license (he was a professor of zoology), police interference, the dismissal of a teacher who cooperated with him, and threats of being fired from his own position. Our investigators had to retreat from only three sites because of opposition: one in Kansas City, a suburban community in Oregon, and a shopping center in the South. The opposition came, not from the citizenry, but from the operators of the shopping malls who feared offending customers or from husbands of female field agents who objected to their wives' approaching strange men with a proposition of such nature as ours. The research firm had prudently planned alternate sites for every location and therefore did not sacrifice any area of the country as part of the study.

A few of the men asked to take home the handwritten portion of the questionnaire, and returned it the following day. Each participant, in addition to answering four "essay" questions at the testing site, received a sheet of four additional "essay" questions with a postage-paid envelope to complete at home, if he wished. The replies we received by mail were usually among the most thorough and interesting, and though only one subject in ten sent them in, this was a higher rate than we expected.

When we finally combed the long-awaited data that spewed from the computers, we learned that today's men were essentially in agreement on most of the issues we raised; many of their views, however, were not what we would have predicted and we found that much of the extant male lore, though promulgated widely as psychological fact, belongs more properly to the realm of modern mythology.

We will frequently be pointing out differences in response rates between various groups—old men versus young, black men versus white, uneducated versus highly educated, etc. It is most important, however, to keep the total response pattern in mind; for example, on a particular question, 20 percent of blacks might show a chauvinistic attitude compared with 10 percent of whites. While this would indicate a slightly stronger trend toward chauvinism among the blacks, it must be remembered that 80 percent of blacks did not show such an attitude. It is rare that two subgroups will be found to be at complete odds on an issue.

Finally, let us say we were amazed and gratified by the directness with which men answered our questionnaire. Out of the thousands of handwritten responses, only two rejected the questionnaire with obscene language and one respondent mailed in a blank answer sheet. We received one form via the mail that had been completed by a subject's wife, who criticized the survey, doubted we were secure in our own gender identity, and concluded with: "I thought you women's libbers had better things to do." We suspect she thought we were Shere Hite.

Almost all of the men, however, answered our questions with refreshing candor and seemed to share the feelings of an army sergeant who volunteered his name and address and said, "If I knew what magazine this was for, I'd answer at length and mail it to you. If you want to, you can let me know: my address is:—————. I'd like to know what magazine this is, and I'd probably buy it, as it seems to have a good attitude towards life."

As soon as the handwritten replies began pouring into New York from across the country, we knew that the American male was indeed a complex, sensitive creature with definite feelings, attitudes, and ideals, once he doffs his armor. Perhaps he would prove to be a knight, perhaps a knave; but, in any case, at the end of our quest, we knew we would find a man.

# The Power to Turn Men On

DON JUAN: I came to believe that in her voice was all the music of the song, in her face all the beauty of the painting, and in her soul all the emotion of the poem.

—GEORGE BERNARD SHAW, *Man and Superman*

The "turn-on" is where it all begins. It is the ticket of admission to the wide arena of sexuality, and as such is understandably sought by every woman interested in heterosexual activities ranging from innocent flirtation to marriage. Some women seem to radiate this power, drawing men to them like moths to a flame. Others focus it selectively like a radar beam, enticing one man out of an otherwise oblivious crowd. No matter how casual his demeanor, the charmed man cannot help conveying the attitude that he finds the woman interesting and appealing not just as another person, but specifically as a female. From the point of the turn-on, the relationship may progress to romance, to passion, even to marriage; without the turn-on, the encounter is no more than a polite interchange.

Hollywood called it "sex appeal," and it's hard to think of a better term for that elusive quality that men worship in women and women try to achieve through clothes, cosmetics, coiffures, and calisthenics. It's something that goes beyond beauty, beyond sexiness. It is more than the ability to arouse erotic desire in a man; "I wouldn't kick her out of bed" is one of the weakest compliments a man can pay a woman. It's the ability, perhaps, to inspire a man, to set in motion the romantic reveries, the awe of women, the physical excitement, and a genuine liking, all at once. It is the power to conjure

21

up all the magic that a man has found in women since puberty or even earlier.

Madison Avenue would have us believe that the whole secret is in grooming. A man, they tell us, cannot resist a head of smooth, shining hair, or the fragrance of an exotic perfume, or the glossy flame of the latest shade of lipstick. The men's magazines glorify the body, emphasizing the perfect set of measurements, long, trim legs, and the robust glow of youth. The feminists cynically claim that men are attracted to subservient, compliant women who will meet men's sexual demands and make few of their own, sexual or otherwise.

Yet it is readily apparent that many women succeed in attracting and holding men better than others who seem to be prettier, more expensively dressed, impeccably groomed, and desperate to please. It is this secret of female fascination that we tried to define, the essence of the turn-on that sparks a man's interest and keeps it burning.

## Mothers, Whores, and Lovers

"I like a responsive woman, one who tells me what she likes, one who is obviously turned on to me. I like a woman to touch me and want or come after me from time to time. I like tight-fitting tops and lacelike see-through nightgowns. I want a woman with company and a whore in bed."

Like the man quoted above, a number of the participants in the survey, in response to different questions, cited some variation of the old adage that a wife should be a lady in the living room, an economist in the kitchen, and a slut in bed. Some were lucky enough to have found such a woman; others apparently wound up with a lady in the kitchen, a slut in the living room, and an economist in bed. In addition to these maxim-quoters, many more men used the terms "whore" or "slut" to describe how they wanted or did not want their women to act. The concept of women as "whores" plays—or did once play—an important part in most men's view of sex, and may be a positive or negative factor in the all-important area of turn-ons.

Some men do not need much of a turn-on because they can respond sexually to almost any woman, regardless of her personality, mentality, and congeniality; and many men are capable of having sex with any woman they don't find wholly repugnant. While women are capable of having sex with any male at all, most of them will not be aroused by a man they do not find attractive. They are confounded by the ease with which a man can physically be aroused by so many different women. A man's ability to be aroused by a woman who might be expected to turn him off emotionally, such as a seedy prostitute or a hostile spouse, depends on his denial of the total woman; he approaches her as a series of body parts: an object rather than a person. He compartmentalizes; sex in one box, love in another. He does not find sex under these conditions as gratifying as a loving relationship, but he can manage it because he has been compartmentalizing since the dawn of his sexual awareness.

A woman's sexual awakening in puberty is a gradual one. It usually begins with complex romantic fantasies quite remote from any sensations in her pelvic organs, and her first intercourse is likely to be with a man she feels she truly loves. An adolescent male, on the other hand, suddenly notes a heightened sensitivity in his penis, erratic changes in its size, and its remarkable reactivity to almost any female in the vicinity—all of which is beyond his control. Sisters, and even his mother, are not exempted from such unwelcome sexual responses. This is more than the boy's conscious mind—already at odds with his independent organ—can bear, so he quickly divides his thoughts about women into two compartments: thoughts about mother (and similar taboo females) that are entirely nonsexual, and those about other women, which are sexual.

But here another problem arises. Any woman who is sensitive, sentimental, caring, or maternal in any way is likely to remind him of mother, and therefore she gets mentally relegated to the respected-but-not-coveted compartment. The only women who can remain securely in the category of potential sexual partners are those who are or can be imagined to be the opposite of a good mother—seductive, insincere, lustful, vulgar, bad—in short, prostitutes. So, fairly early in the sexual game, men develop what psychiatrists call the "prostitute-madonna complex." A mature man comes to realize that a sensitive, intelligent, caring woman can be desirable as a sexual partner, but the less well-adjusted man becomes sexually inhibited in the presence of a "good" woman and, because of his guilt, avoids her or must reduce her to a "prostitute," as he did all sexually desirable women in his early teens. We will be discussing this "prostitute-madonna" complex again because it affects most men's thinking to some extent in their relationship with women. It is important for a woman to remember that it is a part of normal psychosexual development for all men; and while most men get these troublesome feelings under control as they mature, the complex is not limited to highly neurotic men.

# Much Ado About Macho

An offshoot of the prostitute-madonna complex, though its roots are rarely acknowledged, is the machismo ethic. Though the word came into our language from the Spanish cultures, "machismo" or "macho" values have been as much a part of Anglo-Saxon cultures as they have in the Latin world. The meticulous Victorian banker might have seemed worlds apart from the thick-booted, pistol-toting Mexican guerrilla, but in both the Georgian mansion and the adobe hacienda, the same order prevailed: the man was master and made all decisions; the woman served his needs and acquiesced to his wishes. At the heart of the macho ethic lies a contempt for women. Even if such a man is a good provider, a nonviolent husband, and considerate in some of his ways, he definitely regards females as creatures inferior to males and dehumanizes them accordingly.

Since the feminine is equated with inferiority and weakness, the macho must appear masculine and unfeminine at all times. He dresses in leather and coarse denim, affects a tough swagger, never cries or appears emotional, denigrates artistic works, pursues rugged sports and physical activities, and modifies every noun with an obscene adjective. He regards women as "dumb cunts" with only one function, and moves quickly from partner to partner with no trace of emotional involvement.

Yet Archie Bunker is as macho as Arthur "Fonzie" Fonzarelli, though his middle-aged potbelly limits his typical activities to beer drinking at the local tavern, bullying his wife, and belittling the liberal views of his son-in-law and daughter. You don't need big muscles or an insatiable penis to be macho; if you believe women are basically weak, overemotional, impractical, untrustworthy, shallow, and nonintellectual, the black leather jacket is strictly optional.

There is one woman, however, whom the classical macho does not regard with contempt. Rather, he reveres her and will fight to the death any man who impugns her—and that is his mother. He reveres her as a saint. Sometimes, if she is compliant and fertile enough, the macho will treat his wife with the same devotion; he will cheat on her incessantly, of course, and will expect unquestioning gratification of all his desires, but the wife will be held in the highest esteem, as such a marvel of mechanically efficient servitude undoubtedly should be.

The macho's credo is based essentially not on his faulty perception of males, but on his perception of women as "whores." They are sexually desirable, but otherwise contemptible. They are objects, not people. He will not let himself view them as people, for if he ever gets to like or respect them, he will not be able to have them as sexual partners. He moves on quickly, before he can begin to really know the woman, or keeps her at a distance with his cynical, boorish behavior. His wife either receives similar treatment or is elevated to a position where any sexual activity is dutiful and unimaginative.

Like the prostitute-madonna complex, the macho problem will crop up repeatedly and will be discussed again. Most books on male sexuality discuss both these phenomena, but they never seem to connect the two. They somehow fail to realize that there cannot be a neurotic glorification of the masculine unless there is a correspondingly strong devaluation of the feminine. Such a strong contempt for females is not based on mere ideology, but rises from a desperate male need to protect his sexual functioning by preserving his primitive defense against anxiety and guilt, the prostitute-madonna complex.

## In the Beginning

For a woman, the stage of orgasm may well be the most important aspect of sex; it is certainly the most widely discussed and often elusive. For a man, the stage of arousal is the most important, for orgasms usually come easily and often more quickly than desired.

The turn-on may not be as simple as a pretty face or a nice figure, and it may be different things to different men. We had 4,066 different men. Here are some of their answers:

*Essay Question: What turns you on about a woman? What things about her body, her personality, and the way she acts would you find exciting?*

"A pretty face is nice but it's not *that* important. A soft warm body with lots of curves, soft round breasts. I like a woman with a sincere smile and lots of white teeth. I like a woman that acts a little naïve but also a little sexy at the same time, a quiet sort of woman not too bold and brassy, quiet, warm and sincere."

"Long dark hair, full lips, big boobs, shapely legs. Self-confidence and happy self-control. Carefree and adventurous. Able to play any social role as a great actress who knows who and what she really is: a special person, a fulfilled, aware individual."

"Decency, outgoing nature, pleasant to be friends with whether male or female, easygoing person with rare ability to honestly discuss your/her feelings/beliefs. Bodies, like minds, must not be messy and uncared for. Even a depraved body which is well cared for and well presented is excellent. Sense of humor is great asset."

"Small, but well-built. Good clothes sense, but not too 'trendy.' Friendly, warm, outgoing personality. Intelligent but not 'know-it-all'. Somewhat independent but still conscious of needing someone (me). Well-groomed appearance—knowledgeable of makeup, hairstyle. A good body: breasts, rump, legs, pretty but not necessarily beautiful facially."

"A woman can do almost anything in a female way and make herself attractive to a man. It's not what she does, but how she does it."

"First, the face and body and then her personality. A self-assured woman who knows herself is the greatest turn-on."

In *Understanding Your Man*, Dr. Theodore Isaac Rubin says that very often men tend to see and evaluate a woman on the basis of her looks, while women see men's looks for what they might represent (strength, fatherliness, wealth, etc.). This common oversimplification leads many women to an obsessive concern with their physical beauty, which, as we have learned from our survey, is irrelevant to most men. The replies from our subjects across the nation confirmed that attraction was based on a great deal more than looks. Their first priority is a quality of self-assurance in the woman, an air of confidence in herself that enhances every aspect of her appearance and personality. The "cactus flower"—the late-bloomer who blossoms by whipping off her glasses and letting her hair down—reminds us that, if plain women cannot always be beautiful, beautiful women can always appear plain if feelings of inadequacy are reflected in poor grooming, body posture, and social withdrawal. The psychiatrist frequently encounters pretty women with low self-esteem and consequent lonely lives; we also see average-looking women who are convinced they possess extraordinary beauty and actually do find themselves surrounded by admirers. In the animal world, mates are chosen, usually by the female of the species, not on the basis of beauty, but on aggressiveness, apparent strength compared with others, and receptivity. Male animals of our species, who seem more preoccupied with performance and practicality than beauty in their machines and other belongings, ultimately judge a woman not on what she has, but what she does with it.

The modern man is more turned on by naturalness and poise that is not a product of affectation, quite the opposite of the image conveyed by the heavily made-up models who dominate magazines and billboards. In a new world where natural foods are gaining favor over those laced with chemical preservatives and color enhancers, where practical compact cars are replacing ostentatious gas-eaters, and television heroines race around in comfortable pant suits instead of being hobbled by skin-tight sheaths, men are seeking a freshness and spontaneity in women rather than the artificial beauty concocted by the makeup mongers.

"I like women who have not lost their femininity, yet are mature and intelligent. Time spent in bed with a woman is only a small part of the total time spent. I like attractive feminine figures, but it's probably true that the mind is the sexiest part of the body."

"Nothing about her body (as long as not grotesque)—simpatico, friendly, clean—(and all other Girl Scouts requirements.)"

"I like an alert woman, an aware person—physically, emotionally and intellectually. One who takes care of her body and is in good shape. I find alert eyes very beautiful and I like women who are witty and self-actualized."

The term "self-actualized" is sometimes used by psychologists to describe people who have reached the peak of their potential, doing the best they can within their limitations and their range of options. Throughout our study we found that men did not demand exceptional looks in women, but did expect her to take care of her body and keep it slim, poised, and clean.

"What turns me on, so to speak, about a woman is if she is clean in appearance and has the so-called 'natural look' (from head to toe)."

"The more appreciative, sincere and understanding, the more attractive she becomes. A plain woman that exhibits these characteristics becomes more attractive. A beautiful woman who is cold and callous becomes repulsive."

"A body that is kept in fine shape shows that a woman cares about herself as well as what pleases others."

What men desire today is not the sheer physical sensuality extolled by the glossy publications directed at the modern woman, but rather a show of genuine attentiveness, a responsiveness based on honest regard and a desire to communicate and give mutual pleasure.

"If she acted like I was the most important person to her and yet not a worship attitude."

"I must be able to just sit and talk to her and know that she is really listening and really cares."

"If she pleases my individual tastes. Personality can change with the individual woman, she would have to care more for me than herself."

"I like a woman able to conform to my many moods."

For some, the promise of a good sexual relationship was important from the start; however, many qualified their desires with warnings against a female attitude that seemed "professional":

"An aggressive woman. Someone who knows a little about what's going on, but can still be kind and not a whore."

"I like a friendly, outgoing type of woman who is not afraid to show her sexuality."

"One who is responsive to my gestures. I like for a woman to flirt a little, but not to turn on and off like a faucet."

"Her intelligence and if she acts like a lady in her motions and her talk. She must be daring but not too daring and she must be honest."

"Dress sexy—not lewd."

"Nice dresser, clean, easygoing, willing partner. I want someone who wants sex as much as myself."

Note the word "clean" in the above response. The biggest surprise
in these answers was how often that word came up: one would not
expect women in this era of preoccupation with soaps, deodorants,
mouthwashes, antiseptics, and other chemical aids to achieving a
nearly germ-free state to be suspect in the slightest of being less than
scrupulously hygienic. Yet, this fresh-scrubbed aura is quite in keeping with men's desire for a natural appearance and an honest, open
attitude:

"Body cleanliness and physical shape (takes body tone exer-
cises)."

"Being with a woman who is clean."

"Neatness, regardless of fashion. Very clean, clean, clean."

"Clean, healthy, affectionate."

What, no male chauvinist pigs in our sample? Okay, we did have a
few, but they were amazingly rare:

"Her butt and her boobs."

"Large breast and a firm ass. Very friendly. Moving hips and
rubbing her breast on my back and such when she walks past."

"Her build—big boobs!"

"Nice ass, teeth, lips, jugs, twat, 100 lbs. or less, long hair; not
fake or phony."

"Her nude body—everything about her body."

And many men responded gallantly that what turned them on about
a woman was "everything."

In general, we agree with what actress Loretta Young casually told
a reporter 25 years ago: "Being pretty is an advantage; you attract
attention without trying. But after the first five minutes, you're on
your own."

# Setting the Stage

The heroine alone cannot ensure the success of the hero—the setting, lighting, and even music may play a key role in the drama, along with whatever has happened in the previous acts. While a woman's ability to grip a man's attention at first meeting and make him feel there is something special about her is essential, this turn-on must be sustained throughout the ensuing sexual activity, where the man's body comes to reflect the excitement he has already experienced in his mind. This is vital; if a man is not physically aroused, he cannot participate in sex at all. A woman can take part in sexual relations with a man whether or not she is truly attracted to him. Once she gets involved in the act, she may even find herself responding with an enthusiastic orgasm. Not so for a man. While experts point out that he can still receive and give sexual satisfaction in other ways, we have found (see Chapter Four) that men regard intercourse as their prime source of feeling manly, and the prospect of a sexual encounter without an erection would be as distressing as entering a golf tournament without a club.

It is the erection that transforms the man from a plodding workhorse into a fiery unicorn, that fabled beast whose horn grew steadily in length from 18 inches when the ancient Greeks described it to a staggering 10 feet in the scholarly writings of the Middle Ages. The unicorn has a huge advantage over man, however; its head totally controls its horn, whereas in man head and horn are physically separated and often seem to be going their separate ways.

At puberty, when a male first becomes acutely aware of his penis, it's invariably a source of embarrassment. The sight of a girl, a fleeting thought, or no apparent stimulus at all can leave him with a bulge in his trousers, a lump in his throat, and a block in his mind. Notebooks and jackets acquire the new function of a modesty shield. As he gets older, he may have the opposite problem—the belligerent organ that used to intrude on his tranquillity with hardheaded impetuousity now may refuse to rise to the occasion when its ineffectual master wishes to please a lady. A man can neither will an erection to occur nor to vanish, a fact women frequently forget.

One of the most curious theories in the history of medicine was the widely held belief that hysterical behavior in women was actually caused by a detached uterus wandering through the body. ("Hysterical" is derived from the Greek "hysteros," meaning uterus.) It is easier to understand how intelligent people like the Greeks of Plato's time could have given credence to such an absurd notion when we realize it was their frustration over the independence of their penises that led them to conclude that a woman's internal sexual organs could cause irrational behavior by similar irresponsible actions. Plato thus wrote:

> In men the organ of generation—becoming rebellious and masterful, like an animal disobedient to reason, and maddened with the sting of lust—seeks to gain absolute sway; and the same is the case with the womb of women; the animal within them is desirous of procreating children, and when remaining unfruitful long beyond its proper time, gets discontented and angry, and wandering in every direction through the body, closes up the passages of the breath, and by obstructing respiration, drives them to extremity, causing all varieties of disease.

So, there exists in every man an uneasy truce between head and penis. A woman can detach her brain completely from her body in a sex act (prostitutes do it daily), but a man must bring his head along. Though his brain sends pleasing signals to his penis based on the sights, sounds, and smells it encounters, it occasionally transmits negative vibrations triggered by the unhappy memories and fears that are an integral part of his conscious and unconscious mind. The sight of a well-shaped woman may be enough to turn him on, as it did in early adolescence; but associated negative feelings of fear, guilt, inadequacy, or disappointment could turn an erection into a comedown. The turn-on must be a total package, assuring him that a woman who excites him in one way won't turn him off in another.

*Essay Question: What could a woman do to excite you more? What would you prefer her to wear, what kind of atmosphere do you like, and how would you like her to act?*

We never expected so many men to request things one might term conventionally romantic, such as soft music, dim lights, and provocative nightwear:

"Wear perfume and sexy clothing. Soft lights, soft music— I'm a romanticist. Soft and feminine."

"Music & candlelight mood with plenty of time to enjoy everything. A see-through gown which can be easily removed."

"Come to me nude, lots of perfume, nice soft skin, soft music, candles and mirrors."

"The atmosphere should be quiet and a dim light (blue). Also soft music playing in the background (sort of a relaxed atmosphere)."

"I'd prefer her to wear thin negligee with a semi-dark (soft lights) room with soft rhythmic music and I'd like her to act uninhibited, letting herself enjoy and become aroused."

"Let her feel and tell her emotions. Wear nothing. Atmosphere quiet, alone, soft music, a little wine, and a fireplace."

"Dress in sexy bedclothes and act very sluttish, only with me, in bed. I like it semi-dark with many mirrors around the room. On the ceiling, too. Satin sheets are nice, too."

"Be less inhibited; be sexy. Wear something that compliments her the most, go somewhere that has good food, quiet soft music, act like a lady, then go home and fuck like a mink."

A Boston marriage counselor tells the story, quoted in a recent book on increasing your man's "sensitivity," of the husband of a client who came home to a candlelight dinner and exclaimed, "I knew we had an energy crisis, but this is ridiculous!" We wonder if that counselor is aware that there are men out there who actually want to make love by candlelight.

A few men preferred an atmosphere conducive to intrigue and fantasy:

"Many things such as wearing underclothing, a towel or anything to allow me to expose her body. I prefer a strange place, such as a motel, friend's apartment, etc. Soft lights, music."

"I think role playing prior to sex which could include simulated pick-up, dressing as a teenager, etc. Atmosphere would depend upon the role played."

More men, however, encouraged their partners to be natural, relaxed, and informal:

"Be warm and affectionate. Sexy underwear. Nice quiet surrounding. Any way she pleases so long as she is in a positive mood and do what she wants to have enjoyable sex."

"Articles of clothing, actions all must be natural. Anything can be stimulating, given the right atmosphere and a loving and caring partner."

"Show that she is interested in subtle ways. I prefer her to dress nicely. A sexy woman looks sexy in anything she wears. Any atmosphere. Women should act normal."

"Being herself and letting herself enjoy what is going on. Hopefully she won't have to wear anything or create an atmosphere to excite me. She should be able to do this with whatever equipment she has."

"What she wants without guilt feelings. Clothes she is comfortable in. Being alone secluded from the world. Natural with no hang-ups."

"More? More?!? Are you kidding . . . I can hardly function as it is. [Wear?] Nothing! [Atmosphere] 80% nitrogen, 19% oxygen, 1% argon. [Like her to act?] No acts please."

Most psychiatrists would agree with Theodore Rubin that a woman who takes the initiative in sexual relations is creating a serious challenge to her partner's manhood and that many men are very threatened by aggressive, or even assertive, women. Yet, contrary to this widely prevalent belief, we found that most of our men welcomed an aggressive, active partner. They want women who will sometimes initiate sexual activity, who are uninhibited in their enjoyment of sex, and who are open to the idea of adding variety to their lovemaking. Many women are undoubtedly holding back in their degree of active participation for fear of appearing unfeminine and turning off the man, and thereby undermining the enjoyment and success of the relationship through adherence to obsolete beliefs about what men want:

"Sometimes I feel I want them to be more aggressive. There are times (and I can only go by my own experience) when I feel that the woman feels the man should be the aggressive one *all* the time. I'd like the woman to be herself, to be relaxed; comfortable. I don't want her to pretend to be a great sex goddess. Just simply herself."

"I like her to be fairly aggressive. Bikini pants or nothing—soft lighting and I don't like coy."

"To grab me by the penis and drag me to the bedroom. Confident about who she is."

"Take things in her own hands! Use her own imagination, discover and search for new ideas herself. Sexy lingerie never hurt. Atmosphere (such as woods) can and can't stimulate. I can't change her actions. They're inherited."

"Be a little more aggressing [sic], boots and black underwear, relaxed, passionate and very responsive."

Some men didn't even need aggressiveness to satisfy them. They apparently would have settled for just a little more participation:

"Most women that I have known (not enough) seem to be very timid and just lie there. I want someone to take the initiative with me, to please me instead of me doing all the work."

"More oral sex. No clothes, casual and more aggressive. Women today are so damned worried about 'their' sexual needs the man gets shortchanged."

"I would like her to return my love and not just lay there."

"love love love love love love love love love love love love love love love love love love love love."

"I want her to kiss and hug me. I like her to lick my ear."

"Wear sexy clothes. Look good. Like a lady not a cunt."

## Foreplay—More Than a Warm-up

Between the surge of arousal and the peak of orgasm lies a plateau. Physiologically, the plateau phase marks the congestion of the sexual organs with the increased blood flow resulting from sexual excitement and ultimately makes orgasm possible. In men, this phase is generally automatic, except in cases where the man has a potency problem and quickly loses his erection before coitus can occur. Psychologically, this intermediate phase gives a man's body time to catch up with his aroused brain; even if he already has an erection, his body can undergo more far-reaching changes, including an acceleration of heart rate, an increase in respiration, and generalized flushing of the small vessels of the skin. The turn-on is mainly a mental phenomenon at the start, but quickly precipitates a man into the first stage of sexual excitation, that of arousal, whether or not he is fortunate enough to have access to intercourse then and there. Arousal can occur in a man without any sort of physical contact; not so the subsequent stages of plateau and orgasm. Since all the stages of sexual excitation are pleasurable, it would seem logical for men to desire those precoital activities that enhance their excitement prior to orgasm—though many critics accuse them of approaching foreplay as a chore rather than a pleasure.

In her survey of women, Shere Hite printed 76 female responses to the question "How have most men had sex with you?" and not a single one was complimentary to men. Many criticized men for lack of foreplay, lack of imagination in foreplay, or failure to understand a woman's needs. Another recent book patronizingly explains that many men have hang-ups about sex because it isn't "useful," takes up time, and exposes the body, which is a source of embarrassment; therefore, men want to get the sex act over as quickly as possible.

We know what "experts" think—we wanted to find out what the typical American male thought. Is it true that he wants to proceed to his orgasm as quickly as he can, just as he would attack any task, or might he conceivably really enjoy foreplay?

*Question 8: What sexual activity gives you the most pleasure during foreplay?*

| | |
|---|---|
| Kissing and caressing | 36.9% |
| Oral sex | 26.5% |
| Touching and sucking breasts | 22.2% |
| Touching female genital area (sex organs) | 19.1% |
| Looking at partner's nude body | 10.6% |
| Don't like foreplay | 1.6% |
| No answer | 0.8% |

The first very evident finding is that there are very few men—less than 2 percent—who don't like foreplay; while it may have been true at a time when women were raised to be inhibited about sex and suppressed orgasms and excitement, the modern man, with the help of a cooperative, eager partner, is interested in using foreplay to increase his own pleasure, as well as his partner's.

We asked men to elaborate on their feelings about foreplay through an essay question:

*Essay Question: How important is foreplay to you? What do you enjoy doing and what do you do to please your sexual partner?*

Their answers indicated that they deemed it a highly enjoyable, integral part of every sex act:

> "Foreplay is essential to a satisfying experience. Stroking/caressing the entire body is pleasurable for both of us, leading to oral sex prior to coitus. The extent of foreplay is limited only by mood—sometimes we carry on for hours, sometimes only for a few minutes."

> "Foreplay is the whole thing. I wouldn't consider intercourse without it. I enjoy oil massages and oral sex."

> "Foreplay is very important. Both partners should be actively involved. Kissing, caressing the entire body, and holding my partner close to me are the main areas I use during foreplay."

That more men selected kissing and caressing as their greatest pleasure will surprise many people, for men have somehow acquired the reputation of being interested only in a woman's sexual parts. That presupposes that most men do not relate to their partners as total people when having sex, and pursue gratification in a manner devoid of any affection or tenderness. This may be true of a man who feels threatened by a partner he barely knows and certainly would apply to his behavior with a prostitute (most of whom firmly draw the line at kissing their clients), but it does not hold for the average man, who apparently feels isolated and lonely enough in the competitive world outside without conducting his sex life under similar conditions of alienation. Kissing and caressing was the first choice for every age bracket, all races, and all educational, income, and occupational levels. Only those men living with a partner, unmarried, gave oral sex a slight edge, 39 as against 34 percent for hugging and kissing. (Percentages over 10, here and throughout the book, have been rounded to the nearest whole number.)

Some respondents felt that a sexual encounter without adequate kissing and caressing would result in an act that was lacking in warmth and full pleasure:

> "Foreplay is important to the extent of having a warmth for the sexual act. Kissing her in many places to bring about the warmth of her body that will bring about a perfect satisfaction."

"Sexual foreplay is very important to me in order to get full sexual pleasure. I like it when a woman caresses my penis. I enjoy massaging her breasts, also licking them."

One of the most striking findings of the study was that the percentage of men under 40 who consider oral sex the most pleasurable part of foreplay is triple that of men over the age of 55. In both the 18–29 and 30–39 age brackets, 31 percent of men liked oral sex best, but only 22 percent of men 40 to 54 and 11 percent over 55.

While we did not ask any specific question in our study about the practice of fellatio (acts involving the penis and mouth), we did ascertain (see Chapter Seven) that 80 percent of our respondents perform cunnilingus (using their mouths on vaginal areas) and we can assume that a similar number enjoy fellatio. The wide acceptance of oral sex is remarkable in view of the fact it was considered a perversion by most a generation or two ago, and that most states still have archaic sodomy laws that make it a crime. Kinsey reported in the 1940s that 15 percent of high-school-educated married males and 43 percent of college-educated engaged in fellatio. Hunt reported in 1972 that 54 percent of high-school-educated and 61 percent of college males were employing fellatio in marital relations. (Corresponding figures for cunnilingus were the same or within 5 percentage points higher in these studies.) Hunt's estimates of incidence of oral sex were even higher for younger college-educated men, with more than 80 percent of those under age 35 and over 90 percent younger than 25 regularly enjoying it.

We did not see drastic differences in preference for oral sex based on education (20 percent for less than high school graduates, 24 percent in high school graduates, 27 percent in college graduates). Both Kinsey and Hunt found blacks to be less accepting than whites of oral sex; in our study, too, the blacks showed an 18 percent preference for oral sex while white men reported a 28 percent preference.

In their answers, many of our subjects made it clear that they enjoyed cunnilingus as much as fellatio:

"It [foreplay] is a very important thing for me and my girl friend. It enhances the sex act a lot. We both enjoy oral sex; especially me. I enjoy doing it as much as receiving it; she especially likes receiving it."

"I think it's real important. It gets both partners more relaxed so you can enjoy yourself more. I enjoy oral sex and like to perform it on my partner."

Why are men today so interested in oral sex? It seems to reflect a willingness and an expectancy on their parts for their women to be more active in sex, along with a desire to be passively stimulated at times, instead of being the perpetually active partner. In most instances of fellatio, the man will lie recumbent while his partner stimulates him with her tongue and mouth. A generation ago, a man might have found this position threateningly passive and feminine, but most men today feel they are entitled to a pleasant respite from constantly proving their prowess. Of course, fellatio may occur in the position glamorized in pornography literature, with the male standing erect, legs spread like a conqueror, his partner kneeling, preferably naked, at his feet, giving industrious lip service to his manhood. There are obvious sadomasochistic elements here, but to a degree that is often perfectly acceptable to both partners.

We did not ascertain the prevalence of simultaneous fellatio and cunnilingus, colloquially numbered "69," but from our indication of the number of men eager and willing to perform cunnilingus, it seems many would elect this joint endeavor in which both partners can be equally active and passive.

Oral sex is on its way, if not already there, to becoming the new standard of intimacy. Now that many women give themselves more casually in intercourse, oral sex becomes the next logical frontier for proof that the woman "really cares."

What about the woman, perhaps happily married for years, who abhors the thought of oral sex and finds that her husband, intrigued by glowing accounts of the practice in respectable publications, decides he's not going to leave this earth without a taste of this previously forbidden passion fruit? One can always fall back on the tried truism, "Any sexual activity is fine, provided only that it is mutually pleasurable and neither partner is opposed to it." Fine, but it may be worth avoiding the risk of a disappointed, restless mate by asking the woman to examine her opposition to the act, which is usually on either aesthetic or moral grounds.

Most aesthetic considerations stem either from viewing the penis as a "dirty" excretory organ, or from an actual fear of it. In a man who is circumcised or who has a retractable foreskin, the organ can be scrubbed as clean as a finger—cleaner. And urine, though an excretory product, is normally absolutely free of bacteria, whereas the mouth is loaded with them. So, even as a urinary organ, the penis, shielded as it usually is, is one of the cleanest areas of the body.

Fear of the penis is common in young girls. The little girl perceives the adult penis as unusually large and may first fantasize intercourse in terms of anal penetration, since her vagina has not been experienced yet as a receptive organ. In women's dreams, penises become symbolized by knives or snakes. Even a woman who is accustomed to intercourse with the penis undercover may be threatened by an eye-level confrontation.

On moral grounds, we can only remind women that, while perversion has many definitions, none of which the courts can agree on, it is most commonly defined by psychiatrists as an activity that substitutes for intercourse or uses an object other than a consenting adult. Oral sex need not be used as a substitute for intercourse, and can be most enjoyable as a means of enhancing the ultimate satisfaction of the sex act via foreplay.

The breasts, focus of foreplay for only 22 percent of our sample, have always been a source of erotic arousal to a man, and the profusion of topless bars and magazine fold-outs would indicate that their appeal has not waned. Yet our survey shows that younger men place less emphasis on the breasts during foreplay: 27 percent of men over 40 cite the bosom as the source of most pleasure during foreplay, with a drop to 21 percent in the 30–39 age bracket and to 18 percent in the men under 30. Many women do complain that their partners do not devote as much time to caressing, sucking, or licking the breasts as women would like. Why in the world, they are apt to wonder, after all the ogling of tight sweaters and low-cut dresses, all the surreptitious patting and rubbing, does he now, with full access to those precious orbs, virtually ignore them? Are they too small, too droopy, too imperfect?

Probably none of the above. With our more liberal attitudes towards sex, we are seeing a shift in attention from the breasts to the genital area in foreplay. Touching the female genital area was cited as the main turn-on by 19 percent, and coupled with the 27 percent who selected oral sex, we find a total of 46 percent who focus on the vaginal area in foreplay.

Some men do not find the sight of female genitals stimulating, contrary to all the expected laws of nature, because children are taught that pelvic areas are dirty and should not be looked at. Rather than risk loss of parental love, the child actually convinces himself that the normal objects of fascination are repulsive and substitutes other parts of the body as focal points for his sexual interest. In the early 1940s, when decent magazines would not show bare breasts, men bought and drooled over "cheesecake" photographs of women's legs. As the bikini became acceptable, leg men had to be content with a truncated section of thigh, as cameras zoomed in on navels and cleavage lines. As bare breasts became less obscene, pin-up girls lost half of their bodies, except when an occasional rear-view was posed for variety. Now that the vaginal area is no longer considered taboo, we can expect to find fewer men obsessively preoccupied with legs, buttocks—yes, even breasts—and more interested in whole women.

The decreasing inhibition in our society will ultimately mean not only a franker acceptance of the genital organs, but also a wider interest in a variety of sexual behavior, including increased attention to other erogenous zones:

> "Foreplay necessary. Oral-nipple and oral-genital contact as active and passive partner. Sometimes anal contact for both. Wife enjoys friction in genital area without use of hands or mouth. I enjoy the passive/female role occasionally. Would enjoy anal sex as passive partner with wife but don't because I don't know how to suggest it without embarrassment."

Some men may equate breast sucking with infantile behavior, which would then cast his partner in a mother role. This brings up incest anxieties and, under the rules of the prostitute-madonna complex, he gets turned off. Most men, however, are not adverse to mouthing the breasts, and the partner's erect nipples are a reassuring indication of her increasing arousal. With the trend we have observed in our younger men to shift their interest to the genital zone in foreplay, a woman can best insure the man's continued attention to her breasts by reciprocating with manipulation of his penis in her hand or against her sexual organs—this not only gives him more direct genital gratification, but also avoids putting him in a possibly threatening childlike position where the erect penis that confirms his manhood is ignored. Visual arousal, by the breasts or other sources of stimulation, can produce an erection; but once the penis is ready for action, the man wants it included in the activities of foreplay. As women have become less inhibited and more willing to touch and mouth the penis, breast play, by itself, has become a second-class type of foreplay, much as it was back in the days of petting when a "good girl" wouldn't let a boy "go below the waist."

The prevalence of nudity in movies and magazines has not dimmed its fascination for some men, and one respondent pointed out that the eyes, as well as the hands, are capable of caressing:

> "To kiss, to deep kiss, to caress the body by looks and touch, to feel warm, open, responsive."

> "I like hugging and kissing followed by undressing. I like to have my partner undress me. If she's not too heavy, I enjoy picking her up and carrying her to bedroom."

Looking at the partner's nude body was not the major foreplay pleasure for many, nor did we expect it to be. After all, sex is not primarily a spectator sport. Most men who responded to our question about how women could excite them more mentioned wearing some sort of seductive nightclothes rather than nothing at all. The most interesting aspect of this visual element of foreplay was that only some 10 percent of all respondents chose it, with the percentage remaining consistent throughout all age groups. Men 55 to 65 years old were actually the highest, with 13 percent. In other words, older men, most of whom would be having sex with older women, still found nudity a turn-on.

There is something very stimulating to a man when a woman offers her body openly, without shame, revealing her secret and vulnerable areas. Trust is a powerful aphrodisiac.

## At the Summit

Byron wrote: "All who joy would win must share it—happiness was born a twin." Certainly, in the pleasure of orgasm, the woman's response is frequently as essential to the man's enjoyment as his own sensations, and we will explore the female orgasm at length in Chapter Six. Here, however, we will limit our consideration to the man's own orgasm, although, as we shall see, the twin responses often cannot be easily separated.

One of the reasons men found foreplay very important is that it improves their orgasms. Women find it difficult to understand that a man's orgasms differ in intensity, despite the fact that their own are so variable. Similarly, they interpret the sight of a man's erection as evidence that he is as aroused as he can possibly get. A good orgasm for a man, just as for a woman, should involve his entire mind and body, not just his penis. His penis can get aroused ahead of everything else; a man with an erection may be quite capable of fixing a car engine or solving an intricate math problem (many men feel they went through high school with a constant erection), something that a totally aroused woman could not do without "turning off."

*Essay Question: Do your orgasms differ from time to time, and how? How could your orgasms be improved? . . .*

"Yes—some are stronger. The longer the foreplay, the better the orgasm."

"Yes—the intensity varies. Longer foreplay, when I'm better rested, and my wife is more responsive—all of these result in a more intense orgasm."

"My orgasm, a lot of time, improved by some foreplay. The only difference is when I'm tired and ejaculated without much of the pleasure."

With adequate foreplay, a man can proceed from a simple erection to an overall state of physical excitement short of ejaculation, with acceleration of heart rate and breathing, flushing of the skin, and a near-delirious brain. He senses a building pressure in his testicles, and his already erect penis seems to stretch and expand to the bursting point, so that penetration and thrusting in the vagina is accompanied by a sense of great energy and power, with the ejaculation seeming to be a veritable explosion, draining his entire body and being.

In responding both to this question on orgasms and the preceding one about foreplay, many respondents said that the attitude of their partners was an important contributing factor:

"My orgasms differ in intensity. They could be improved by a more passionate and responsive wife."

"Not too much different. Each orgasm is usually emphatic. [Improved] by more response and passion from the woman and oral sex by the woman and lip caressing on my neck, behind my ears, tongue in my ears, etc."

"It has taken about 8 years to liberate my wife's feelings about foreplay. She now actively enjoys it."

"Foreplay with the *right* person is very important. With the wrong person there isn't much 'heart' in it. As to what type, anything goes."

"I enjoy touching and kissing wherever wife will allow—my wife puts limits on what I can do."

Consideration of the woman's needs and desires often was said to improve the quality of the sex act:

"My orgasms differ. Exactly how goes by how I feel at the time and the amount of stimuli affecting me. I think my orgasm can be improved by understanding my partner and teaching her what stimulates me."

"Yes, some are more intense. With my wife they are better than with other girls. When I am more unaware of the pleasure I'm going to receive because of the desire to give pleasure, they are better."

"Foreplay is very important. I enjoy the feeling that I get when I make my partner very excited and I enjoy making her have an orgasm or more than one if possible. It is very important that my partner be satisfied."

"It's extremely important to 'feel' your partner out occasionally. I think touching, kissing, hugging, sucking, etc., is a very emotional response which displays a great deal of consideration and love. I enjoy any and all of the above. I think consideration is extremely important in pleasing my sexual partner."

"I enjoy making out with my partner on my lap. I like to undress her. As for her, I do whatever she asked, and give in if there is a conflict."

"Difference in intensity—I think I am *overly* concerned about the woman's response.—I have read reports such as *The Hite Report* and I am not sure what the hell I'm doing any more."

The time element is an important factor to many, the pleasure increasing proportionately as the act is prolonged:

"They differ in intensity. The more prolonged the sex act the better and more intense the orgasm."

"Orgasms come very quickly each time. Could be improved with more 'practice.'"

"They differ from time to time—different positions with the unnormal time element causes them to be better."

"Yes, it depends on the mood of the partner. By having plenty of time and not be in a hurry to get through."

"Foreplay is as important as climax and I use it extensively preceding and following!"

The man's state of mind prior to intercourse can have a profound effect on the quality of his orgasm:

> "If I have a lot on my mind or am very nervous for one reason or another my orgasms are less intense—if I have one at all. My orgasms could be improved if I were more relaxed."

> "Yes, better when I'm not tired or something on my mind."

> "Yes. Depending on the physical condition of my body. It could be improved if my body has had the proper rest."

> "I find marijuana heightens the pleasure of orgasms. Could be improved by more of it."

Not all men were overly concerned about stimulating their partners sufficiently. A few were unenthusiastic about the benefits of foreplay:

> "A certain amount of foreplay is fine, but it can get boring. Different girls like different kinds of foreplay. Caressing or oral sex before intercourse are the usuals."

> "Foreplay is not that important to me. We both choose intercourse. Once in a while foreplay will enter the picture."

> "Not important for myself but seems to be very much so for my wife. Enjoy oral foreplay."

> "I like foreplay, but I could fuck without it. I enjoy doing anything and enjoy everything that is done to me."

> "It depends. Sometimes you just want to rip the clothes off !!!"

> "Sex is good with or without foreplay."

> "Who wants to fool around with foreplay? Get right down to business."

# The Lady or the Tigress?

*Question 9: What could your partner do to make you more excited?*

| | |
|---|---|
| Be more active during sex | 34.4% |
| Use more oral sex | 24.3% |
| Touch penis more | 17.8% |
| Wear sexy lingerie | 15.7% |
| Display nude body more | 11.2% |
| Use exciting words | 6.7% |
| No answer | 3.0% |

These answers confirm the finding that was suggested earlier by the essay question about what sort of atmosphere and actions would excite a man more. The top three answers, all involving more active involvement by the woman before or during intercourse, total more than 75 percent. Men today do not want a passive partner; they want a woman who shows her interest and enjoyment, who is an active participant during intercourse, and who is not timid about touching a man in intimate fashion. This is a new attitude compared with the generations of men who wanted only compliance from their women at a time when female satisfaction was considered irrelevant at best and unladylike or downright sluttish at worst.

In their responses to the previous essay question on the topic, men welcomed an attitude of enthusiasm and adventure in their women:

"I am excited by a woman who actively seduces me. I am turned on by erotic or flimsy clothes. I like a softly lighted room with soft music and drinks. I like a woman who acts as if she wants me as actively as I want her."

"Woman should feel at ease in exploring my body and not be inhibited in trying whatever she likes. Enjoy it when she reassures me on my performance without obvious lying. Don't like it when a woman feels she must act as if she was coerced into action to preserve 'respectability' and acknowledges she's into it."

Single men, the married, the divorced, and men living with unmarried partners all wanted increased activity from their partners during sex more than any other choice. The youngest men asked for it more than the older groups, and students made this request more frequently than any other group.

Activity is closely bound to reactivity. It's not just a question of taking the lead, it's how well you finish. The intensity of many men's orgasms, as we have seen, depends on how active and responsive their partners are. A woman need not be a Nadia Comaneci in her gymnastic ability or come to bed encumbered with bowls of ice cubes and cans of whipped cream as long as she remains a participant—not a spectator—in the ongoing activities.

Twenty-four percent of the men wanted more oral sex, and 18 percent wanted their partner to touch the penis more. Thus, a total of 42 percent wanted women to become more involved with their penises, which again requires more activity on the woman's part. The oldest men (18 percent) did not choose more oral sex as much, but compensated with a slightly higher (21 percent) request for more touching of the penis.

We have already talked about women's early aversion to the penis, one that is often difficult to overcome. The penis is a phobic object for society, as well. We accept nudity in publications and on stage—even finally an exposed penis; but an erect penis is still considered pornographic. Thus boys grow up with easy access to statues, photos, and movies of nude women; but girls are never permitted to view a penis in the state in which they ultimately encounter it.

Even married women with years of sexual experience may find themselves reluctant to touch the same penis to which their vaginas have played hostess innumerable times. As the devotees of clitoral orgasm well know, the vaginal vault is almost devoid of sensitive nerve endings; handling the penis gives the woman a whole new perception of it.

Seeing a woman in sexy lingerie would excite men more than seeing her totally nude. Half the fun of a gift package is still unwrapping it. Older men as well as younger, and poorly educated men as well as graduate students chose lingerie more often than nudity.

There are several reasons why men like suggestive garments at bedtime, which may range, as we have seen in our men's response to the question about what their partners could do to excite them more, from ladylike gowns to bikini panties and black boots. Dressing specially for a man signals him that his woman is making a special effort to arouse him, and affirms that she truly desires him. Secondly, scanty or revealing underthings, garter belts, fancy stockings, or sheer negligees transform a spouse from a dutiful, practical housewife and mother into a wanton object of lust, the prostitute of his adolescent fantasies, the antithesis of the good mother he would be too intimidated to approach. Finally, it seems men undergo a certain "imprinting" during their years of sexual awakening. Up until a few years ago, magazines catering to sexual interest did not run pictures of entirely nude women, but presented them in some type of scanty and provocative dress. Thus, most adolescent boys had daydreams or masturbatory fantasies about women so garbed, and the sight of a real partner so attired reawakens the vivid reveries of their lost youth. Whether or not pantyhose and *Penthouse* will ultimately put Frederick's of Hollywood out of business remains to be seen.

The confusion of some women between men's attraction to lingerie and fetishism causes them considerable distress. Even Dr. Theodore Rubin, in his latest book, falls into a basic error when he says, "The man who likes to see his wife in lingerie is a fetishist," and compares him to a man who enjoys kissing his wife's shoes. True fetishism involves the substitution of an object or a body part (unusually an unconventional one, such as feet or hair) for the total person as love object. While undergarments may be classified as a fetish if sex is impossible without their use, especially if they must be left on, the man who becomes aroused by his partner wearing lingerie and then removes it and engages the partner—not the lingerie—in sexual activity has not displaced his interest from his partner. He is not to be equated with Dr. Rubin's shoe kisser unless he starts kissing the panties.

Though generally not deemed very important by our sample, use of "exciting words" can certainly add to the intimacy of the sex act and make it as much a union of minds as bodies. Some people become remarkably uninhibited, and their speech may sound like anything from the babbling of an infant to the comments of a sailor who finds the town's brothel closed. Most men welcome some vote of approval *viva voce,* but we would caution women against using frequently deleted expletives unless your mate is accustomed to your using them, or takes the lead in using them himself. For one thing, erotic words are considered "dirty" words and just as many men are turned off by women who are not freshly bathed or have unshaven armpits or legs, they are also repulsed by "foul" language. Just as the madonna must bring a bit of the prostitute to the bedroom, the prostitute must not leave the madonna behind. Then, too, most of our sexual vulgarities do double duty as words of anger and are used to insult others, attack people, or complain about things. Hence, a man hearing such words from feminine lips is confronting not only sexuality but aggression of the most hostile sort.

So, unless a man shows a distinct preference for this type of "oral" sex, as indicated by his own enlistment of fighting words in the service of Eros, be wary. And modify them with words that lack ambivalence, such as "You have such a *beautiful*———" or "I just *love* to———." Come to think of it, words like "beautiful" and "love" are pretty erotic themselves.

# Great Expectations

> In sex, supposedly, men know what to do: they initi-
> ate and carry out the main activities. We 'respond' to
> them. But what men have generally initiated has had
> little to do with our needs for orgasm. And even
> worse, being necessarily passive gives us no sense of
> our strength and autonomy.
>
> —SHERE HITE, *The Hite Report*

The problem with social changes is that by the time writers get around to documenting them, they have changed again. Although Shere Hite's contention that men desire to initiate sexual activities while the women remain necessarily passive might have been valid in her not-too-distant youth, our survey shows that quite the opposite is true with today's men. Ms. Hite is in good company with regard to her misperceptions; most writers today fail to perceive the change that has taken place in men over the past few years, and expect males to persist in the traditions that governed them more than a decade ago. Some even blame the increase in impotence on female aggressiveness; we will deal with that fallacy in Chapter Seven.

As you may recall, one of our respondents answered a question about how he would like a woman to act with "Act very sluttish, only with me, in bed." That answer characterizes the feelings of most of today's men. While the prostitute-madonna complex is still very much in evidence, the sexual revolution, with the increased availability of sexual knowledge presented by the press and movies, offers a woman considerable expertise which she does not have to gain firsthand through sexual experience. Besides, men, to take advantage of the increased availability of sexual partners offered by women's liberation, have conceded women the option of some limited experience without branding them as prostitutes. Under the old standards, a "good" woman, with no access either to experience or information, was supposed to know nothing about sex and therefore could not be expected to contribute much. Men, experienced or not, had to bear the burden of successful lovemaking, assuaging their anxiety with the knowledge that the naïve woman would not know the difference between a good and bad performance.

The rise of a more sexually sophisticated woman has given men renewed hope of finding the ideal combination of prostitute and madonna in the same woman. The average man's fantasy is that of a woman who puts up a gallant but losing struggle against his overpowering allure, and having fallen into his arms and bed finds him so sexually fulfilling that she would never leave him for another man. Prostitutes are characterized by their availability, not their responsiveness. A man has already typed a woman before their first bedroom encounter; how long did it take him to get her there, how well does she seem to know him, has he demonstrated sufficiently his particular masculine charms to account for her sexual compliance? Once she is in the bedroom, he wants her to demonstrate her interest and satisfaction by bringing to the relationship the ideas and techniques that would not have been available to her a decade ago.

The majority of the men surveyed wanted more active, aggressive women. Some stressed the importance of the woman's expressing her own desires and fulfilling her own needs; others seemed to want this increased activity in service of their own gratification. But they certainly did not want their women to be "necessarily passive."

*Essay Question: How do you like a woman to act during sex? Do you want her to be passive, or to do various things to you? What would give you the most pleasure?*

Many of the men felt that their own pleasure would be increased by knowing that their partner was satisfied:

"I want the woman to be more passionate. I would like her more active and do whatever she felt like rather than being inhibited by convention. Having my partner happy would give me the most pleasure."

"Responsive and active and tell me what she wants. Multiple orgasms on the part of my partner seem to please me as much as my own. Passive partners are a pain."

"Would like her to be very affectionate. Would like various sex acts—not just the basic one. The most pleasure would be to completely satisfy the woman I'm with."

"I prefer a woman to be concerned with pleasing me. If all she wants is satisfaction for herself she should find it herself. I am at least 75% given totally to pleasing any partner—the more I like her, the more I forget myself. When I have sex with my wife I am giving at least 98% of myself for her."

"Excited and responsive. Do as much as possible to indicate degree of involvement and pleasure—hand, foot, head motion, etc."

"I like for a woman to be as aggressive as I am. If she wants sex to ask for it or be suggestive. I get the most pleasure from seeing my partner really enjoy the experience."

"Like she is going crazy with enjoyment. Use her imagination, be free to do what she wants without guilt."

Some men, in their responses, focused on the enjoyment they would receive from a perceptive and uninhibited woman who could anticipate their desires and comply with them:

"I don't like women who try to be exceedingly dominant during relations. However, I don't like passive women, and enjoy a woman who is spontaneous in actions (tries different things without asking) and who continues actions which she feels satisfy me."

"Should be willing to assist with erection when necessary."

"I like my women to be aggressive and responsive during foreplay and intercourse. I get the most pleasure when a woman gives me oral sex without me asking for it."

"She could act very loving; as the saying goes, 'a lady in a restaurant and a whore in the bedroom.'"

Some men, in accordance with the spirit of the equal rights movement, expressed a desire for an egalitarian relationship between the partners:

"Equal partners, various positions and roles. Male doesn't need to always dominate. An uninhibited partner."

"I prefer a sharing, give-and-take relationship. I enjoy being a sex object also."

"I do not like a woman to be passive during sex. It has a tendency to make me feel inferior sexually or even socially."

There were only a relative handful who preferred passive partners. The usual motivation in such cases is a fear on the man's part that he will not be able to satisfy the demands a more active partner might make on him. Some are frank in confronting their sensitivity to rejection and failure; others take refuge behind the macho facade and express the feeling that a woman's satisfaction is irrelevant, thereby freeing themselves of any sort of obligation to measure up as lovers:

"To caress me as I do to her, and passiveness is preferable. I never tried oral sex (because of fear) but like to try if circumstance is given. Straight intercourse with my partner reaching climax at the same time I do would be much of my pleasure."

"I want her to be compassionate and understanding; also tolerant and patient. No worry or recrimination or being embarrassed."

"Very tenderly. One time to be able to wear her down before she does me, in an all-night session."

"Keep her mouth shut and don't say a word, various positions. Do not know, because haven't found most pleasurement yet."

"The way a woman acts during sex doesn't really bother me as long as I'm satisfied. I think most people like someone who is flexible but as I said before, as long as I'm satisfied that's what counts."

A few had rather unconventional tastes:

"I want a woman to be very lively and active during sex. An unresponsive woman is the worst. My greatest pleasure would come from administering a severe spanking on a woman's rear end. I would also like to engage in various bondage and discipline and S&M sessions with the woman being submissive."

"A woman should be a tender combination of active madness and passive feeling. To make love on a hang-glider."

"I would want her to act as if she was mad."

"Loving and enjoying it as much as I do. Being very responsive to the point of sadistic ideas."

"I enjoy having my back clawed."

While most men opted for aggressive women, some firmly refused to cast their partners in a single role and stressed the need for complete mutuality:

"If a woman was totally attuned to her man's feelings and needs during sex, she would react sincerely and just as that particular man needed her to be. Please understand I mean this in a two-way sense."

"A woman should have the freedom to do whatever she wants. Sometimes I want her to be passive, sometimes not. But you must communicate what you want."

"Variance between passive and active would be the best. If it is always one way or other it would take a bit of the fun and intrigue out of it."

Thus far, our survey shows that most men expect their women to be anything but passive. Now, the logical rebuttal from those who accuse men of initiating and running everything would be "Sure, they want women to be active—active in giving them better orgasms. But it's still fellatio they're after, and intercourse will always be in the old missionary position, man on top, woman down under. Right?"

Wrong. Several of the men quoted above did mention that trying new positions would give the most pleasure, but we have more evidence than that. We've got the returns in from 4,066 men.

# New and Different

*Question 10: What would you most like to do more often?*

| | |
|---|---|
| Different sexual positions | 54.5% |
| Oral sex | 21.6% |
| None | 10.9% |
| Sex with more than one woman at a time | 10.6% |
| Anal sex | 4.2% |
| Homosexual activity | 1.6% |
| Sadomasochistic activity | 1.2% |
| No answer | 1.5% |

This was one of the few questions in our survey where over 50 percent of the men selected a single answer; it was more remarkable because they were offered the option of checking "none" if they were content with their present practices.

Apparently, we can consider unjust the accusations by those, particularly the militant feminists, who charge that men always assume the "dominant" position in sex, the "missionary" position which keeps the woman on her back, him on top, and him in control. Such critics hail the "woman-superior" position as infinitely more gratifying for her, since her increased freedom for activity allows her more clitoral stimulation during intercourse—and men will not allow it.

Our men stand acquitted. They not only would welcome different sexual positions, but would even choose such variety over oral sex, the most rapidly growing turn-on in the country, and more exotic adventures, such as group sex, anal sex, and sadomasochistic activity.

If more than half the men in America truly desire more variation and are not employing it, it is entirely plausible that women prefer the missionary position. This conservative stance might be due strictly to the same puritanical attitudes preached by the apocryphal missionaries who brought the natives face-to-face with a more morally, if not physically, upright approach to sex. Yet, much has been written about women's need for cuddling and body closeness, and men, as we have seen in the foreplay question, also have a high desire for caressing, though they tend to suppress needs that they consider childlike. The missionary position offers maximal total body contact, matched only by the side-to-side position which impedes a man's thrusting and his bringing his partner to orgasm. The argument for the universal adoption of the female-above position is based on the questionable theory that women using other positions do not have orgasm. The trade-off of close body contact for orgasm would be more than fair; but if, as studies other than Hite's have indicated, most women do experience orgasms in the traditional sexual position, we can well understand why most are content to lie down in arms rather than rise up in arms.

But as important as women's preferences are, we are dealing here with men's desire for variation in sexual position, as a change of fare if not a steady diet. Today's men have indicated to us that they want more sexually active and aggressive women. Perhaps they are tired of being responsible for everything and are less threatened by ceding responsibility for mutual gratification to their partners. The "female-superior" position, ignoring its sociopolitical implications allows the man to lie back while his partner, kneeling or squatting, does the maneuvering. He does not have to be totally passive any more than his partner did back in the male-superior position; and their combined activity, with sporadic thrusts from him as she builds her own rhythmic stimulation, can heighten the pleasure of both. As she increases her excitement, a full view of his highly responsive partner can be a tremendous turn-on for the man.

"Rear-entry" is often opposed by women who find the position assumed by the rest of the animal kingdom dehumanizing. In fact, part of the turn-on for men is its subtle "dirtiness," for the posterior area has been a source of gratification, conflict and merriment from age 2 on up. Potties, passing gas, spankings, and parental cooings over bare-bottomed photos imbue a mixed attitude about the buttocks and associated orifices that lingers for a lifetime. From a visual point of view, the buttocks of a woman are usually more provocative to a man than her pubic area. The man who uses this approach as an occasional variation can offer his mate a pleasant change of course, with the advantages of freedom from the weight of a heavy partner, a possibly greater sensation of fullness and penetration in the vagina, and a more imaginative and responsive man.

These positions, along with sitting and standing variations, cannot be easily performed undercover, except for a blanket of darkness, and the shy woman might initially feel ill at ease. Her man's increased arousal should quickly restore her security, sans blanket.

All of these alternatives, along with some of the acrobatic ones attempted by frustrated iron-pumpers and skydivers, may add to variety, but there is no need to believe that the popularity of the missionary position has been due to people's basically religious nature. Laurie, a twice-divorced patient, had been on a three-month sex spree since her latest split, and confided, "I've been trying everything, every position, every variation. You know, the missionary position's still best." But Laurie added, "It's better, though, with my legs inside his, not outside as usual. Tighter penetration." One can always add an innovative touch even to the most tried and true of old recipes.

We've discussed oral sex previously, but it's interesting to note here that among those who wanted most to have oral sex more often, there was little variation in the age brackets, even though we had previously seen how young men find oral sex the most pleasurable form of foreplay far more often than the older ones. This new finding would seem to indicate that many older men get less enjoyment from oral sex in foreplay not because they don't like it, but because their partners are less willing to engage in it.

Having sex with more than one woman at a time was the favorite goal of 11 percent of our sample. (We avoided the term "group sex" because of its homosexual implications.) When there are several men, as well as women, involved, participants do not set up preliminary rules as to who has the right to do what with which and to whom, and things often become a unisexual blur. The impersonal nature of it and the presence of active females make the homosexual elements acceptable to men who subconsciously desire contact with other males, but are too inhibited to seek an intimate relationship with just one other man. Some men would avoid group sex because of the unacceptability of homosexual aspects, and others go along with the unconventional practice seeing the other men as a tolerable drawback, knowing that a room full of nothing but lascivious women cannot be found outside *The Arabian Nights*.

Our question sought to bypass homosexual anxieties by merely mentioning women. The older men (age 55–65) understandably declined this feat of endurance, except for a hardy 4.4 percent, but other age groups showed equal enthusiasm. There were no great differences between married and single men here. We suspect that many had never actively engaged in sex with more than one woman, but even the fantasy would indicate that men are less preoccupied with the penis as their sole source of gratification since, in either an active or passive role, the organ could not be involved with more than one woman at a time.

Hunt reported in 1972 that 16 percent of all males and 3 percent of females have had multiple-partner sex. Figures were higher for those who had at least once been involved in "group sex"—which could be defined merely as having sex in the presence of other people, though not involved physically with more than one partner —and 40 percent of single men and 23 percent of single women surveyed in that study had that experience, though frequently they had engaged in group sex on only a single occasion. In *Playboy's* (1976) college campus poll, 7 percent of male students had tried group sex and 5 percent liked it. Another 47 percent said they were willing to try it. And 14 percent of the students in our sample—the highest of any occupational or income breakdown—indicated that what they would want most to do more often is have sex with more than one woman at a time—but we do not know how many had actually experienced it.

Just as Oriental potentates acquired more wives and concubines than they could possibly handle, so, too, do modern men fantasize about a harem of available females to bolster their own sense of worth. The dream of sex with more than one woman at a time frees men from the constant threat of competition with other males. They've shared mother with father and their siblings; they've shared girl friends with other men, and wives with their children and in-laws. For once, even if only for a few minutes, they would love to have two or more women sharing *them*.

Anal sex is the bane of sexual therapists. In *Everything You Always Wanted to Know About Sex*, David Reuben discussed it only in terms of homosexual activity, and said cynically that "determined assault by the homosexual penis, generous amounts of lubrication and intense pain on the part of the 'recipient' ultimately result in 'success,'" though at the cost of sphincter muscle tone. Dr. Theodore Rubin, who is a little more liberal, but not more enthusiastic, characterizes anal intercourse as possibly harmful, with psychological overtones of anger, mastery, and conquest, and physically leading to urethral infection in the male and tearing of the "vital anal sphincter muscle" in the woman.

There is a great temptation here to report that only 4.2 percent of our men wanted anal sex more often, dismiss it as insignificant, and move on to the next question. But recently a male mental health assistant, only months away from receiving his master's degree in psychiatric social work, asked at a supervision seminar, "How could you persuade a woman to have anal sex if her husband wanted to and she didn't?" Now, we have been accustomed to hearing this sort of question from family doctors dealing with older wives who refuse to try oral sex, and our advice has been to confront the reasons for the women's inhibitions and help her to experiment. But in cases involving anal sex, our counsel is, if the woman is unwilling, work with the husband on *his* problem in demanding it.

The problem is compounded by the profusion of popular literature that presents anal sex as a routine, desirable form of sexual variation. The author of *The Sensuous Woman* tells her readers to "stop wailing like a banshee or playing Purity Raped" at such a devious proposition, and *Redbook* magazine reported that 48 percent of young women in one of its surveys engage in anal sex, a particularly disturbing statistic because it indicates that women most thought of as "liberated", are involved in what one male author described as "the ultimate act of submission for a woman, short of sadomasochistic acts."

So, is the woman who participates in anal sex very liberated or very dominated and exploited? And how prevalent is the practice? Whereas anal intercourse between men and women was regarded by Kinsey as "not frequent enough to make it possible to determine the incidence of individuals who are specifically responsive to such stimulation," Hunt estimated in 1972 that about 25 percent of couples under 35 used the technique and over one-sixth of single people under 25 had tried it, but only 9 percent of the men within the past year. *Playboy's* 1976 campus poll indicated that 20 percent of college males have tried it (14 percent liked it) and 41 percent would be willing to try it for the first time. In our survey, only 4 percent of students cited it as the thing they would most like to do more often.

Shere Hite, who changed her questionnaire three times during the process of her study on women and asked questions about rectal contact of only 1,609 of her claimed total sample of 3,000, reported only 146 women who enjoyed anal intercourse. Another 215 of the 1,609 polled apparently did not answer the rectal questions, but if we assume they did not enjoy anal sex, we can calculate that only 11 percent of Hite's sample, drawn largely from the militant ranks of National Organization for Women, found the technique pleasant.

Theodore Rubin notwithstanding, the number of women sustaining lacerations of their anuses or other complications is really quite rare when you consider the number of experimenters; the incidence of rectal gonorrhea and other venereal diseases is much more common. Since women in therapy find it difficult to discuss anal sex and many claim subsequent feelings of having done something dirty or shameful, the psychic trauma is apparently more common than the physical. Still, a woman should never feel she is being prudish or unreasonable in her refusal to comply. The woman who enjoys anal masturbation, who delights in enemas, or has stimulating reveries about anal sex will probably enjoy the act and, with a patient partner, runs little risk. But for the woman not so inclined, we reiterate that 96 percent of the men in this country are *not* panting for more anal sex, and we suggest that she find one of them.

Sadomasochistic activity is actively desired by only 1.2 percent of our men, although nonwhites averaged 3.7 percent in this response. (Black men outranked white in preference for anal sex as well—7.5 percent to 3.9 percent, though "other" races were low at 2.2 percent) Since men are more interested in fantasizing about sadomasochistic activities than in acting out the urge, our discussion of S-M will be covered in the chapter on fantasies.

## Gay Choice or Sad Plight?

Despite a recent backlash, there is now a more widespread accept-ance of homosexuality by society, antidiscrimination legislation, an increased popularity of group sex, and a generalized decrease in inhibitions along with an increasing demand for sexual variety. Does this mean that homosexuality is increasing?

Since Kinsey's report that 37 percent of men have had one or more homosexual experiences, an estimate he based on many reports of transient experiments early in adolescence, investigators have gen-erally agreed that the number of thoroughly homosexual men in the country ranges between 1 and 4 percent. Psychiatrist Irving Bieber, co-author of *Homosexuality: A Psychoanalytic Study* (1962) says that 1 to 2 percent of American adult males are exclusively homosexual, and another 3 to 4 percent are bisexual. Hunt's 1972 sample yielded 1 percent homosexual and another 1 percent bisexual.

These are the findings from our own sample:

*Question 11: With what type of partner do you usually engage in sex?*

| | |
|---|---|
| Women only | 93.4% |
| Men only | 1.3% |
| Women and men | 3.1% |
| No sexual experience | 1.2% |
| No answer | 1.1% |

Our survey coincides closely with Bieber's estimates, with our findings of 1.3 percent exclusively homosexual and 3.1 percent bisex-ual. Of our men who reported themselves living with a partner to whom they were not married, 4.6 percent were homosexual, 8.6 percent bisexual. Among blacks, 9.2 percent claimed to be bisexual, as opposed to 2.6 percent whites and 5.1 percent "other races." There were more exclusive homosexuals among the blacks; 2.5 per-cent against 1.1 percent for whites; "other races" had 3.6 percent homosexuals.

In the previous question about what men would like to do more often sexually, homosexuality was the fondest wish of only 1.6 per-cent of our sample, virtually identical to the 1.3 percent of our re-spondents who declared themselves exclusively homosexual. And 5.7 percent of those living with a partner to whom they were not mar-ried chose this answer. Many of these responses may have come from homosexuals living with a male partner. Single men wanted increased homosexual activity in 3.0 percent of the cases, against 1.6 percent divorced/widowed and 0.8 percent married.

This book is about relationships between men and women. We did not believe that a homosexual could meaningfully answer our questions by applying them to his relationships with male partners. Therefore, most of our questions made specific references to women. No attempt was made to deter homosexuals from accepting the questionnaire, since it was presented as a study of men's attitudes about sex. At least 1 percent of the respondents did not answer each of the computer-tabulated questions, and we assume homosexuals accounted for many of the "no answers."

This makes our approach drastically different from that of Shere Hite, who apparently designed her questionnaire so that it could be answered easily by homosexuals as well as heterosexuals. In the 58-item questionnaire (the final one of four) she presented to women, she always used the asexual term "partner," never used "male" or "husband" and used the word "men" only three times. Questions were sometimes addressed specifically to lesbians. The word "penis" appears only once in the questionnaire, and she used the term "penetration" in a way that allowed for the use of fingers or dildos.

Hite is not only tolerant of bisexuality, she is absolutely militant about it, something few of her readers have commented upon. It's possible most readers failed to get through the 35 pages on the six types of female masturbation or to notice the following passage on page 276:

> Any woman who feels actual horror or revulsion at the thought of kissing or embracing or having physical relations with another woman should reexamine her feelings and attitudes not only about other women, but also about *herself.* A positive attitude toward our bodies and toward touching ourselves and toward any physical contact that might naturally develop with another woman is essential to self-love and accepting our own bodies as good and beautiful. As Jill Johnston has written: " . . . until women see in each other the possibility of a primal commitment which includes sexual love they will be denying themselves the love and value they readily accord to men, thus affirming their own second class status."

The above is not just a plea for understanding the lesbian viewpoint. It is a statement that unless the woman agrees with it, even if she does not engage in homosexuality, there is something wrong with her. The quote from Johnston, a gay spokesperson, implies that the love that women receive from men in return is worthless and that "first class" love comes only from other women.

Hite uses the "homophobe" attack on heterosexuals popularized by those homosexuals who believe the best defense is a good offense. The homosexual turns the tables on the "straights" by saying that their refusal to have relations with partners of the same sex is based on a neurotic, self-demeaning fear or phobia of members of the same gender. Those psychiatrists who regarded homosexuality as a mental illness always argued that the choice of same-sex partners was not a true choice, because the homosexual was, in reality, neurotically repulsed by partners of the opposite sex. Now Hite uses the same line that homosexuals have contested for years as biased and unscientific.

Before anyone can evaluate the Hite report objectively, one must understand her bias. We need not object to her views on lesbianism, but we must know that she holds these views. Then, the disproportionately low percentage of married women in her sample (38 percent) and high percentages of women single (29 percent) and living with "lover" (12 percent) suggest the possibility of a disproportionate input from homosexuals and bisexuals. Add to this bias her curious categories of "boy friend" (9.5 percent) and 1 percent "celibate" and her ranks of single women swell to 42 percent, not counting the divorced and widowed living alone. She herself sums up the book with: "It must have been clear throughout this book how tired women are of the old mechanical pattern of sexual relations, which revolves around male erection, male penetration, and male orgasm." She asks the rhetorical question, "Do men need intercourse?" and extols lesbian sexuality as involving the kind of extended intimate physical contact one respondent claimed she was not getting from her male lover. Whether or not the entire Hite report is regarded as a lesbian polemic, her own prohomosexual views are never in question.

While we do not intend to advise people on how to improve homosexual relationships, we do want to address the problem of gay or bisexual men who profess to want marriage or a steady relationship with a woman. Should a woman risk involvement with a man who has a history of homosexual activity? The first consideration must be when his homosexual activity occurred and under what circumstances. Many adolescents, during a period of high sex drive and unavailability of female partners, engage in homosexual experimentation; some investigators even consider group masturbation a homosexual phenomenon, even though it does not truly involve an act between two men, only a solitary act witnessed by others. Such episodes are so common that they can be virtually discounted if the male has enthusiastically and exclusively accepted female partners, once they became available. Adult males who engage in homosexual acts in settings where there are no females—such as prisons, naval ships, war zones, and isolated expeditions—may be acceptable risks, although it should be pointed out that most men will resort to masturbation, but not homosexuality in the absence of women. Men who enjoy a broad range of sexual activities, including group sex, anal sex, and exotic variations, are likely to engage with male as well as female partners. Here, the problem for the woman may prove to be the man's promiscuity rather than homosexuality. Psychiatrists use the term "polymorphous perverse" to describe people who crave or accept all manner of sexual activity—"polymorphous" means "many forms" and "perverse" means away from the normal; it's tough for a woman to be all things to such a partner, so unless she's a free-wheeler herself, she had best not try.

Men turn to other men for two main reasons. The first and most classical one is a fear of the female, so that the man could not have intercourse if he tried. Such men have usually been raised by pathologically seductive mothers and rejecting or threatening fathers. The possibilities of incestuous intercourse and paternal retaliation are so vivid that the boy repudiates all attraction to females. The second major reason is a fear of men, not women. The boy feels so inadequate that he dares not compete with other men for fear they will angrily destroy him. Even a woman with no current lover cannot be approached for fear some other man might want her and attack him. Ultimately, the man with such a conflict becomes homosexual in an attempt to win, through his passive compliance, the approval and protection of the men who threaten him. Men operating through this fear are more likely to be able to have intercourse with women than the ones with deep incest conflicts and castration anxiety.

With the increasing confusion about male ideals in society and the ever-increasing demands for male performance on competitive jobs and in the beds of assertive women, psychiatrists are seeing more men with a syndrome termed "pseudohomosexuality." Such men have never engaged in homosexual acts, but suspect they are homosexual, have erotic fantasies about other men and homosexual dreams, feel compelled to look at other men's sex organs, and feel extremely uneasy around homosexuals. These men are not true homosexuals, because in an actual homosexual situation, they would not become sexually aroused and certainly would not perform; they are neurotic heterosexuals who feel they fail to measure up to adequate standards of masculinity, and they equate inadequacy with homosexuality.

The man who has lived an exclusively or mainly homosexual life has an extremely difficult time changing. "Bisexuals" are usually men who prefer homosexual relationships, but believe that heterosexuality is healthier and more acceptable; female partners are often sought to maintain the man's self-respect and give the impression that homosexual activities are a matter of free choice. Irving Bieber, more successful than most psychiatrists, is justifiably proud of a 30 percent rate of permanent conversion to exclusive heterosexuality through intensive psychotherapy. Homosexuals have done as well with him as bisexuals, but the fact remains that 70 percent of his homosexual patients fail to change despite their sincere motivation.

For the woman determined to take the risk, we pass along Dr. Bieber's indications for a more hopeful outlook. Men under 35 have a better chance of converting than older men. Men who have at least attempted intercourse with a woman or who have heterosexual dreams fare better than those with nothing but good intentions. Positive feelings held toward his father improve the homosexual's chances (Catch–22: Not one of 106 patients treated by Bieber had a warm, constructive relationship with his father). A history of effeminate voice and gestures in childhood or of a mother who openly preferred her son to the father are danger signs.

Unfortunately, under stress, bisexual men tend to resume their quest for a strong, loving, hypermasculine father figure, deserting their wives at the time when they need each other most. A devoted wife may ultimately win out over another woman, yet feel totally unequipped to compete with another man.

## The Impossible Dream

An anonymous philosopher once said, "The worst sex I ever had was still pretty good." While this may represent the opinion of most men, it does not stop them from forever imagining some improvement in their sex lives. This was apparent in the response to our previous question about what men would like to do more often sexually—only 11 percent of the men indicated by answering "none" that they were perfectly contented with the variety of sex they enjoyed. Contentment with the status quo increased with age, so that nearly a quarter of the men over 55 did not desire more experimentation of some sort —three times the number of contented men in their twenties. The oldest men had either found the formula for sexual happiness through years of experience, or were too worn out to continue the search. Married men were least interested in adding to the variety of their sex lives, while men living with partners out of wedlock were most adventurous.

According to the myth of the new impotence, men are finding it difficult to relate to independent and sexually assertive women, so that they are seeking sex less frequently or, in increasing numbers, avoiding it completely because of emotional conflicts over the potency problems brought about by the threatening modern woman. If this were true, we would expect men to desire intercourse less frequently than in the past. On the contrary, we found men desired intercourse more often than ever:

*Question 12: Ideally, how often would you want intercourse?*

| More than once a day | 13.1% |
| 5 to 7 times a week | 25.3% |
| 3 to 4 times a week | 34.6% |
| 1 to 2 times a week | 18.2% |
| 2 to 3 times a month | 5.9% |
| Once a month or less | 1.7% |
| Never | 0.4% |
| No answer | 0.8% |

We did not ask our males how often they actually had intercourse because adequate statistics based on large samples are already in existence and we preferred to limit our questions to what women most wanted to know about men. Women are less concerned with what men do than with what they really want. When Morton Hunt compared the weekly frequency of intercourse reported by husbands in 1972 with Kinsey's data accumulated from 1938 through 1949, he found an increase in coital frequency, especially in men under 35, who had gone from intercourse twice a week to 3 or 4 times a week. Now, if we add to these figures our own data on what men in each age group consider the ideal frequency, we see that throughout life man's goals always outstrip his actualities:

| Frequency per week (Kinsey) | | Frequency per week (Hunt) | | Ideal Frequency | |
|---|---|---|---|---|---|
| *Age* | *Average** | *Age* | *Average** | *Age* | *Average** |
| 16–25 | 2.3 | 18–24 | 3.5 | 18–29 | 5 to 7 |
| 26–35 | 1.9 | 25–34 | 3.0 | 30–39 | 3 to 4 |
| 36–45 | 1.4 | 35–44 | 2.0 | | |
| 46–55 | .8 | 45–54 | 1.5 | 40–54 | 3 to 4 |
| 56–60 | .6 | 55 & over | 1.0 | 55–65 | 1 to 2 |

*The figures for Kinsey's and Hunt's reports are the medians for each age group, the middle value when all responses are ranked from highest to lowest. The "average" for our study is the ideal frequency range chosen by the greatest percentage of men in the indicated bracket.

We see that as men grow older, they lower their standards for the ideal frequency of sexual relations; but since their actual sexual activity also decreases, they forever think they should be having intercourse more often. The Kinsey and Hunt figures are for married men, who theoretically should be most active because, as George Bernard Shaw noted, marriage "combines the maximum of temptation with the maximum of opportunity." Our own figures, broken down by age, include single, divorced, widowed, married, and living-together men, but the concept of an *ideal* would not likely be modified by either temptation or opportunity.

Married men in our study actually did desire intercourse less frequently than their less-committed colleagues; married men most often opted for intercourse 3 to 4 times a week, whereas singles most often chose 5 to 7 times a week as the ideal. Those living with a partner, unmarried, and the divorced/widowed living alone were very close to the singles in their ideals. More than one married man in five considered intercourse once or twice a week as ideal, but only one unmarried man in eight would be content with that frequency. Of men who wanted sex more than once a day, the living-togethers were highest, with a 23 percent representation; about 18 percent of the divorced/widowed and unmarried men living alone wanted this high frequency, but only 10 percent of married men had such ambitions.

Nonwhites averaged 20 percent in choosing sex more than once a day as ideal, compared with 12 percent of whites; but for the more realistic ideal frequencies, there was no racial discrepancy. Every occupational, income, and educational group selected 3 to 4 times a week as its most frequent response, with 5 to 7 times a week second. Overall, 70 percent of the men wanted sex ideally at least three times a week.

Kinsey did not give any figures, but he stated, in the 1940s, that many younger husbands desired more frequent intercourse, but in the later years of marriage, it was often the wives that wished for increased frequency. Hunt's reported study in 1972 said that 40 to 50 percent of husbands were desirous of more frequent sex. Men at 45 surpassed younger ones in their desire for more frequent intercourse.

Using Hunt's data to estimate the frequency of actual intercourse, we can gauge from our survey that 51 percent of men under 30 and 40 percent of men in their thirties would ideally want sex more frequently than most of them actually achieve; the same is true for 65 percent of men 40 to 54 and 38 percent of all men over 55. Some of these men may, of course, be actually living up to their ideals; but since the number of men in each age group who desired sex *less* frequently than the known medians ranged only from approximately 9 percent (men 40 to 54 who felt the ideal was less than once a week) to 27 percent (men over 55 who felt the ideal was less than once a week), we can again conclude that most men do not quite measure up to their own standards.

The fact that men's ambitions in this area often exceed their grasp is not necessarily unfortunate. For one thing, it indicates that most men find intercourse satisfactory, or they would not want more of it. When partners find intercourse extremely pleasurable, they are likely to silently berate themselves for not having it more frequently. They lose sight of the fact that it was the waiting until they had reached a peak of desire and had encountered the right circumstances that made the act such a positive one. Factors such as lack of privacy, fatigue, and illness may dampen enthusiasm or rain out the action altogether.

Some men are calendar watchers, just as others are clock watchers. The clock watcher is obsessively preoccupied with how long he can delay his orgasm during actual penetration, and tries to beat an arbitrary standard, such as ten minutes, or break his own current record. The calendar watcher schedules sex for certain nights in the week or is very careful to maintain a weekly or monthly average. In this way, he reassures himself that he is normal and adequate. As with all routine acts, however, scheduled intercourse becomes an automatic thing where little thought or imagination is required. Just as continuous exposure to the same noise or same odor tends to extinguish its perception, automatic sexual patterns are perceived less vividly on all levels of consciousness.

Spontaneity and variety are more important than frequency; they are actually quite likely to lead to increased frequency as intercourse becomes more pleasurable. Sexual variation should not be limited to positions and techniques; a different room, a different hour, or a different mood can be just as refreshing. If the woman never takes the initiative in a relationship, a female advance on a customary off-night can double the couple's sexual frequency; her interest will usually be enough to ignite fires that would otherwise take several days of smoldering to rekindle spontaneously. But always beware of routines, even frequent and pleasurable ones. Men tend to settle into them and expect the woman to do regularly what came as such an invigorating surprise, turning unscheduled charter flights of fantasy into dreary shuttle runs. Women should consciously attempt to keep their mates pleasantly off balance so that sexual encounters will be too unique to lump together in weekly bunches.

Men will apparently never be entirely satisfied with their frequency of sexual performance. One wishes that every man could have a Shaw's jird for a pet; this obscure North African rodent has been observed to copulate 112 times in one hour. After exposure to a jird, men might give up striving for new highs in sexual frequency, and settle for improving the distinctly human aspects of lovemaking with which no jird could ever compete.

# What Makes a Woman a Good Lover?

Does lovemaking come with experience or is it an outgrowth of natural feeling? Do men expect their lovers to be sophisticated in sexual matters, or do they seek out women who appear innocent and naïve?

*Essay Question: What makes a woman a good lover? Should she be aggressive, a little shy, tender, eager to try new things? How much experience should she have had?*

This question was similar in some ways to the one about how men liked a woman to act during sex; however, we hoped here to get men to discriminate between casual bed-partners and women they considered lovers by virtue of a greater depth of feeling and a more committed relationship—if, indeed, such a distinction existed. We have seen previously that most men today desire an active, aggressive woman. Did they equate this with considerable past experience?

Some men felt the nature of her relationships and her own emotional makeup were as important as experience:

"If she has a feeling that she is loved, she will make a good lover. She should act in ways which come naturally to her. She need *not* have had any experience."

"She should be able to empathize totally during the sexual experience. Communication is the name of the game and for that reason, experience or a lack of really doesn't come into the picture."

"Kind, considerate person who is happy and independent in her thoughts and attitudes. She can have any amount (or none) of experience and should always be willing to experiment on highly personal basis. (No group.)"

"A good man. She should be able to determine what she must be at the time. With each partner she should be a different woman. Experience? It isn't how many times or lovers, it's quality."

"Understanding and a knowledge of her own needs and a willingness to work for them. What was before is none of my business."

"What is important is how the two of you can grow together."

Some respondents felt variety and lack of inhibition in a sexual relationship was the essence of being a good lover:

"I feel that the lack of sexual variety between a couple is the death of many a sexual relationship. I feel that a small amount of meaningful sexual experience goes a long way. The quantity of sexual experience isn't as important as the quality."

"I appreciate tenderness, with willingness to keep intercourse from becoming routine by varying the techniques of foreplay and coitus. Sex, like anything else, loses its appeal if the act becomes routine, boring."

"Reading, trying, being uncritical, becoming orgasmic, freer in love making. Experience really doesn't matter. Involvement does."

"A woman should be uninhibited, willing to satisfy as well as be satisfied, able to enjoy her own sexuality (not be hung up on guilt or inferiority trips)—a capacity for innovation is also important."

"I think my views have changed here as I've gotten older. When I was younger I had to have a virgin; as a matter of fact, in my first marriage (divorced now about 1½ years) when I found out she wasn't a virgin I became unbelievably upset and ended up that evening in a hospital after wrecking my car. But my views have changed today, I expect a woman to have had experience but hopefully not too much! I appreciate a woman who is tender, but at the same time one who gets turned on rather than acting unconcerned about the whole thing."

"Intensely warm-blooded—goes all the way. Very aggressive. Does not need experience. Should be born a good lover."

Are good lovers really born that way? Isn't experience still the best teacher? Well, even without experience, there are always plenty of men around willing and eager to teach:

"An appreciative, active, emotional and loving woman. Should be moderately aggressive and willing to try new things. Lots of experience is unnecessary since most women are fast sexual 'learners.' (Teach your own.)"

"I like mine to be shy at first then become very aggressive, but always tender. I like to teach her new things."

"Affectionate and willing to try new things, sometimes aggressive, sometimes shy, but always willing to please me as I would to her. Experience—a little helps however as long as she has an open mind and willing to learn or teach."

"The partner has a lot to do with a person being a good lover or a bad lover. I think I should be dominant in my relationship during sex and do most of the leading. Experience is not really essential any more, she should just do what comes naturally and shouldn't hold back."

"A little shy letting me be the aggressor but enough experience not to be afraid."

Some men accepted experienced madonnas, but stipulated that prostitutes need not apply:

"A good lover is attentive, shares in sexual activity. Experience is not undesirable. Promiscuity is undesirable."

"Aggressive, not critical, uninhibited, able to have fun in bed. Experience is irrelevant although I might feel threatened by a former hooker."

"Imagination; boldness; stimulating; agile and coordinated; adventuresome; some experience helpful but professional activity undesirable."

"She should be partly aggressive, but not too much so. She should be willing to try new things and offer to please her partner with sexplay he enjoys. Too much experience can make her jaded and dissatisfied."

Being a lover is probably the only occupation in the world (at least according to some men) where experience is a drawback:

> "Women who I know are experienced or let me know of their experiences tend to intimidate me. Understanding, eager but still cognizant of my needs and fears, but most importantly, comfortable to be with."

> "A woman is a good lover if she tries to be herself and show consideration to her partner. I would prefer no experience. There is nothing more beautiful than exploring sex together."

> "Overaggressiveness turns me off. Aggressive in terms of suggestion, touch, sexy clothing—*wanting* to make love and openly showing her joy during pre-intercourse and intercourse. Experience—I would feel uncomfortable if she was 'experienced.'"

> "She doesn't have to be experienced. You learn this with your husband. The longer you are together the better everything gets. You learn each other's likes and dislikes."

Men today have repudiated the old traditions that demanded passivity and unemotional compliance in sexual relations from a good and virtuous woman. If they are becoming more insecure in their own masculinity, men at least seem willing to admit that they are not born with all the answers and, if women have more freedom and knowledge these days, they are expected to use it with responsibility in the quest for mutual sexual harmony and gratification. Men want an active and aggressive partner who is willing to communicate her needs and understand those of her man. The supreme position of the missionary has been shaken, and men are willing to risk security for something better than the old routine—even willing to admit that perhaps sexual satisfaction can be questioned without simultaneously questioning their virility.

The expectations may seem unrealistic at times but, as Browning said, "A man's reach should exceed his grasp, or what's a heaven for?" Men may not reach heaven on earth, but some of the earthly delights aren't half bad.

# Satyrs and
# Other Legends

DON JUAN: Do you not understand that when I stood
face to face with Woman, every fibre in my clear
critical brain warned me to spare her and save myself. My morals said No. My conscience said No. My
chivalry and pity for her said No. My prudent regard
for myself said No. . . . And whilst I was in the act of
framing my excuse to the lady, Life seized me and
threw me into her arms as a sailor throws a scrap of
fish into the mouth of a seabird.

—GEORGE BERNARD SHAW, *Man and Superman*

Don Juan here portrays himself as a man overpowered by lust, even
at times when his clear and critical brain is opposing it vigorously. He
could only escape the grip of passion after he had managed to put
some distance between himself and his newest lover, and he became
as notorious for his retreats as for his conquests. Don Juan became the
myth of male insatiability, the embodiment of the compulsion to
mate with every desirable female encountered.

To the mind of woman, man's lust is wild and formidable. The first
piece of sexual counseling that she is likely to get from her mother
is the axiom, "All men are after only one thing." Her father, if he can
stifle his embarrassment enough to talk to her at all, reinforces that
axiom with a set of rules restricting dress, cosmetics, late hours,
secluded places, and anything that might abet her escort's single-
minded assault on her body.

Her more experienced peers describe the terrible pressure of male
needs, the excruciating gonadal pain for men who are aroused and

71

unsatisfied; the male himself makes all the predicted advances in predictable sequence, and when suaveness, cynicism, and romance fail, he is not above pleading for merciful relief from his agonizing lust. Many a virgin has succumbed not out of ardor, but compassion. The image of the man with the loins of an animal pervades mythology: the roisterous, stallion-limbed centaurs; the lascivious, goat-haunched satyrs; the fierce lion-loined manticore; and the benevolent but potent bull-bodied lamassus that guarded the temples of the Orient. Satan himself is usually depicted with the head of a man, but the lower body of a goat, bristling with phallic symbols—his horns, his long tail, his pointed goatee, and his pitchfork.

Men, in truth, have been rather flattered by comparisons to sex-driven animals, and delight in labels such as "wolf," "stud," "tomcat," and "tiger." Words that demean their size and brute strength, such as "ape" and "gorilla," are not considered very offensive, and epithets that revile their callous treatment of women, such as "rat," "skunk," and "cur," may be met with snickers of bravado. One fashionable New York men's store recently sold neckties decorated with the monogram "MCP" (for "male chauvinist pig"), some with the actual image of the macho mascot.

Is sex the most important thing in men's lives? If it isn't, would they admit it? And what in the world could be more important to them?

*Question 13: How do you feel about sex?*

| | |
|---|---|
| Not the most, but a very important pleasure | 61.2% |
| It's the most important pleasure in life | 19.8% |
| It's important only as a means of expressing love | 11.4% |
| It's strictly a physical pleasure | 4.2% |
| Other things are more important, such as business or hobbies | 1.7% |
| It's not very important to me | 1.4% |
| It's something you have to do | 0.7% |
| No answer | 0.5% |

We also asked an essay question that enabled our respondents to elaborate on their feelings about sex and its relative importance in their lives:

*Essay Question: How do you feel about sex? What does it mean to you? How important is it and how would you compare it with other things in your life?*

For 80 percent of men, sex is not the most important pleasure in life. They not only find other things in their lives more important;

they even find activities that are more pleasurable. It is true that when a man is intensely attracted to a woman or has been without a sexual outlet for a considerable period of time, he may be relentless in his pursuit of gratification; but libido, like any appetite, once whetted, becomes nonexistent for a time. Sexual appeasement is a recurrent but short-lived need, while other pursuits, such as success and security, do not periodically die out. Even an unusually susceptible man like Don Juan who could not resist a woman when he approached her would always follow the dictates of his cool and rational brain once the heat of the moment was dissipated.

In our previous chapter, we saw that men feel they should ideally be having intercourse more often than they actually do. In reality, there are invariably more pressing needs or commitments that force the sex drive into a secondary position of importance. Their desire for more aggressive women indicates that, in order to ensure an active, fulfilling sex life, they need a partner who can entice and divert them from the other concerns that dominate their lives.

Man embodies within him the elements of the gods Dionysus and Apollo. Dionysus is the god of wine, a lusty, reveling fellow who leads a troupe of satyrs and nymphs; Apollo is the god of light, a rational, poetic type. When Dionysus holds sway, a man will find his sexual urges often overpowering and will be oblivious to reason; but ultimately the Apollonian aspects will prevail, as dependably and predictably as the sun rises each morning while the revelers slumber in an unconscious stupor.

Most men (61 percent) considered sex an important pleasure, though not life's most important one. Some men affirmed this belief without specifying what pleasures or priorities ranked higher:

"A satisfaction of horny desires. Depending on girl—sometimes good, or nothing. As part of life but not a fulfillment. Life is full of too much to see and do, than just sex."

"Sex is for me a pleasureful experience, perhaps a bit more psychologically fulfilling than eating a dinner—but not the 'cream of the crop' experience by a long shot. For instance, watching a sunset in solitude or with someone is very fulfilling but on a different level."

"Sex is fantastic, it is the best way for one to relieve inner tension (that, of course, is for self) and is the best way to express your love and creativity to the one you love and cherish. It is about the third or fourth thing on my list of priorities, but it is there."

For those men who said there were more important things, these priorities fell into two major categories, one being success in work and financial affairs, and the other being love and satisfying interpersonal relationships with a woman:

> "Sex is not as important as a sound life philosophy and is only a form of sharing affection and love. Friendship is the most important thing in life."

> "Biological and emotional need. Very important in the sense of personal need and contentment. Not the most important thing, but may have strong effects on other more important things."

> "Important part of life and marriage. Second only to my children."

> "I like sex very much and yet, it means less than companionship."

Sex as biological need, sex as psychological drive, and sex as an act of free choice involving a highly personal relationship between two human beings are all realities, although some men approach sex as though it had only one or two of these three components. We were not surprised that many men ranked work and achievement ahead of sex, for in our society such voluntary pursuits often assume the intensity of biological drives. One respondent not only ranked his "striving" for career success above sex, but was even able to rank it above strictly biological needs, such as eating and sleeping:

> "Sex is necessary and fun! I would rather engage in sex with the 'girl of my dreams,' but I wouldn't pass up an opportunity to have intercourse with an attractive lady at any time. As far as importance, at this particular time in my life and with the individual I have chosen to live with, I would rank my sex life about #4, behind: (1) Striving for a successful business career (2) Consumption of food and beverage (3) Need for seven hours of sleep per night (4) Participation in sex, regularly."

> "I do not distinguish between sex and love as a desire, and I desire love intensely, but I also desire other aspects of life intensely, e.g., productive, enjoyable work. Within a romantic relationship, I desire sex as often as contextually (and emotionally) possible."

"Sex is a reaction to a biological and less emotional craving. It is important and necessary but other things like money, status, children occasionally take first place. Sex was more important *before* I got married."

"Enjoy it. It comes a close second behind flying as a job. I can spend a hell of a lot more time flying than I can screwing."

"Sex is cool, but not the most important aspect. My respect for sex acts stems from discerning the right to have it and the maturity to deserve it. Drag racing is more to my attitude."

When we examine men's psychological attitudes toward sex, we might initially feel that many emphasize work and career ambitions as drives totally apart from their sex lives. The last few answers indicate how men often feel they must earn their sexual prerogatives, as in the case of the respondent who spoke frankly of "the right to have it and the maturity to deserve it." Arousal depends not only on the reaction of the man towards his female partner's attributes, but also upon his perception of himself in that situation. Hence, it is not uncommon to encounter cases of impotence when a man confronts a woman he deems himself unworthy of: one with superior intelligence, a more successful career, a great deal of sexual experience, or even a particularly voluptuous figure. Neurotic men may have difficulty with maternal or cultured women, feeling that a sexual act would debase these madonnas. And sometimes a man's worthiness may not involve a particular partner, but all women. Psychiatrists commonly see men in their twenties who cannot even picture themselves in a sexual encounter because they feel physically unattractive, are intimidated by other men, have failed in school, and hold menial jobs or none at all. Acceptance or rejection by a woman is irrelevant; they will not even risk an encounter because they cannot accept themselves as true men.

Women, after all, have a recognized need to see themselves as sexually desirable. Weight control, hair conditioning, figure-flattering clothing, and careful hygiene are concerns of the married as well as single woman. Many women are aroused by pictures of nude females in men's magazines; not out of any homosexual element, but through identification with this irresistible object. Women who feel they are not desirable generally make apathetic partners; however, even the ungainly woman can view her man's erection as indisputable proof of her desirability.

Men cannot rely so easily on their bodies as criteria for desirability.

Also, evidence of a woman's arousal in the initial stages is not readily discernible. Observation has led men to the indisputable conclusion that the man who is most desired and pursued by women is not the beautiful man, but the successful man.

Not all of men's emphasis on work and money relate to a quest for sexual supremacy. Our society's emphasis on settling down with one faithful partner gives a man a lot more energy than males of less monogamous species to devote to other pursuits. Then, as our pilot said above, "I can spend a hell of a lot more time flying than I can screwing." Men are acutely aware of their physical limitations. A highly erotic woman might fantasize about an endless series of orgasms with one superman or a harem of lovers, but a man knows that his penis could no more manage endless sexual activity than his gastrointestinal tract could accommodate all-day eating. Career ambition is limitless, but sexual drive is not.

Thus it is not surprising that 61 percent of our sample said that sex was not the most, though a very, important pleasure. The 1.7 percent that selected the answer "Other things are more important, such as business or hobbies" are probably the type termed by psychiatrists obsessive-compulsive, men who tend to overvalue the rational and reject the emotional. They dissociate ideas and experiences from the associated feelings and rarely show outbursts of temper or passion. They love orderliness and routine. Strong emotion of any sort represents the threat of loss of self-control.

One respondent said, "My feelings about sex are mostly for pleasure, but at times it is to satisfy my need for achievement. Sex is very important although sometimes I rank business obligations or objectives first." His questionnaire showed that he considered many casual partners the ideal sex relationship and he would like most to engage in group sex more often.

This respondent demonstrates that while some work-oriented men may seek limited, conventional, and unimaginative sex lives, others are less inhibited, but apply standards of achievement—rather than pleasure—to their sex lives and seek partners in quantity, rather than striving for a solid relationship with one woman.

While the percentage of men who specified that interests such as business or hobbies were more important was small throughout the sample, the number was greatest among the oldest (2.5 percent over age 55) and youngest (2.4 percent under 30) men, possibly reflecting diminished sexual drive in the seniors and intensified career ambition in the juniors on their way up. Single men (3.0 percent) chose this response more than married (1.3 percent) and those living with a partner (1.4 percent). Divorced men were intermediate (2.3 percent).

One in five men (20 percent) did consider sex to be the most important pleasure in life:

"Most important thing in life—with it, everything else falls into place."

"I enjoy sex very much. It means making your partner happy and a way of expressing love to one another. To me it is the best thing in life."

"Sex is *life*. The greatest pleasure. The only thing that gives me a sense of well-being."

"Most enjoyable thing there is. It means almost everything at this time. Compares with being a father for the first time."

Some men saw sex not as occupying a linear position on a hierarchy of priorities, but as a central focus around which other aspects of life revolved:

"It is central—no less or greater in general than food, work, play, etc."

"I think that sex is an important part of our lives. It rounds out for me a complete relationship. If things are going well for me sexually, everything else goes well."

"[It] is the one thing you can do for free and the pleasure it returns is great. It doesn't compare with other things in life, because it is life itself."

What sort of man considers sex the most important pleasure in life? One would be tempted to say the macho, whose preoccupation with his masculine image, the foundation of his entire identity, requires sex for its verification. One respondent wrote, "It makes me feel like a man. I'm macho and I'm glad." However, on the objective portion of his questionnaire, he indicated that other things are more important, such as business or hobbies. While he believed the ideal sex life would be marriage with outside activity and had cheated on a few occasions, he felt the ideal frequency of intercourse would be 2 or 3 times *a month*. He seems rather pseudo-macho. Yet our respondents who considered sex to be number one often expressed concern for their partner's needs and did not seem emotionally detached from their sexuality.

Education seemed to be the biggest factor in distinguishing men who regarded sex as their greatest pleasure, i.e., the more the education the less weight given to sex as pleasure. Of those who did not complete high school, 30 percent had this attitude, which decreased as schooling increased. The percentage for high school graduates was 21, with 17 for college graduates and those with postgraduate education. Students were the lowest occupational group, only 14 percent choosing sex as most important, the next lowest being 18 percent (managerial). Blue collars and retired/unemployed were highest with 23 and 22, respectively. Nonwhites ranked this attitude much higher than whites (29 percent of blacks, 28 other races, 19 white), possibly another reflection of education, since whites have distinct advantages in schooling and subsequent job stature.

Those living with partners, unmarried (24 percent), and the married (20) tended to view sex as the greatest pleasure more than the single (18) and divorced/widowed (17). With regard to age, there was not much variation.

But education and occupation still emerge as the main governing factors, indicating that men find sex their number-one pleasure when other areas of life cannot give them fulfillment, as in the case of the respondent who said sex *was* life because it was the *only* thing that gave him a sense of well-being. Don Juan understood this when he said, "The ploughman lives as long as the philosopher, eats more, sleeps better, and rejoices in the wife of his bosom with less misgiving." Still, the educated man may make the better lover because sex does not assume ponderous implications for his entire identity and existence, and his relationship with a woman does not cave in if he or she should become temporarily incapacitated for physical or emotional reasons to engage in intercourse. The educated man is more at odds with his lower parts; but the human head was able to convert hybrids like Chiron and Pan from half-human monsters into demigods and gods.

Eleven percent of the men said that sex is important only as a means of expressing love. We might have expected this attitude chiefly from the oldest men, but 14 percent of the men under 30—highest of any age bracket—chose this answer, as opposed to 8 percent of men in their thirties. Single men scored slightly higher than the others, with 14 percent. Either we are seeing early idealism that wanes in the thirties, or a backlash against the more liberal attitude toward sex without love that prevailed at the start of the 1970s. The latter is more probable, since the number of men who felt that sex is important only as a means of expressing love in the 40–54 group (12 percent) and over 55 (11 percent) was higher than for men in their thirties (8 percent). Nonwhites chose this answer slightly more often than whites, belying the generalization that they are all machos. Among the romantic sentiments voiced were:

"Sex is the most intimate way to express your feelings. Words and gifts go only so far. My life would be very empty without a loving companion to share it with."

"I feel that sex is at the bottom of almost every marriage breakup. I feel a definite need, more than the average male. A woman and even men require affection, love, even some lust, but sex should be with love, not just cut and dry [sic]. One-night stands are bullshit, you may as well masturbate."

"[It] is a very important part of my life. It relieves me of tension and brings me closer to my wife. It isn't the most important but it does play a big role in our marriage and life-style. Sex is a time where we can both open up to each other both physically and mentally."

"Sex is not the upmost [sic] relation in life, but is a God-given gift to be used between two partners as an ultimate expression of affection toward each other."

"Sex loosens me up. My sex partner usually inspires me if we have a good relationship. I can have sex with not so gorgeous girls, if I decide I like them and trust them very much. Sex is the fulfillment of friendship and love. Everything else is just like masturbating."

"I think it's very important to marital stability and keeping a calm, harmonious marriage going. Too bad women make it so humdrum after having children."

"When having sex with someone you discover another person behind the facade we all hide behind. You finally get to see the real person, with all their inhibitions thrown aside. Sex is probably 50–80% of my life in one form or another."

The man who claims sex is important only as a means of expressing love solves the prostitute-madonna complex by giving all to the madonna. It is not necessarily a bad solution, for if he marries, he will usually be thoroughly faithful to his wife, though their sex life is likely to be unimaginative; black lace and exotic sexual positions coupled with lofty sentiments of spiritual harmony and devotion would make the couple feel as though they were dubbing *Deep Throat* with the sound track from *Love Is a Many-Splendored Thing.* The man who is on better terms with the strictly physical side of sex, with the help of his partner will be able to give rein to the sheer biological drive at times, tempering it with the humor and empathy that enable humans to harness the energy of the animal within and use its power and energy to gratify the loving mind that guides it. Lust and trust make good bedfellows.

The man who believes sex can have importance only as an expression of love may wind up deceiving women, himself, or both. If his need for sexual release is strong enough, he may convince himself that he is in love with a woman to whom he is attracted just to justify physical intimacy. Women had been in this bind for centuries, believing that they could engage in sexual relations only if they loved their partner enough to marry him. Every love affair had only two possible denouements: marriage or a breach of promise suit. The clergy and the jurists got some relief with the invention of the "meaningful relationship." Many women were capable of engaging in several different meaningful relationships a week. This sort of overuse led, in short time, to a loss of meaning for meaningful relationships.

Women may be deceiving themselves less these days, but men are perhaps deceiving themselves more. As women have become willing to take a man to bed without a mutual profession of special affection, more men have assumed the old female burden of constructing a backdrop of romantic visions against which the love scene may be played. The man who engages in sex only with a woman he truly loves may be making a sound and healthy choice. He blunders only if he underrates or disregards purely sexual feelings. Like wild dogs, they may be set free, chained up, or tamed to serve those he loves, but they should never be considered harmless or unimportant.

Then, there were those few men (4.2 percent) who regarded sex strictly as a physical pleasure. This type, too, fails to weld prostitute with madonna, and gives the whole pie to the prostitute. This does not mean he is incapable of love or of having sex with his wife; however, his sex acts will not be punctuated by declarations of love nor will he regard his partner, in that context, as much more than a body. Some of these men may expect lace and leather, X-rated home movies, and mechanical aids. Others may be so embarrassed by their "physical needs" that they keep marital encounters as brief as a station break. While percentages of men who expressed this attitude were small throughout the sample, the oldest men were slightly higher with a 7 percent and the 40–54 year olds were second with 5 percent.

Blacks gave this answer 9 percent of the time, as opposed to 4 percent for whites. But we saw earlier that blacks also were most frequent in expressing the sentiment that sex is important only as a means of expressing love, an apparently opposite viewpoint. How do we reconcile this? The biggest discrepancy in black-versus-white opinion came in the attitude selected most frequently by both groups, "not the most, but a very important pleasure": 64 percent white, 41 percent black. This difference coincides with the education gap on the same response: 65 percent college graduates and 48 percent less-than-high-school-graduates who said "not most, but important." Thus, the more educated man is better able to take a moderate position, to make compromises in his own head. The less educated man is not necessarily macho; he may just as readily turn out to be a puritan, depending on influences from his home and his subculture. He is more likely to relate to the madonna or the prostitute exclusively, never realizing they are really the same woman. Likewise, while the older man may view sex as a purely physical pleasure as a result of the erosion of romantic ideals, such an attitude might also reflect a more puritanical upbringing that relegated sex to the carnal side of his nature.

Only 1.4 percent said that sex was not very important. Men in the 55–65 age bracket gave this response 4.6 percent of the time, with no other age group higher than 1.0 percent. Blacks, again given to extreme positions, topped whites, 2.5 to 1.3 percent. Divorced/widowed men living alone said "unimportant" in 2.6 percent of the cases, probably due to greater age, against 1.8 percent of singles, and 1.1 percent of those living with partners, wed and unmarried. The lowest frequencies of potential celibates occurred in the highest income (0.6 percent) and highest educated (0.8 percent with postgraduate education) groups. Retired/unemployed (2.6), lowest income (1.8) and lowest educated (1.9) men were least interested in sex, as gauged by this answer.

None of the men elaborated on why sex was unimportant to them in the essay questions, nor did they speak of sex as a strictly physical pleasure, though many described it as a "need." Only 0.7 percent checked "It's something you have to do" as a response. This option was intended by us to mean "a duty," although we later realized it could be interpreted as a biological mandate. Of course, either answer regards sex as an imperative, not an act of choice. However, those who saw it as a necessity did not find it at all burdensome:

"Sex is a necessary part of adult life and rates high among my important things in life. [It] is a natural high and should not be abused."

"Need it. Makes all other things fit into the scheme of things and motivation of everyday life."

"Sex to me doesn't always mean intercourse. Feeling a 'oneness' with your partner is great, intercourse bonds it."

"It is something that I can live without for a fairly long time (3–4 months) but it sure is hard to pass up when available!!"

"Sex is an important and needed physical act but should not rule or dictate one's way of life."

"Sex is more open than ever. An exchange of emotions, needs and wants. I crave it. It's natural. If it feels good, do it."

How do men feel about sex? There are as many answers as there are men. For some, the answer is weighty and muddled; for others, the answer can be reduced to a line or two:

"I love it! I spend a lot of time trying to meet girls."

"Once a week is enough."

"I'm all for it, holds major importance. It's more fun than playing tennis."

"It's here to stay."

Sex may be many things to men, but it is not all things to man. In his "great expectations" (see Chapter Two), he wants it to be more and seeks to enlist women in bringing their newfound knowledge and experience to a more aggressive pursuit of a richer sex life for both genders. For four men out of five, sex is not the most important pleasure in life. Yet, every man must confront not only the prostitute-madonna dichotomy in women but the human-animal split in himself, accepting the dual natures in both so that sex becomes not an encounter between nymph and satyr, but between a man and a woman.

# The Test of Time

> I had certain things I always said. One of them was
> that even when I was eighty, one white hair of the
> woman I loved would make me tremble more than
> the thickest gold tress from the most beautiful young
> head.

—GEORGE BERNARD SHAW, *Man and Superman*

Does sex improve with age like a good wine, or does it depreciate with time like an automobile? Do men's attitudes towards sex vary with time, or are they formed immutably in adolescence? Are older men less interested in sex because of aging or more interested because the world around them is becoming more liberal? Do married men get bored with their partners, or does decreased inhibition and increased familiarity with each other's needs enrich their sex lives?

In the retinue of Dionysus, according to the old legends, was Silenus, a potbellied and gray-bearded roisterer, more preoccupied with wine than women. His affinity for the grape has led people to confuse his images with Dionysus, though Dionysus is young, beautiful, and virile. Silenus is the prototype for the modern myth that contends sexual interest and enjoyment decline with age, and that the young man, to whom sex is all, quickly ages into a listless and unimaginative creature more preoccupied with commerce than congress.

We wanted to explore this belief, to learn whether or not it was true that men find sex less enjoyable with time. We wanted to ascertain how their feelings about sex had changed, and we set a time limit of five years, which seemed sufficiently long to include significant changes that were recent though not just in the immediate past, and short enough in duration to disregard the inevitable changes that occur between puberty and adulthood or age-related crises over an entire lifetime.

*Question 14: How have your feelings about sex changed over the past five years?*

| | |
|---|---|
| Find sex more enjoyable than ever | 40.3% |
| Not at all | 26.0% |
| Have changed attitude, want to experiment more | 13.3% |
| Vary my sex practices more | 10.7% |
| Sex seems more routine | 6.5% |
| Find it less enjoyable | 4.6% |
| No answer | 0.6% |

The figures above apply to all the men we surveyed. What is more interesting is how the men in the different age brackets replied. According to conventional beliefs, older men would be highly unlikely to report a growing enjoyment in sex; we found this was not true.

While it was true that men in the oldest bracket, 55 years and over, were the only ones that did not select "more enjoyable than ever" as their predominant response, they most frequently said their feelings had not changed at all, rather than indicating that their enjoyment had declined. More than twice as many of these older men said their enjoyment had increased compared to those who reported a decrease. And while they were lowest in wanting more variety and experimentation and highest in finding sex more routine, the percentages giving these responses were no more than one in ten.

Men under 30 ranked highest in sexual variety and desire to experiment, and least often found sex to be routine. While the percentage of men who found sex less enjoyable did increase with age, it never rose higher than the 12 percent in the oldest age bracket.

Married men seemed more stable in their attitude, though they were as apt to find sex more enjoyable than ever as any other group. Men who had never been married hardly ever reported sex less enjoyable with time, but their youth may have limited their sexual activity to a period of time too short for significant changes in attitude to develop.

More educated men tend to find sex more enjoyable with time than those who do not complete high school. Despite their youth, students were the occupational group that least reported no change in attitude over the past five years, and were, by far, the lowest in saying they found sex less enjoyable. One-quarter of the student group characterized their attitude as "want to experiment more," considerably more than the next highest group, the blue collars.

We backed this up with an essay question:

*Essay Question: Have your feelings about sex changed over the years? Do you find it as interesting and important as ever? Are you less inhibited and more adventurous, or have you become more conservative—and why?*

Most men who found sex more enjoyable attributed it to being more liberal in their attitude:

"Yes. It is definitely more pleasurable for me in the last 5–6 years. Perhaps because I've attained some of my professional and financial goals and have been more relaxed and have more free time away from home—I feel more experimentative and liberal. Much freer!"

"My feelings have changed. Sex answers both physical and emotional needs. Now I can just use sex to satisfy my physical needs and I won't get hung-up. Even my fantasies are getting more pleasurable."

"I am less inhibited as concerns my view of how a woman views my body, and I find sex more interesting, with added changes and dimensions."

"For the past few years I have come through a few changes. I am now less inhibited because of marijuana usage."

"I have changed as I have grown older. It used to interest me because of what I didn't know. Now it interests me because of what I know."

"Have become more liberal. I enjoy a woman swallowing my semen now which I thought was sickening when I was younger."

"Yes. My age reminds me of how much I have missed. This also has made me less inhibited and to be more adventurous. You can never get back what you didn't get."

But it was not only those who were interested in a variety of partners or strictly physical gratification who found sex more enjoyable with time. Some who were committed to one partner found they could become adventurous without losing tenderness; others found that more concern for and understanding of women's needs brought increased satisfaction:

"Find it more interesting. Find that women have improved in their knowledge of what makes men happy and how men can make them happy."

"Sex is a beautiful gift from God (Proverbs 5:19); it has always been very enjoyable for me. My wife and I try new things that we both feel comfortable with and know the other likes."

"The importance of sex in my life is less now than before, but still quite important. I am less inhibited and more adventurous, but practice is limited to those for whom I have genuine emotional ties. Perhaps in this I am more conservative in that it used to be purely physical on my part."

"My feelings for sex have not changed. It fulfills the need of love of life to enjoy everything of beauty around us. I have become more conservative at age 64 and enjoy it no less."

Some defined themselves as "more conservative" because they had become more monogamous; however, they were not necessarily less happy than the "liberals":

"I feel now that sex should be with one person and I should love that person. I feel I'm more conservative now than two years ago."

"More conservative—because I like what I have at home."

"Become more conservative due to womens' lib more than anything."

"As I get older, I become more concerned with quality (e.g., emotional and personal interrelation) than with quantity."

"Less curious because I have more experience. More realistic—less illusions [sic] of grandeur—recognize women's need for sex. Desire more adventure to heighten sensation."

Some of the men who said their feelings had not changed usually indicated that some aspects had changed after all:

"The intensity of the drive has diminished but not the interest —don't think about it as much—reasons: contentment; availability of partner; need is satisfied; age."

"Not much change in ideas. Just as interesting except limited to marital partner. I am somewhat inhibited in revealing what I would like in regards to playing passive role. Since marriage, I take extra care not to force demands on my wife that I would have on casual partners."

"My wife does not like anything new, so it limits the amount of adventure one can put into the sex life."

Most of the few men who reported sex to be less enjoyable or interesting related the problem to their age:

> "When I was younger and hornier, sex was a domineering [sic] factor which controlled much of my emotions. As I have gotten older I am much less inhibited. I attribute this to increased experience." (This aging gentlemen was in his twenties.)

> "I am older and don't crave it as much. It's harder to do different things now, although I'd like to."

> "As I have become older I feel that sex is not quite as important or as exciting. I am less inhibited though as I use my mouth and tongue extensively."

> "Yes. It seems the older one gets it's important to you to prove yourself to your partner."

> "I have changed in the last two years because my partner can take it or leave it and I got to think it isn't worth the hassle so I don't push unless my need comes up."

> "It gets old with the same old hump."

It is interesting that in the objective question about change in attitude over only a five-year period, 40 percent of our entire sample reported an increase in sexual enjoyment despite the short time span specified. While we would expect young men to become less inhibited with experience and recently married people to find increased enjoyment through learning about each other's needs and preferences, we cannot readily explain why men of all ages should express such positive changes. The sexual revolution has been waged far longer than the past five years, so we cannot credit it with the fact that men grow happier rather than bored or discontent with sex as time goes by.

Perhaps we can reach the happy conclusion that, five years from now, we can expect the same sort of response. For most men, interest in and enjoyment of sex flourishes in a lifelong growth process. Venus, goddess of love and lust, shines as constantly as the morning star that bears her name and it can be said of her, as it was of Cleopatra, "Age cannot wither her, nor custom stale her infinite variety."

# The Ultimate Druther

Cartoonist Al Capp once created for Li'l Abner and the denizens of Dogpatch an irresistible food called "druthers." No one could pass up a bowl of this commendable comestible because anyone would "druther" eat it than anything else. Of course, we in the world outside of Dogpatch never get to eat druthers and, most of the time, never get to see, experience, or own the "druthers" we would select if our choices were limitless.

Suppose men could have any sort of sexual relationship they wished—what would their ideal be?

*Question 15: What do you consider the ideal sex life for yourself?*

| | |
|---|---|
| Marriage, wife being only sex partner | 50.5% |
| Marriage, with outside sexual activity | 19.9% |
| Living with one female partner, unmarried | 10.6% |
| A few regular partners | 9.3% |
| Many casual partners | 6.3% |
| One female partner, but living separately | 4.1% |
| No answer | 1.1% |

We also asked the men to tell us why they would consider their particular choices as the ideal sexual relationship for a man:

*Essay Question: What would be the* ideal *sexual relationship for a man? Would you prefer marriage, steadily dating one woman, having a variety of sexual partners—and why?*

We found that despite the increased availability of sexual partners outside of marriage, the rising divorce rate, and the increasing number of unmarried couples living together, men were still overwhelmingly in favor of marriage.

A majority of all the men—51 percent—considered monogamous marriage (wife being only sex partner) as the ideal condition. Add to this the 20 percent who wanted marriage, but with outside sexual activity, and we have a total of 71 percent of men who felt that, ideally, men should be married. There were 11 percent who chose living with a female partner but without marriage, so 82 percent of our sample wanted to live with a woman, rather than maintaining bachelor quarters. Every type of man in our sample selected marriage without other sexual partners as their first choice, except, as expected, those who were living with a woman to whom they were not married. However, only 31 percent of the living-togethers considered their state the ideal one—26 percent of them felt monogamous marriage was best and another 10 percent elected marriage, with outside partners; including the ones who wanted some outside sexual activity, 35 percent of the living-togethers felt, ideally, they should be married—more than the 31 percent of them contented with their present unwed status.

Sixty-one percent of the married men—by far the greatest percentage of any subgroup—felt that monogamous marriage was best. Twenty-six percent of the married men chose marriage plus outside partners, so that a total of 87 percent of married men still believed that wedlock was the best option. Thirty-one percent of the divorced and widowed would still elect monogamous marriage, and those who were single and living alone picked monogamous marriage in 32 percent of the cases.

The ideal of being a faithful husband, however, is losing popularity as time goes on. Sixty-eight percent of men over 55 held this value, but it dropped steadily in the younger brackets: 58 percent of men aged 40–54, 51 percent aged 30–39, and only 40 percent under age 30. White males chose monogamous marriage in 52 percent of the cases, and nonwhites, lower at approximately 38 percent, nevertheless also made this their first choice.

Students selected monogamous marriage 36 percent of the time, while all the other occupational groups were between 51 and 56 percent. The students brought the low-income (under $10,000) group down to 41 percent advocating marriage with fidelity, the other groups ranging from 51 to 55 percent, but the educational brackets did not show significant variation.

Marriage plus outside sexual activity was the second choice of our total sample, though at 20 percent it ran far behind monogamous marriage. Married men chose this as the ideal state 26 percent of the time, the next highest group being those living with a woman, unmarried, at 10 percent. Thus married men preferred a marital contract, with or without fidelity, in 88 percent of the cases, far ahead of the next group—the never-married—with a total of 41 percent who chose marriage with or without outside activity.

In terms of age, marriage with outside partners found most favor with men in their thirties (26 percent) and middle age (22 percent), the older ones preferring monogamy and the youngest either monogamous marriage or living with a partner, unmarried. The desire for marriage with outside sexual activity climbed steadily with earning power, from 12 percent under $10,000 to 27 percent at $25,000 or more. Professional men topped the occupational ranks, with 26 percent choosing marriage-plus, the other employed groups averaging 21 percent, with the students lowest at 13 percent.

Of the men who selected marriage, without mention of outside activity, many spoke of it in terms of the love and companionship it offered:

> "Marriage—for me to fully develop my potentials and personality, I prefer to have a wife to work for and with. It's great to allow each to develop in his or her own way and remain and become closer together."

> "Marriage, security, I believe in a family life and sharing, building together. It can go *beyond* sex in that two people have pledged the security to build a much better life together than they could have apart."

> "I think that most everyone reaches a point in the maturing process where a monogamous relationship seems the most appealing alternative—the successful realization of this depends on the willingness of both partners to sacrifice some of their 'freedom'—self-centeredness—to achieve a harmonious relationship."

> "A woman . . . a wife. One reason I'd have a woman as my spouse for life is because in addition to all her other outstanding attributes, I, myself, deem her the absolute finest fuck in the entire civilized world! I am monogamous. Just an idealist, I guess."

> "Marriage is it. Everything else creates frustration, confusion, fear and uncertainty."

> "I would prefer marriage so we could work and play as one (this we would strive for). It would be too complex for me to have more than one girl on the string."

A few men chose monogamous marriage because they felt it would provide a partner who would be sexually uninhibited, available, faithful, and tolerant:

> "Ideal for me would be a marriage with a woman who likes to be somewhat adventuresome in sex—about 3 or 4 times a week —sometimes submissive, sometimes aggressive."

"I would prefer marriage because usually you know where your loving is going plus if it is the right lady you feel good to go home to her after a hard day's work."

"Marriage with a woman who *would not* cheat under any situation."

To some, marriage should wait, although it was the final goal from the start:

"I prefer a good sexual relationship outside of marriage till 25–30, then settle down with a good lover. Emotional is most important though."

"Age 20–40 Sex Partner. 40–60 Marriage."

Since we are devoting a chapter to marriage later, we will not pause here to discuss in depth the reasons so many men opt for monogamy and marriage today. Yet, it is important to emphasize that most men not only want it today, but consider it the ideal sexual relationship. Theodore Rubin maintains that at the present time, marriage holds "no great virtues or rewards" for men, and remains substantially more inviting for women. Our study proves this contention to be wrong. While we asked men to tell us about the ideal sexual relationship, many of those who chose marriage and fidelity responded to the question in terms that went far beyond the sexual. They spoke of developing their potentials, of building a much better life, and of working together.

So we ask a question about sex and get answers that discuss the need to change, to develop, to build and grow, from men who do not want to confront this life task alone. These are not philosophers or clergymen talking; these are the average men of America. They deal with the weighty questions of purpose and partnership because if they fail to they must face each morning alone, regardless of how many women were available to share their beds the night before. Against the problems of loneliness and alienation—the "frustration, confusion, fear, uncertainty," as one man put it—the arguments against monogamy seem shallow, for they promise spice, never sustenance.

There are, of course, men who envision other ideals. And in the men under 30, 6 out of 10 reject marriage to one sexual partner as the ideal sexual relationship. They are far from being in agreement about what *would* be ideal, with 17 percent of these younger men choosing a living arrangement without marriage and 16 percent selecting marriage with outside sexual involvements. Of course, the living arrangement might imply monogamy, raising to a respectable 57 percent the number of men under 30 who might be content with one partner.

Then, too, remember we are dealing with ideals; many men might consider marriage with outside sexual activity as the perfect arrangement, yet settle for monogamy rather than risk rocking the boat in matrimonial seas, which, with our rising divorce rate, are perilous enough. The main point we wish to make here—to be pursued later —is that the arguments for marriage and monogamy were rarely presented in purely sexual terms; they therefore take on more formidable dimensions since they apply not just to sexual man, but total man.

Those men who wanted marriage with some outside partners generally indicated that they would feel love for their wives, and would regard the outside activities as impersonal and recreational:

> "Being married to a woman you truly love, that fulfills all your ideals of attractiveness and sexuality. But the need for friends outside of marriage should not be limited to those of the same sex. People need to have friends of both sexes, and the spouse should accept the need and recognize it in themselves. Sex is not dirty and need not be done only for self-gratification. Sex is a means to express emotion and bring pleasure to the other person as well as yourself. It should not be engaged in lightly, but not necessarily only in the context of strong love feelings either. People, and women in general, need to learn the middle road of sex, not only love (but best in that context) but not for the 'hell of' it either. To express friendly feelings for some one you enjoy being with is enough reason, but to feel horny and grab the first person you meet is not nearly enough reason."

This respondent, a married white-collar worker in his twenties, was atypical in that he stressed feelings of friendship for the outside partner, not just a physical attraction. He had indicated on his questionnaire, however, that any "cheating" he had done was with his partner's knowledge and consent, so he apparently had an open marriage. Other men were not so "middle-of-the-road" in their view of sex and seemed to cross that primrose path often, finding love and security on one side and uncomplicated physical gratification on the other:

> "Being married for security and love yet able to have several other women for sexual intercourse for physical satisfaction. Sex

mostly is a state of mind and different partners other than your wife is most satisfying without loss of love for wife."

"Marriage for family life and children. Occasional long-lasting sexual (interpersonal) encounters with different partners for sexual fulfillment. Marriage, if a good one, makes two people as one but does *not* fulfill *completely* the sexual fantasies."

"I am happily married, but still appreciate other women. If a man finds a compatible partner there's nothing wrong with being married even if he enjoys the presence or intimacy of other women."

Some men appreciated the obstacles to ideals that matrimony usually imposes:

"Marriage with opportunity to have other sex partners. Ideal but difficult to handle. I would prefer marriage with proper partner after having a variety of sexual partners."

"Ideal sexual relationship can vary depending upon family situations. Without my children I would seek new partners."

Some men did not see marriage as an obstacle, because they fully expected their wives to have outside partners, too:

"I feel that ideally marriage is the answer; however, monogamy seems to be a very boring approach to sex. I feel that both partners should at some point seek other casual relationships with similarly interested partners."

"To re-energize myself, I believe that marriage to a liberated, understanding partner with an occasional diversion on either mate's behalf would or could be possible."

"I feel a married man has the ideal sexual relationship. I do however feel that exchanging of partners with other couples strengthens a marriage and brings a man and a woman closer together."

A few men, however, specified or indicated that forays outside the marital boundaries were limited to men only:

"Marriage, with some variety. However would expect wife to be loyal."

"Variety of sex partners without my wife knowing."

"I like being married but I still like to fool around. I never have relations with my wife for at least three days after I've had another woman, just to make sure I don't have any social disease."

The considerate gentleman above is not aware that gonorrhea may take eight days or more to produce symptoms and syphilis always takes at least ten days; but his heart seems to be in the right place, even if his penis often is not.

If men could have their "druthers," many would seek an occasional outside partner just for the physical pleasure and satisfaction of curiosity. Now, a woman may well wonder why a man who has had experience prior to marriage and has an enjoyable sex life at home would feel a need to explore and experience women who are not likely to provide him with either new knowledge or new sensations. The man himself would have a great deal of difficulty explaining it. The key lies in the nature of the outside liaison—it is outside the sanctions of matrimony, the constancy of love, the bounds of conventional morality. It is transitory, lustful, and wicked—an interlude with a prostitute. As one respondent noted, marriage does not completely fulfill the sexual fantasies. For such men, they have found in their wives only half of the dream, the madonna without the prostitute. As medieval courtiers dreamed of perfect romantic love, modern man often dreams of the prostitute who promises new heights of sexual gratification, free from the anxiety and guilt he unconsciously brings to the madonna in the marital bed. Since the women who provide his outside diversion fail to measure up to this demon-goddess, the wandering husband is often adrift on an endless extramarital odyssey. Some wives can accept the "purely physical" argument, although it is disturbing to be told there is some physical need in their husbands they cannot satisfy. The problem with "open marriages" is that they are generally advocated by men with a compulsive need to philander and a rationalization of the guilt by granting their wives freedoms that men do not really believe in. If the wife strays, she becomes the prostitute, not the madonna, which deprives the husband of the more stable half of his required pair before he has found the elusive perfect prostitute. We will return to this complex quandary in our chapter on cheating.

For some men, it is not the monogamy of marriage that threatens them, it is the permanency of that state. Of the 11 per cent of our sample who believed living with a partner, unmarried, to be the ideal condition, the reason invariably cited was the relative ease of escaping that ideal state:

"I find nothing wrong with steady relationships with one woman like that present in a traditional marriage. It's the 'forever' concept of the traditional marriage that I feel is unrealistic. I feel that a steady relationship is in fact very desirable, but people change and so do their needs and when two people do not meet one another's needs they ought to separate."

"Steadily dating, and possibly living with a woman is to me an ideal relationship. I can't see perpetuating a relationship by contract. When the relationship ceases to be satisfying to me, it's time to move on."

"Living together. That way there would be no bad feelings or heartbreak when it is over."

"Do everything for me. Only dating or living together."

Ours is one of the few studies that has garnered data on couples living together without a marriage license. We were interested not only in how many there were, but also how the attitudes of such men differed from those who were living alone or in conventional marriages. Of our total sample, 6.9 percent were men living with a partner to whom they were not married: 4.2 percent had never been married, 2.4 percent were divorced or separated from legal spouses, and 0.3 percent were widowers. Of these men 60 percent were under 30, 19 percent were in their thirties, 14 percent were between 40 and 54, and 7 percent were over 54. Nonwhites and whites chose this living arrangement with approximately equal frequency. Lower-income males chose to live together without marriage more than the higher income brackets: 36 percent of males in households without marriage were earning under $10,000, though only 22 percent of our total sample were in this income range; 20 percent of living-togethers made between $15,000 and $24,999, and 9 percent $25,000 and more, though these high-income brackets represented 31 and 17 percent of the total sample, respectively. We can probably attribute this to lower incomes among younger men, for if we look at the living-togethers by occupation, there is completely proportional representation of every career group among the men who chose this life-style:

| Occupation | Total Sample (4,066) | Living with partner unmarried (280) |
|---|---|---|
| Professional | 25.3% | 21.8% |
| Managerial | 16.2% | 15.4% |
| Other white collar | 12.9% | 12.1% |
| Blue collar | 17.9% | 17.5% |
| Retired | 3.1% | 3.6% |
| Unemployed | 3.5% | 4.6% |
| Student | 11.6% | 14.6% |
| Other | 6.8% | 7.1% |

The 6.9 percent of the men in our sample who are living with a partner, unmarried, do not represent a very large group, but show that Rubin's belief that such men constitute an "infinitesimally small percentage of all male-female relationships" is a gross underestimate of the magnitude of this growing life-style. More significant is the finding that 11 percent of our sample regarded this arrangement as the ideal sex life, but 20 percent of unmarried men and 22 percent of the divorced/widowed saw it as the best. Married men, secure in their choice, picked this response in only 4 percent of the cases. Those already living together predictably were highest with 31 percent, but it is interesting that over two-thirds felt the ideal life-style would be something else—marriage in over one-third of the cases.

In designing our study, we had considerable difficulty finding a designation for this category. Even "living with partner, unmarried" is unsatisfactory; we mean the partners are not married to one another, though, in fact, both might be married and separated from legal spouses. At one point, we facetiously suggested to our research firm "living in sin." But this bantering produced another insight; people choose to live together not for the sexual opportunities involved, but for the domestic benefits, just as they choose marriage for that reason. We have seen divorced or widowed middle-aged female patients who have been living in asexual unions with men for many years, though there had been intercourse at the beginning. The women provide meals and laundry, the men companionship and (in some cases) money. The women often experience guilt about how the neighbors regard their "living in sin," though any carnal sin here would have to be sloth, not lust.

Even where the partners are sexually active, the motivation for living together is generally economic. When a doctor in residency had to give up his room in a hospital building and asked to move in with his steady girl friend, a divorced nurse, there were few advantages for her: crowding of her limited living quarters with his books and belongings, fixing him meals and snacks, potential hassles from the landlady, and an end to the occasional casual date she could enjoy while he was studying. She capitulated, nevertheless, for although she professed acceptance of his lack of commitment, the dreams she reported in sessions were filled with brides, including herself, and the living arrangement might bring her a step closer to the aisle. The immediate benefits for him and the potential benefits for her were clearly nonsexual.

And if the benefits are domestic, so are the disadvantages. The biggest difficulty encountered by a footloose divorced college professor when his girl friend moved in was accepting the way objects in "my kitchen" would wind up in areas other than their usual resting places.

"If the prisoner is happy, why lock him in?" protests Don Juan. "If he is not, why pretend that he is?" And so indicate the men who select domesticity sans marriage as the ideal state; they want a clean escape without a "messy divorce." But it is this open-door policy that causes considerable anxiety in partners, particularly women, like the nervous customer in W. C. Fields's film *The Bank Dick* who approaches a teller wearing a hat and demands to withdraw all his money because "you lookin' like you's 'bout to take off." Some men are naïve enough to believe, as our respondent, "there would be no bad feelings or heartbreak when it is over," simply because no contract was drawn up. Heartbreak can be avoided by limited emotional investment, but one then wonders why a couple would endure the invasion of privacy, the loss of independence, and the inconveniences and demands of someone they did not care much about.

Of course, many women find themselves living with a man they would never have dreamed of marrying on such short acquaintance. As overnight stays progress to weekend visits, more of his belongings take up residence in her closets and medicine chests. Late weekday dinners lead to more nights in her bed than his, and before either knows it, only the two separate rents belie their common dwelling-place. The economic absurdity of renting a barely used apartment forces the final step of jettisoning one domicile, and two independent souls who would never have dreamed of rushing into marriage are suddenly sharing a life remarkably like wedlock, except for documentation. Of course, that detestable piece of paper shunned by many modern couples sometimes becomes replaced by reams of agreements, waivers, and permissions needed to cover such situations as sudden illness of a partner and management of joint funds.

With the advantages to the man, it is surprising that so few men would choose this way of life. Rarely will a man and a woman share household chores equally, and the woman invariably winds up cleaning and cooking for two, relieving him of this responsibility while adding significantly to his income. He can subtly use the open door to ensure his happiness, for the whole point of the arrangement is that it can be dissolved whenever satisfaction wanes.

A living-together arrangement, however, is like a marriage in every way. Spending a night with a woman and leaving in the morning is like a liaison with a prostitute. Spending every night and day with her elevates the woman to a madonna-wife, and the threat of her suddenly leaving this role for another round of lovers is often more than the average man can bear. It would be like playing house with a prostitute. A man wants to drive *his* car, bowl with *his* bowling ball, root for *his* team, and live with *his* woman. Thus, we see living-together as essentially a way station leading to marriage or turning back to single life, not as a terminal for most men. It should be pointed out that while 6.9 percent of our sample were currently living with a partner, unmarried, many more might have been in that situation at some previous time in their lives. Since only one-third of our respondents living with an unmarried partner felt this was ideal, we can suppose that, at most, 2 percent of our sample will remain in a state of unwedded bliss. This may change in years to come since one-sixth of our men under 30 preferred this life-style in theory, but our society is still far from rejecting conventional marriage.

Should a woman live with a man to whom she is not married? The chief advantage of the situation is that it will give her a fair idea of what kind of a person he is to live with; whether he will share cooking and cleaning chores, does he come home at a reliable hour, is he messy, does he have a bad temper, etc. Many of the other professed advantages sound fine in theory but never work out from a practical point of view, the main one being the illusion that there are "no strings attached." A newspaper columnist recently cited a case involving a man who wanted to break up, against her opposition, with the woman he had lived with for several years; his lawyer actually advised him to marry the woman and then get a legal divorce so that he could make a respectable financial settlement with her and avoid the real danger of subsequent embarrassing lawsuits that could disrupt his life and his business.

The woman living with a man occupies a strange non-status, with problems ranging from what to call him ("boy friend" sounds juvenile, "fiancé" implies future marriage, "my man" sounds like something out of a jungle movie, "my lover" obscene, and "cohabitant" sounds like a legal term) to their lack of being able to sign medical consent forms for one another in the event of emergency illness. Some choose this arrangement on the grounds that people need sex, but not marriage; yet you can have sex without living together, but not marriage, and there is nothing quite like cohabitation to take the glamour and fantasy out of an affair. Just as people do not marry primarily for sex, they don't live together for that reason, though it takes some couples a while to realize it. It is far from an ideal state. A woman should enter into it with the attitude that the relationship can evolve into a marriage if all goes reasonably well. She should never presume that such an arrangement will leave her free from commitment, responsibility, quarrels, crises, and the pleasures and pains of domesticity; it may take a marriage certificate to legitimize all this, but it takes more than a lack of one to avoid it.

There was a small percentage of men who liked monogamy but disliked domesticity; 4.1 percent wanted just one female partner, but not under their roof. Such men were few and seemed to equate living together with threatening both their own independence and the stability of the relationship:

"Prefer steady girl with different address than mine. Would enjoy different girl every now and then just for sex. Can't stand the thought of getting married and losing identity and goals in life."

"Steadily dating one woman. To me, a relationship is more important than sex. Marriage destroys most good relationships, I think."

"Sexual relationship with the one in which I'm in love—one-on-one relationship."

Of our sample, 9.3 percent picked "a few regular partners" as ideal. The married men (4.7 percent) brought down the percentage; about 18 percent of the nonmarried made this selection. Some specified a more-or-less steady girl friend, plus occasional variety, a modification of the madonna-prostitute dichotomy:

"The ideal sexual relationship would be a variety of women, but to have a 'steady.' The reason explains itself, the man wouldn't lose his interest in them if he had a variety of women."

"Several girl friends is more interesting because I find the difference between girls intellectually stimulating. I feel as if I am not tied down. And because I am not with just one person I can react emotionally to others. I grow bored with one person after I get to know her—so far!"

"Ideal situation would be 4 or 5 women who you could have sex with on a regular basis without fear or worry of jealousy on their part. Also without fear of the women wanting to become more serious than a friendly and fun relationship."

"I would like to try two women at a time, hooked up together all three of us."

"Ideally, a group marriage by totally involved partners who are willing to share responsibility."

Finally, we come to the "satyrs," men who wanted many casual partners; 6.3 percent saw this as ideal, but again the married men (3 percent) pulled the percentage down, the nonmarrieds averaging 12 percent. Since the youngest men, especially students, led those who felt that many casual partners was the best option, we feel these few exceptions to the majority of men who wanted more committed sexual relationships chiefly represent a phase men go through before settling down. Rather than abandoning the logical, goal-directed aspect of their personalities in favor of the pleasure-driven, genital-centered portion, they are merely deferring the work of finding and settling down with a permanent partner, knowing their youth will afford them a few years' respite. Ultimately, most of these satyrs will shed their horns and join the majority of men in responsible relationships.

Most of those who chose many casual partners gave answers that read like impossible dreams or wild fantasies:

"I would prefer a woman who is willing to try everything but that doesn't seem to be possible, so up to this point I have 'used' a variety of partners."

"Having a variety of sexual partners because there are so many different women around."

"Being rich and having a harem."

"100 women."

"I would like to make love to all the women in the world for about one month per each."

As the last answer indicates, the ultimate fantasy might require immortality to make it work.

In the animal kingdom, monogamy is the exception. Wolves and foxes usually select lifelong mates; fox breeders have sadly learned that the vixen is not as promiscuous as her human namesake. The industrious beaver and majestic eagle have been cited as monogamists, but this is more romance than zoology, according to most experts. But man is a different breed of animal. He is quite capable of mating with any female, and the modern female is usually cooperating toward that end; however, he often chooses not to. In Shaw's play *Caesar and Cleopatra,* Caesar says to the sphinx, "I am he of whose genius you are the symbol: part brute, part woman, and part god—nothing of man in me at all." Caesar sees in himself the appetites and raw emotions of a beast, the gentleness and sensitivity of a woman, and the intellect and greatness of a god, and concludes that there is nothing of man in him, failing to realize that it is the sum of these parts that makes not a sphinx, but a man. The lusty, lascivious, impulsive, selfish carefree brigand that women often envision, to the clandestine delight of men, is not a man at all—he is a satyr, a myth.

Neither psychological enlightenment nor the demise of organized religion, nor the alleviation of sexual guilt will lead monogamous men into bacchanalian revels, for their life-styles are based on a simple principle mastered by every toilet-trained two-year-old, the sacrifice of immediate pleasure for an anticipated greater compensation. Don Juan protests, "The confusion of marriage with morality has done more to destroy the conscience of the human race than any other single error." Strip away all of the moral exhortations and prohibitions, and most men will still choose marriage.

As Mae West replied to the woman who said, "Goodness, what pretty jewels!": "Goodness had nothing to do with it."

# Viewing Women—
# Ad Lib

The women . . . are become equally dangerous: the
sex is aggressive, powerful: when women are
wronged they do not group themselves pathetically
to sing *"Protegga il giusto cielo"* [May the just
heaven protect us!]: they grasp formidable legal and
social weapons and retaliate.

—GEORGE BERNARD SHAW (1903)

It seems that as long as women have been around, there have been
men complaining that females have too much control over things.
Call the roll of influential women in history and literature and you
will find heroines and villainesses in every age who either had direct
power or manipulated men as personal power sources: Eve, Cleopatra, Helen of Troy, Lysistrata, Medea, Lady Macbeth, Queen Elizabeth I, Catherine Di Medici, Lucrezia Borgia, Madame Pompadour
—we can continue *ad lib, ad infinitum.* The problem has never been
an absence of women wielding influence and holding responsibility,
but rather the scarcity of them. Another problem that will become
apparent in scanning our all-time list of notable females is the taint
of notoriety that sullies each fair name. Even capable rulers are
generally deemed to be either ruthless bitches or wily *femmes
fatales* who barter sex for power. The only women in history truly
revered by men as virtuous were those who faithfully served and
abetted their husbands, sons, or fathers, such as Calpurnia, Portia, St.
Helena, Cordelia, and Penelope—most of them fictitious.

It is obvious that women have been oppressed by men. It took
black men less than a century after the signing of the Declaration of

Independence to get the right to vote, while women were denied that right for over 140 years. It seems almost as incredible now to have denied a human the right to self-government on the grounds of being female as for one human being to buy and sell another because his skin was black. Yet, within the memory of many of our parents, women were held to be inferior despite a complete absence of biological or psychological data to support that contention.

But what is curious is how women accepted their second-class status. They were not kept in servitude by whips, chains, and prisons. In fact, exceptional women throughout history were able to become rulers, writers, warriors, and scientists—against formidable opposition, perhaps, but with ultimate acceptance. The way man kept woman subservient was by threatening to withhold the one thing she could not bear to lose—his love. As Byron noted: "Man's love is of man's life a thing apart; 'Tis woman's whole existence." It was not the love of one man that achievement-oriented women risked losing; it was the regard of *all* men. The woman who rose to the top in politics, business, or science was "unfeminine" and almost assuredly threatened with an old-maid existence, or a kind of ostracism.

In the past decade, something has happened to change that. While the leaders of the Women's Liberation Movement played a key role, we cannot attribute the revolution only to those who wrote in its behalf, for even women who read nothing but *TV Guide* were affected by it. Oral contraceptives, abortion reform, a plethora of labor-saving household appliances, and emphasis on population control made large families undesirable and housework less than a full-time occupation. For the single woman, who had previously avoided sexual relations, there was no longer fear of the three threats that guarded her chastity: infection, conception, and detection. Antibiotics, improved contraceptive methods, and legal abortions eliminated these obstacles. The greatest deterrent to premarital sexual activity, however, had never been social disease but social sanction. The new permissiveness arose from a combination of factors, most of them disseminated through the mass media: Masters and Johnson's writings on female orgasmic potential; the advocacy of sex without commitment by leading feminists; graphic depiction of sexual acts and nudity in major movie theaters; and more easy accessibility to sex education, contraception and abortions, even in adolescence.

It was probably the vast increase in available sexual partners that sold men on the Women's Liberation Movement. This was essential, for the revolution was not a war. Lysistrata and her cohorts achieved their demands by withholding sex; modern women advanced their cause by giving it. It was the promise of freer and more varied sexual experience that motivated men to take seriously a world where ERA no longer referred to pitchers' earned run averages and the co-worker in the next office was a potential sex partner. And what was sauce for the gander sweetened the bargain for females as well, because the sexual freedom that was as vital to the recipe as the meatier equal rights provisions insured that the movement would bring men closer to women, not drive them away.

We are about to explore men's attitudes toward "today's women." The woman of the 1970s is living in a society that is constantly changing its concept of her, so even if she herself does not choose to change, she cannot escape the shift in attitude towards her. "Today's women" is not just a nice rhetorical phrase; they are different, if only to the degree that their potential to be different has infinitely expanded. Among the female leaders there is dissension—one will advocate political activism and uncommitted sexual activity; another wails that they have been coopted, and urges a return to the old morality; a third sees lesbianism as the only viable answer. How are the men taking all this?

We have heard the warnings of the social scientists that an "epidemic" of impotence is sweeping the country; it is all the fault of the modern woman, who is threatening the devil out of men who cannot cope with her new independence, sexual freedom, and equal status. Not only do men dislike this new female breed, we are told, they are actually terrified of her.

*Essay Question: How do you feel about today's women? Have they changed for the better or worse, and why? Do they make good wives and mothers and why?*

We found that most men admire the new woman and actually are enthusiastic about the changes she has undergone. About two out of three men surveyed expressed positive views and felt the modern woman had changed for the better. They are no longer withholding their collective love from active, intelligent women, but rather find them more satisfying as companions, as well as lovers!

"Today's women are nicer and better than ever. They were always good, but today they are much better. They have definitely changed for the better, because, due to better education and opportunity and the fact that they have more of a voice and they are more independent and self-reliant, self-sufficient, and self-confident, due to women's suffrage, women's liberation, and more job opportunities, many more working women and career women, capable of earning their own living, etc. They make good wives and mothers, definitely, because they are more capable, more qualified, and have much more know-how."

Independence was considered desirable by most of the men who praised the new women, although some tempered their accolades with reservations about abolishing the differences between the sexes altogether:

"I think women today have become more independent which in many ways is good. I do, however, object to Radical Women's Lib groups demanding they be treated like men. I believe there should be a distinction between the sexes, masculine and feminine. A female construction worker turns me off! . . . Women of today are more aware of what's going on around them, which makes them more understanding and aware in their own marriage."

"I cannot establish much of a relationship with a 'helpless female.' However, I do appreciate treating a woman like a lady and I prefer to be treated as a gentleman. Androgyny is for the birds."

"They are more confident and willing to try different things. They have a harder time with both because of more choices, but both can be done, and the few who make it are probably more innovative, adventurous, and do a better job."

This respondent's reference to "a harder time with both" refers to being a wife and mother, but also seems to imply combining these roles with a career. Several respondents were aware of the inherent conflicts for the married working woman:

"I believe they are making startling professional advances in a male-oriented work environment. They take more responsibility. I believe their maternal lives may suffer somewhat."

"They have changed for the better. They do more, such as work to help the family. They make good wives and mothers, but their independence often sets up a conflict."

"Today's women are becoming more intelligent and aware of what is going on around them. The only objection I have is when a woman uses a man knowingly to her advantage. Yes, they make good wives and mothers, but so do a lot of *men.*"

This man confronts society's relegation of the task of meeting needs, or nurturing, to the female sex, and acknowledges that men, too, can be supportive and caring. Many of the men commented on the abolition of the old, limited roles and the emergence of women as better companions because of the new equality:

"Women today are easier to communicate with, possibly because they are more assertive and more able to talk with a man at the same level; therefore, I am more comfortable because I do not have to play a role."

"I think there are a lot (majority?) of women who are probably better equipped—education, experience, etc.—than ever before to be companions and helpmates in the adventure of life."

"Oh, much better today—intelligent, competitive, stimulating, enlightened and much more open and responsive to today's living—much better 'partners' to their spouse in all ways."

"They seem very smart and know what they want whether it is accepted by a society which calls itself moral or not. They seem to prefer the truth at all times and I think it makes for a better relationship between men and women."

"I feel in most ways things are better since they have more interest than before, but I still feel that I should be the boss, but this isn't always so since they are financially able to see their own way."

Not all the men responded so enthusiastically to the changes in today's women. By far the biggest complaint was women's increased independence:

"Today's women are becoming more secure and independent, including the married women and single-parent women. They have changed for the better as far as *they* are concerned, but as far as a man is concerned, the change is worse. Most of the women are too independent to make a good wife. In other words, the husband would *not* come *first* if he is the breadwinner. . . . Most, 95% of them, do not make good mothers. They spoil their kids, giving them whatever they want, no discipline. The kids seem to run the family, instead of the mother."

"Women are too liberalized. They should be more considerate of their man's needs and work towards making their relationship sound and happy."

"Women today are too independent—the pill has helped bring on this situation—I don't think today's women want children."

"As far as children and home maintenance go—they are worse. Knowing there is a possible better life one may tend to stray from home leaving all loved ones behind."

"Today's women are more aggressive. Better, because more so than ever they choose you instead of reverse. They don't make good wives, mothers yes—you just can't trust them for wives. Good mother because it's a mother's instinct."

"I think women have gotten too independent and want to work at jobs instead of staying home and taking care of the children. I believe a mother's place is at home."

Our questionnaire obviously had the fringe benefit of letting respondents blow off steam in a world that attacks men with words like "chauvinist." Some men expressed a more quiet frustration, wondering whether they could meet the demands of the new woman:

"Women are much more intelligent. Which makes it difficult for a man to please a woman."

"They are worse on account of Women's Lib. They want too much."

"They have forgotten that they are a sexual mate. They are too preoccupied with taking care of No. 1 first."

A few (surprisingly few) berated women for being too sexually permissive:

"Most women today don't have the good morals that they had when I was growing up. They don't seem to be ashamed of anything, especially sex."

"Too independent, dress, talk, and promote sex. Most who have problems get what they ask for, deserve it. Are not seeking companionship, only pleasure."

"For the most part that women have become too promiscuous. However, I do not relate it directly as a change in women's values but more as a repercussion of our society's changing values."

"Much too loose morally, too 'I'-oriented, and not concerned about other people."

"Horrible wives—castrating mothers."

There were also some who regarded women as in a process of transition, complicated by the problem that the society which was pushing the transition was itself still changing:

"Because of society's changes, and because women had farther to progress in society, I feel many of today's women either try to grow up too fast or are caught between the old and new ways. They are confused."

"Women are becoming more independent but most (at least some) are too dependent and lacking in ambition. They are still brainwashed by society."

"I don't really feel today's women are any different. They have just been allowed to express publicly and openly the emotions and opinions they have had for generations."

"Women today are on the verge of becoming themselves—haven't quite got everything together yet."

## Free and Equal

With all the complexity of their responses, our men had predominant impressions about today's women. A clear majority expressed positive sentiments, and the most enthusiastic were the men under 30 and those who had never been married.

*Question 16: How do you feel about today's women?*

| | |
|---|---|
| They are too independent | 23.3% |
| They are better company | 22.5% |
| They are more intelligent than ever | 18.2% |
| They've become more loving and giving | 16.9% |
| They expect too much from men | 11.4% |
| They are too promiscuous ("fast") | 8.2% |
| No answer | 3.2% |

There was nothing to prevent our respondents from checking more than one answer, but on 4,066 questionnaires, there were only 151 additional responses, so that most men were content to select the one given answer that best typified their attitude. Three of the given responses (more intelligent, more loving, better company) were positive ones; three (too independent, expect too much, too promiscuous) were negative. 58 percent of the responses were positive, and 43 percent were negative. (Multiple answers and the 3.2 percent who did not answer account for the percentage total in excess of 100.)

Percentages were remarkably consistent throughout the various age and occupational brackets. The biggest difference was found in the more positive attitude of the men under 30. Only 19 percent of them thought women today were too independent, against a consistent 26 percent of all older men. Married and divorced men exceeded by about 4 percent the singles or living-togethers in condemning women's independence, perhaps due to the younger age composition of the more liberal subgroups. Blacks showed a slightly higher tendency to complain about women's independence (28 percent versus 23 for whites), and men in the highest income bracket (18 percent) were less threatened by it than men in other income brackets (23 to 27 percent). Twenty-nine per cent of those who did not finish high school and 30 percent of high school graduates saw women today as too independent while the most educated men made this complaint only 17 percent of the time. Students (15 percent) were least likely to hold this opinion and the retired/unemployed most likely, with 29 percent, followed by blue collars at 27.

We therefore see a clear pattern wherein the men who have achieved the most in terms of education or earning power are the least threatened by women's independence. To the man who is insecure about his social status, a woman's dependency becomes a virtue, assuring him she will not depart for a better life on her own or with a man who can offer her more. "Liberty"—the prime American ideal, the word emblazoned on every U.S. coin—loses its virtue and becomes a vice.

One respondent expressed the fear behind the devaluation of liberty: "Knowing there is a possible better life one may tend to stray from home leaving all loved ones behind." Abandonment is one of the first fears experienced by any child. And, most paradoxically, independence becomes equated with irresponsibility, whereas it ultimately means responsibility for one's actions. The woman without education, money or earning power has no options other than marriage and motherhood; she cannot easily flee the home, but since she did not truly choose her responsibilities, her motivation to perform is not likely to be strong. The woman who has been better prepared to fend for herself in life is likely to be overwhelmed with options—she can choose when to marry, whom to marry, how many children to have and when, and whether to pursue a career after marriage. A woman today actually has more options than a man, for men cannot realistically decline to work, whereas it is still quite respectable to be an unemployed housewife, even without children. Men frequently envy women's new freedom of choice.

Men today have turned to women more for companionship. A companion is usually an equal; a spouse or lover is not necessarily so. Our youngest men gave as their predominant impression that today's women are better company more frequently than older men, and white men cited women as better company more often than did nonwhites. As the men's education increased, men valued women more as companions, and high-income men were more appreciative in this regard than men with low earning power.

These differences in men's attitudes about the value of women as companions may be due to the company they keep. The more educated man will be associating with more educated women; the younger men will be exposed chiefly to younger women, who have generally been better educated than their mothers. Companions are people to share experiences with, and empathetic sharing requires nearly equal sensitivity and intellectual perception. We are beginning to see here not only an acceptance of women as equals, but a desire for them as such.

Eighteen percent of our respondents were most impressed by the intelligence of today's women. The esteem correlated with the man's schooling; 21 percent of college graduates gave this response, compared with 14 percent of high school graduates. Divorced men were slightly more negative in their overall view of women and praised female intellect least, and the living-togethers were most impressed by intelligence.

The greatest discrepancies were observed in the racial break-downs; 13 percent of blacks cited intelligence, against 19 percent of whites. The other races gave this response 25 percent of the time. Asiatic women of the upper classes not only vie with but often surpass the men in completing postgraduate education, and Hispanics, while rarely seeking college degrees, receive a far more thorough education in the United States than they would have in their native lands, where girls from poor families were routinely pulled from grade school as soon as they were old enough to care for the newest additions to their burgeoning families.

Education and intelligence are not synonymous, but education is needed to bring an intellect to its full potential. Through television and reading material, even women who do not attend college have access to a wider world than those of a generation ago.

One feminist writer complains of her own education: "I was told I was 'sensitive' and 'perceptive'—nice things to be, and much more suitable for a girl than solid achievement. I swallowed that kind of claptrap, and found myself, as I grew older, actually getting less and less smart. By the time I was a sophomore in college, I was literally incapable of rigorous intellectual work." Women were never less intelligent, but they were often subtly—or not so subtly—discouraged from developing their intellects. The old adage, "Men seldom make passes at girls who wear glasses," was not a denigration of the myopic, but of the brainy. Men's acceptance of intelligence in women is the natural result of seeing women as allies, not competitors.

The youngest men were most apt to characterize today's women as having become more loving and giving, the percentage decreasing with age and reaching a low in the over–55 group. Single men and the living-togethers (again, chiefly men in their twenties) most often saw women as more loving, with married men giving this response least often. High school graduates and men with some college focused on this reply more than those who completed college or had postgraduate training, but this is probably only because the most educated men placed the highest premium on companionship instead.

This response indicates that men view the increased sexual activity on the part of women in a positive way; twice as many saw women as more loving and giving compared with those who viewed them as "too promiscuous." The youngest men are most likely to benefit from the increased availability of partners, and it is not surprising that they emphasized most this positive aspect of today's women.

The uneducated man tended to complain most that women expect too much of men, with twice as many of those who did not complete high school voicing this complaint compared with the college graduates. Divorced men gave this response most often of the marital status subgroups, and married men least. Blacks lodged the complaint more often than whites. Whether the demands perceived as unreasonable were sexual, economic, or emotional is not clear, although the correlation of this response with education would indicate that the demands were chiefly psychological ones which the more intellectual and self-fulfilled man felt confident to meet.

Do men feel the new woman is promiscuous? Apparently not, for fewer men selected this response than any other. Men over 55 were more apt to feel this way, but men in the 40–54 bracket did not feel so any more than the younger men. If women are more liberal in their attitude toward sex, men may be threatened by their independence, or praise them either as better companions or as more loving and giving; but men today do not regard women, in general, as too loose with their favors. This does not mean that the archetype of the prostitute has been finally laid to rest—only that men have become more aware of women as total persons and are less likely to regard them as two-dimensional stereotypes.

Theodore Rubin says, "After years of treating men, I have come to realize that most men really do not *like* women." Our study seems to indicate quite the opposite—a sincere regard for women in many men, a concern for their welfare, and a growing awareness of their potential as equals. There are the germs of hostility in every man; they arose in puberty when he was struggling with his ambivalent sexual urges and needed to see women as wily demons who would overpower his embryonic ego if his conscience did not fend them off. *Any* psychiatrist could conclude from years of treating men that most really don't like women—but that's like concluding after years of practicing dermatology that most people have skin problems. Neurotic men see women in shades of black and white, wearing the inky skirt of the prostitute or the snowy veil of the madonna. Most men, however, can appreciate the full spectrum of a woman's true colors, and while subconscious traces of the prostitute-madonna split lie unperceived at either end of that spectrum, like invisible infrared and ultraviolet rays, they do not color man's judgment enough to preclude healthy relationships with women.

When man relates to woman as a typical member of the species, he summons up his archaic adolescent notions of the prostitute, usually reserving the madonna classification for his mother and her surrogates. When man relates to woman as an individual, he can view her realistically because he apprehends what is unique in her, not what is common. The more choices women have and the more freedom to make those choices, the more individual they will become—and the more likeable.

# Feeling the Part

In his play *No Exit*, Sartre envisioned hell in very unconventional terms. A man named Garcin finds himself locked in a comfortable sitting-room with two women: Estelle, a flirtatious and superficial lady, and Inez, a cynical lesbian. Garcin had been a revolutionist who deserted his comrades when the going got rough. In hell, he tries to convince the women that he was not a coward. Estelle tells him what he wants to hear, but he realizes she is flattering him because of her own dependent need for the love of a man; in fact, her weakness makes her incapable of forming any sincere judgment of Garcin, one way or the other. Inez berates Garcin and tortures him with her taunts, causing him more distress than any of Satan's horned henchmen could have managed. Yet, when the door of that elegant torture chamber opens unexpectedly, Garcin cannot leave. While the odds of his ever convincing Inez that he is a real man are infinitesmal, she is the only remaining creature in his universe who can validate his fading hope that he was not a weakling, after all.

The way that men regard women also has a great influence on how men regard themselves. Men have always, to some extent, sought to win women's esteem as a way of validating their own worth as men. Under the macho ideal, however, the man gets his primary validation by being a man-among-men, respected in the eyes of other males; since he views women as intellectual inferiors, he resorts to deceit and flattery to win their favors, and basically holds their opinions in scorn. As the modern woman has grown in responsibility and education, and as man has come to accept her as a true companion and peer, her esteem of him has taken on a powerful new validity. She is no longer viewed as weak and gullible. She has acquired the wisdom—and the role—of a judge.

Women usually fail to appreciate how important they are to men's impressions of themselves. The man on the make may seem totally secure in his projected image of a self-assured, intrepid hunter; he can, indeed, handle seductive responses or timid feminine protestations with equanimity—but let a woman respond in an unconventional way, such as with amusement or with logical arguments against his illogical declarations, and the smooth line often collapses into chaotic gibberish. Men need women, not only as lovers, mothers, maids, and companions, but also as mirrors. This became strikingly apparent when we asked our sample:

*Essay Question: When do you feel most manly—when you are making love to a woman, socializing with other men, competing in sports, on the job? When do you feel least manly?*

A large majority of the answers showed that men's concept of their own masculinity evolved from having intercourse with women and feeling they have satisfied their partners:

"When I'm making love to my wife and she's enjoying what I'm doing I feel most manly. Least manly when I see other men further advanced in their careers than I am."

"When I'm with a very feminine woman. I think a woman makes a man feel like a man, and she can also make him feel less of a man."

"Most manly when I am doing things for my family. This would include making love but also when relaxing with the family and when hunting or fishing. I do not have any feeling of manliness when I am 'doing things with the boys.'"

"Feel most manly when a woman is performing fellatio on me. Least when a woman refuses sexual advances."

"I feel manly most of time. Only put-down is in pickups in single bars where girl turns me down."

"When 'courting' a woman; i.e., candlelit dinners, dancing, etc. (if she acts interested). Least manly when doing something simply to please a woman (attending church, going shopping, etc.)."

"Making love to a woman—I feel less manly when my judgment is bad and my wife is correct in her opinion."

"Loving a woman until she is completely exhausted—Socializing with men, being a leader—In sports being a winner. Least manly—weak—recessing [sic]—lacking aggressiveness."

"When I've had a hard day at work and come home and can

give my wife good enjoyment in bed I feel most manly. I feel the least manly when uncontrollable situations happen that I can't avoid."

Some said they felt the least manly when they were impotent or otherwise failed to please their partners:

"Most manly when I am making love to a woman. I feel least manly if I'm impotent at times."

"On the job. [Least] when I have trouble completing the sex act due to pressure or too much to drink."

"Making love to a woman I love. Least manly when she makes a joke of my loving her."

"I feel mostly man when I'm in bed with a woman. Feel less manly when I'm physically ill and don't care for the sexual act."

A small number felt least manly, not in the bedroom, but when doing domestic chores, or feeling intellectually or socially inferior to a woman, even though performance sexually gave them the strongest validation of masculinity:

"During lovemaking. Least manly when doing women's work."

"Making love and having ego boosted by wife or other women. Least manly when doing domestic duties."

"Competing in my job. Feel least manly when being led, ex: woman paying on date, going dutch, etc."

"I feel most masculine when I'm in bed with a woman—least manly when I'm with an emotional or intellectual superior."

For a few, the worst feeling was having no woman at all:

"When I have two women working on me at once. Least manly when she's not there."

"No special time to feel manly. Least manly is when being serviced by prostitute."

"Fucking a woman. [Least] when preparing goddamn tax reports. Also, when I have to get most of my fucking by jacking myself off."

"When I pick up a girl someplace and fuck her that night. I feel least manly when I get turned down by more than 3 women."

There were some men, though in the minority, who did not regard sex as the prime source of masculine identity. For these men, masculinity was usually equated to achievement or competency in other areas:

"Does 'manly' mean dominant? Probably while on the job, but don't normally feel 'dominant' or 'manly' per se. I would like to feel I am in control of things, but I rarely do."

"I feel manly when competing in sports and on the job. When walking alone in an undesirable neighborhood, the least manly."

"When providing for the needs of wife and children. I feel least manly when I lose temper and control."

"I feel most like a man when my family recognizes that I am the man of the house. Least when I am confronted with a problem I can't seem to handle."

"When I am at work because I am the boss I feel most manly. Least manly when I am talking to a woman that dominates the situation or is overly confident."

"Least manly at work—stocking shelves. I can make most of my activities manly."

"When I'm socializing with other men like at a 'stag' party. [Least] when I'm lost in a large crowd of men and women with no companions."

"I suppose I feel most manly when competing in sports. Of course, you cannot discount feeling manly when you're making love to a woman; and I also feel quite manly when running my office and my three secretaries. I feel least manly when socializing with other men."

"Sports, by all means, makes me feel more manly. I feel least manly when I can't answer a woman's question correctly."

"Most manly when I am peaceful (state of mind). Feel least manly when I feel I have made an ass of myself in public."

"[Most] competing in sports. [Least] afraid of snakes."

For men, manliness may stem from a feeling rather than a particular activity. These feelings, however, are often tied in to particular accomplishments:

"I feel most 'manly' when I've done something which reflects my attempted maturity—something which helps me to hold myself in higher personal esteem. I feel least manly when I've allowed myself to give in to anger, pettiness, immaturity or jealousy."

"When I've accomplished what I have set out to do I feel most manly. Least manly when I have failed in something."

"When sick I feel the least manly. [Most] on the job doing what I'm supposed to do to support the needs of a family—supplying all the demands of the home and family."

There were a few men who rejected the concept of masculinity entirely, although even more of them detailed when they felt manly but said they never felt unmanly:

"I'm not really hung up on 'feeling manly,' hence I feel the same way about it most all of the time. I *know* I'm a man; I act and react as such, and I don't really recall feeling otherwise in the past 15–20 years."

"These concepts do not enter into my life. I feel comfortable in my masculinity even when washing dishes and changing diapers."

Masculinity can only be conceived as one of a pair. Its opposite is femininity, and anything that is unmasculine is therefore feminine. As a pair, one cannot compare them to earrings or cufflinks, which are identical, or to shoes, which are mirror-images, for they are totally different in every way. Most European languages divide all of the world's objects into two genders: masculine and feminine. The ancient Chinese conceived two elemental forces, the male principle yang and the female yin, dividing the world between them. Yang had dominion over what was positive, spiritual, active, light and lively. Yin was left with the negative, earthy, passive, dark and dead.

In our society, most of the characteristics considered masculine are desirable: strength, activity, hardness, intellect, courage, and industry, although brutality, insensitivity, and coarseness are also likely to be deemed masculine. Femininity reaps the questionable qualities of weakness, passivity, softness, emotionality, timidity, and domesticity, along with sensitivity, tenderness, nurturance, and gentility. No rational man would want to be thoroughly masculine by the above standards—although the macho is so eager to avoid the stigma of femininity that he conducts himself in an unnecessarily brutal and insensitive manner. Similarly, women who abhor the weakness and fear that femininity denotes may reject the more desirable traits of consideration and emotional sensitivity.

In the past, men turned to other men for validation. Men's clubs, athletic teams, the corner tavern, fraternities, and veterans' associations formerly held great importance in men's lives. It was among his buddies—his fellow men—that a man received his validation that he was, indeed, one of them.

But technological changes in our society and the changing roles of women in the family have made mutual male validation practically obsolete. Few men today earn their bread by the sweat of their brow and the brawn of their arms, and machines have put the strength of Samson within the reach of anyone with the ability to push a button or pull a lever. Television and professional sports have turned us into a nation of spectators; nobody in Mudville is going to watch Casey strike out on a sandlot when they can watch Dave Kingman do the same thing in living color on a major-league ball field. Men grow up in smaller families; they have fewer brothers, uncles, and other male clansmen, and the demands of the jet age and the corporation often compel them to move away from the few they do possess. A man is now expected to share the obligations of child rearing and not spend long hours on weekends or after work in bull sessions at the neighborhood bar or bowling alley—if, indeed, there is one in the suburban neighborhood he commutes to. His fellow males would be small comfort, anyway. They are more likely to be viewed as competitors rather than supporters, for the man who might have been his own boss in a small business 50 years ago is more likely to be now a small cog trying to be a big wheel in some vast industrial or business machine, acutely aware of those above him whom he must displace and those at his level who compete with him for the limited space at the top.

Having lost the sports arena, the military battleground, and the job field as his proving grounds, man is left only with the bedroom as the testing site for his masculinity. Woman becomes his judge and validator, as well as his conquest or companion. The more man sees woman as ally and peer, the more independent and intelligent she becomes, the greater is the value of her judgment.

Many men, therefore, are seeking not just reassurance that they are good sexual performers, but that they are men in the broadest sense of the word; and since masculinity concepts are so intrinsic to men's identity, the question of their whole existence hinges on their sex life. This should not be simply dismissed as a manifestation of feelings of sexual inadequacy; the lack of opportunities that our society offers for other sources of validation and other validators contributes to the overloading of the sex act and the sexual partner with the full weight of the male ego, its other supports having collapsed with those pillars of patriarchal society: independent enterprise, craftsmanship, athleticism, family ties, paternal authority, and self-sufficiency. Surrounded by other men who are equally lost, men are turning to women in their search for a new identity. Ironically, as more women are finding identities, more men are losing theirs. Thus, women must add one more role to their growing repertoire, that of guide—or, at least, fellow searcher.

The woman should regard the man, not as someone with all the answers, but one with many questions—interesting and important questions. She must get to know him as someone who relates to a wider world beyond the bedroom, as a man with goals, work, and problems. The love and friendship of a concerned female companion may be the only stimulus to lead him into the sort of self-exploration that will organize his own unique outlook and free him from some of the old masculine-feminine conventions that prescribe and restrict his behavior. Together, they may find not different identities as man and woman, but a common identity as humans.

## Reaching the Goal

If women have attained new importance as validators of manliness and if successful lovemaking is the main way to win a woman's validation, a man must determine how to be a good lover. If the bedroom has become the area in which he finds not only sexual gratification but the esteem of a woman that confirms his worth as a man, so, too, does the bedroom have the potential of becoming his Waterloo. Failure as a lover means more than the loss of mutual pleasure; it can mean a far-reaching loss of self-esteem.

Much has been written about men's approach to the sex act. Attainment of orgasm for themselves, it has been claimed, is the goal line, and they are depicted as engaged in a mad scramble to reach that end zone as quickly as possible, with no concern for teammate or obstacle. Shere Hite charges that the prevailing pattern of intercourse "has institutionalized out any expression of women's sexual feelings except for those that support male sexual needs."

Preoccupation with performance, another favorite topic of contemporary male-watchers, indicates the man's concern with his partner's satisfaction as well as his own; delaying orgasm, prolonging penetration, cunnilingus, and trying to bring his partner to multiple orgasm are as much a concern to him as progressing toward his own orgasm. But we cannot talk about a variety of techniques to enhance female response without talking about the existing needs. Being a good lover involves more than sex technique just as football involves more than pushing toward one end of a field. Our men were quick to point out that you have to know what your partner needs before you can satisfy her; you need a game plan before you start playing the game:

> *Essay Question: What do you think makes a man a good lover —understanding women's needs, performing well in bed, making a woman feel secure? What's most important and why?*

Overwhelmingly, our respondents stressed understanding women's needs over performing well in bed, although many noted that good performance was usually bound to follow, just as good execution generally follows good planning:

> "I think that understanding a woman is most important. If a man understands a woman's needs and lets her know it—the other things will follow—she'll respond better in bed—whether or not he's a great performer, and she'll feel secure in the knowledge that her needs are understood and her man is making an effort to meet those needs."

> "Understanding a woman's needs—if he doesn't even attempt, then he doesn't care for her. It is when the man is stuck in his egotism that he treats women as objects. No true love can be

had unless both partners fully understand their needs and wants as well as their partners'."

"Tenderness and trust are most important attitudinally. Of course, a man might theoretically have these qualities and still be unable to render physical sexual satisfaction. Therefore, a knowledge of what works in giving partner satisfaction must be acquired."

"Yes, understanding women's needs because of her constant change in her body chemistry."

Some stressed the importance of making a woman feel loved and wanted:

"Making a woman feel like she is special, not just another lay. Good performance is part of it, but good performance with little or no emotional contact makes a woman feel cheap."

"Understanding a woman's needs and making her feel secure. Don't make her think you only want her for sex. Let her make the advances."

"My greatest satisfaction in making love is when I feel I have given and received love. Giving is most important."

"Understanding and comforting a woman when she is in depression or at indecision. The most important is making a woman feel like a real beautiful woman at all times."

"She needs to be loved and know that she is loved."

Some felt that honest communication was the basis of trust, which would then lead to a feeling of security:

"Making a woman feel secure ranks high with me. Performing well in bed is important, but only a woman can tell you how good or bad you are, and it's been my experience that most won't. It takes time for two people to be good lovers and open up to each other. Unfortunately, today it is all too frequent that two people meet and end up in bed that night. Never has such a relationship lasted for me. And don't believe that men cause this either—I feel it's just the opposite in many cases."

"Understanding a woman's needs—reasoning behind this is that you must have a two-way street through communications, before you can be a good lover."

"Being able to talk in bed makes your partner feel relaxed and open-minded. Important to be able to talk about the act."

"Empathizing is an integral part of a relationship and I find when I truly listen to a woman, she feels good and so do I."

A few were defensive about their views, but felt that ideals considered old-fashioned by many still were valid:

"Love her—old-fashioned idea, but then if problems and needs arise, if you love her, you can cope with them."

"Even with women's lib, the majority of women, I feel, like to take care of and be taken care of by their man. By this, the man should do his best to make the woman feel secure and comfortable."

"Remembering special days and really wanting to please."

As Don Juan pointed out, without a brain you would enjoy yourself without knowing it, and so lose all the fun. His adversary replied, "But I am quite content with brain enough to know that I'm enjoying myself. I don't want to understand why." Most of the men we encountered, however, were introspective, and likely to view lovemaking as something more than one-dimensional, even if their recurrent analogies to food suggested an equation of the sex drive with other appetites:

"To love a woman physically and emotionally is the most. Man can't live by bread alone—emotions come into love, too."

If physical satisfaction is the daily (or, more likely, semiweekly) bread of sex life, the overwhelming majority of our men took it for granted and concentrated on the meatier elements of a relationship. A few did mention the physical side of sex as important to a man's being a good lover, occasionally with considerable sensitivity:

"(1) Treated his wife or girl friend with compassion and tenderness. (2) Knowing what a woman likes and giving it to her. (3)

Slow and gentle stimulation of her clitoris, kissing and sucking her breasts, preventing premature ejaculation."

A few others answered or dismissed the question with macho brusqueness:

"When she is paid for giving good head."

"Having a big prick."

"9 inches."

"Don't know and don't particularly care."

"Don't know. I'm not a woman."

But men with such attitudes formed a tiny minority, and most were not only concerned with being good lovers, but felt that success required more than physical attributes and competent technique.

If we compare the men's answers to this question with their responses to the one about what makes a woman a good lover (Chapter Two), we are struck by the difference in the way the questions were approached. Whereas men rated women as good lovers solely on their attitude towards the sex act, even though that attitude might encompass feelings of love and respect for the man, they saw men's obligations as lovers to include understanding and meeting a realm of women's needs that extended far beyond the bedroom. While this reflects men's appreciation of the complex interweaving of emotional and physical needs in women, it also underscores men's tendency to segregate sexual needs from other dependency needs in themselves, even when the same woman is trying to meet them all.

# The Age-Old Question

Traditionally, a woman will not be older than her mate. Since men originally receive love and gratification from an older woman—mother—why are they so reluctant to accept it from older women as adults?

"The Oedipus complex!" you exclaim, knowledgeably. But we must ask: If Oedipus killed his father and married his mother unknowingly, what did he feel so damned guilty about? And how could the gods blame him?

The question is not that trivial, for if Oedipus is viewed as a passive victim of circumstances, the myth loses its meaning. According to the story, Oedipus had been told by the oracle at Delphi that he would kill his father, marry his mother, and sire children by her. While Oedipus might not have been able to avoid killing a man in self-defense, he could have beaten the terrible prophecy with one simple precaution: under no circumstance should he marry a woman older than himself. Yet, with the added inducement of the throne at Thebes, Oedipus was unable to resist the allure of Jocasta and knowingly broke the taboo.

For the young man, his preoccupation with still younger women is not based on a distaste for older women, but on the anxiety that their attraction for him arouses. Since sexual feelings stem quite naturally from other warm and powerful emotions, the adolescent boy has, through the prostitute-madonna complex, forced himself to react in a way quite opposite to his natural inclinations and regard older women to be thoroughly inconceivable as potential sex partners. The young man automatically follows the law Oedipus flaunted, the one rule that gives total peace of mind: avoid any woman old enough to be your mother or to remind you of your mother.

Beyond the male myth of writer and analyst, is the adult male still under the tyranny of Oedipus, as well as a society that values only youth and compliance in women? Now that men are offered a greater number of available sex partners, will they take advantage of a wider age range or restrict the quantity by the qualities of age? If aggressiveness is more acceptable in women and passivity less objectionable in men, are men now able to benefit from the experience and maturity of an older partner without fear of losing their virility?

*Question 17: How do you feel about having sex with older women?*

| | |
|---|---|
| Age does not matter at all | 38.2% |
| The woman must be my age or younger | 16.4% |
| The woman could be 5 years older, not more | 16.3% |
| Age doesn't matter, but she must not look older | 12.8% |
| The woman could be 10 years older, not more | 11.3% |
| Prefer an older woman | 3.5% |
| No answer | 2.2% |

Only one out of six men insisted that their sex partners be no older than themselves. This attitude was most prevalent among men over 55, where more than a third made this demand. Preoccupation with youth was least marked in the youngest, and increased with age. Married men exceeded the unmarried, the living-togethers, and the divorced/widowed in limiting themselves to women the same age or younger.

Acceptance of older women as partners increased with education; almost a quarter of men who did not complete high school would not consider older women, compared with less than one-sixth of college graduates. Students were most accepting of older women, followed by professional men. The retired/unemployed, like the least educated, were the least tolerant.

Of the 38 percent of men who said that age did not matter at all, 41 percent of men under 40 gave this response, as did 33 percent of those over 40. The divorced/widowed were least concerned with age, followed by the living-togethers and trailed by the singles and married. Those with college education, whether or not completed, averaged 40 percent in disclaiming concern over age, considerably more than the less educated.

Of the men who said they would accept a gap no greater than 5 years in excess of their own age, there was not much variation in the age brackets of respondents; men in the 40–54 range chose this response as often as men under 40, and men over 55 only a little less often. When the gap increased to 10 years, there was little drop in acceptance among the youngest group and those in their thirties, but a definite decrease in the 40–54 bracket and an understandable precipitous drop in men over 55.

"Age doesn't matter, but she must not look older" is the response many women believe lies closest to men's true feelings, although only one in eight made this choice, with not much variation among the subgroups. Men who are concerned enough with age to want the woman to look younger are likely to go whole hog and demand that she *be* younger. Men liberal enough to accept a woman of any age are apt not to be threatened by her showing her age. Only 3.5 percent actually preferred older women, with equal percentages in the very youngest and very oldest brackets. Nonwhites preferred older partners (6 percent) twice as often as whites. (Racial groups showed no variation in age criteria otherwise.)

These findings show that men are not as preoccupied with youth as women might tend to think, bombarded as they are with Madison Avenue copy that extols the importance and beauty of youth. Even among the oldest men, we have found, nearly two out of three would consider a partner older than themselves, and only one man in ten under the age of 30 would reject a woman on the basis of age. Women may protest that men are indeed willing to take almost any woman to bed, but will not consider an older woman seriously as a permanent partner. We have not really been in this era of sexual liberation long enough to determine the validity of this contention; however, men who believed in a strict standard of monogamy, with intercourse limited to one partner within or just prior to marriage, were far less likely, being restricted to one woman, to explore relationships with those who were older. We see this attitude reflected both in the older age brackets and in those men who are married.

Laurie, whom we spoke about in Chapter Two, is a 34-year-old patient, divorced for the second time. She frequents a neighborhood bar whose clientele is unattached, known to one another, and respectable, so she is not afraid to go home with men she meets or take them home with her—which she usually does. They always ask her age immediately; years ago, men wouldn't have dreamed of such a question, but then they wouldn't have asked for sex right away, either. Laurie never lies about her age; it never deters any of the men still in their twenties, which most of her lovers are. Her youngest was "the kid," a 20-year-old; she considers that a mistake because he was too unsophisticated to understand the rules and acted too possessive the next time they met.

Not all women are as frank as Laurie. They feel that by knocking 5 or 10 years off their ages, successful men in their late thirties or older will show more interest. The dilemma here is that most men will not reject a sex partner on the basis of age and will seek sincerity and honesty in a woman they would consider for a more serious relationship. Embarking on a deeper phase of a relationship by confessing a lie often goes over with the same effect as stripping off a heavily padded bra. One might argue that without the lie the couple might never have become intimate enough to confront the moment of truth; however, we know the odds are only one in six that a man will disdain a woman for aging—we have no statistics on how men feel about being duped, but we would bet they resent it more than 16 percent of the time.

For centuries, women managed to maintain the prerogative of keeping their ages a secret; ceding that right was foolhardy. Dropping one's inhibitions with regard to chastity offered pleasure in return, but disclosure of age offered nothing but dilemma. If a woman does not want to reveal her age to an impertinent questioner, she should fall back on the time-tested ploy of secrecy under the rights of genteel women. She may come off somewhat old-fashioned and coquettish, but many men will find this curiously refreshing. A little mystery keeps a man coming back in hopes of learning more. In any case, sooner or later, the woman who lies will face a sticky confrontation if she is at all serious about the man; and if she just wants a casual sexual affair, age is rarely likely to block the way. One glamorous middle-aged actress said it well: "I would rather tell people my age and have them say, 'How young she looks!' than tell them I am ten years younger and have them say, 'How old she looks!' "

Youth in women has been a commodity for exchange in sexual liaisons approximately equal in value to wealth in men. According to one story, a group of women were gossiping about an affair between a wealthy old man and a young attractive woman. "I don't believe much ever comes of these May-December affairs," one meowed. "December can find youth and freshness in May, but what can May hope to find in December?" Her more knowledgeable friend replied, "Christmas."

Don't blame Oedipus for the older man's pursuit of the young. Both sexes want love and admiration to bolster their own egos, and love is worth more when it comes from a worthier person. In men, the standard of desirability is success and its usual concomitant, wealth. In women, it is youth and its usual companion, physical beauty. It is pointless to hurl epithets such as "gold-digger" and "lecher" at the participants, who may be genuinely seeking a valid love relationship from a partner assumed to be strongest and most secure in his or her own identity, and hence best able to love and protect.

But as the modern woman dares to develop her intellect, her ambition, her earning potential, and her identity as a complete human being, she will have new currency with which to barter in the sexual marketplace. Youth has never been particularly valued in men, not because it is unattractive, but because the years invariably allow men to acquire more desirable attributes. With our society's more liberal attitude toward sex, the older woman can gain the benefit of experience and have the opportunity to share it in an endless spiral wherein each day's pleasures augment the promise of tomorrow. Hopefully, she will grow in nonsexual achievement and experience as well.

In Don Juan's hell, where women could appear any age they chose, the fashionable age was "forty—or say, thirty-seven." Such a situation on earth would be deemed more of a heaven than a hell to most women—but once the earthly delights remain readily available for those of all ages, as they now nearly seem to be, the joys of heaven will not be far off.

# Communicating– Man to Woman

"Then you should say what you mean," the March Hare went on.

"I do," Alice hastily replied; "at least—at least I mean what I say—that's the same thing, you know."

"Not the same thing a bit!" said the Hatter. "Why, you might just as well say that 'I see what I eat' is the same thing as 'I eat what I see.'!"

—LEWIS CARROLL, *Alice's Adventures in Wonderland*

A captionless cartoon printed several years ago in a magazine depicted the familiar scene of the driving of a golden spike to mark the completion of the Union Pacific Railroad. On one side were the men who had been laying track in the westward direction, on the other those who had labored eastward. Beneath the festive banners, there were only looks of dismay and consternation, for the two sections of track lay side-by-side, several feet apart, at the planned junction point.

Communication between men and women sometimes parallels this frustrating scene. Each party moves toward the other, but somehow they never quite manage to meet. Even if men and women come from different worlds, is it necessary for them to remain worlds apart? Can communication bring them together, or are there too many obstacles to prevent derailment en route?

*Essay Question: Do you feel that you communicate well with women? Can you make them understand the way you feel? If not, what do you think the problem is?*

At least two-thirds of the men said they could communicate well; however, these men were not as adept at communicating why they could as were the men who claimed they had difficulty communicating. We wonder if the many men who responded to the question with a simple "yes" might not be as terse in their interactions with women. One can communicate an "S.O.S." effectively with a flashlight, telegraph key, or any audible sound, but one would hardly want to transmit a love letter by the same media.

Most of the men who admitted difficulty attributed part of the problem to their own shyness:

"When I first meet a new woman, I'm kind of shy—I actually have to make myself go up to them and introduce myself; then, if I want to take her out, I almost have to force myself to ask her —the rejection syndrome, I guess. It would be so much better if people didn't have to be so 'plastic.' Honesty is my policy, but how do you say to a girl, 'You turn me on'—and if you don't get put down then, where do you go from there?"

"I feel my communication level with women is at a poor level, due to my family background. If I overcome my shyness in interpersonal relationships, I can make a woman understand me. Sometimes I become frustrated because of all the superficiality surrounding courting behavior, and then I will stay alone for a period of time and reflect and wait for change. Then try again. I would like to see a breakdown in the present sex roles which are prevalent in male-female relationships, a more egalitarian approach would suit me."

"I can communicate well with one woman, my wife, only her. I have always had a problem with women, basically due to lack of self-confidence."

"Only with my wife—the rest scare me."

Some of the men who didn't communicate well blamed it on the women:

"The more I try to see myself through a woman's eyes, the more I realize that she doesn't understand herself. I mean her psyche, emotion, concepts, physique, etc., and then I'm thrown off. Instead, I tend to communicate with women their ideas, feelings, images; of course, I don't understand these concepts about myself either, so it's impossible to communicate the understanding of my feelings with a woman unless she stands in a personal relationship with me."

"No. Most are screwed up with visions of having a beautiful family but yet they've got this 'women's lib' in their head. To top it off, they say men treat them unfair."

"It depends on the woman. If I feel at ease I can communicate, but if I suspect I am dealing with a snooty person, I begin to stumble and get self-conscious."

"I can communicate but 75% of them don't receive. They seem to me that they can make it on their own and their goal is to be president of the firm instead of trying their best to be in bed."

A few respondents made it clear that they did not expect men and women to communicate on an eye-to-eye level:

"I never express too many of my feelings to a woman. I have a basic sense of superiority to most women I engage in sex or conversation with. I feel they would not understand, so I do not try."

"The women that don't understand me I don't want to know. Those who do have certain insights that I have as well and therefore roughly the same intelligence."

"Yes. I can make women understand the way I feel. Most men don't want women to understand, just accept."

Even men who felt that they could communicate well noted that our society induces certain gender-linked attitudes and that a man must work to overcome these obstacles and improve relationships:

"I do feel I communicate well with women. I think there are certain 'male' and 'female' attitudes toward sexuality that are difficult for the opposite sex to understand, but it goes both ways."

"Roles in society cause us to play certain parts, which is good, but too often the roles being played are ones using past morality standards."

"Yes, I do feel women are as easy to communicate with as men, if they would slow down and don't run at jobs. I am afraid women are going to die with heart attacks and nervous breakdowns more then men."

"I can because I understand that all women are not alike. This something you have to find out yourself and only with time and patience will you ever find out."

Some summed up the secret as kindness, consideration, and honesty:

"I feel I do. I feel that if you are willing to open yourself, your true self, fully, and to share in the lives of others, then you will be very loved, or hated; but not ignored. [Women] are very eager to know how I feel, because I am very patient and understanding, and demonstrate that I'm willing to understand how they feel, and cooperate with their needs."

"Yes. I communicate better with women than men. The only problem I experience is that women are often scared away by a man who can be open and honest—it's something most women have not experienced."

## The Unanswered Riddle

Going for the $64,000 question is a lark compared to what Oedipus had at stake. He had his life on the line when the Sphinx asked, "What creature goes on four feet in the morning, on two at noonday, on three in the evening?" Fortunately, Oedipus figured out that he himself was the answer. When he replied, "Man," the Sphinx not only spared his life, but inexplicably took her own. Was she guarding the secret of her own riddle? Having brutally demonstrated that men who could not unravel the riddle of their own existence were not fit to live, did she fear Oedipus might fathom the female as well?

Today's men, unlike Oedipus, have access to many books and articles on female psychology, so one might think that there are few female riddles still unanswered. With all men's exposure to psychological expertise, is there anything they still don't understand about women?

*Essay Question: What do you find hard to understand about women? What would you like to know about them? Do you understand them well, or are they a mystery to you?*

Probably the biggest puzzle to most men is how frequently women change their moods and opinions:

"How they can be a very mature adult one moment and very childlike the next. I would say most remain a mystery."

"First, what they want out of life is the biggest question. Why they can't be satisfied easily. And no matter how you figure them out, there always seems to be a change in them, over and over."

"I don't understand them at all. Sometimes they want to be near you and then when you try to get close to them, they push you away. I'd like to know what makes them change so fast, and, yes, they are a complete mystery to me."

"Since women are cyclical (menstruation periods). It's sometimes hard to keep this in mind when a woman is 'moody.'"

"I find it hard to believe how women can gossip and cut one another down to their backs and still face the person. I believe most women are hard to understand—hot and cold on the same issue."

"Women are easier to understand than men, if they would watch their nerves, and laugh and be jolly as they were back before the women's lib."

"Women seem to be very unstable about making up their minds. But I like it. Take away the mystery, you lose the women."

Men also tend to see women's minds as operating in illogical fashion:

"I don't understand the way women think. I am somewhat of a logical person myself and women's reasoning always fails to escape me. I would like to know more about what makes a woman tick so I could relate to my wife better."

"Their reasoning or inability to. Followed closely by lack of common sense. I would like to know why they can feel that they have accomplished something after a full day of sitting and talking to their neighbor and let the housework go to hell. I don't understand women and don't believe anyone does."

"I often wonder if they worry about the same things as men, for example, whether or not there is any sense of purpose (philosophically)."

"I believe their sense of humor is hard to understand. One day they have it, the next day they don't. I believe I understand them well enough."

Some men felt that women's inconsistency implied a lack of honesty, which further interfered with male attempts to understand them:

"They are a puzzle. One minute they are warm and open—the next they are a mystery. They seem hesitant to be honest. They seem to always be holding back making you the one that must make the moves."

"Women don't lie as much as they 'don't tell the truth.' They don't seem hard to understand or seem mysterious. I think they want to seem that way."

"Some women I know seem to like to tease and fool men. I will never understand why they can't be more honest."

"I think it's hard for most women to really trust a man enough to lay bare her innermost emotions. Women remain mysterious in many ways."

Many felt they did not really understand women's feelings about sex:

"Many women 'today' fall in love too fast or are just too 'easy' —most men are not looking for this. Perhaps women feel that is the only way they are going to catch a man."

"Why they get hung up on guys so fast. Why can't they just fuck one night and forget you the next."

"Not much [hard to understand]. I would like to know what the average woman likes about sex, dislikes, not just some glorified ideas by *Playboy*, etc."

"Why they generally think that a man must always be the initiator in sexual approach. Do they generally 'size' a man up at first meeting as to whether he would be a desirable sex partner?"

"Their attitudes about sex. They can develop a close personal relationship with a man but will turn him down to have sex with someone who is not as in touch with them as a friend."

"I sincerely wish that women were like the ladies of the thirties and forties. That they would treat men like men, and not just a tool for lovemaking. They feel that they can conquer a man with just spreading their legs!"

"Young girls today give themselves so easily to men, and *after* they marry, you have to *drag* them to bed to have intercourse, avoiding under different excuses."

"The thing I find hard to understand is why a woman, when she is single, and a virgin, is not too crazy about sex before marriage, but goes crazy over it after marriage. Why is that?"

Sometimes exactly what the woman wanted and expected was the hardest thing for men to understand:

"It's hard to understand their standards for judging men. And it's hard to understand what they want from men."

"It's not always easy to understand what drives women, what their desires are, and what they expect from you personally."

And there were a number of lesser mysteries and complaints, wanting solutions:

"Women in general are a mystery to me. I try to make them fit into male roles and it doesn't work worth a damn. They seem to live in an equal but separate world."

"What I don't understand is why women allow themselves to be taken advantage of."

"They are very complex and dependent, too dependent at times."

"Their insecurities amaze me. I think many still envy the male species."

"The thing I don't understand is why a woman would cheat on her man."

"I find it hard to understand why they always worry so much about 'not being dressed for that' or 'I'm not in the right clothes for such an occasion.'"

"Why some women cock-tease?"

"I have been married three times and am now 31. It seems like when you get married the woman takes the attitude that she has you and forgets that you still need to feel loved and needed."

"Women today seem to be a mystery in that at first glance you don't know whether a woman is a feminist or a more 'traditional' woman. I find it awkward in that I don't want to say or do anything that would insult the woman no matter what her beliefs are."

## Safe at Home

Charlie Brown's best-known definition is probably "Happiness is a warm puppy." And though we think of his pal Linus as the expert on security, who would undoubtedly define it as a warm blanket, Charlie once gave another perceptive and near-unbeatable definition. According to Brown, security is falling asleep in the back seat of a car after a long evening out visiting, knowing your parents in the front seat will take care of getting you home. We never, he noted sadly, recapture that degree of security in later life.

Even if adulthood means we are all in the driver's seat, security makes the road a less lonely one. From an emotional point of view, it is the reassurance that someone consistently cares and will be there when you need them. From an economic point of view, it means someone will put their earnings or services towards covering your mutual needs. It's a blanket that covers a broad spread of desires and needs—and according to the men we asked, security was what women wanted most from them.

*Essay Question: What do you think women want most from men, and why? Do you think they want love, security, children, a home, sex—and which do you think is most important to them?*

Security was the overwhelming first choice of our respondents, with love a strong second. Love is, of course, a prime component of emotional security, although men and women can love without making the sort of commitments that try to ensure the stability and permanence of that feeling. It is difficult to segregate the economic and emotional components of security, since a commitment means pooling all resources—psychical, physical, and fiscal:

"In talking with various women on this subject, I have found varying answers. However, I do find for the majority they seem to desire emotional security. They are willing to participate in sex in order to achieve this. If they do happen to enjoy sex with their partner, so much the better!"

"Security. For all their flirtation in economic independence, most young women still want it both ways. Home and children are forms of security; most women can love any man who provides them with security, and sex is just too casual."

"I think most women want security first, love, then children. This satisfies their dreams and they put up with things they dislike to keep their marriage together."

"I feel they want sexual security. Many women are afraid they aren't attractive or appealing. Marriage insures consistent sexual activity."

"Women want support in their endeavors. They want someone who believes in them as individuals and partners."

"They want to be married because they see their brothers and sisters and friends doing it and they don't want to be left out."

"I guess I would have to say security because once they've been hurt, they have a difficult time trusting again. Trust and security mean pretty much the same to me."

"All—mostly security. Let's face it, women still like money to spend on themselves and family."

"Security and home—they are compulsive homemakers and spenders."

"Security—money—they couldn't give a damn about sex."

Men who stressed security disagreed about the importance of sex:

"Women want attention and kindness. Women subconsciously want security and submit to sex to gratify male partner."

"Protection and security. Security is most important to women. Once children are born, the children become important and sex less important."

"Security because they don't want to be alone and like sex and don't want to raise bastard children."

Several of the men who deemed love to be what women want most from men specified that love had arisen as the priority of this particular generation:

"My generation of women, specifically those with college educations, are much less hung up on the security-home-children trip. I think they want a man whom they can love without submitting to, cooperate with rather than compete against."

"I feel that most women want love, security, children, a home and sex. Which is the most important? I would think at this time, day and age, love. The rest they can get from any man or provide for themselves."

"Everyone, man or woman, wants and needs love and understanding—someone to rely on in times of crises and to share happiness with in times of joy. Security, children, a home and sex are all important, but need not be shared with or provided by a man in an emotional sense. Love, however, must be emotionally shared and is, therefore, the most important thing a man can 'give' to a woman (and vice versa)."

"I think women are confused, for at this time there is not a prescribed role for them. Should they be wife and mother, mother and career, etc.? Women most want from men the feeling of being appreciated and accepted."

There were a few men who had a more cynical point of view:

"Some women don't want men at all. Some want sex, some want just money. A lot of the younger ones want just to marry a man just to get them away from their parents."

"Women want men to do their bidding, fix broken things, paint, etc."

"Security—wish to be free from worry at the man's expense."

"I think in the past decade women's attitudes have changed from seeking love and security to just having a good time and finding men who will show them a good time."

"Today's women are unpredictable. Some, or I should say very few, want love, security, etc. They seemed to enjoy having affairs with strangers and they forget about it."

"I think girls today are out for what they can get from a guy. Most girls today don't think of getting married, just living together so that way they can go from one to another."

"A man with a big dong."

## Hard Shells and Thin Skins

If women are often a mystery to men, men are no less an enigma to women. Men often appear emotionally withdrawn and incredibly stoical. Many women conclude from the failure of males to display emotion that men are insensitive and rather brutish creatures—losing sight of the fact that men have been responsible for most of the literature, philosophy, art, and poetry that has shaped our civilization. In the social sciences, men have described and analyzed the anxieties, conflicts, and emotional states that they usually fail to display in the company of women.

What a man is and how he acts are often discordant with one another. One psychologist, after studying the upbringing of children in America and five European countries, concluded that boys are encouraged to control emotion, while girls are encouraged to control aggression. Any woman who was urged in her formative years to act like a little lady, or any boy admonished against being a crybaby has reached that conclusion without the time and expense of an exhaustive study.

But women must not confuse the man with the mask. While the neurotic man may throw himself into the role of the superboss, the jock, or the Don Juan with such abandon that he loses touch with his basic identity, the average man still sweats behind the mask and chafes under the costume and, in the presence of those he loves and trusts, is quite happy to strip off the padding of the jock for the comfort and freedom of his jockey shorts.

We asked men to drop their defenses long enough to share those aspects of themselves that they felt women did not understand:

*Essay Question: What do you think women don't understand about men? What advice would you give women to help them understand men better?*

Our respondents showed little hesitation in stripping off their armor and revealing the vulnerabilities that some experts claim men hide even from their own conscious minds. Our survey showed not only that men are sensitive and vulnerable, but that they themselves very frequently pointed out how women failed to perceive how sensitive they really are. In this era of sexual permissiveness, women confuse physical with spiritual intimacy and take their bed-partners at face value. Never getting past the shell, they conclude that men are more mineral than animal, hard and unfeeling. We find in these responses a candor women rarely encounter in their relationships with men, a frankness that belies all the expert contentions that men are walled off from their own feelings. We found, for the most part, not the leather-clad hide of the macho, but the warmth of flesh-and-blood men:

"I don't think women understand the vulnerability of most men —women are deceived by the stereotyped 'masculinity' roles and attitudes attributed to the male population; a little more understanding and compassion would be helpful."

"That most men cannot express emotions for fear of being less masculine."

"Men have egos that must be recognized. They are very emotional but in many instances try to hide their emotion to avoid looking soft."

"Men are more fragile than women. Men need the ego boost a woman can give just as a woman needs positive strokes from a man. Many 'liberated' women emasculate men badly."

"Men generally are very sensitive, easily hurt. I wish women would be more honest and up front with the men they meet.

They should tell how they feel towards them and not lead them on."

"Some women don't seem to realize that men are also only mere human beings—not demigods—and that they, too, therefore learn by trial and error—same as women. My advice to women is to kindly give men the same 'break' ('fair shake') they demand for themselves and to 'take it easy' and to 'go slow' on unfairly criticizing men, but to try to help them along the rough spots."

"That liberation scares most men. That men will sooner or later accept feminism after they have become better educated and aware."

"Men are getting somewhat worried and uptight about the growing women's independence and the women should reassure the men that while they, the women, demand and need their wants, the women have not forgotten the men's needs."

"Men would like to be mothered a little."

"Some don't realize the affection a man needs. A kiss without asking means a lot."

"We (read that 'I,' I can't speak for all men—I don't match that well) don't want to be on a pedestal, as in years past; neither, however, will I worship at the foot of womanhood. I dislike gutters and I'm afraid of heights."

Many felt that the need to be dominant was so ingrained in men that women should accept and gratify it; others felt that women could help them modify it:

"Men (in general, if I may) have a more swollen ego and need to be assured occasionally that they are useful; this is not to say they are conceited, perhaps more insecure and this is why they try to be extroverted."

"The male image is one of dominance and being in command of things at all times. If women can see that this is not always true and that there are needs of men to be fulfilled. These needs are overlooked because of the male image. Not all men are chauvinistic or women-chasers."

"Women are aware that men have an ego hang-up when it comes to competition. I'm not sure women understand that this is learned, and can be unlearned by men. It is a very painful existence when men themselves are unable to become close to each other without some awesome fear that that is not allowed."

"That a man considers himself a little superior. That they should let a man feel that way so he doesn't feel inferior."

"Women should let men win a little more."

Some felt women did not appreciate the pressure that men's jobs imposed:

"Life-style and working in 'the big jungle.' Let them work in it first, then decide whether home life for approximately 10–15 years is suitable to them."

"Their sense of responsibilities and obligations. Advice: Be in a man's shoes for one month."

"Sometimes they don't seem to think we are tired when we get off from work and they are all ready to go some place. I'd rather rest at home at night."

"Still don't understand some of the daily stress a man lives under, and are not as understanding of money or the lack thereof."

Men also wanted women to understand that they often felt a need to be alone or with other men, but this did not indicate dissatisfaction with their women:

"Men have a different physical makeup than women. A man, at times, must be alone or away from normal pressures to recoup. A woman, theoretically, will look for outer meaning, not inner strength when things get too wound up."

"That at times we are totally separated from them both in body and mind. That this doesn't mean there is a loss of affection, but merely an effort to do something uninvolved and separated from the partner."

"That a man, regardless of how much he loves his wife and family, needs time to himself."

"Some don't understand men like to go out with fellows once in a while, and I mean to stag parties. I feel they should be more trusting in their men."

"Their need for a release of pressure at home, to get out and enjoy each other in different activities."

"They don't understand that certain things will always be for men and men only."

Some men felt that women erroneously regarded them as preoccupied with sex; they also felt women should not press relationships men were not yet ready for:

"Women should understand that not every man is out to take them to bed. (There are, of course, exceptions to the rule.) I think that some women stray away from relationships with men because they are afraid of being taken advantage of, or that they would become involved in a deep relationship that the man never intended. My advice would be for women to be more friendly with men. If a relationship gets more involved than they would like, they should inform their male friend. Women should learn to communicate, let their feelings be known to men, and men should do the same."

"Women always think men are out only for a good screw. I'm sure many men are, but since women expect it from all men, I find many women turning me out because they think everything leads to sex. What's wrong with a good bullshit session?"

"I think sometimes women force men into commitments before the men are ready so sometimes come on too strong in terms of the *finality* of the relationship."

"How much a man can really love a woman. That there are men that can love just one woman and not cheat."

There were many men who wanted to emphasize, however, how important sexual activity was to them:

"That men always relate love to good sex. I would advise making love less of an issue and being as creative as possible while participating and enjoying sex."

"I believe that women fail to understand a man's desires fully. I think that women should be more open to experimentation in sexual matters. They should also discuss their desires *more.*"

"All men don't want a family too soon. Try to be better a lover than a wife at home. Let man have last word sometimes."

"Men in general are more physically oriented toward sex. They generally require less emotional involvement than most women to have a satisfactory relationship. Man is by nature not monogamous."

"Most men want to be around more than one woman. She should become aware of this and she should let a man have other women! *But* there is a difference between love of wife and *sex!* He might want to find more *sex.*"

"Many men are selfish, they want to have affairs with other women but want to limit their partners to themselves."

"That they are preying animals, always looking for something different."

It is apparent from the answers we received that men are complex creatures but, more important, they are aware of their complexity and eager to share their difficulties with communicative women. They have been raised in a society that teaches them men should take the dominant role, but they often feel overwhelmed by responsibility. They acknowledge their need of women and hope women will begin to comprehend the depth of their need. They want women to be more open with them, and not force them to play intellectual games involving the old conventional role-playing. Their sexual drive is strong, but they do not want women to feel that they are primarily seeking sex in every approach to a female. In fact, some feel women pressure them into a sexual liaison before men are ready for it.

Throughout their answers, we found new evidence that the modern man is more sensitive than ever, aware of his psychological conflicts, and desirous of improved communication with the women in his life.

## Strategy Sessions

One psychiatrist related the story of a young woman who felt men were terrible lovers and accordingly rebuffed them because they never stroked her ears the way her father did; she never asked them to—they were supposed to know what she liked. And, if women are loath to talk about their favorite among their several dozen erogenous zones, men may correspondingly oversimplify their sources of gratification, humorously described by comedian Alan King as "one erogenous zone—often inoperative."

How many men actually tell their partners what they most enjoy?

*Question 18: Do you tell the woman you have sex with what you'd like her to do?*

| | |
|---|---|
| Yes, discuss it as we have sex | 28.0% |
| No, I do what she seems to enjoy | 25.3% |
| No, I just do what I enjoy | 19.6% |
| Only after considerable experience together | 15.8% |
| Yes, talk about it before we start or after we finish | 9.1% |
| No, I'd be too inhibited or embarrassed | 3.0% |
| No answer | 1.1% |

Just over half of all the men discuss their preferences in sex with their partners sooner or later. Just under half never do. One-quarter of all the men took their cues from what the woman seemed to be enjoying, in opposition to some feminists' contention that men dictate the pattern of sex according to their own desires. One-fifth took the chauvinistic attitude of doing whatever they themselves enjoyed. While only 3 percent admitted to embarrassment over talking about their likes, 16 per cent would not broach verbal communication until they knew the woman quite well—talking is apparently a more intimate form of intercourse than copulating.

Rubin abhors discussing preferences during lovemaking: "But, as if things weren't bad enough, some people try to discuss the issues *during* lovemaking, rather than before or after. I don't mean to suggest that the topic should be raised at the dinner table or while shopping in the supermarket; just not *during* lovemaking."

More than half of the men who discuss their pleasures with their partners do it during the act, and it is difficult to understand Rubin's objections. Granted, a calm, intellectual discourse might seem ludicrous and dispel any atmosphere of romance, but a couple locked in an amorous embrace can communicate without the resulting dialogue sounding like labor negotiations or tennis lessons. Simple phrases such as "Like it?" or "Like that!" mingled with gasps and purrs are more conducive to romance than a frenetic silent scene that cries for the superimposed message: "We have temporarily lost the audio portion. . . ." It's certainly easier to teach and experiment during the heat of the action than to attempt a cool-headed mental reconstruction later.

Besides, what's so terrible about a couple taking time out to talk things over? Many couples who had their first intercourse after marriage will hold among their fondest memories the warmth and humor of honeymoon moments of shared delight and frustration. That was before Erica Jong glorified the "zipless fuck," the incredibly smooth, wordless melting together of two strangers, their agile bodies exploding simultaneously in an overpowering, flawless orgasm after an eternity of spontaneously choreographed movements ascending in concatenated steps to ecstasy. This is an admitted tongue-in-cheek fantasy, never really attainable.

Younger men are much freer about communicating with their partners. Adding the percentages of those who communicate during, before, or after intercourse plus those who communicate only after much experience, we find 60 percent of men under 30 confide their preferences, as do 55 percent in their thirties, 49 percent of those 40–54, and only 35 percent of men over 55. Perhaps older men are married and have become so accustomed to their partners that talk is unnecessary; however, 4.6 percent of this oldest group, more than any other, said they would be too inhibited or embarrassed. In every age group there were more men who did what the woman seemed to enjoy than who followed their own inclinations.

Men who were living with a partner, unmarried, were most open in communication, only 34 percent answering that they did not discuss their likes. Married men responded in 51 percent of cases that they did *not* talk to their wives, higher than single noncommunicators (45 percent) and divorced/widowed (39 percent).

The more educated a man was, the more likely would he be to tell his partner what he liked. Only about 39 percent of men without high school degrees communicated, compared to 45 percent of high school graduates, 58 percent of college graduates and 61 percent of those with graduate school education.

Some men, it is true, do not like to engage in intimate discussions. Since questions about how their mate might make their sexual enjoyment greater may imply there is something left to be desired, they will be reluctant to say more than "Everything is fine." Therefore, direct feedback during lovemaking itself often is the woman's best source of information. By acquainting herself with her partner's preferences, the woman will create the opportunity to discuss her own preferences without sounding critical or reproachful.

# A Measure of Precaution

Contraception, that vital ounce of prevention, is a disturbing factor to many men. It intrudes a harsh note of reality on a siren song. He is desirous and excited, she is eager and willing, and their bodies are ready to meld in a carefree union that transcends all worldly woes. Under such wonderful conditions, what could possibly go wrong? The devastating news of an unwanted pregnancy, like a late-exploding time bomb, can mean the squeeze of insufficient space or funds for the married or the secret anxiety of abortion for those who cannot even consider an alternative. Thus, except for those couples truly desiring pregnancy, there hangs a threat over every blissful union and the man who is complacent may find his sexual triumph becoming a sudden disaster.

In the innocence of the 1950s, male responsibility for contraception was one of the facts of life and the condom had an element of macho glamour about it. The most adventurous 14-year-old in the crowd would, in contrived fashion, flip out his wallet and dig out a "scum-bag" to show his buddies he was ready for action if the opportunity came up. In reality, he was somewhat like an old, obscure comic-strip character who always wore a large iron shield on his head to protect him from falling meteors—the protection appeared adequate, but it was never really put to the test. The "pill," however, seemed to shift the responsibility to woman. With oral contraceptives, she was always protected, not just when she made a conscious decision to have sex with a particular man. The intrauterine device (the IUD or "coil") similarly offered a *semper paratus* status.

Men are as prone as women to dream of "zipless fucks," encounters not only without zippers, but without messy creams and clammy "skins," so the unseen guardians of sterility, including the out-of-sight-out-of-mind diaphragm, understandably appealed to many men's desire for an act that at least had more the appearance of wild abandon than rational prudence. Hostility certainly played a part in the rejection of the condom by some macho types who had previously viewed it as a shield to protect the seduced woman from the shame and pain of an unwanted pregnancy risked out of devotion to her man. Now that woman had the means to keep herself in a state of permanent protection, which meant ever-ready for any man she chose, as well as access to abortion which made every child she bore a truly wanted one, some men discarded their condoms in a thin-skinned pique and said, in essence, "Let her manage the whole thing."

Do most men feel this way? Will they still take responsibility for birth control? How many don't believe in birth control at all?

*Question 19: Who should take responsibility for birth control?*

| | |
|---|---|
| Preferable for women to be responsible, but men should have protection ready | 35.9% |
| Both should use protection methods | 32.2% |
| Women should take the sole responsibility | 19.7% |
| Men should use protection (condoms) | 6.0% |
| No birth control measures should be taken | 4.1% |
| Withdrawal method should be used | 1.5% |
| No answer | 1.4% |

Eighty-eight percent of men felt the woman should be partially or totally responsible for birth control. Of those who felt that men should be solely responsible, the married men 7.9 percent) far out-numbered the rest, with 4.2 per cent of the divorced/widowed tak-ing this stand, and only about 2 percent of the singles and living-togethers.

Condoms are becoming anachronistic; 12 percent of the oldest men advocated their exclusive use, with drops to 8 percent in the 40–54 group, 5 percent in the thirties, and 3.6 percent in those under 30. Men under 40 (about 35 percent) believed that both should use protection methods more than those over 40 (27 percent). Thirty percent of black men felt women should assume sole responsibility, versus 19 percent of whites.

It is difficult to interpret the response of 32 percent of the sample that both should use protection methods. It is unlikely that they meant both condoms and some female device should be employed in every encounter. While this might be advisable for the single man who worries about venereal disease, the double coverage seems un-warranted in the case of monogamous partners. While single men did advocate joint responsibility in 38 percent of their responses, mar-ried men advised it in a hefty 32 percent, divorced/widowed in 29, and the living-togethers in 25. A few of these men might indeed be obsessively cautious—like the fellow who always carried a bomb in his airplane luggage, figuring if the odds were one-in-a-thousand that one man would smuggle a bomb on board, they would be one-in-a-million against two bombs—but probably most respondents were merely unwilling to assign responsibility on even a preferential basis to one sex, and felt each partner should have an equal voice in the plan.

The least educated men tended to take stances at either extreme, scoring the highest percentages in the view that women should take sole responsibility (26 percent), as well as advocating use of condoms (10 percent). They also led the other educational levels in opposing birth control entirely (7 percent). College graduates said most often either that both should use protection methods (37 percent) or men should have protection ready although female responsibility was preferable (36 percent). Five per cent of high school graduates did not believe in birth control, nor did 3.1 percent of college graduates and 1.7 percent of those with postgraduate schooling. Students were the greatest advocates of mutual responsibility, with 41 percent, and were least likely to delegate sole responsibility to women (16 percent) or men (2.3 percent). All other occupational groups said it was preferable for women to be responsible, but for men to be ready— with mutual responsibility a very close second.

In addition to the authors who claim men have thrust full responsibility for birth control on women, there are experts who contend that men are threatened by woman's increased power over her own impregnation. The single woman, they say, who is "on the pill" or harbors an IUD in her pelvis is viewed as promiscuous and available to every man; the married woman, likewise, cannot have her infidelity checked by the fear of pregnancy. We certainly have not seen in our sample any desire to remove control from the women nor to keep them continuously encumbered by pregnancy.

Birth control often fails for many hidden psychological motives. Some men seek to impose pregnancy as proof of their virility or as a test of the woman's love for them. Some unmarried people can accept sex with less guilt if they convince themselves it was unpremeditated, which contraception belies. For some, pregnancy fulfills sadomasochistic impulses, as a punishment for the sex act. Others are so apathetic and pessimistic that they disregard the risks of unimpeded intercourse or feel "nothing works anyway." These attitudes, however, are not the rule.

Our study indicates that, at the present time, men strongly believe in the need for contraception and advocate a shared responsibility. They are not threatened by women's increased control of the situation and will not abandon their own responsibility.

Female responsibility for contraception is not new; it dates back at least to ancient Egyptian ladies who put crocodile dung in their vaginas as a postcoital precaution. Of the three most effective methods of contraception, the pill, IUD, and sterilization, two are limited to use by females. However, sterilization now rivals birth-control pills as the leading contraceptive method used by married couples, according to a 1975 survey directed by the Office of Population Research at Princeton University. Among white women under 45 who were married only once to men who were also married only once, 31 percent of the couples had elected surgical sterilization, and nearly as many husbands (15 percent) as wives (16 percent) had been sterilized. The percentage of couples electing sterilization had increased nearly fourfold since 1965. Among couples married 20 to 24 years, well over half (56 percent) involved a partner who had undergone sterilization.

The wide acceptance of vasectomy by men confirms that they do not, in general, equate fertility with manliness, and it seems reasonable to predict that the development of an oral contraceptive for men would be similarly adopted without reservation. We seem to be entering an era in which men are less preoccupied with discovering better methods of contraception for women to employ and more concerned with mutually cooperative solutions.

# Earthshaking Problems

> "It was a pleasure but it was not thus."
> "And then the earth moved. The earth never moved before?"
> "Nay. Truly never."
> "Ay," she said. "And this we have for one day."
>
> —ERNEST HEMINGWAY, *For Whom the Bell Tolls*

Before Kinsey, nobody gave much thought to female orgasms; sex was strictly a masculine pleasure. Since Kinsey we have had the vigorous debate on male versus female gratification. Actually, according to an ancient Greek legend, Zeus and Hera, king and queen of the gods, were arguing about whether men or women got more pleasure out of sex, each claiming the other had all the best of it. To settle the argument, they called in Tiresias. Tiresias had an uncanny knack for offending people, with dire consequences to himself. First, he had been struck blind for looking at Athena in the nude. On another occasion, he killed a female snake who was enjoying an amorous act, for which the gods punished him by temporarily turning Tiresias into a woman. Since he had lived life as both a man and a woman, he was the only qualified expert to resolve the eternal argument between Zeus and Hera. Tiresias answered promptly that women have ten times as much pleasure from sex as men do. Hera, just as promptly, killed him for his honesty.

For all his pains, Tiresias did not settle the question once and for all; controversies persist over how important sex really is to women and how much they truly enjoy it. What does the average man think? Does he feel women are as interested in sex as men are? Or do they engage in relations mostly to please their mates or to gain other advantages?

*Essay Question: How do you think most women feel about sex in general? Do they use it mainly to please men, to get a husband? How interested do you think women really are in sex?*

Most of the men surveyed thought that women today are as interested in sex as men, even for the inherent pleasure in it, independent of any emotional ties:

"It seems that today's woman is more aware of sex as a pleasure to be experienced regardless of the situation. They seem to be experiencing an awakening towards sex as a phenomena rather than as tool or lever in personal relationships."

"Fortunately women are now becoming more aware of themselves sexually. More women I meet are interested in their own gratification which in turn makes them more aware of their partners and their happiness."

"Great—excited. Sex, for the women I know, is for pleasure: first, to themselves, second, to please the man and third, to further her personal growth."

"Today most dig it. No, most of the girls I know enjoy it with no ties at all. Most don't want to get married."

"I think that sex plays a big role in women and that they like to have flings (affairs) to gain confidence and pleasure."

"I find the new generation of thinking has enabled women to show they really enjoy sex and men without being thought of as a tramp or 'loose woman.'"

A few men pointed out drawbacks in women's freer attitudes:

"Too many are seeking only their own pleasure. Their independence inhibits their need for sharing and companionship."

"They definitely enjoy sex and want it for themselves, even though they are often forced into a situation where they are just going through the motions."

"I think women are more interested in sex than in the fifties or sixties. It's not the dirty thing it used to be. I still think they use their 'gold mine' as a weapon."

A few of our respondents thought women enjoyed sex only if love was involved:

"In some ways the old adage that men give love for sex and women give sex for love is somewhat true. However, the more educated and liberal women become, the more they will enjoy it."

"If it's done in the name of 'love' and with some careful tenderness, warmth and arousal, most women enjoy every bit as much as men."

"I think most women are interested in sexual relations, but as a means of establishing some kind of deeper relationship. In that sense, I think women are less interested than men in sex for its own sake."

A minority felt women were more interested in pleasing men than in pursuing their own enjoyment:

"Initially, I find most women so inhibited about sex that they are subconsciously trying to please the man rather than totally freeing themselves and getting the most from the experiences."

"In general, most women have sex to please the man (about 80%), and mainly to get a husband—also for enjoyment. Women's interest in sex depends on the man's ability to stimulate her even long before the sex act."

"When young, women generally enjoy sex most to have children. They don't *use* it for anything! Most women after a few years of marriage or middle age could live without it."

"They like it but not enough, they enjoy it but do it almost as much to please men, because of a lack of men who take time to please them."

"Women feel that sex is strictly to procreate and not for pleasure. I think women are interested in sex but deny their interest in participating."

"Interested but not many seem to really attach a strong meaning to it. Yes, think the way to a man's heart is through his penis."

And a cynical few saw women as users of sex for other gains:

"I think women feel sex is necessary to achieve their particular goals, be it a husband, job or to please a man."

"Women all too often use sex as a tool not only to coerce but also as a punishment (lack of sex). Women are beginning to understand that sex can be pleasurable to both partners."

"Women perhaps use sex as a 'negotiating' item. Probably used mostly for ego reinforcement. Same as men, although most women might describe otherwise."

"Women are trying to change and become a participant in sex instead of tolerating it. They have a long way to go, since are still using it as a means to an end."

## Mission Unaccomplished

If the question of sex's importance to women has never been answered to the satisfaction of men, the men have nevertheless become acutely concerned with the satisfaction of women. Shere Hite contends that women are pressured into using emotional orgasm as a substitute for *real* orgasms; she claims that male orgasm is the focal point of conventional sexual activity and women who do not have orgasms during intercourse must either ask for extra stimulation or try to send subliminal messages to a partner who often is unaware of her dilemma.

Are men really as insensitive as Hite implies? Are they not concerned about whether their partners have orgasms? How do men feel if a woman does not have an orgasm—and what would they do about it?

*Essay Question: How would you feel if the woman you are having sex with fails to have an orgasm? What would you do to help her have an orgasm?*

An overwhelming number of respondents—about 98 percent of all the men surveyed—felt that it was important for a woman to have an orgasm. This major finding was completely contrary to the widely publicized feminist complaints that men are selfishly concerned only with their own orgasms and are not interested in a woman's gratification. Even more surprising was our finding that over half of the men were self-critical if their partner did not respond fully. Failure of the woman to achieve orgasm would turn the sexual experience into one of frustration and dismay for them, and they were willing to go to any lengths to ensure their partner's satisfaction:

"Very inept. Communicate with her to try and find what the problem is. Hopefully if I'm doing anything wrong, she would be able to correct this."

"Feel I've neglected her desires, depending on the level of my affection towards her. Try to make her feel at ease (often failure is due to nervousness), and engage in more caressing of various erogenous zones (i.e., nibble ear, fingertip massage) and oral and manual stimulation of organs."

"Very embarrassing, inferior in sexual capability. The next time I would make sure that I have enough foreplay for her to get the feeling of close to climax, then have intercourse."

"I would feel disappointed in her and somewhat in myself. To help her have an orgasm, I would warm her up by French kissing her, tonguing her nipples and if her pussy (vagina) was clean, I would give her oral sex."

"Distressed. I feel that I have not lived up to my part of the bargain. A sexual experience is to be shared by both partners. [Would do] almost anything!"

"I kind of feel like I'm cheating her. Sometimes I realize that she just won't come no matter how long or well I perform. I would often complement intercourse with oral sex to help her come."

"It would depend on how active she was during sex—if she was very active but failed to have an orgasm, I would have a tendency to feel inferior; however if she was passive, I would think that she was probably nervous about something and try to relax her by talking quietly to her or trying different techniques to relax her so she could have an orgasm."

"Like I'd forgotten something. Anything she wanted—anything at all."

"Worried about our relationship. Talk to her about why."

"Very let down, inadequate. [Would do] anything she wants. (She quits though.)"

"Like I failed in my job."

Men also used the following words to describe their feelings if they failed to bring a woman to orgasm: "Bad . . . a little empty . . . at fault . . . unfulfilled . . . hadn't done my duty as a husband . . . guilty . . . selfish . . . lousy."

Some stressed that they needed communication from the woman:

"I want the woman to get as much pleasure out of sex as possible. I am not certain that orgasm is as important to a woman as to a man. I would help the woman in any way she wanted, but she would have to communicate to me what I'm supposed to do, because I'm not a good guesser."

"If woman's satisfied, orgasm not really all that important; can always ask what would make her feel better or what she would enjoy, and do it."

"Not cheated or guilty, but if she's willing to tell me, I'm willing to do whatever it takes."

"I would not feel badly if she did not orgasm. I would communicate with her. I would want her to teach me what stimulates her. What she likes. I want to help her because that stimulates me as well."

Some men said they would not feel bad personally and some even felt the woman had a problem; however, they would be glad to try again, if the woman wanted to. Note, however, that some men feel they must have another erection and bring her to climax through intercourse, unlike the majority, who were amenable to using other techniques:

"This wouldn't bother me during that particular time—I would just reassure her of my love and next time give more attention to a favorite foreplay and give more to help her along."

"If she said she wasn't horny and didn't bitch about it, I would feel okay. If she wanted one and I had climaxed, I would manually stimulate her."

"I'm not responsible for her orgasms. I'm willing to help by doing what she suggests. Don't feel like a failure when, if, she doesn't have an orgasm."

"I would feel that she has a problem stemming from childhood. I would treat her very gently and passionately and we would talk about her feelings."

"Not too bad, women sometimes are too messed up in the head about it. But I would try anything to help her."

"Some women are too uptight and can't. Most women who are interested can have an orgasm. More foreplay and affection."

Some men were very determined indeed to bring their partners to orgasm:

"If she didn't have an orgasm, I would go at it till she did, no matter how much time it would take. I would do whatever gets her off."

"I would make her have an orgasm before I would leave. I would go crazy."

"If the woman is willing, I'm willing to go all night until she does have an orgasm."

"Unless I was 100% exhausted I would do everything possible to bring her to orgasm. Probably by more cunnilingus and kissing her whole body."

Some men did not concentrate on their own feelings, but rather simply outlined their formulas for bringing a refractory partner to orgasm:

"This has happened before even though you try your hardest. Oral sex, if you really appreciate your partner and it is very pleasing for her this usually does the trick."

"I try to get the woman off first, usually by massaging her clitoris, sometimes by having intercourse dog-style and massaging at the same time. It's tiring as hell, but it's good to both of us. Sure gives us both a lot of pleasure."

"Manual stimulation or vibrator or oral. If she doesn't seem to mind, I don't either, as long as she seems satisfied."

"Eat her and talk nasty to her and get her involved and talk about what I'm doing to her."

A few men seemed pessimistic and negativistic about the situation:

"I feel a little disappointed if she fails to have an orgasm. I am not sure there is anything I can do to help her have one that I don't normally do."

"Disappointed. I would do whatever I could to help her but unless she is responsive and communicative, it might be difficult."

"Almost anything, but a great deal depends on her attitude or mood."

"I don't know, I would like to know what to do myself."

There was a handful of men who did not feel orgasm for women was very important, although many qualified their answer to indicate that there was a problem if the woman did not share this viewpoint:

"If a woman doesn't (or won't) have an orgasm: roll over, kiss her on the forehead, put your arm around her, fall asleep. It works every time."

"I always like for the opposite partner to have orgasms. Sometimes it doesn't occur but it isn't because I don't last long enough or am interesting—just one of those things."

"Failing to have orgasms isn't that important, it's the feeling of mutual satisfaction that's more important."

"I probably wouldn't know or even ask unless she told me."

"Not offended."

"If her head is that screwed up I'd just let it go at that."

"Get mad. Dump her."

The overwhelming majority of men do care very much about a woman's sexual satisfaction. Since so many of them reported feelings of deep distress if a partner fails to achieve orgasm, it would seem accurate to say that female orgasm has displaced male orgasm as the focal point in a sex act in the minds of most men today.

## Ladies First

"Nice guys finish last."

Leo Durocher was talking about the New York Giants at the time, but his advice could just as well apply to bedroom athletes.

We have seen that the overwhelming majority of men today want to bring their partners to orgasm. Shere Hite says, "We are taught that if we are anything but helpful (or at least noninterfering) during intercourse, it is tantamount to castrating the man. This is nonsense. Our noncooperation with men in sex is no worse than their noncooperation with us." Our study shows that men not only want to cooperate with women, but that they feel terrible if they fail to bring their partners to orgasm. If a woman wants to try a little vicarious castration, she doesn't even have to interfere with the man's orgasm—just making him feel responsible for her own lack of gratification will emasculate him.

Hite's ladies play a very cutthroat (or lower level) game; she lauds the example of one woman who breaks off sexual activity in the middle if she feels disinterested or dissatisfied. We wonder how many women—how many human beings—would throw down a bridge hand in progress, leave a restaurant, or walk out of a movie without consulting their companions just because things were not going quite as well as they hoped. Protesting something is one thing, but quitting is quite another. If the woman does not know or like the man well enough to communicate her dissatisfaction, one may well ask what the devil she is doing in bed with him in the first place.

While *The Hite Report* repeatedly castigates men for arousing women only to a point short of orgasm, the author herself keeps advocating sexual activity that does not result in orgasm, or even avoids genital stimulation entirely. While she harps on "the almost hysterical emotional fixation on intercourse and orgasm currently prevalent," the closest she comes to a viable alternative is lesbianism; she thus avoids neither orgasm nor genital stimulation, eliminating only men.

Hite quotes Rollo May: "The pleasure in sex is described by Freud and others as the reduction of tension; in eros, on the contrary, we wish not to be released from the excitement but rather to hang on to it, to bask in it, and even to increase it."

Most men, as we shall see, agree with the old travel slogan, "Getting there is half the fun," but not many with Hite's suggestion that they forgo the other half. Of course, if women follow Hite's advice and try to abolish male orgasm, the men may well heed a different piece of advice from Rollo May, describing an abused man who used anesthetic cream on his organ to prolong further his ten-minute penetrations: "By all means the man was impotent in this hideous caricature of a marriage. And his penis, before it was drugged senseless, seemed to be the only character with enough 'sense' to have the appropriate intention, namely to get out as quickly as possible."

Our first concern here, however, is not whether men *should* delay orgasm, but whether they, in fact, *do.*

*Question 20: Do you deliberately try to delay your orgasm and for how long?*

| | |
|---|---|
| Yes, until partner has orgasm | 31.4% |
| Yes, as long as possible | 24.8% |
| Yes, until partner seems satisfied | 23.6% |
| No, don't try | 14.7% |
| Yes, up to 5 minutes | 5.4% |
| No experience in intercourse | 1.2% |
| No answer, | 0.5% |

Four out of five men are making a conscious effort to delay their orgasms as long as possible. The "five-minute" response was something of a trick question, because we felt that what appeared to be a positive response was actually a negative one, five minutes of penetration being insufficient for many women—and not many men gave this response. While we know for certain that only about a third of men succeed in consistently bringing their partner to orgasm through intercourse, some of those who delay until their partner seems satisfied may be dealing with multiorgasmic women— at least 5 percent, according to our question about when a sex act ends, discussed next in this chapter. Only about 15 percent of men make no attempt whatsoever to delay orgasm.

Men over 55 were the least likely to attempt to delay orgasm, although perhaps at that age their naturally retarded ejaculation made conscious effort unnecessary. Men under 55 were uniformly more conscientious in their efforts to delay orgasm than this oldest group.

There were more black men than white who made no attempt to delay orgasm. More educated men were more considerate lovers; the percentage of those who did *not* delay was twice as great for those without high school degrees as for those at the postgraduate level. Income level showed a similar pattern, with the highest percentage of nondelayers among those with the lowest income, and the lowest percentage in the group making $25,000 and over. By occupational status, professional men were fewest among those who did not try to delay, and the retired/unemployed highest.

Those who delayed until the woman had orgasm were found most in the high achievement groups: income of $25,000 or more, postgraduate education, and professional occupational status, although every single subgroup gave this as their most frequent response, with the exception of students who gave a minimal edge to "as long as possible."

One-third of married men delayed until their partners reached orgasm, as opposed to one-quarter of single men, though only one bachelor in six did not delay at all.

This question gave us some incidental findings on male virginity. Of our men between the ages of 18 and 29, only 2.3 percent reported no experience in intercourse. Kinsey, in 1948, reported that at age 29, 5.3 percent of men were still without sexual experience. At age 39, 1.4 percent of Kinsey's male subjects were still virginal, whereas in our sample only 1 of 927 respondents in their thirties (0.1 percent) had no experience in intercourse. We actually had more virgins between 40 and 54 (0.6 percent) and over 54 (0.9 percent) than in the thirties, reflecting the virtual extinction of celibacy by the sexual revolution.

The willingness and ability for a man to delay his orgasm after vaginal penetration is very important if female orgasm is to be attained in actual intercourse. In a 1966 study by Gebhard, it was found that when penetration lasted less than one minute before ejaculation, only 25 percent of wives nearly always achieved orgasm; 50 percent did so if penetration or intromission lasted one to 11 minutes, and 65 percent between 11 and 15 minutes. If the husband could sustain penetration and erection for 16 minutes or longer, almost all women had consistent orgasms.

Foreplay was found in this same study to have as significant an effect on female orgasm as duration of penetration. With less than 10 minutes of foreplay, 40 percent of wives nearly always reached orgasm; 50 percent did when foreplay lasted 15 to 20 minutes, and 60 percent with even longer precoital stimulation.

Kinsey estimated in 1948 that about three-quarters of males reached orgasm within two minutes of intromission. In his *Sexual Behavior in the Human Female* (1953), Kinsey disparaged the advice of marriage manuals which advocated delay, saying that rapid ejaculation was a sign of biological superiority. Dr. Abraham Stone corroborated Kinsey's estimate of an average male ejaculatory time of one to two minutes in 1952. In 1974, however, Morton Hunt reported that the median duration of intercourse as estimated by both white males and females was about 10 minutes. Hunt concludes that motivation is the prime factor affecting delay of ejaculation, for young men took longer to ejaculate than older ones, contrary to biological expectation. Helen Singer Kaplan reported at the American Psychiatric Association's annual meeting in 1977 that cases of uncomplicated premature ejaculation had become so rare that she had difficulty finding 20 cases for therapists in training to treat.

Masters and Johnson delineated four distinct phases in both male and female orgasm: excitement, plateau, orgasm, and resolution. In the excitement phase, the vaginal walls become lubricated, the clitoris, labia and breasts swell, and the inner two-thirds of the vagina lengthens and becomes wider. In the plateau phase, the tissues around the outer third of the vagina swell, reducing the vagina's diameter by as much as 50 percent.

It is important to realize that women must reach the plateau phase before they can proceed to orgasm. In the excitement phase, the woman may seem "ready," but there is not enough engorgement of the genitals to give sufficient traction on the clitoris when the penis thrusts between the labia. In the plateau phase, the clitoris is less accessible to direct stimulation because it has been retracted under the hood formed by the apex of the engorged labia minora. If a woman complains that she gets no satisfaction from penile penetration, but her clitoris is exquisitely sensitive to manual manipulation during intercourse, there is a good chance she had not reached plateau phase when the penis was inserted.

While both men and women experience the same four cyclical phases, there is one great and significant difference in the resolution phase. Once a man has orgasm, the blood quickly drains from his penis and it may take considerable time for him to get another erection. Women's pelvic organs may remain congested for an extended period, as long as 20 minutes, after orgasm, which explains why women can often have a series of rapid multiple orgasms. Since men are more familiar with their own physiological responses than female ones, men are very reluctant to bring their partners to orgasm during foreplay. Hence, they often stop stimulation even short of the plateau phase for fear of crossing the orgasmic threshold. However, the man who brings his partner to orgasm before penetration has a double advantage: first, his partner has already had one orgasm, so there is no danger of the session being a total shutout for her; second, having had one orgasm, she may actually proceed more rapidly to orgasm during penetration, her vaginal tissues being back at plateau phase, than if she had no orgasm. Even if the woman is unable to climax during intercourse subsequently, this way of "taking turns" is more pleasurable than ignoring the "ladies first" rule. A man who has already experienced orgasm is in his resolution phase and is bound to be a less enthusiastic lover than when he was excited and his partner's orgasm could augment his own arousal; furthermore, the congested organs of a woman who has just had orgasm will give her richer sensations of vaginal fullness than in a state of insufficient arousal.

Granted, some women may have a short interval between orgasm and resolution, but every couple should experiment with the possibility of bringing the woman to orgasm during foreplay before penetration. The man should be reassured that the woman will not quickly lose interest and capacity for arousal directly after orgasm, the way men do from a physical if not a psychological standpoint. With experience, the couple can even gauge the timing of the woman's progression from excitement to plateau to orgasm, so that penetration can be effected precisely when she will be most responsive.

There will always be some women who require direct clitoral stimulation to reach orgasm—and partners of both sexes who feel it is undesirable. Women equate manual stimulation of the clitoris with masturbation, which by definition is the stimulation of the genitals *outside of* intercourse; they might accept clitoral stimulation as a prelude to intercourse, but feel guilty about including the once-taboo activity as part of sanctioned, mature relations. Men may feel that the finger is replacing an inadequate penis. Both partners should be aware that, directly or indirectly, the clitoris must *always* be stimulated—the question is merely how, not if, it should be done. Friction between the pubic bones may provide the needed clitoral traction and even subtle shifts in the "missionary position" may suffice, although the female-superior position allows the woman more body flexibility, as well as providing either partner's fingers easier access to the clitoris. The direct way is generally the fastest, but in intercourse, speed kills—desire, pleasure, and imagination.

# In Conclusion

According to conventional assumptions, most men have an orgasm, roll over, and go to sleep, often leaving their partners unsatisfied and frustrated. A sex act, it is widely believed, may be initiated in various ways and may be enhanced by a variety of foreplay techniques, but the conclusion is unvarying and predictable—the male orgasm always signals the end of the act. We found, however, that more than two-thirds of all the men we surveyed regarded the woman's satisfaction as the criterion for terminating sexual relations.

*Question 21: When does a sex act end?*

| | |
|---|---|
| When we both have an orgasm | 40.9% |
| When I have one orgasm | 18.2% |
| When the woman wants to stop | 17.7% |
| When I want to stop | 10.8% |
| When the woman has an orgasm | 5.2% |
| When I have more than one orgasm | 5.1% |
| When the woman has more than one orgasm | 5.0% |
| No answer | 1.3% |

If we add all the percentages that include female orgasm (single, multiple, orgasm for both), 51 percent of men do not consider a sex act over until their partners have experienced orgasm. If we add the 18 percent who wait until the woman wants to stop—an answer that implies female satisfaction though not necessarily orgasm, we find 69 percent (about two-thirds) focusing on female gratification.

Older men were more likely to hold the view that the sex act ends with a single male orgasm; well over a quarter of men over 55 gave this response. It decreased in frequency as the men got younger, to a low of one in nine in men under 30. However, a majority of the oldest men indicated that the woman should have an orgasm or "want to stop," rather than using male satisfaction as a criterion. More than two-thirds of all the men under 55 gave similar female-oriented replies.

Married men answered "when I have one orgasm" far more often than those in the other subgroups. However, married men said least frequently "when I want to stop," so when it came to giving female-oriented responses, there was not much difference between married men and the others in basing the end of the act on female satisfaction.

Single men and those under 30 were the leaders among men who wanted more than one orgasm. Black males wanted multiple orgasms for themselves twice as frequently as whites, and were similarly more interested in multiple orgasms for their partners. While a clear majority of blacks gave a reply based on female satisfaction, they were lower than white males in giving female-oriented answers.

Men living with a partner to whom they were not married were more interested in providing multiple female orgasms than the others. Age did not make much difference in the man's desire to elicit multiple orgasms from his partner.

Less educated men were more preoccupied with their own orgasms than the highly educated. One-third of those without high school degrees ended an act when they had one or more orgasms, compared with one-quarter of high school graduates and even fewer college graduates. Mutual orgasm was deemed the desirable end point by only one-third of the least educated, and considerably more of the college graduates.

In every subgroup, more men selected "when the woman wants to stop" than "when I want to stop."

It is important to remember that men who answered "when I have one orgasm" or "when I want to stop" do not necessarily fail to bring their partners to orgasm. The striking finding here is that two-thirds of the men took their cues from the women, not ending a sex act until the partners indicated they were satisfied.

It is not clear what motivated 5.2 percent of the men to choose "when the woman has an orgasm" over "when we both have an orgasm." It is doubtful that these men were not experiencing orgasm themselves; perhaps they routinely brought their partners to orgasm after they ejaculated.

Can men be good and active lovers after they have ejaculated? Or do they become exhausted, apathetic, and let down? Also, we have seen that 80 percent of men try to delay their orgasms, but do they do it primarily to enhance their own feelings or to gratify their women? How do men feel prior to and after climax?

*Essay Question: . . . How do you feel after an orgasm? Do you try to delay them and why?*

Most men who delayed their orgasms did so primarily to please their partners, although her responsiveness contributed to mutual pleasure. The predominant feeling for the man after orgasm was one of relaxation and contentment:

"Relieved and content after an orgasm. Yes, I try to delay my orgasms in order to give the woman more satisfaction, more orgasms so that her requirements are fulfilled."

"Contented. Try to delay for mutual pleasure."

"I feel very happy afterwards. I try to delay them until my girl friend has had one or two—because if I don't I feel bad—like I used her for my own purposes."

Some felt tired or sleepy afterward—and a few had negative feelings:

"Usually I'm tired after orgasms because I do delay them until my partner has had one or two orgasms. I don't think they could be improved because they're very intense now."

"After orgasms I'm content to talk or sleep, I feel good. I try to delay, because I want my partner to feel as good as I do."

"Completely wrung out and satisfied. Delay so my wife can climax more. (That is erotic to me.)"

"Sometimes there's a slight letdown after orgasm. I try to delay them to help to satisfy the woman."

"A bit depressed. More fun for everybody if I delay."

"I usually feel good but sometimes if I 'come' too soon I don't feel that good anymore."

"Often I feel a bit regretful the pleasure given could not be extended in more experiences outside the sack."

A few felt excited rather than tired or let down after orgasm:

"Afterwards I feel exhilaration. I delay them for the prolongation of our mutual pleasure as long as possible."

"Usually content and euphoric. Yes, it [delay] makes a better orgasm and to let partner get more orgasmic."

"Feel like having another. Delay when partner is a slow arouser."

"[Feel] very well—thank you! Always [delay]—to assure my partner has been sexually satisfied and achieved as many orgasms as desired."

"Fulfilled and ready to go again if they are ready."

Feelings of love and tenderness were sometimes increased after orgasm:

"[Delay] at times, when it will give more pleasure to my partner, but I'm slow and normally need to try and hurry them a bit. If the girl does not feel satisfied I feel a bit guilty. If she doesn't reach orgasm but tells me and appears to be content then I feel like staying close and trying to make her feel even better emotionally. If we both have orgasms then I feel great, and my reaction usually follows the mood of the reaction of my partner—excited, happy, deep-down content, tired, satisfied."

"Loving. I feel that I've given part of myself to my partner. Yes [delay], so that my partner can experience the same elation as I do."

"After, feel very content and like to admire partner, evaluate feelings towards some. Will try to delay for partner's pleasure."

"Afterwards, if my partner is close to her orgasm, my whole being concentrates on satisfying her and getting her as high in emotion as possible. As far as delaying orgasms, I mostly just try to control myself and know myself well enough to be ready for one. Recently I've bought some delaying cream to see if I can achieve longer periods of sex without climaxing."

Some men delayed orgasm because it increased their own pleasure. Their feelings afterward ranged from exhilarated to depressed, though most felt calm and contented:

"Yes, [delay] because I enjoy the actual union between myself and partner and the closeness of her nude body!"

"Content. Longer the fuse—the greater the explosion."

"I try to delay orgasm to get the full effect. Half the fun is the build-up."

"Very tired, feeling depressed."

"Improved with a young chick. [Afterward] terrible. [Delay] absolutely."

"Feel relaxed. I purposely delay so our sex act will continue for an hour or two."

"After, I am content and like to relax or often I feel a kind of energy and like to use it on other things."

The minority of men who did not consciously delay their orgasms felt much as the others afterward:

"Feel content and good, like to keep on cuddling after. Never tried to delay them, never been a problem."

"I feel like I have had a beautiful high. No, there is no delay, whenever it comes, it comes and I let go."

"Feel very relieved (tension)—satisfied. I do not delay them— no willpower."

"I feel very good and also satisfied. I don't try and delay them, that would deprive me of the pleasure."

"Exhilarating—high, never try to delay."

"No. Wife has problems and never has orgasms."

"The feeling is light and relieved. I only tried to delay them very few times previously thinking it would give more pleasure, but not gaining any more I then let go."

# The Contented Rooster

The great Greek physician Galen said, approximately 2,100 years ago, "Every animal is sad after coitus except the human female and the rooster."

Kinsey took exception with those who had "distorted" Galen's statement to imply that sadness follows coitus: "There is neither regret nor conflict nor any tinge of sadness for most persons who have experienced orgasm. There is, on the contrary, a quiescence, a calm, a peace, a satisfaction with the world which, in the minds of many persons, is the most notable aspect of any type of sexual activity."

Now, Kinsey, a professor of zoology at Indiana University and the owner of a gall wasp collection numbering 4,000,000 specimens, probably knew his animals a lot better than Galen. Galen, on the other hand, probably knew more about depression—he invented the term "melancholy," derived from the Greek words for black bile, which Galen believed to be, if present in excess, the cause of depression. Which of the two experts was right? After orgasm, does a man feel like the rooster, fit to crow—or more like he has just eaten crow?

*Question 22: How do you usually feel after climaxing?*

| | |
|---|---|
| Content | 45.2% |
| Very loving | 23.9% |
| Exhilarated/high | 15.9% |
| Very drowsy | 15.5% |
| Somewhat depressed | 2.2% |
| Somewhat guilty | 1.5% |
| No answer | 0.7% |

We couldn't survey other members of the animal kingdom, but as far as human males go, Galen loses this round to Kinsey.

"Content" was the response given most frequently by every subgroup except the blacks, who showed a more romantic tendency, with 37 percent answering "very loving."

The divorced/widowed, perhaps more sensitive for having had loved and lost, led the rest in "very loving" responses with 29 percent, followed by the never-married at 25 percent, living-togethers at 24, and married at 23.

Physical endurance may have a lot to do with postcoital feelings; 21 percent of the youngest men felt "exhilarated," but the number decreased with age to a low of 6.3 percent of men over 55. Conversely, 13 percent of men under 30 felt "very drowsy," with an increase to 22 percent at age 55 or more. Age might have been the reason that 22 percent of unmarried men, living alone or with partners, reported exhilaration, compared with 16 percent of divorced/-widowed and only 13 percent of married men. Married men claimed postcoital drowsiness in 18 percent of cases, compared with 14 percent for divorced/widowed, 12 percent living-togethers, and 10 percent of singles.

The least educated men gave the response "very loving" with 29 percent, more than any other educational level. Among retired/-unemployed men we found the highest percentage answering "very loving"—29—of any occupational group. Throughout the study, it had been our experience that the least educated and least productive men were least sensitive to women's needs and held the typical macho attitudes; yet here they seemed to feel closest to their partners when other men were in the process of detachment. It may be that these men, generally least preoccupied with their own performance, experience a more uninhibited, basic spiritual fusion with their partner, while the more sophisticated man cannot regress to the same level of subjective intimacy.

Depression was reported in small percentages throughout the subgroups. Men of races other than black or white were highest of any subgroup with a five percent reply, against 2 percent for the rest. The oldest men, possibly because of waning performance, were depressed in 3.9 percent of cases, the next age bracket highest in depressive responses being the men under 30 at 2.7 percent. Men who had never married were twice as prone to postcoital depression as married men, but those living with a partner, unmarried, had the least depression.

Students and those with college degrees or postgraduate education reported depression more frequently than other occupational and educational subgroups. While the uncertainty of youth might have been responsible for such reactions in the students (depression was higher in the men in their twenties than in men 30–54), we cannot correlate age with the findings in the more highly educated. The student generally reads more and becomes more aware of sexual norms and potential problems in interpersonal relations. This makes him more introspective and prone to self-criticism; he may become overly preoccupied with performance and suffer pangs of inferiority.

Guilt was the feeling least reported, with a 1.5 percent response. It will undoubtedly surprise some women that men *ever* feel guilty about sex. The figure was as high as 3.2 percent in men who did not complete high school, 2.4 percent in men who had never married, 3.3 percent in blacks, and 4.3 percent in other races. Guilt waned with education (1.2 percent in college graduates) and earning power (0.6 percent making at least $25,000).

What in the world do men feel guilty about—unless they're cheating—women wonder. Women are used to feeling postcoital guilt themselves; most were raised with the idea of guarding their virginity with the zeal employed by Ebenezer Scrooge towards his cash the week *before* Christmas, and the idea of sex changing from the blackest sin to the purest expression of holy love with a flick of the ring finger is hard for a new bride to assimilate. Though male virginity is more of an embarrassment than a source of self-esteem, men experience sexual guilt earlier than women because of conflicts over masturbation, an earlier and more prevalent phenomenon in males. Psychoanalysts claim that the guilt has nothing to do with parental prohibitions or religious beliefs; it stems from unconscious incestuous fantasies associated with masturbation and can therefore occur even in boys raised to believe that masturbation is natural and desirable.

In *Lover: The Confessions of a One-Night Stand,* author Lawrence Edwards writes: "The sex in such situations was pretty good. But the moment I'd climaxed, I'd turn away from whatever woman was with me and lie on my back staring at the ceiling and wonder what the hell I was doing there." The man being "used" by a liberated woman for sexual gratification has a mind and body at war; his brain finds abhorrent the idea of his serving as a plaything for a woman who might choose never to see him again, but his body is nevertheless aroused—if it isn't, the sexual liaison would be impossible. Once the man has climaxed, however, desire diminishes as the penis detumesces to usual size, and the brain, which objected to being there in the first place, finds itself unopposed but trapped.

It takes considerable courage for a man to verbalize feelings of guilt. The idea of a man turning down sex from a desirable woman seems, to the traditionalists, positively prissy. But now man can no longer simply have sex either with a woman he loves and respects with his mind or with a prostitute he can reduce to an anonymous price-tag; his unemotional brain is now confronted by women it can neither accept on the most intimate terms nor ignore, women he can neither fully control nor willingly serve. And once his penis has fired its volley and fled the field, his troubled head views an alien woman who is captor, conquest, judge, mistress, adversary—and seeks refuge in the sleep of oblivion.

Guilt and shame may be translated into depression, especially if the man is not consciously aware of the mental opposition to the pleasure his body is craving. Depression may also arise from feelings of not having satisfied the partner, failure of the experience to meet precoital expectations, or an unconscious yearning for some other person, including a parent or homosexual partner.

Man's quicker resolution phase with loss of penile erection and return of heart and respiratory rate to basic levels may be experienced physically as a letdown; one suspects that men who report postcoital exhilaration do remain, in fact, physically excited longer and can maintain partial erections, with rapid recovery capacity and frequent orgasm. The female phasic cycle in orgasm is supposed to conclude with a resolution (letdown) phase and a period during which the woman is incapable, like a man, of subsequent orgasm; yet it has been shown some women can have repeated sequential orgasms by prolongation of the plateau phase of high arousal rather than experiencing resolution, and now experts claim that all women have the physiologic capacity for multiple orgasms, though psychological factors can negate this. It is not that uncommon for a highly excited man to maintain an erection after orgasm and proceed to a second orgasm without withdrawing from the vagina—certainly not within a matter of seconds like the multiorgasmic woman, but in apparent defiance of the neat four-stage model with its "refractory" period during which men cannot regain erection.

Sex therapists should follow the example of the law professor who would begin each semester by placing a small thin book and two thick volumes on his desk: holding up the thin book, he would say, "Gentlemen, these are the laws." Then, indicating the two thick volumes, he would add, "And these are the exceptions." Biofeedback studies have shown that heart rate and brain waves can be brought under voluntary control and we will undoubtedly find that many of the body's neat physiological patterns in sexual behavior, particularly orgasm, can be modified consciously or unconsciously by the number one erogenous zone, the brain.

The postorgasmic male who has brought his brain and penis to truce terms will feel content; the man in conflict will feel depression or guilt, or, more commonly, take refuge in sleep. The man who regards woman as an adversary will sense himself overmatched by her fabled multiorgasmic capacity, like a man with a rifle up against a machine gun. The man who regards his partner as friend and lover will linger in her embrace, still sharing the communication their spent genitals have abandoned. For the man who has achieved such rapport, lovemaking will never be a trial and his postcoital feelings will always render him not guilty.

## Come One, Come All!

Our survey has shown that most men believe sexual gratification is as important to women as men, that men want desperately to bring their partners to orgasm, that they consciously and successfully delay their orgasms, that most do not consider a sex act over until the woman is satisfied, and that men feel content after orgasm, but not excessively sleepy or depressed. They seem to have an excellent attitude and strong motivation toward bringing women to orgasm.

Now, for the big question: how successful are they in practice? We asked what percentage of the time men's partners had orgasms during intercourse, and also what percentage of the time the women had orgasms either before or after intercourse (presumably by manual or oral stimulation).

*Question 23: What percent of the time does your partner have an orgasm during intercourse?*

*Question 24: What percent of the time does the woman you're having sex with have an orgasm either before or after sexual intercourse?*

| % of time woman has orgasm | % of women with orgasm during intercourse | | % of women with orgasm before/after | |
|---|---|---|---|---|
| | Total | Cumulative | Total | Cumulative |
| 90% or more | 29.8 | 29.8 | 17.4 | 17.4 |
| 60 to 89% | 26.0 | 55.8 | 18.6 | 36.0 |
| 40 to 59% | 14.9 | 70.7 | 15.1 | 51.1 |
| 10 to 39% | 10.8 | 81.5 | 18.5 | 69.6 |
| 0 to 9% | 4.5 | 86.0 | 13.3 | 82.9 |
| Not sure | 13.0 | | 15.0 | |

The "cumulative" columns in the tables above show how many women have orgasms *at least* that often. Thus, if 30 percent have orgasms during intercourse 90 percent of the time or more and 26 percent of women have them 60 to 89 percent of the time, a total of 56 percent of women will have orgasms at least 60 percent of the time, and so on. The cumulative columns do not reach 100 percent at 0 to 9 percent of the time because of the men who answered "I'm not sure when she has an orgasm."

Our study shows that nearly one-third of the men brought their partners to orgasm *through intercourse* nearly every time, and more than half succeeded 60 percent of the time. Even if we count the partners of all 13 percent of the men who were not sure about female orgasm as being unable to climax during intercourse, only 18 percent of the men consistently failed to elicit orgasm.

Our study, therefore, contradicts Shere Hite's contention that only 30 percent of women are capable of achieving orgasm regularly from intercourse without additional direct manual stimulation of the clitoris and 16 percent can achieve "regular" orgasm with the added assistance. Hite gave her respondents only three choices: "regularly," "rarely," and "does not orgasm" (Hite considers "orgasm" a verb, but we will wait until the dictionaries catch up); if we accept a frequency of 60 percent or more as "regular," we find that 56 percent of our respondents achieved this frequency with their partners, 10 percentage points higher than Hite's findings, even if we include her women who needed additional stimulation. If we define 40 percent as "regular" rather than "rare," our sample's success rate surpasses Hite's by 25 percentage points; 71 percent compared with Hite's 46.

Even though our findings did not agree with Hite's, her study has raised the question of whether or not women's orgasmic potential has changed since 1972, the year the Women's Liberation Movement achieved new prominence with the publication of widely read books by Millet and Greer. It was conceivable that marked changes in attitudes of women and men could have had a significant effect on sexual relations even within a short span of five years. However, comparing our survey's findings to those reported by Morton Hunt in 1972, we found only a remarkable similarity, refuting Hite's contention that today's woman has become dissatisfied with her sex life. Since Hunt used "married women" for the figures cited below, we are comparing them with the responses given only by the married men in our sample.

| Hunt's Survey (1972) | | Our Survey | |
|---|---|---|---|
| Orgasm frequency | % of wives | Orgasm frequency | % of wives |
| All or almost all of time | 53 | 80 to 100% | 48 |
| About ¾ of time | 21 | 70 to 79% | 10 |
| About ½ of time | 11 | 40 to 69% | 23 |
| About ¼ of time | 8 | 20 to 39% | 9 |
| Almost none or none of time | 7 | 0 to 19% | 9 |

In calculating our percentages for the above table, we discarded the 11 percent of married men who were not sure when their partners had orgasm and the 0.8 percent who did not answer the question, taking the remainder of the sample, those that gave a percentage, as the total sample. Other studies do not seem to allow for men who do not know whether or not their partner has climaxed—and 20 percent of men who had never married admitted they were not sure; this poses a problem in validity when such men are forced to make an estimate.

If we recalculate our percentages for our total sample as we just did for our married men, eliminating from the sample those who could not give an estimated frequency for partner's orgasm, the total sample and married segment do not vary:

| Orgasm frequency | Partners of married men (%) | All partners (%) |
|---|---|---|
| 80 to 100% | 48 | 47 |
| 70 to 79% | 10 | 12 |
| 40 to 69% | 23 | 24 |
| 20 to 39% | 9 | 9 |
| 0 to 19% | 9 | 9 |

Here is an interesting new finding, for in Kinsey's time, the frequency of married women's orgasms increased with the time they were married. (He found that 50 percent of wives were having orgasm "regularly" during the first year of marriage, 59 percent by the tenth year, and 64 percent by the twentieth.) We have found that now partners who are not married to their lovers have orgasms just as frequently as wives who have had years of experience with the same man.

Thus, it would seem that with the increased sexual freedom enjoyed by single people today and the abundance of written material about sexual theory and technique, experience in terms of years of marriage is no longer as important for women to reach orgasm. Below, we have compared the frequencies of orgasm for the partners of married men in our study with those reported by Kinsey and Hunt. While Kinsey's figures are for women in their fifteenth year of marriage and Hunt's are for women with a median duration of 15 years in marriage, our sample consists of all married women, without regard to duration of marriage. Yet our percentages coincide nearly exactly with those of Hunt, indicating that in the 1970s duration of marriage has little bearing on the frequency of female orgasm.

| Kinsey (1948) | | Hunt (1972) | | Our Study | |
|---|---|---|---|---|---|
| Orgasm frequency | % of wives | Orgasm frequency | % of wives | Orgasm frequency | % of wives |
| 90–100% | 45 | Almost all | 53 | 80–100% | 48 |
| 30–89% | 27 | 50–75% | 32 | 40–79% | 34 |
| 1–29% | 16 | About 25% | 8 | 20–39% | 9 |
| None | 12 | Almost none | 7 | 0–19% | 9 |

Our figures above are based on the respondents who gave a percentage, eliminating those who were not sure when their partner had an orgasm.

In 1973 Seymour Fisher reported findings based on a study of 300 married women that 39 percent always or nearly always had orgasm during intercourse. The relative youth of his sample may account for his estimate's being lower than the larger studies quoted above. Fisher's study is of particular interest because he did ask how many needed direct manual clitoral stimulation during intercourse for orgasm: about half of the women (19 percent) required it; 20 percent did not.

It is not clear why Hite is so terribly concerned about clitoral stimulation during intercourse, since no other investigator has made an issue of it. The most publicized finding of *The Hite Report* is that only approximately 30 percent of the women surveyed could have orgasm regularly from "intercourse"—which Hite goes on to define as copulation without manual stimulation. If she included her 16 percent who could have orgasms "regularly" with this assistance, her 46 percent would be more in line with our findings and those of Kinsey and Hunt. Since only 38 percent of Hite's women were married—a totally unrepresentative sample—many of her subjects might have felt embarrassed to request or engage on their own in direct clitoral stimulation, but if men readily accept cunnilingus and non-traditional coital positions, they should be—and apparently already are—quite amenable toward adding direct clitoral stimulation to their repertoire.

Helen Singer Kaplan says that at least 40 percent of women will require direct clitoral stimulation for orgasm during intercourse and agrees with Hite that no more than 30 percent of women can have orgasm without this assistance. Kaplan, however, has found that up to 20 percent of women with the complaint of needing clitoral assistance can learn to have orgasms on direct intercourse, which would raise her estimated maximum to 50 percent, quite comparable to our figures.

Hite states that 12 percent of her female sample has never had orgasm, not much greater than Kaplan's estimate of 8 percent chronic anorgasmia; however, Hite's claim that one-quarter of women are incapable of orgasm during intercourse does not agree with anyone else's findings, and seems to reflect the bias of her sample.

One puzzle in comparing the data from other investigations with our own is why the women in Kinsey's sample had such success in reaching orgasm regularly if Kinsey's contention that "for perhaps three-quarters of all males, orgasm is reached within two minutes after the initiation of the sexual relation" was then valid. While there has been some improvement in the frequency of female orgasmic response since Kinsey's time, particularly in the decrease of women who rarely or never have orgasm, the improvement has not kept pace with the increased duration of the average sex act and men's increasing interest in bringing partners to orgasm. Among his innumerable tables, Kinsey does not present any specific data on speed of male orgasm, so we may question the objectivity of his estimate.

The psychological climate of Kinsey's time might have contributed more to women's increased satisfaction than did men's performance. Around 1900 some estimates of frigidity in married women ran as high as two-thirds or three-quarters. In 1929 about half of married women were estimated to be almost totally or completely lacking in orgasmic potential. By 1938 Terman was able to report that two-thirds of married women usually had orgasm. Women born in the 1920s were reaping the bounty of women's suffrage and the later independence and responsibility of the war years. Thus, for all our sophisticated knowledge and technique, the psyche still holds sway, and women in the 1930s and 1940s seemed to move spontaneously toward greater orgasmic potential just as men in the 1950s and 1960s spontaneously changed their pattern in intercourse from speed to endurance.

Whereas our survey has shown that neither many years of marriage nor marriage itself has an effect on increasing the frequency of female orgasm, male experience is a significant factor. Only 23 percent of men who had never been married reported that their partners reached orgasm 90 percent of the time or more, compared with 31 percent of married men and living-togethers and 34 percent of divorced/widowed. Age was somewhat less important, though only 26 percent of men over 55 reported that their partners had orgasm nearly always, compared with approximately 31 percent of men between 30 and 54, and 29 percent of the men under 30. Twenty-four percent of blacks reported that their partners nearly always climaxed during intercourse, compared with 31 percent of whites; only 38 percent of blacks reported female orgasm at least 70 percent of the time, compared with 51 percent of whites.

Educated men were more successful in bringing partners to orgasm. A level of 70 percent success was attained by over half of the college graduates, while it was 41 percent for the men who did not finish high school. And 9 percent of the least educated men reported that their partners had orgasms less than 10 percent of the time, compared with 3 to 5 percent in the more educated brackets. Men in the highest income bracket reported near-total success in 37 percent of cases, female orgasmic response decreasing with male income to a low of 24 percent (for 90–100 percent response) at the under-$10,000 level.

Men also frequently bring their partners to orgasm either before or after intercourse, through manual or oral stimulation. Correcting for the 15 percent of men who were unsure when their partners had orgasms and the 2.2 percent who did not answer the question, about 56 percent of men bring their partners to orgasm by stimulation outside of intercourse in at least half of their encounters, and 21 percent do so at least 90 percent of the time. Only about one out of six men today fails to give his partner orgasm outside of intercourse.

Highest income earners (24 percent making at least $25,000), men with some college (19 percent) and professional men (20 percent) constituted the subgroups highest in bringing partner to orgasm outside of intercourse 90 percent of the time or more; no subgroup, however, fell below 13 percent. Single men were lower than others in frequently bringing partners to orgasm without intercourse, and men over 55 were significantly lower than their juniors in using such technique with 90 percent success. In no subgroup did more than 17 percent of the men report that they never or almost never (0–9 percent) brought their partners to orgasm before or after intercourse.

# Faking It

If men were once indifferent to female orgasms, many are now overzealous. Some regard the partner's failure to achieve orgasm as an affront to their masculinity and will press on into the night hoping to generate the heat of passion by the sweat of their brow. Other men may be sincerely considerate of the woman, and though their egos are not overinflated enough to burst at the point of failure, their air of quiet desperation might move the woman to such pity that she feigns orgasm to give the partner happiness and herself some sleep.

Men find it very difficult to conceive that a woman would pass up the chance for an orgasm. Once males get aroused, unless they have a problem with psychological impotence, orgasm is intensely desired and virtually inevitable. Since a man must be *fully* aroused to have intercourse, he cannot identify his own experiences with those of a woman participating happily and lovingly in intercourse without full arousal.

Theodore Rubin warns: "I believe that sexual lies almost invariably lead to difficulties. Even for those women who make the effort in an attempt to foster greater intimacy with their partners, the treat to precisely that intimacy they seek far outweighs the possible—and probably temporary—gains to be achieved."

The sooner a man understands that women do not bat 1.000, the less tension there will be on both partners. If the woman later proves to have orgasms nearly all the time, the man will feel he is an exceptional lover. If she does not have an orgasm, he will not reproach himself, and if he finds ways outside of intercourse to excite her to climax, the explorer will experience a wild surmise like stout Cortez upon his peak.

On the other hand, if he believes a woman should have an orgasm each time, an encounter can bring only defeat, not victory. And if he should catch the woman in deceit, he will never again be sure whether he has truly pleased her or been so inept that she must protect him from confronting the truth.

The notion that men want only to penetrate, thrust, and ejaculate is, as we have seen, outdated, if, indeed, it was ever true. Men today rarely object to foreplay, cunnilingus, manual stimulation of the clitoris, changing sexual positions, postcoital activity, or eliciting multiple orgasms. The one thing they do seem averse to in some cases is bringing a woman to orgasm prior to penetration; this is not because they are inconsiderate, but because they equate female orgasm with their own and know they quickly lose feelings of arousal after ejaculation. In the woman, however, the clitoris returns from its retracted position to its normal accessible one (a plus), while the outer third of the vagina decongests more slowly, retaining the "plateau" formation required for effective orgasm through penile thrusting (another plus). Female orgasms during foreplay won't guarantee orgasms during penetration, but neither will they inhibit subsequent climaxes. An orgasm may not be a necessity, but it is never a drawback and, considering the number of women who counterfeit them, orgasms should be deemed highly valuable.

The prevalence of extracoital female orgasm reported by our subjects should successfully refute Hite's contention that men define sex as intercourse and that "intercourse *is* the pattern (at least insofar as it ends with male ejaculation and this ends sex)." Hite accuses men of "almost hysterical fixation on intercourse and orgasm," and then goes on to advocate disregard of male orgasm and more lesbian relationships—somewhat akin to throwing out the baby with the bath water, which is perhaps understandable if one didn't like babies to begin with.

Hite's problem seems to be her sample. Basing a study on a sample of chiefly unmarried women who are eager to write long answers to a 58-item questionnaire and expect these women to be representative of the general population is the *height of folly*.

To advocate the restructuring of sexual relationships on the basis of such findings is the folly of Hite.

# Turn-Offs—Thorns
# in the Rose Bed

DON JUAN: My ear, practised on a thousand songs
and symphonies; my eye, exercised on a thousand
paintings; tore her voice, her features, her color to
shreds. I caught all those tell-tale resemblances to
her father and mother by which I knew what she
would be like in thirty years' time. I noted the gleam
of gold from a dead tooth in the laughing mouth: I
made curious observations of the strange odors of the
chemistry of the nerves. The visions of my romantic
reveries, in which I had trod the plains of heaven
with a deathless, ageless creature of coral and ivory,
deserted me in that supreme hour.

—GEORGE BERNARD SHAW, *Man and Superman*

A team of medical students was performing a routine experiment on
an anesthesized cat. One studiously monitored the animal's heart
rate, breathing, blood pressure, and muscle tension on a polygraph,
a kind of a miniature lie-detector. While the other students applied
various chemical and electrical stimuli to the oblivious creature, the
row of levers on the machine clicked furiously, tracing waves and
spikes on the paper that gushed endlessly from the mechanical bowels. One frantic student tripped over the machine's cord, dislodging
the plug, and the electrical marvel, alive and clicking an instant ago,
became immobile. The student who had been watching the machine's every movement looked up in consternation and moaned,
"Who turned off the cat?"

179

Maybe that scene sticks in mind because a turn-off for a man can be just that abrupt; one minute his heart is racing and he's panting with enthusiasm, and the next, he's as cold and inert as if someone pulled out his plug. What amazed Don Juan was how, with all the things he found unattractive in women, he was, nevertheless, unable to resist them sexually. This is probably true for the average man, although some seem to have a particular hang-up that catapults them out of a potentially amorous situation like an ejection seat; it may be something physical about the woman, something perceived in her attitude, or even something as benign as her age or how far away she lives.

If there is anything that concerns a woman more than what turns a man on, it's what turns him off. If she hasn't found the right way to turn on a particular man, there's always hope that she will gain ground later; being still in the race is the important thing. A turn-off can mean she is out of the running for good. If a man is vulnerable to a particular turn-off and a woman has the misfortune to demonstrate the fatal flaw, their chances of romantic success are as poor as the probability of a marriage between Premier Sadat of Egypt and Golda Meir.

The men we surveyed had no difficulty identifying the things about women that turned them off. Some of their answers read like shopping lists—of products they wouldn't buy.

*Essay Question: What things about a woman turn you off? What things about her body, her personality and the way she acts would make you lose interest in her?*

The one answer that we expected to see often appeared only once or twice: ugly, homely, or unattractive. Men did not demand exceptional or even average beauty, but they emphatically expected a woman to take pride in her appearance, groom herself well, and not let herself become fat:

"A woman who doesn't take any interest in herself turns me off totally. If she can't take care of herself, then to hell with her. Her sex is probably just as bad. She cannot be demanding and she must like to try different things in life and not be afraid."

"I like a neatly dressed woman. If she's not put together on the outside, something tells me she's not put together very well on the inside. I like curves but not flat. Too heavy not good. If a woman is giddy and silly too much."

"The biggest turn-off is an unkempt appearance. An attractive woman turns me off if she acts like she knows it."

"Obese, dirty, coarse, crude, cruel, ignorant, egotistical factors turn me off. Tall, proportionate, healthy-appearing women with nice, sincere smiles and laughs turn me on. Too much makeup turns me off."

"Too strong a perfume and the taste of perfume on her breast. Excessive stretch marks on her tummy or sagging stomach. Overweight women also turn me off. Being too demanding to continue intercourse after an orgasm."

The physical defects for which women were criticized were essentially those that were totally or partially under their control, obesity being the overwhelming complaint, along with bad teeth, poor complexion, dirty hair, and poor posture. It was incredible to see so many mentions (nearly 25 percent of all respondents) of bathing and personal hygiene in a sample with such a high representation of middle-class and upper-class men:

"Fat. Bad hygiene . . . (like not bathing for 11 or 12 days!). Nagging bitch who argues to convince herself and others of her own self-worth. A phony. Super self-indulgence."

"Unmitigated dirt in the wrong places would do it, so would disturbing sanity. The really consistent gold digger could also not hold my interest."

"Stuck-up, spoiled, dirty. Has VD and won't do anything about it but spread it. Bad teeth, drinks too much, loud mouth, foul mouth, shows her ass to everyone."

"An unfit or unclean body. An overconfident or 'cocky' attitude. A woman (or man) should have pride in the way she/he looks and should be aggressive, but feminine."

"Doesn't take a bath before hitting the sack."

"Her smell before a bath."

It is difficult to envision so many American women coming to bed encrusted with dirt, and, as we will explore later, this complaint may reflect some deeper male hang-ups about odor. Men also might be influenced by the disproportionate amount of television time devoted to commercials for soap of all kinds, though these are aimed primarily at women through the daytime "soap operas." When women are too distressed by video assaults on their personal hygiene, they can displace some of their anxiety from their bodies on to their laundry and be obsessive about ring-necked collars and gray-bellied undershirts. Their ubiquitous soap commercials have, in the past, been populated by such virile fantasy figures as a charging white knight, a brawny genie looking like a cross between Yul Brynner and Arnold Schwarzenegger, and a giant who would periodically thrust his mighty arm up from the washing machine in which he dwelt, leaving the rest of his masculine attributes to the imagination. The women in the laundry commercials, far from being exotic counterparts of these dream men, are apparently selected for their plainness, so that the most drab housewife can identify with them and believe that the secret way to love is through the door of her washer-drier. "Clean is sexy" is the subliminal sales pitch; and a lot of men have bought it.

A woman's attitude could be a big deterrent for many men, if she were domineering, possessive, or apathetic:

"In one word, 'bitchyness.' If she acts indifferent or tries to punish me sexually, I lose interest very quickly. Also, if she starts to compare me with other men or try to make me compete for her."

"Always arguing and making demands, expecting too much, and not helping make a better life."

"Too domineering and forceful—doesn't keep herself in good health and not very friendly to my friends."

"An openly aggressive grabber would turn me off. Her complexion and oral health would be a first notice to me. A helpless type turns me off."

"Being fat, sloppiness, too much self-confidence, career mindedness, too much shopping for junk, negligence toward children, financial irresponsibility, sexual disinterest."

"A woman with poor hygiene is a turn-off. Also too much makeup or too concerned with her physical appearance. I can't stand self-righteous people. And I don't enjoy a woman who thinks that when she has sex, she's being taken advantage of—it's a sharing experience. I also abhor possessive women."

"A woman instantly turns me off if she talks stupid or way off base. I don't like a woman to hang on me or watch every move I make."

"Bad personality (know-it-all, one-sided), nice body—bad face. Voice of a little girl. Someone who doesn't know how (or when) to keep her mouth shut when we have done sexual acts or knows what I have done with someone else."

"It turns me off when a woman seems cold, indifferent or distant. If I can't intelligently talk to her about the things I'm interested in, I would tend to seek out someone with whom I could. A woman who is too dependent on me turns me off completely."

"I think a woman who was unaware of her environment and herself would make me lose interest in her. A woman who was not happy with herself would also turn me off, for a woman of this nature would not be prepared to be happy with me."

"Loud, stupid mouth. Bossiness. Sloppiness. Lack of general interest in doing something and becoming somebody."

"A lack of interest in the sex act, or trying to put on an act of enjoyment. Also a bad personality can turn me off very quickly!"

Men seemed to dislike most of all women who seemed conceited or who put on airs:

"A woman that tries to be what she's not. A woman that tries to hide everything about herself. And a woman that plays a part of life that she made up that's not natural."

"I dislike women who try to pretend to be what they are not and who are greatly status conscious. I dislike women who allow their physical appearance to fall apart without taking the same efforts to preserve appearance that they did before marriage."

"Fat, not intelligent enough, having too high an opinion of herself, expecting a long engagement or dating period before

really getting to be friendly. Expecting to own me, even if it is
just when I'm with her. Having the attitude that she is doing me
a favor by going out with me.—By trying to act like something
she's not. By acting like she's leading me on for her own kicks.
By expecting me to conform to her ideas of what I should be
like."

"Vanity, or a woman putting other women down by compar-
ison. Example would be derogatory statements made to another that seem to make themselves look or seem better."

"A girl who is too well built and knows it and throws it at you
and if her first and only thoughts are her."

"If she feels she's better than most. If she only enjoys one type
sex. Not open-minded."

"Excessive beauty. Obesity. Strong perfume. Lack of warm
feeling for other people. Excessive interest in self or family."

"An immature girl and/or a sloppy appearance turn me off. An
ugly girl turns me off. I would lose interest in a girl only interested in herself or in me."

"If she seems too sure and independent about herself. If she
continually wants to diet when she really doesn't have to."

"Body proportions out of align. Smoking and swanky walk burn
me up. Nose in the air, tone of voice, New England accent."

"Dirty women who swear. Talk too much about their self and
how good they are."

"Some snooty cunt who's 'too good for you.' "

"A big ass turns me off most. . . . A woman that is too emotional
or childish also turns me off."

Dirtiness, coarseness, insensitivity, and unladylike behavior all suggest that by-now-familiar shady lady that haunts the imaginations of
men, the archetypical prostitute. A few men stated more openly that
they were turned off by a woman who seemed promiscuous, and they
did not mince words:

"Do not like someone who is an obvious flirt (what we call a 'prick-teaser'). A woman with extreme emotional swings. Someone who looks and/or acts cheap (like a prostitute). A 'swinger' or one who needs/wants more than one partner—that's the biggest turn-off."

"A drunk, mouthy, know-it-all turns me off. I lose interest in bad odors, poor teeth and too promiscuous."

"I don't like stuck-up woman. Nor do I like women who dress like whores."

"Blatant sexual appearance, overaggressiveness. Heavy perfumes. Limited fields of interest and knowledge. Closed-minded attitudes on life and people. Hang-ups about sex."

"Crudeness, lewdness and ignorance. Flab, excessive crotch hair, uncleanliness and unpleasant odors. Habitually negative attitudes. Amoral attitudes. Promiscuous behavior. Continuous, compulsive talking. Preoccupation with 'girl talk.' "

"When she says on the first time, 'You want to fuck.' It's okay if you've been together awhile though or if you are really close because it's cute. If she just lays there and expects the guy to do everything."

Not many men passed up the chance to catalog their complaints about women who turned them off. Only one said, "Nothing in particular" and another, "Not much."

One happily married man said, "When the man and woman are free from inhibitions and fears, with a true understanding of each other and continued willingness to understand, then no physical characteristics can affect that glorious spark of passion between them, which is love, as exists with my beloved wife and I."

Then, there was the guy who found himself confronted by the ultimate turn-off: "If she says, 'Get lost.' "

## The Bad Madonna

Having read many of men's previous answers to our questions, you probably noticed an abrupt change in tone when they started talking about turn-offs. The sympathy toward women and the unexpected emotional sensitivity apparent throughout their other answers are not seen here. Here we cannot generally distinguish the educated man from the uneducated, the old from the young, the upper economic strata from the lower; there is a primitive, gut-level, unvarnished quality to the answers. Granted, we did not expect men to say nice things about women in response to a query about negative points; yet often we see here a list of gripes that adds up to a picture of a woman that is so foul, obnoxious, and repulsive that it becomes a caricature, so ludicrous and out of character that one does not want to take it seriously.

These women who are composites of purely negative qualities with nothing of redeeming value in their makeup are archetypes—unconscious images or conceptions common to every man, based on universal experience—like the madonna and the prostitute. Are these terrible women, then, the "prostitutes" that coexist with the "madonnas" in men's conception of women? Not really, for the prostitute has considerable allure and appeal for men, whereas these "turn-off" women are totally repugnant. They are the negative half of a much earlier dichotomy or "split," one which precedes by many years the prostitute-madonna split, a product of puberty. The components of this earlier split, one that begins in infancy, are the ancestors of the madonna and the prostitute: the good mother and the bad mother. The mother is the first source of gratification for the child; she provides nourishment, warmth, comfort, and affection. She is also the first source of frustration, when she fails to materialize immediately with the milk, when she refuses to hold the squalling infant, and when she later makes demands on the child for his bowels and other parts to conform to standards of conduct that oppose his natural inclinations. Given his utter dependency on the mother and the primitive state of his ego development, the child experiences intense rage and hostility towards his mother when she frustrates his desires; he would devour her, annihilate her if he could, at times. Yet, he must reconcile these feelings with his love for his mother as the very source of his life and sustenance. He, therefore, comes to think of her as two entirely different people, a warm, good, nurturing mother and a demanding, rejecting, depriving mother. In the Oedipal period, around age 4 or 5, the bad mother adds some sexual components to her nature. The good mother gives her first allegiance to him; the bad mother to his father, who offers her the mysterious adult relationship he cannot.

All of the turn-offs men cited are basically rejections. Physically, the obese, unbathed, poorly groomed woman is refusing to keep herself as men would like her. The homely woman who is neat, clean, and thin keeps herself presentable, and men are turned on by her receptivity. The domineering woman places herself ahead of the man; the dependent, helpless woman is unable to nurture him; the lazy, apathetic woman does not care about him; the conceited woman is too self-centered to give to him. The promiscuous woman will gratify other men instead of devoting herself to him. It always comes back to a woman's interest in a man and her willingness to gratify him as a good mother would.

Sex appeal tends to boil down to a woman's ability to project herself as a self-confident, competent person and as someone generally interested in others, especially her man. If she does not seem to please herself, how can she please a man? A woman can guard against turn-offs by visiting her shower twice a day, her health spa twice a week, her hairdresser twice a month, and her dentist twice a year, but the main secret in doubling her pleasure is to be able to approach a man with two firm attitudes, confidence in herself and concern for him: "I'm okay" and "Are you okay?"

## Too Good to Be True

For all his experience and alleged coolness, today's male is still threatened by rejection and competition. Thus the very qualities in a woman that would normally be considered highly desirable may arouse anxiety in him for fear that she will reject him because he is inferior to her or because he cannot meet the competition from a large number of other males. If his anxiety level gets high enough, the turn-on may become a turn-off.

*Question 25: What type of woman makes you feel most nervous?*

| | |
|---|---|
| Beautiful woman | 24.7% |
| Very intelligent woman | 21.4% |
| Virgin | 14.0% |
| Woman with much sexual experience | 12.7% |
| Wealthy woman | 11.7% |
| Woman with high-paying job | 9.0% |
| No answer | 8.4% |

The financially independent or successful woman, a growing phenomenon in our society as more women enter graduate schools and sexual discrimination in business is reduced, does not unnerve men as much as the exceptionally attractive woman. We are familiar with scenes from both movies and life where a mature, competent male is reduced to a blushing, stammering boy by a radiantly confident, sweetly sympathetic beauty; we witnessed on the screen not only such classic confrontations as Jimmy Stewart versus June Allyson and Donald O'Connor versus Debbie Reynolds, but, even earlier, Dopey versus Snow White, Bambi versus Faline, and Jiminy Cricket versus the Blue Fairy. Put a man up against a pretty face and, on their first encounter, his legs will turn to rubber and his brain to jelly.

The man sees beautiful women as having an infinite range in the choice of partners, which throws him into competition with just about every male on earth—odds that would intimidate the most inveterate gambler. He may have his own strong points, but she already has an ace showing. Even if he is as gorgeous in his own way as she is, male beauty is devalued currency, and pound for pound, he will come up a few shillings short in the exchange.

Younger men are more intimidated by beauty than older ones; 25 percent of men under 40 cited it as being most nerve-wracking, against 19 percent of men over 55. The oldest group was more put off by high intelligence, with a 23 percent response here.

Understandably, men with poor educations were more threatened by very intelligent females than highly educated men were: 35 percent of those without high school diplomas chose this, followed by 28 percent with diplomas, and so on down to 12 percent with postgraduate educations. Blue-collar workers (29 percent) and the retired-/unemployed (24 percent) were most threatened by intelligence, students (18 percent) and professionals (18 percent) least. Blacks (27 percent) were more threatened by highly intelligent women than whites (21 percent); this is probably a reflection of education, since high school graduates cited high intelligence 28 percent of the time against 19 per cent of men with some college.

The most highly educated men said beautiful women made them the most nervous (26 percent); those without high school diplomas picked beauty 21 percent of the time. Perhaps intellectual men are less at ease with women who arouse them on a more physical level —on the other hand, since so few of the highly educated ones picked intelligence as a major threat, some were bound to choose beauty, the first or second most commonly picked factor by every subgroup.

Married men named beautiful women first (24.1 percent) and intelligent women second (23.5 percent), leading the other marital status subgroups by at least 5 percentage points in citing intelligence. The older age of married men, less accustomed to college-educated women, is a factor; they were also not concerned with a woman's abundance or lack of sexual experience and tended to be more monogamous.

Single men (18 percent) were more threatened (than those who had been married or in living-together relationships) by women with much sexual experience, probably because of their own relative inexperience. Students (18 percent) likewise were more threatened than men established in professions. Men in their thirties (10 per cent) were most comfortable with experienced women, the oldest (15 percent) and youngest (14 percent) subgroups least so.

Virgins were most threatening to the divorced/widowed and those living with a partner (20 percent for both). Older men were more at ease with them than the younger, having been acquainted with them long before they became an endangered species. Nonwhites (19 percent) were less at ease with virgins than whites (13 percent). Highly educated men were more threatened by virgins: only 9 per cent of men without high school diplomas cited virgins as anxiety-provoking, against 16 percent of postgraduate men.

Women with high-paying jobs were most threatening to the oldest men (13 percent), least to the youngest (7 percent).

A woman blessed with beauty and brains is bound to arouse anxiety in nearly half (46 percent) of men. The brainy woman is not likely to blow a good prospect unless she's dumb in her actions—in which case, she's probably not all that intelligent. If she asks intelligent questions rather than making brilliant statements and otherwise sounding like she's at a quiz show tryout, she can make a man feel smarter than he is. The timid man avoids intelligent women because he fears they will not accept him; if the woman demonstrates her acceptance of his thoughts and opinions from the start, he no longer will feel threatened when the degree of her intellect becomes apparent.

The superbly endowed beauty will never lack for men in quantity, but may have problems in the quality of what she dredges up from her sea of admirers. She will always be the target of the Don Juans who feed their egos on the company of the best-looking women in the crowd; because they spend so much of their time and energy in such pursuit, they do not generally achieve much in other areas— besides, they are interested in quantity, as well as quality, so their attentions should be as welcome as moths who obscure the flame they cluster about. Ironically, the very attractive female may find she has to hunt down the really desirable specimens on a one-to-one basis, prize bucks often shying away from the wolf pack. Wonder Woman may cut a wide swath of devastation in her most revealing costume, but in the prim guise of Diana Prince she can often get a lot more done with a lot less unwelcome attention; an alter ego may be indispensable for the superbeauty—she can always let her hair down when she's with the good guys.

# An Air of Unpleasantness

As it commonly happens, a man has been neither overly repelled by a woman's deficiencies nor threatened excessively by her attributes, and has propelled himself into her bedroom without being turned off somewhere en route. Finally ensconced in their bower of love, everything is bound to come up roses—including a few thorns, of course.

*Question 26: What is the most unpleasant aspect of sex for you?*

| | |
|---|---|
| Having an unresponsive woman | 58.5% |
| Odors and discharge | 24.6% |
| Feeling guilty | 6.1% |
| Woman making demands | 5.8% |
| Engaging in foreplay | 3.6% |
| No answer | 3.3% |

Contrary to popular myth and feminist folklore, men are not indifferent to their partners' responses and concerned only with their own satisfaction. Rather, how much their partners seem to be satisfied by them is apparently the single most important aspect of a positive sexual experience.

Responsivity should not be confused with orgasm. It is possible for a woman to have consistent orgasms and still appear unresponsive to her mate. Conversely, she may never have orgasms and still convey a deep enjoyment of sex. Initiating the sex act indicates to a man that his partner enjoys it. Moving her body actively during intercourse, emitting vocal sounds (a shriek isn't necessary—an erotic gasp or moan will do just fine), or even flexing her vaginal muscles by rhythmically contracting the anal sphincter will signal the man that she's "with it." Suggesting different positions or variations is another indication of interest.

A woman lying on her back during intercourse can wrap her legs around her partner's back at the peak of her excitement, clutching him in a strong, all-encompassing embrace that drives his penis to a maximum depth. Even an occasional playful "thank you" after intercourse or a contented smile validates his performance. Responsiveness need not involve a metamorphosis into a clawing tigress, a screaming banshee, or, most frightening of all, an insatiable nymphomaniac. The burning question for him is not "Did you come?" but "Are you glad you came to bed with me?"

Rather than taking their wives for granted, married men were the most concerned about partner's response, with 60 percent; then, singles and divorced/widowed at 55, and living-togethers at 54. Men in their thirties were the leaders (63 percent) in this category; other groups registered 57 percent for under-thirty-year-olds, 58 for age 40–54, and 56 percent for the oldest group.

White males found an unresponsive woman to be the most unpleasant aspect 60 percent of the time, but nonwhites only 45 percent.

The more educated a man became, the more concerned he was with his partner's response: 44 percent of those without high school diplomas, 56 percent for high school graduates, 62 percent for college graduates, and 65 percent for the postgraduates. Higher-income men were more concerned than the low earners, the least concerned group being the $10,000–$14,999 bracket with 55 percent, against a top of 62 for those making at least $25,000. (Students tend to skew the lowest income group, which registered 57 percent, in the direction of high earners.)

Odors and discharge was the second most frequent response, 25 percent of men rating this as the most unpleasant aspect of sex. Odors were also commonly mentioned in men's replies to the essay question about what turned them off. This complaint seems related to a complex of biological, social, and psychological factors.

Divorced/widowed men (32 percent) and those living with partners, unmarried (30 percent), complained of odors most frequently. Married men (24) and singles (23) were lowest in percentage. For the married, familiarity with a partner over the years may desensitize them to particular odors, while partners of unmarried men are likely to engage in sex under least informal circumstances, with more scrupulous care about hygiene. Men with little schooling (31 percent) objected to odors more than those who had graduated high school, 22 to 25 percent of more educated men giving this response. Nonwhites, at 30 percent, took exception to odor more often than whites (24 percent).

In every other animal, the smell of a female not only arouses rather than repels a male, but is usually essential for sexual activity. With a few exceptions, like the chimpanzee, male animals never copulate with a female unless she is in her fertile period (estrus or "heat") when she emits certain odors, chiefly around her genital area. Animals have a highly developed sense of smell, not only for sexual purposes, but to enable them to tell friend from foe.

If men are repelled by odors that other male creatures would naturally be attracted by, it is probable that there are strong psychological factors involved. Little boys automatically equate the vagina with the anus—it's the only orifice they have in the pelvic area, so they assume the similarity. Both male and female children equate pregnancy and birth with the digestive system, and believe mother carries the baby in her "stomach." It would logically follow that she would give birth through the rectum, and possibly become pregnant through the mouth. Vaginal discharge becomes, by association, something akin to feces, an excretory product to be considered with repugnance. (Small children are not repulsed by feces and have to be taught that excrement is dirty and foul.) There are many men who do find vaginal odors stimulating and who consider the smell of women's used underwear very erotic. The great differences in attitude among men would indicate that we are dealing mostly with psychological, rather than biological factors in man, who routinely suppresses much of his olfactory (smelling) powers.

Socially, of course, advertisers wage an incessant war against odors —body, breath, foot, and now vaginal. Vaginal deodorant sprays are openly advertised in popular magazines, and no sooner did we get rid of the douche bag after several generations than we are faced with this new bane. Most doctors do not recommend vaginal sprays because of the high incidence of local allergic reactions. Advertisers may soon stop recommending them because of widespread feminists' reactions.

Unfortunately, we must call this indelicate preoccupation of men about odors to women's attention. Cleanliness was mentioned often in the essay question, close to odors (not godliness) in frequency. The average man wants his woman freshly bathed, and a hint of perfume adds the final touch. Don't go overboard on the fragrances; "smelling like a whore" is a phrase widely applied to a woman who reeks of perfume.

Guilt feelings, discussed in the chapter on orgasm, were mentioned as the most unpleasant aspect of sex in 6.1 percent of our sample. Single men gave this reply in 13 percent of cases—one in eight. Even married men felt guilty 4.1 percent of the time— whether this is guilt of the psychoanalytic variety related to primitive taboos or less esoteric guilt related to cheating on their wives is unknown. Nonwhites referred to guilt in 10 percent of replies, compared with 6 percent for whites. Men between 30 and 54 were least guilt-ridden, those under 30, despite the liberal attitude of their peers, most so (9.4 percent).

Only 3.6 percent of men considered foreplay a chore. Men over 55 (6.9 percent) disliked it most. Blacks (7.5 percent) resented it more than whites (3.2 percent). Foreplay was found to be unpleasant mostly by the least educated (6.4 percent), the retired/unemployed (6.1 percent) and the lowest income earners (4.9 percent). All of these percentages indicate that no more than one man in 20 from any subgroup objects to foreplay. Women do not have to worry about starting a sex act with a turn-off.

## Critical Issues

Women may say, "It's great that men want responsive women—don't you think that *we* want to enjoy sex to the fullest? But are we supposed to come right out and tell a man that he doesn't spend enough time in foreplay or that we prefer one position over the other? Isn't a man going to consider that bossy and see it as a criticism? After all, men do have their pride—don't they?"

*Question 27: What most irritates you during sex?*

| | |
|---|---|
| If the woman seems cold or disinterested | 60.1% |
| I never get irritated | 16.6% |
| If the woman criticizes you | 11.5% |
| If the woman makes demands | 4.9% |
| If the woman is "too easy" (seems promiscuous) | 4.8% |
| If the woman made the first advance | 2.8% |
| No answer | 0.9% |

As in the previous question where an unresponsive woman was cited as the most unpleasant aspect of sex, a cold and disinterested woman was most apt to irritate men. Again, the least educated men showed least concern about their partners' attitudes, as did the retired/unemployed. Blacks selected this response less frequently than whites, though it was still the first choice by a wide margin.

Many women are unnecessarily leery about making suggestions to a man about how to satisfy them better. Women have read so much about men's colossal egos built on shifting sands of inadequacy that they fear a nudge in the right direction will demolish him. Yet, only 12 percent of men said that the most irritating aspect of sex was "if the woman criticizes you" and 4.9 percent selected "if the woman makes demands." In our previous question about the most unpleasant aspect of sex, a woman making demands was named by only 5.8 percent.

Suggestions during intercourse or foreplay are not likely to be rebuffed as criticism, especially if phrased in terms other than "don't." If a little praise is added, the offer is one he can't refuse; for example, "I love it when you kiss my body—try putting your mouth right *here*." Don't say, "Ugh, you're so heavy," try, "Hey, lift up a little, lover, you're big *outside*, too."

There were even as many men who said they *never* got irritated during sex as there were men who chafed under criticism or demands. (Note that the relatively few men who did express irritation with directive women were objecting to actions phrased in the most negative terms—not mere suggestions or attempts at guidance.) Men living with partners, unmarried, apparently often were on relaxed terms with their partners, for they most often (21 percent) denied irritation compared with other marital groups; singles were least complacent, with 14 percent reporting they were never irritated. Retired/unemployed men were most complacent (21 percent), students (15 percent) and those in managerial capacities (16 percent) least so. Men over 55 were the most patient, and men under 30 most likely to find some irritating aspect in the course of their relationships.

Women who made advances or who seemed "easy" did not irritate many of our subjects. This does not mean necessarily that men have abandoned notions that women can be "fast and loose"—it just means that, if they object to such behavior, it will be when a woman acts that way toward other men.

# Downers

Grace Slick once recorded a song that opened with a line about one pill that made you larger and one that made you small. It was called "White Rabbit," after that frantic character in *Alice in Wonderland;* the subject was drugs, not children's fantasies, but watching a pill-head juggle the stimulants ("uppers") and sedatives ("downers") he takes in an attempt to get his "head just right" does remind one of Alice cautiously nibbling one piece of mushroom, then the other, to regulate her height to its ideal dimensions.

It's too bad we don't have pills to regulate the size of body parts instead of "heads," although there wouldn't be much call for "downers" among men. Men have sought the perfect "upper," an effective aphrodisiac, with the zeal of the old alchemists in their quest for gold —without success. As Shakespeare's besotted porter noted in *Macbeth,* alcohol may increase desire, but decreases performance; and, though it's a crime, marijuana use has become as indispensable as contraceptives to only a few who are very high on its value as an aphrodisiac.

"Downers" are not swallowed, they are encountered. Deflate a man's ego and his erection will suffer the same fate. Thanks to our readily adaptable language, he can now say, "I got totally turned off," which sounds a lot better than "I was impotent." Still, a rose by any other name still bears thorns—here are some to watch for:

*Question 28: When are you likely to be so "turned off" you can't complete a sex act?*

| | |
|---|---|
| If the woman seems unresponsive | 45.6% |
| If you've been quarreling | 18.2% |
| I never get "turned off" | 16.2% |
| If the woman seems physically unattractive | 12.5% |
| If the woman tries to control things | 4.8% |
| If it's the first time with that woman | 3.0% |
| No answer | 1.6% |

Only 16 percent of the men—about one in six—replied that they "never get 'turned off.'" Since the question specified inability to complete a sex act, this indicates that about 84 percent of men today have experienced some sort of potency difficulties. Most psychiatrists have concluded from their clinical experience that impotence is increasing, in spite of the availability of copious literature on the latest findings from the sex research labs and clinics and popular guidebooks to failproof technique. This voluminous information probably has contributed to—as much as helped—potency problems, for as women became more aware of their untapped potential for gratification and men had the opportunity to match their experiences vicariously with those of other men, sexual behavior lost much of its spontaneity and the bedroom became a testing grounds in which to experience, not mere pleasure, but the thrill of victory and the agony of defeat.

The incidence of impotence is difficult to gauge from past studies, since most investigators and therapists are interested in cases where the man is impotent all or most of the time. Helen Singer Kaplan does say in *The New Sex Therapy* that approximately half the male population has experienced occasional transient episodes of impotence. Kinsey said that erectile impotence occurred in 0.4 percent of males under 25 and about 1 percent of men at 35. The incidence rose to 2.6 percent at 45, 6.7 percent at 55, and 25 percent at 65. These percentages refer to cases "which are more or less totally and, to all appearances, permanently impotent." Kinsey did add, at least with reference to the younger men, "in only a small portion of these is it a lifelong and complete incapacity."

Hunt documented a rise in the rarest form of impotence, failure to achieve orgasm. Kinsey referred to this as a very rare phenomenon, occurring in only about one man in a thousand. In 1972, Hunt found that 8 percent of men 45 years old or older missed orgasm anywhere from occasionally to most of the time, 7 percent between 25 and 44 failed at least a quarter of the time, and 15 percent under age 25 failed to have orgasm at least 25 percent of the time.

There are some men who reach ripe ages without ever having experienced or even considered erectile failure, and when it does occur, they are about as shaken as if they had noticed their heart was no longer beating. One man in his early fifties, a blue-collar worker, came to the mental health clinic in dismay, having failed to achieve erection with his wife for the first time. "Do you mean," he was asked incredulously, "that you've *never* had this happen before?" He thought awhile, then said, "About thirty years back, when I was in the Navy, I was very drunk and had the same problem with a whore in Shanghai." Then, he brightened. "But I got it up about twenty minutes later!" He did not need the new sex therapy.

Without reassurance, however, many men go on to develop a fear-failure-fear cycle, dreading the next sexual encounter for fear of failure, failing out of fear, and eventually avoiding sexual situations altogether. And, even if a man does rebound from an occasional loss of erection, it can usually be avoided entirely; while the man with impotence all or nearly all the time generally has a deep psychological problem and would have difficulty relating to any woman under any circumstances, men who get "turned off" at periodic intervals are reacting to some specific—and often remediable—situation.

As usual, the more educated man is more sensitive and more likely to have potency problems. Only 13 percent of college graduates were immune, compared with 20 percent of high-school-educated men. Men under 30 less often reported never being "turned off" (15 percent) than the older men, including 17 percent of those over 55. Those living with regular partners, married or not, were less prone to episodes of impotence than those living alone.

An unresponsive woman was once again the biggest turn-off, and married men (47 percent) had as much of a problem with this as the others, although the living-togethers cited it only 37 percent of the time.

Quarreling was more of a problem with men who lived with wives or partners (20 percent) than it was for the divorced/widowed (15 percent) or singles (13 percent).

Physical unattractiveness was cited more often by the singles (20 percent), where a man's interest may drop when a new partner drops her clothing along with her defenses. It's been said that the more a woman takes off, the better she looks, and the more a man takes off, the worse he looks, but Maidenform and Playtex have often guided the destinies of women, offering support and shaping their ends. Even married men (9 percent) complain of finding their partner physically unattractive; it is important to remember that attractiveness is not something a woman has or doesn't have, but something she can acquire or discard through apparel, grooming, and cleanliness. Men under 40 were more preoccupied with physical attractiveness than their seniors, especially in the case of men under 30.

Five percent of single or divorced/widowed men experienced "opening-night jitters"—sexual difficulties when it was their first time with a woman. College graduates (3 percent) felt more confident in this situation than uneducated men (6 percent of those without high school diplomas).

Even if a woman was perceived as trying to control things, only 5 percent of men would be drastically "turned off," one-tenth of those put down by an unresponsive woman. With the most capable of lovers, the average sex act lasts less than an hour; the feeling about himself that the man brings away from that act lasts considerably longer. He can tolerate constructive criticism, direction, and ceding control more than he can tolerate indifference. A negative number has more value than a zero.

## Not Bloody Likely

There are women who refer to menstruation as "the curse" and who refuse to touch flowers and plants while menstruating for fear of killing them. Men, too, regard menstruation with a mixture of distaste and bewilderment. Doctors often defer pelvic examinations on patients who are menstruating. Linnaeus, the great botanist, named a plant after the female genital organs, *Chenopodium vulvaria,* because it smelled like human menstrual blood—it was commonly called stinking goosefoot.

Our survey showed that menstruation is still a significant turn-off, and one-half of all men are deterred from intercourse by this natural phenomenon. Women have sometimes used male repugnance toward menstruation as a means of avoiding intercourse without discouraging the suitor. One coed claimed menstruation so often, her boy friend didn't know whether to kiss her or transfuse her. Some women might find it difficult to believe men are put off at all; their lovers are as regular as postmen in seeking intercourse, and are deterred neither by snow, nor rain, nor massive hemorrhage in the gloom of night from the hopefully-not-too-swift completion of their appointed rounds.

*Question 29: How do you feel about having intercourse during partner's period?*

| | |
|---|---|
| Enjoy sex as much | 31.4% |
| Do not have intercourse, but engage in other sex play | 19.3% |
| Limit contact to hugging, kissing | 18.9% |
| Have sex, but do not enjoy it as much | 13.2% |
| Avoid partner physically | 11.0% |
| Have sex only to please partner | 5.0% |
| No answer | 1.8% |

Just about half the men in our sample reported having intercourse during their partners' menstrual periods, although only about one-third have no loss of enjoyment. More educated men reported that they enjoyed sex just as much: 35 percent of postgraduate men, 28 percent of high school graduates, and 24 percent of lesser educated men. There was a wide gap between men under 40 and over, the younger men (38 percent under 30 and 36 percent in their thirties) reporting equal enjoyment more often than the middle-aged (23 percent between 40 and 54) and the elderly (20 percent). Black men were not as likely to enjoy relations during menstruation as white men (24 percent versus 32 percent).

Men over 55 tended to avoid a menstruating partner completely in 27 percent of cases, far more than the 15 percent of middle-aged men giving this answer, the 9 percent in their thirties and 5 percent under 30. Education was also a big factor: 21 percent of men with less than high school degrees avoided their partners physically, compared with 14 percent of high school graduates and 9 percent of college graduates.

Married men were the least likely (29 percent) to experience equal enjoyment and most likely (13 percent) to avoid physical contact entirely. This seems to be a reflection of age (51 percent of our married men were over 40, as opposed to 39 percent of our entire sample being over 40) more than any other factor. Any other speculation we might advance, such as having a partner readily available for intercourse at a more aesthetic time, is contradicted by our finding that those living with a partner, unmarried, were least concerned with menstruation (45 percent enjoy sex as much) and least likely to avoid their partner (4 percent). The living-togethers were generally young (61 percent under 30) and obviously liberal in their thinking. Single men (27 percent) were most likely to engage in sex play other than intercourse, since the partner possibly might not be available one to five days later.

Many women do not desire intercourse during their menstrual periods and therefore do not mind if their mates are temporarily turned off. (When a feminist group opened a women's bank in New York, the running chauvinist joke was that it would fail because the night deposit vault would be closed five nights a month.) Some women, however, are more sexually aroused and desirous of sexual relations during their periods. As we have seen, more educated men not only engage in relations during periods, but also they suffer no loss of enjoyment. According to popular myth, the less educated man, the coarse laborer or drifter, is reputed to be a desirable sexual animal, always eager, potent, and uninhibited; however, our study shows throughout that highly educated men use more variety of lovemaking techniques and have fewer hang-ups. Ignorance may cause men to shy away from the menstruating woman, believing that she will suffer pain or injury if intercourse is attempted. After all, with the exception of childbirth, menstruation is the only occasion of bleeding that is not indicative of injury or illness.

Some men may have their old castration anxiety aroused. Seeing blood all over their prized organs, even though they know its origin, may unnerve them considerably, and quite a few may be unable to emerge bloody, but unbowed.

The insertion of a diaphragm can ensure a bloodless encounter, and then even oral sex is perfectly feasible, since the external genitalia, including the vagina, don't bleed; the vagina only pools the blood from the uterus. Clitoral stimulation is usually thought of as involving hands or tongues, but the erect penis makes a fine "dildo": the woman can hold it and stimulate her own clitoris, simultaneously stimulating her man. By taking things into her own hands, not only the menstruating woman, but any partner, can control the pressure, location, and amount of stimulation without excluding her partner from pleasure or participation. If more women brought themselves to orgasm during foreplay in this manner, more would probably achieve subsequent climax during intercourse as well, having once reached the required plateau phase of swelling of the mouth of the vagina.

Menstruation has always been one of woman's secrets and, if she wants an uninterrupted sex life, she must help her man accept it more as a harmless part of nature and less as a bloody mystery.

# Shameful Areas

An attractive 22-year-old first-year medical student looks at her male partner across the cadaver they are sharing and asks studiously, "Is the female urethra anterior or posterior to the vagina?" Her male partner, who has been poring over atlas illustrations, dutifully answers her query after giving her the sort of look you give an anatomy student who asks you to differentiate between the olecranon process and the gluteus maximus; forever afterward, he will marvel how women can enter adulthood without any awareness of the construction of body parts outside their line of vision.

Not that the average man is that much more knowledgeable, of course. As a young child, the female genitals were more a void than an entity—a lack of a penis, with not much to compensate for the loss, as if anything could! Once he is informed there is an opening there, the boy equates the vagina with some new form of anus, equally taboo and dirty. Some men never outgrow the child's images of mutilation and excretory organs. One homosexual patient cynically described the vagina as "a hatchet wound." Others regard the whole area between the female thighs as a muddle of discharges and excretory products, a mammalian cloaca.

Feminists are quick to point out that female animals are more advanced on the evolutionary scale and, therefore, biologically superior to males because they have complete separation of their genital and excretory systems. According to this viewpoint, we find on the bottom rung of the evolutionary ladder birds, amphibians and reptiles who have cloacas (from the Latin term for "sewers") which receive the waste products of kidneys and bowels, as well as sperm or ova. (We'll ignore more primitive creatures such as the clam, who is not only bisexual, but has its rectum overlying its heart. Feminists ignore it, too, except when liberating it from its shell.) Next come male animals of all mammalian species, which pass urine and sperm through the same channel. At the top of the heap are female animals, fortunate enough to have separate tracts and orifices for urinary, sexual, and digestive functions. Male chauvinist pigs (see rung two) may argue that if biological superiority is based on the number of orifices, the sponge would be king of the beasts, but at least the feminist line of argument does tend to make both sexes a little more aware of basic anatomy.

As we have seen, many men complain of body odors (not necessarily sexual ones) and avoid intercourse during menstrual periods. So, for the woman who enjoys cunnilingus, there is often doubt in her mind about her partner's true feelings. How many men do it? Do they enjoy it, or do they engage only to receive fellatio in return or to please their partner?

*Question 30: How do you feel about stimulating a woman's sexual organs with your mouth?*

| | |
|---|---|
| Enjoy it | 54.5% |
| Don't mind it, but do it mostly to please the woman | 22.5% |
| Don't do it | 15.1% |
| Think it's unnatural | 4.8% |
| Find it boring or unpleasant | 2.9% |
| No answer | 0.9% |

Adding the percentages of those who enjoy it, don't mind it and find it unpleasant, we get a figure of 80 percent of men who do engage in cunnilingus. We assume that those who think it's unnatural do not engage or seldom do so.

Age is an important determining factor: 34 percent of men over 55 said they don't do it; among men aged 40–54, 20 percent didn't have cunnilingus, and the percentage dropped to 10 for men in their thirties and 9 for those under 30. Similarly, 15 percent of men in the oldest group thought oral sex was "unnatural," compared with 6 percent of the middle-aged and about 2 percent of men under 40.

Thirty-three percent of blacks said they did not do it, versus 14 percent of white males. If we consider those who thought the act unnatural to be nonparticipants, we find approximately 82 percent of white men employ cunnilingus, but only 57 percent of blacks.

Single men, perhaps because of their youth, engage in cunnilingus more frequently than married men; about 84 percent versus 77 percent. The living-togethers, having the advantages of youth and intimacy, reported that 90 percent practiced cunnilingus, only 0.7 percent finding it unpleasant or boring.

About 69 percent of men who did not complete high school practice cunnilingus, against 74 percent of high school graduates and 84 percent of college graduates (based again on adding responses of "enjoy it," "to please the woman," and "find it boring or unpleasant.")

If we compare our findings to those of Kinsey's 1948 study, it is apparent how much more accepted and practiced cunnilingus has become in just one generation:

Users of Cunnilingus

| | Kinsey ('48) | Hunt ('72) | Our Study |
|---|---|---|---|
| High school males | 15% | 56% | 74% |
| College males | 45% | 66% | 84% |
| White males | — | 63% | 82% |
| Black males | — | 49% | 57% |

Kinsey's figures are based on males who said they had *ever* used cunnilingus; Hunt's on whether it had been used in the last 12 months. Our study considers as users any man who did not report abstaining or thinking it's unnatural. Kinsey's and Hunt's figures are for married men only; ours are for all men.

Hunt added that 80 percent of married couples under the age of 35 were using cunnilingus and among couples under 25, 90 percent were using it. Our study, less than a decade later, agrees with these rising percentages.

For the woman who enjoy cunnilingus, we can assure her that, far from being an exotic variation practiced by few or some sort of special service, it is fast approaching intercourse itself as a universal sexual outlet. More important, we have learned that less than 3 percent of the men who practice it find it boring or unpleasant, so she need never feel that her mate is being imposed upon to perform some onerous chore.

While fellatio is usually not practiced to orgasm by couples wishing to follow oral sex with intercourse, we believe cunnilingus as foreplay should generally continue to orgasm. The more experience in attaining orgasm that a woman has, the more easily she will be able to have orgasms during intercourse. Some women feel so drained after an orgasm that they may not desire one during foreplay, especially if they routinely reach climax during intercourse; each couple can find their own optimal pattern without becoming too preoccupied with performance and orgasm tallies. Still, it is generally better to err on the side of too many orgasms than too few.

Far from being a turn-off for men, cunnilingus can be a potent turn-on for both partners. Because of the direct, gentle-but-intense clitoral stimulation received, even women who have difficulty reaching orgasm through intercourse have easily attained climaxes through this activity. And, since most men find it truly enjoyable, it is, like Portia's "quality of mercy," an act that truly blesses both giver and receiver.

# Can Love Survive?

He beheld
A vision, and adored the thing he saw.
Arabian fiction never filled the world
With half the wonders that were wrought for him.

—WILLIAM WORDSWORTH,
"Vaudracour in Love"

The 16-page index for Kinsey's 804-page work, *Sexual Behavior in the Human Male*, does not include "love" as an entry. In the index for Hunt's *Sexual Behavior in the 1970's*, "L" is for "lesbianism," "D.H. Lawrence," and *"Last Tango in Paris,"* but not for "love." Helen Singer Kaplan notes at the end of her 524-page *The New Sex Therapy*, "Upon reviewing this book on sexuality, I am struck with the conspicuous absence of the word *love*. And yet, love is the most important ingredient in lovemaking." Dr. Kaplan then proceeds to conclude her book with a half-page discussion of love.

As Charlie Brown, who is fast becoming the last sane spokesman for our society, once observed, "You not only can't explain love ... actually, you can't even talk about it." It has become the ultimate four-letter word.

Since this book is about sexuality, not just sex, we set our sights on what Shakespeare described as "the star to every wandering bark, whose worth's unknown, although his height be taken," hoping to learn about love's worth in a world where sexual gratification seems so highly prized.

Do men want love most of all from women, or primarily sex? Or are there other things even more important?

*Essay Question: What do you think men want most from women—sex, a good homelife, companionship, love? What is most important to men?*

Theodore Rubin says that even the most realistic of men are generally incurable romantics who feel that love is the universal antidote. Along with many other experts, he also claims that men avoid expressions of love because they do not want to seem vulnerable, even to themselves.

In the answers that follow, we noted that while men chose love over sex as what they want most from women, even more men spoke of companionship and homelife as their prime desires. In some replies, and rightly so, one really could not distinguish between companionship, love and homelife, but the ideas seemed to come not from "incurable romantics," as Dr. Rubin contends men to be, but from practical men who placed compatability over romance. Also, we failed to find Rubin's alleged denial of vulnerability in our men, for they spoke very frankly about having needs and did not seem at all inclined to hide their vulnerability. They wanted most of all a companion with whom they could be honest, so that she would accept a man with all his inadequacies and foibles.

We have already seen in Chapter Two that men today want their women to be open and uninhibited in their sexual activities, rather than playing the role of a pursued, reserved object of desire. In Chapter Four, we noted that many men today find women to be better companions, and welcome the increased education and independence that have made possible the acceptance of women as true equals. If the liberation of women has enabled them to abandon the old roles in which they were passive, sexually repressed, and dependent, men have been freed from the equally onerous role of the one who bears sole responsibility for all major decisions, who initiates all sexual activity, and must answer for the fulfillment of his partner's sexual drives and her life satisfaction in general. In Chapters Nine and Ten, men likewise indicated that sincerity was sought in a potential wife far more than sexiness, and that they would marry far more often for companionship than for regular sex or even a homelife and children.

In their answers here, we find a frank acknowledgment of modern man's need for empathetic companionship, and his hopes of finding it in the modern woman:

"Mainly, I prefer a companion who I can get along with, who wants to be with me, who makes me want to be with her. Sex is important, but so is intelligent conversation and an interesting everyday life. Fights and hot tempers turn me off—that's the reason I'm divorced; that, and an indifferent attitude on my ex-wife's part toward sex. Criticism is okay, but constant nit-picking isn't good for anyone's ego. I've heard, as I'm sure you have, that a woman should be an excellent hostess in the living room, a good cook in the kitchen, a very efficient maid, a fantastic baby-sitter, and a harlot in the bedroom. True, to some extent, but she needs to try to understand her man, to help him be what she wants—so many times a man can really blow it because the woman didn't tell him, talk to him. A woman who isn't afraid to speak up is a good woman. The most fantastic time I had was with a woman who literally picked me up in a bar, and we proceeded to spend the next seven months together. She broke it off, and I counted it a good experience." (This extensive reply came from an army sergeant in his thirties, currently living alone. He felt love was good, though one could live a full life without it, considered monogamous marriage the ideal sex life, and would marry primarily for a homelife and children.)

"Men, in general, need that sense of security that female companionship can provide. Sex is a basic physical need but love is a necessity in every man's life, not all the time but at times to make him feel needed."

"Most men probably want companionship and intimacy which involve sex and good communication. Dishonesty or incomplete giving are not wanted."

"To me, companionship is most important. To be friends, lovers and 'buddies' at the same time would be ideal."

"More or less a confidante—a person to share joys and responsibilities with. A melding of the personalities."

"Understanding and tolerance for one's quirks and being able to establish an 'open' relationship, really feeling and knowing how the other half feels."

"A good companion, who understands him, and his needs. A person who's a good lover yet has the understanding of a mother."

"What's important is someone that will support me, emotionally, someone to get up for in the morning."

"Age up to 21 or 20, sex. After that, love. After that, companionship and love."

"An equal relationship with another person."

"The ideal wife is a lover, a friend, a wife and most important, her own woman."

The men who placed love first did not seem to be overly idealistic about it, nor did they disregard other aspects of relationships:

"Love is most important because if you have love, you have all the other aspects falling into their respective positions. None of the other aspects can exist without it except sex. You can have good sex without love."

"I think most men want to be in love with one woman and want to be sure she truly loves him."

"Sex is important but being happy at home is the most important thing. You have to have love to be happy."

"Men want love and a good sex life. They also want a woman who relates to their needs and frustrations but must also be intellectually stimulating to keep the mind alive."

"Gentleness, affection—a source of moderation for man's intensity."

"I don't think that any one factor is most important. Love is important but there wouldn't be much love if there was a lack of sex or a good homelife. I'm not sure that man can be satisfied with one woman. Something dies in a marriage after a while and I'm not sure that anything can be done to prevent it."

"All those men have a big image to live up to but are basically vulnerable so we need extra affection sometimes."

Oliver Wendell Holmes wrote, "Where we love is home," and some of our respondents believed that a man's fondest desire lay in a good home:

"I believe most older men want a good homelife and most younger men want sex from a woman. I believe a good homelife is most important; it makes for a more stable person in being able to cope with the adverse things in life."

"Men want most to be secure. This means emotionally and financially. From this very strong position they can build on to other things they personally aspire to. Sex, homelife, love, etc., all enter into this security, home in the forefront though."

"Sex is very important—but to have a good homelife it takes a combination of love, companionship, and good sex. I doubt if you could have good sex for a long period of time without a good homelife."

"A home that's clean, comfortable—with little friction or fighting among husband and wife. A clean healthy sex life is also important."

"A good homelife, one where a man doesn't have to look any further than his house for a good time."

"Everything above but if a woman acts too whorish and doesn't take care home can be a real turn off."

A very few men said that sex is what men want most from women:

"I think men want a good sex life and companionship from women. The most important thing is good sex—you can find companionship from almost anyone."

"Right now I'm just looking for an occasional piece of ass. I think a lot of it depends on age and future expectations."

"Men, expecting from women a good homelife, and love. But, SEX is *very* important, too. NO ICEBOX partner. *NO* AVOID-ING contact as many women do." This respondent, who signed himself "Gus, the Greek," added, under the heading, "The Ideal Woman," "Four things a woman should know: (1) How to look like a girl. (2) How to act like a lady. (3) How to think like a man. (4) How to work like a dog."

# Is Being in Love Still In?

Men have told us they want women as companions and that they want a homelife, but will they be in love with their partners? Do they want to be? Do men even believe in love anymore or is it an old-fashioned idea, one that is meaningless in our sexually liberated era?

*Question 31: How do you feel about being in love?*

| | |
|---|---|
| It's the most important thing in life | 38.4% |
| It's good, but one can live a full life without it | 25.2% |
| If you're in love sex is better | 21.5% |
| Love is necessary for good sex | 8.9% |
| Sex is better without love to complicate it | 3.3% |
| Love is an old-fashioned idea | 3.0% |
| No answer | 1.5% |

Over one-third of all the men believed that love is the most important thing in life and another 30 percent said love made sex better or was essential for good sex. Only 6 percent felt either that love was an outdated idea or that sex was better without love.

More white men (39 percent) felt that love was most important than did non-whites (31 percent). Education and occupational status made little difference.

We also asked an essay question on the subject of love to ascertain how men defined love and its place in their lives:

*Essay Question: How do you feel about being in love? Do you prefer to be in love with your sexual partners, how important is love in your life, and what does love mean to you?*

While not many volunteered that they considered love the most important thing in life, the answers of the majority made it difficult to imagine anything of comparable importance:

"Being in love is the greatest. Being in love with sex partner is the only way and the best. Love is very important in life. Love means contentment, good sex life and marriage."

"I am an unquestionable romantic. If we live only to acquire pleasures—material ones and others—the hollowness of life is soon apparent. We are here to love and to share—the purpose of life is lost without it."

tant as you grow older, men over 55 said this only 20 percent of the time. The less educated man was less willing to forgo love—22 percent of men who did not complete high school versus 27 percent of college graduates.

Very few men, in answering the essay question, actually said that they "could live without it." Maybe we should have offered a less negatively worded answer for those who felt love was important, but not the most important thing. The second most positive choice we offered was either "if you're in love, sex is better," and the even stronger "love is necessary for good sex." While a substantial number of men did select these responses—about a third overall—some men did feel, apparently, that uncomplicated sexual desire was a part of life, neither better nor worse than sex with a loved one. Love, to some, could be good without being indispensable:

"Take it or leave it, unless sexual compatibility is present. Not necessary to be in love. Love of home, children and life important. Love to me is for the young at heart."

"Love is important if you find the right one. It is not necessary to love your sexual partners but you should feel a lot for them. Love is important if you are planning a family."

"Love to me is very conducive to stable relationships. However, one must keep in mind there is a profound difference between sex-love and mind-love. Ideal or balanced love is one in which a median is established between the two types of love. Unfortunately in many cases, sex-love is prevalent, simply because of the selfishness of our bodies!"

"I love my wife but I constantly lust for other women and hope to get an opportunity with them. Not all of them, of course." (This answer came from the South, but it was from a blue-collar worker in his thirties. We did get one response from Plains, Georgia, but his wasn't it.)

For every man who felt sex was better without love to complicate it, there were 10 who felt love was essential for good sex or, at least, improved sex. Even the divorced/widowed, who were most likely to feel one can live a full life without love, said 25 percent of the time that sex was better if you're in love. If Don Juan regarded his advances as "the outcome of a perfectly simple impulse of my manhood towards her womanhood," most men are not content with such a simplistic approach:

"I believe love is recognizing the integrity of another person and wishing to share life together—to grow. I prefer to be in love with my partner but also enjoy outside affairs in which I enjoy but don't love the other."

"Love means a lot during sex. I feel guilty—in fact, abstain if not involved."

"Love: a difficult word to define; it's more than 'chemistry'—yet 'chemistry' has to be present. Sex without love is not much more than masturbation. I guess love is involvement, commitment—really caring about the other person's total well-being. And vice versa."

"Without love sex is meaningless. Love means that your partner's needs and wants are equal to or more important than your own."

"I prefer to be in love with my sexual partner. Love means not having to be alone."

Some men have known love, and lost it:

"This probably seems to be a very evasive answer; however, I am 33 years old and was married for 11 years and for one-third of my life was a very happy person with a wife who was just as happy. Three months ago, my wife was killed in an automobile accident and since then there has been an emptiness that I never knew existed. I experienced a love for 11 years that many people never reach in a lifetime, so being truly in love and having that love returned was the most important thing in my life. A person doesn't have to love his sexual partner but when true love exists, the sexual experience is a much more meaningful experience. I hope that I have answered your question."

Other men doubt whether they will ever find it:

"Love is important, but as I consider it a rare jewel, I must just have to be content with the 'appearance' that sex can give."

"As in the song, 'Love Hurts,' I've been burnt too many times by what I thought was mutual love, when it turned out the girls in question 'liked me as a friend.' I readily accept their 'friendship,' but am still searching and waiting, overpatiently, for love."

Only 3.3 percent of our respondents said that sex is better without love to complicate it. White males only held this opinion in 3 percent of cases, but 7 percent of blacks expressed it, and 10 percent of other races. However, 12 percent of nonwhites said that love is necessary for good sex, more than the 9 percent of whites. White males therefore had a more moderate attitude, though 22 percent of them felt sex is better when people are in love. Only 3 percent of college graduates preferred their sex uncomplicated, compared with 5 percent from the least educated group.

A small minority of men wrote that they preferred not to be in love, while a few others wanted to be in love with only one partner:

"Being in love is good for some people but I do not prefer to be in love with my sexual partner. . . . What love means to me is heartaches and pains. I feel all men and women should have sexual relationship before they are married, but I prefer staying single and have sexual relationship with different women who are attractive, clean and have a nice personality until I am 50 years old."

"Yes, I enjoy love in all its stages but prefer sex in the discovery stage of love. As love matures, the sexual excitement wanes because familiarity loosens the adventurous feelings and excitement of sex."

"Love is a very important component of life. I do not prefer to be in love with but a small percentage of my sexual partners because it would be very saddening to stop a relationship or affair. Love means security to me."

"Should be in love with your partner but not with the outside sexual partners."

"It is a very important aspect in regards to marriage. Love is the last thread that will hold a shaky relationship together—and is the frosting on the cake with a good marriage. Love is not an essential element of sex. It is a healthy aspect of everyday life —someone who cares."

"Love does not mean being bound by restrictions.—Love with

sexual partner isn't that important, as long as mutual satisfaction is reached."

"I like being in love—but after a while I feel smothered.—I'm not sure I can handle it. I do not need or necessarily prefer to be in love with a sexual partner—to me, love is two people giving their all to each other but at the same time each has his own space/interests—hobbies, etc. Love is sharing everything —experience—troubles—work with each other and helping that other person cope and understand life. Love does not have to be permanent."

Only 3.0 percent of our sample said that love is an old-fashioned idea. Married people (2 percent) expressed this idea least often, while the divorced/widowed were most disillusioned (5 percent). More highly educated men were less cynical—only 2 percent of postgraduate men thought love was old-fashioned, compared with 4 percent of high school graduates and 5 percent with lesser educations. And 4 percent of blue-collar workers and the retired/unemployed were down on love, compared with 2 percent of professional men.

Age made no statistical difference in those who rejected the concept of love, though some respondents thought so:

"In speaking in terms of love, I believe this would be more in line with a younger person than myself. I could have affairs with the opposite sex without being in love, as long as I was attracted to that person. Also, love to me means procreation; young, vibrant idealistic youth would be more receptive to thoughts of love, family, and children. I believe there are many different views of love at different ages of life."

"As an older person, compatibility and common interests rate higher than what we called love."

"Love means less and less the older I get."

"Love is not important to me. It's a business partnership that I want with respect for each other's need and desires."

"Waste of time.—No, not very important as far as a love affair is concerned.—I love my children and my family, not necessarily my wife."

"Love hurts people and makes people jealous and do things stupid. You can't live with it and can't live completely without it."

"It's a farce!"

"This final question is the crux of the questionnaire.—You talk love.—You talk sex. Each one can survive without the other. Amen, eggheads—it's your problem, not mine—you do not need my help."

## What Is This Thing Called Love?

As the uncooperative gentleman above observed, we may indeed be at the crux of our study. If you want to read men's opinions on sex, go to a newsstand, put down $1.50, and you'll get your fill of exploits and fantasies—maybe not from the average man, but at least you also get a few cartoons, jokes, and, if your taste so runs, photos of women in positions that will remind other women to get their annual Pap smear. But nowhere do you find men talking about love, and there are far more men who think sex is better with love than without it. So, we let our respondents ramble on here for several extra pages. The voices of our 4,066 men have been weaving in and out of our text like a Greek chorus, and now we kept them stage center, listening in the wings and trying to learn something.

The experts certainly don't agree about what love is. One professor of sociology, after pointing out that the latest edition of the American College Dictionary contained 14 definitions of love, wrote that most of the social scientists who study the phenomenon of romantic love would describe as its three components a strong emotional attachment toward a person of the opposite sex; the tendency to think of this person in an idealized manner; and a pronounced physical attraction. A psychiatrist in rebuttal, contended that the professor was discussing infatuation, not love, and that mature love is a state of being where the satisfaction or security of another person becomes as significant as one's own.

Now, looking at the responses of our sample, it is apparent that virtually all the men agreed with the psychiatrist's definition of love, even though our question asked about being "in love," a term sometimes equated with strong emotional attachments and idealization. The men spoke of commitment, sharing, overcoming problems together, meeting each other's needs, and empathizing with each other's feelings. They made it sound more like work than fun—and it was what they wanted.

Men are goal-directed creatures. They like to see their educations, their jobs, even their pastimes, leading to some sort of goal or purpose. It was a man who said of drawn games, "A tie is like kissing your sister." They regard the natural world in teleological terms—everything designed for a purpose. Ask a man why a giraffe has a long neck and he'll invariably reply, "So he can eat the leaves off trees." A more correct answer would be that the long neck is determined by the giraffe's genetic makeup at conception; perhaps short-necked giraffes died off more quickly because they could not compete for food, but the length of the neck was originally a random—not goal-directed—phenomenon.

Men expect their sex lives, like giraffes' necks, to have some sort of purpose, too. Turn a man loose in a sexually liberated society and tell him he has nothing to do but enjoy himself, and he is likely, instead, to make up some sort of a contest, such as how many women he can engage, how many acts he can perform, or how well he can perform. There are some psychologists who frown on the concept of love; one wrote an article in *Psychology Today* several years ago entitled "This Thing Called Love Is Pathological." This particular expert has more recently commented that the unmarried and elderly are more preoccupied with love than the young married, and, feeling that romanticism waxes when sexual activity is on the wane, advocates still greater sexual freedom as the "cure."

While unimpeded pursuit of pleasure may be the philosophy of the new sexual revolution, it is not, by any means, a new philosophy. The ancient Greek practitioners, called Hedonists, emphasized finding pleasure in sensual satisfaction. As Rollo May points out, hedonists of that and later eras found their way of life strangely unsatisfying, and one of the early leaders, Hegesias, became so despairing and pessimistic that his lectures in Alexandria were banned because they resulted in so many suicides. Yet, every few decades, someone rediscovers hedonism, like a square wheel.

If men were ruled by their penises, more would probably be hedonists. A penis is very capable of pleasure and incapable of thinking things through. And, indeed, the penis often does seem to hold sway, leading the rest of the man into situations his brain tells him to stay out of. However, once gratified the penis becomes virtually nonexistent; it isn't even susceptible, for a while, to further stimulation. This leaves the cool, methodical brain in command, sitting in the dark, saying, "What the hell did it all mean?"

Our survey has shown that only one man in three thinks love is the most important thing in the world, and only one in five considers sex the most important pleasure; therefore, men will integrate both love and sex into an overall plan for their lives that harnesses these powerful forces into servicing their long-term goals for career and personal satisfaction. To tell a man to give free rein to his passions would be like telling a farmer to let his horses out of the corral—the horses would love it, but it would be hell on the crops.

If a woman wants to win a man's love, she must be part of the blueprint that guides the development of his entire life, providing him not merely with an enticing sexual partner, but with a serious, concerned helpmate, ready to share and give. She must reject the bestial images of the ever-aroused Priapus or the unicorn with one shaft rigidly emerging from its head (even Rabelais could not accept this, and averred that the horn usually dangled down like a turkey-cock's comb, standing erect when the unicorn wished to put it to use). In a more innocent era, when sexual intimacy was a hard-won distant goal instead of the prologue to a relationship, man often put his problem-solving head in partnership with his recalcitrant horn, pursuing the coy lady with all his resources, she defending with all of hers, so that, regardless of the outcome, both parties finally knew each other as full people. Now the unicorn is again a myth, for the head, as the new impotence confirms, is apart from the horn and regards sensual pleasures as bringing it farther from, not closer to, its dreams.

## The New Romanticism

In reading the comments of our subjects on love, some people might say that these men are not romantic at all. Of course, there are almost as many definitions of "romance" as there are for "love," but romantic notions are generally considered to be those that are emotional, sentimental, idealized often to the point of impracticality, and involve an overestimation of the beloved. The men of today do not seem to incorporate physical longings and acts into their definition of love—in fact, many pointed out that love and sex were two entirely different things. One might argue that partnership and love are also two different things, but today's man envisions a mutual devotion, a placing of the partner's needs above one's own, and even a derivation of the meaning and purpose of life from this relationship that are as idealistic in scope of potential gratification as were Don Juan's visions of trodding the plains of heaven with his deathless, ageless creature of coral and ivory. In bygone years, by the time men realized their dreams of physical intimacy, they were already enmeshed in a partnership of empathy and sharing. Now, having bypassed the whole phase of infatuation with a woman's physical potentials, their dreams focus on a state of interpersonal intimacy.

The woman who wishes to be loved can no longer rely on the subtle sexual messages conveyed by meticulous grooming, sensuous body language, and the proper air of mystery. Sex, to paraphrase Shaw, has become no more inspiring than a plate of muffins—you don't get tired of muffins, but you don't find inspiration in them, either. She must project the image of being the reliable, empathetic sort of person who can share something more than the commonplace sexual partner.

The sexual realm, once the dwelling place of romantic ideals, is now inhabited by such mundane considerations as "My place or yours?" and "Do you have protection?" The ideals have moved a step beyond and take refuge, ironically, in the traditionally practical realm of long-term relationships. Romantic ideals and life practicalities make strange bedfellows, but perhaps the fruit of their stormy union is that elusive thing we have come to call "love."

# The Woman He Loves

In courtesy I'd have her chiefly learned;
Hearts are not had as a gift but hearts are earned
By those that are not entirely beautiful . . .

—WILLIAM BUTLER YEATS,
"A Prayer for My Daughter"

In George Orwell's "Hilda," the main character laments: "Well, Hilda and I were married, and right from the start it was a flop. Why did you marry her? you say. But why did you marry yours? These things happen to us." Today, marriage is becoming less a thing that "happens" to men. Neither men nor women are under as much pressure to marry early as they used to be. Unmarried men no longer have to limit their sexual partners to either prostitutes or women they have promised to marry. Single women no longer have to regard marriage as their only option in life, and, perhaps more important, their only respectable way of getting away from their parents. Historian John Demos has estimated that from one-third to one-half of the 18th-century Puritan brides went to the altar pregnant, and there is no reason to assume that, before abortion reform two centuries later, women were any less puritanical; now the shotgun marriage has become as obsolete as the blunderbuss.

Maybe we're jumping the gun here in discussing marriage before we've finished discussing love, but since it is now very easy to have what was once called a "love affair" without being in love, we are virtually compelled to define love in terms of a commitment—either marriage or something close to it regarding exclusive feelings for one partner. Women can no longer barter sex for such a commitment; the only commodity one can get in exchange for sex these days is usually sex.

If a woman wants to earn the love of a man, with or without marriage, what is he likely to want in return?

*Question 32: What type of woman would you most want for a long-term relationship?*

| | |
|---|---|
| A woman with a concern for my needs | 28.4% |
| A sincere woman | 23.0% |
| An affectionate woman | 20.8% |
| An intelligent woman | 16.1% |
| A self-confident woman | 12.2% |
| A sexy woman | 11.1% |
| A woman with a good sense of humor | 10.3% |
| No answer | 0.8% |

We were not surprised that sexiness ranked so far down the list, but we did not expect men to confront their own needs so openly. We think of men behaving like Professor Henry Higgins confronting Eliza Doolittle with "I can do without anybody. I have my own soul; my own spark of divine fire," adding only grudgingly, "I have grown accustomed to your voice and appearance. I like them, rather." Yet, in the play *Pygmalion,* where the author tells us Eliza does not marry Higgins, his parting words to her are unheeded instructions to order some food and buy some clothes for him; in the musical adaptation, *My Fair Lady,* where Lerner and Loewe imply they will marry, Higgins's curtain line is "Eliza? Where the devil are my slippers?"

Lerner adds in the final stage directions: "*(There are tears in* ELIZA'S *eyes. She understands.)*" It is precisely because Eliza understands that Higgins's dependency needs are so great only a true mother could meet them that she does *not* marry him in *Pygmalion.* Lerner and Loewe circumvented the problem to give the musical a conventional happy ending by writing Higgins's mother, a strong character in *Pygmalion,* virtually out of the script. Shaw had thus written a drama about the Oedipal complex in 1912, seven years after Freud's *Three Essays on the Theory of Sexuality* and four years before Freud's *Introductory Lectures to Psychoanalysis.*

Unlike Higgins, the average man acknowledges his needs today and, rather than demanding a woman fill them, requests at least a genuine concern. Men in their twenties and thirties (30 and 31 percent, respectively) were more apt to confront their needs than men in their middle years (27 percent) and those over 55 (22 percent), who may be still under the older Victorian dictates of male self-sufficiency.

We also asked a question about what men sought in a marital partner. Their answers here elucidated the qualities they considered desirable in the question above about long-term relationships:

*Essay Question: What do you think men look for in choosing a wife? What qualities did you, or would you, look for? What's most important—brains, looks, sincerity, being a good home-maker, a good mother—and why?*

Although more than one-quarter of the men specified in the multi-ple-choice question above that they would most want a woman with a concern for their needs, only a few men, in answering this essay question, spoke directly of having needs or wanting security. While they were not averse to acknowledging this desire when confronted with it, they were not inclined to speak directly of dependency or insecurity, probably because such feelings are regarded by our soci-ety as unmasculine. They were able to find expression of these trou-blesome issues in more indirect ways, although a handful spoke with-out reservation about their need for care:

"I like a woman who understands my needs and someone who is faithful."

"A woman who fits his needs and adjusts to his moods. Treats him nice. Looks, sincerity, good mother, it is just as important to me."

"Too many choose bodies. Personality, good looks most impor-tant—caring—good mother—reason: want children—both chil-dren and myself need caring and affection."

"Centering her life around caring for me."

"Can't comment on what others looked for. I wanted and got a fantastic person—who cares and shares."

There were many more men, however, who stressed the importance of communication. Before a woman can fulfill a man's needs, she must understand him, and this requires communication. In accord-ance with their regard for companionship, our men indicated a de-sire to give as well as receive. They understood that needs were common to both men and women, and gave answers such as those below rather than replies which would have stressed a unilateral concern with their own wants:

"I look for a real companion who can stand equally with me. One who asks no more than is willing to give."

"Most important to me is having similar interests and being able to communicate. Intelligence is required for meaningful communication. Looks are definitely a plus, but common interests and ability to communicate are most important."

"Someone who I could understand, who could understand me, who had same religious feelings, mature, honest and complementary character. Loved children and being a mother."

"Probably intelligence, compassion and sensitivity—ability to communicate awareness and an inner strength—(not dependent)—at the same time I prefer a woman who appears attractive within certain limits. Difficult to maintain friend-lover when the woman is not physically attractive to me."

"I looked for and found a woman who is intelligent, nice looking and I can discuss anything and come to some positive understanding of life."

It has been stated often in books by psychological experts that men have been bombarded since birth with demands that they be strong, invulnerable, and totally independent. Well, they obviously haven't bought it. Even in our question on communications where we asked what they thought women didn't understand about men, many of our subjects replied that women did not appreciate how much men needed them. Rather than echoing Professor Higgins's empty boast that he did not need anyone, they endorsed his more honest earlier confession to Eliza: "Independence? That's middle-class blasphemy. We are all dependent on one another, every soul of us on earth."

The second most popular choice was "a sincere woman," with 23 percent. Men do not want a woman who is a mystery to them, or one who will manipulate or deceive them. Life is too complex for men as it is without facing psychological warfare on the homefront.

The battle of the sexes is a cliché, and there's more truth than fiction in it. Men grow up with a basic distrust of women. In the course of normal psychological development, the five-year-old boy gives up his desire for total dependency on and exclusive possession of his mother, and throws his allegiance to his father, henceforth becoming a man and all that is opposite to women. In the years before puberty, he chooses his friends among other boys, excluding

girls and their pastimes from his world and professing a dutiful loath-
ing for them, according to the preadolescent code. When sexual
pressures in adolescence force him to modify his prejudices, the
truce is a precarious one. He seeks to impress girls with a virility and
bravado he does not really feel; and they, in turn, hide their secrets
from him, acutely fearing rejection. In the world of the "singles," the
deception continues; he maintaining a facade of achievements un-
realized and confidence unexperienced, while she constructs a mask
from cosmetics, clothing, and accessories, trying to portray the right
blend of virtue and sensuality, and soon not even sure what the needs
she has been liberated to fulfill really are.

The sexual revolution hasn't made it any easier. Whereas teen-
agers and even couples in their early twenties once had the opportunity for many friends of the opposite sex without sexual involvement
—since intercourse was tacitly understood to be reserved for those
with a commitment, however unstable, to marry—anyone today is a
potential sex partner, and the asexual buddies of yesteryear have
been replaced by sexual bodies with no prior swapping of military
secrets between male and female camps.

Perhaps it is this topsy-turvy inversion of the old order that has led
men to value sincerity and companionship from a woman—in earlier
life, they've rarely experienced it. Our competitive society tends to
offer the working man a field of male rivals rather than a host of
friends. And so, a man finally turns for companionship and understanding to one special woman, she who is sensitive and devoted
enough to show some concern for him.

As Tarzan might say, "Jane, it's a goddamn jungle out there." We
find in the modern male, not the boorish ape-man that some psychologists would have us believe to be the inevitable product of the
macho mystique, but an embattled man searching for an ally, a female counterpart to the Mark Antony promised by Caesar to Cleopatra—"brisk and fresh, strong and young, hoping in the morning,
fighting in the day, and revelling in the evening."

Sincerity was often cited as the most important quality in a wife
by our respondents, and often figured prominently in the answers of
others:

"Sincerity is the most important; if a person makes mistakes,
fails at something or has faults, they can easily be forgiven if the
person is sincerely trying."

"Sincerity because being sincere would make her truthful and
loving."

"Sincerity and a good mother. Being sincere is knowing she loves you and understands you."

"Someone who will be a good mother to their children and who you'll always be able to communicate with. Someone who is charming, nice-looking, and whose company I enjoy both in and out of bed. Sincerity is most important quality, since if sincere, will be good homemaker and good mother."

"I would look for a woman who would be sincere and be able to trust her when I wasn't around. Intelligence is important also."

"A virgin who is pretty and quiet. The most important is being sincere and a good mother (to the kids she is going to have to raise) while the man is at a bar with some chick!" (This was a middle-aged married professional man, whose main reason for getting married was a homelife and children; yes, he had cheated with many different women, apparently during periods of separation.)

It is not surprising that "an affectionate woman" would also rank high among men's preferences in a long-term partner, as it did with a 21 percent response. Affection connotes a genuine liking and respect for someone, which is freely demonstrated. It is distinctly different from passion and would proceed naturally from sincerity and a concern for someone's needs. Don Juan speaks for all men when he confesses:

> It was not love for Woman that delivered me into her hands; it was fatigue, exhaustion. When I was a child, and bruised my head against a stone, I ran to the nearest woman and cried away my pain against her apron. When I grew up, and bruised my soul against the brutalities and stupidities with which I had to strive, I did again just what I had done as a child.

If this sounds like a lot of men are seeking mothering, that's true. But if mothering means sincere concern, attempting to meet needs, and warm affection, we are describing basic human needs of both men and women, and possessing such needs is not a sign of immaturity, but of humanity.

One very successful psychiatrist-author once told his female readers that the secret to winning a man's love was to feed him milk—straight, or in the form of ice cream, custard, etc. His literary career seems to be on the wane, and this piece of fatuous advice, so solemnly pronounced, did not help any; but though milk is dispensable, displays of affection like mother used to make are not. Incidentally, note in the men's answers above how sincerity and motherhood were often equated.

In listing the most important qualities to be sought in a wife, men concentrated on what would make *them* love a woman, but some did mention or imply reciprocal affection:

> "One he can love for a lifetime. A good mother. If she is a good mother, she also is a good wife and loves you also."

> "I know most important to me is someone with whom I can grow emotionally and who 'turns me on' (cute, cuddly, etc.)."

> "Health, brains, ability to make money (good job). Loving."

> "Sex/good looks are the main attraction but after that wears off affection and ability to make a happy home are most important."

America has loved Lucy for decades—and, thanks to syndicated reruns, probably will for generations to come. Lucille Ball went from being an obscure, beautiful showgirl to a millionaire producer by portraying a wife so inept that she always wound up with custard pie on her face. Similarly, Mary Tyler Moore found success by playing a career girl who managed to let her neuroses and inadequacies get her into weekly scrapes that could be resolved in half an hour, less commercial time. Her costars who played females even more disorganized—Valerie ("Rhoda") Harper, Cloris ("Phyllis") Leachman and motherly Nancy Walker—were rewarded with their own shows, all under the aegis of M.T.M. Productions, whose mewing kitten matched the prestige of the M.G.M. lion it unthreateningly emulated. Male comedians have always included masters of sharp, aggressive wit—Don Rickles, Bob Hope, Jack E. Leonard, Jack Carter, and George Burns. Females are portrayed either as dumb, like Gracie Allen, Martha Raye or Jean ("Edith Bunker") Stapleton, or pseudoneurotic and self-denigrating, like Joan Rivers and Phyllis Diller. Even some of our most glamorous stars were made less formidable by being typecast in "beautiful-but-dumb" roles: Jean Harlow, Marilyn Monroe, Barbara Eden, Tina Louise and Marie Wilson (who, for the trivia buffs, virtually started the trend with her movie-radio-television portrayal of "My Friend Irma"). The subtle message to the women of America was that success came to women who were beautiful, cute, funny, even dumb—but don't ever be smart.

Now, happy to relate, more men (16 percent) most value an intelligent woman than they do a sexy woman (11 percent). This was not true of men who did not go beyond high school, but there was an emphatic preference in college-educated men; and those who went on to graduate school even made an intelligent woman their second choice (24 percent), exceeded only by a woman with concern for their needs.

Concern for needs is fine, but though Lucy Ricardo was always trying to be a helpful wife, her scatterbrained approach brought her husband Ricky more bane than boon. And TV's Major Nelson even had a beautiful genie willing to serve his every whim, only her wits had less candlepower than her lamp. Brainless women may get high Nielsen ratings, but as prospective marital partners, few would survive a 13-week season, as some of our men attested:

> "Brains are probably the most important (although looks sure help). Nobody wants a stupid or flaky wife, but it is important that the woman isn't so smart that she looks down on me or is always correcting me in the things I do."

> "I like a woman to have a level head; not necessarily brainy but commonsensical. Of course, she'd have to be sincere and preferably nice-looking. If we have children I'd definitely expect her to be a good mother as I would try to be a good father; *love* is the basic thing to all this, though."

> "A woman they are attracted to physically. Someone with enough brains that when the physical cools down I could talk to her."

> "Brains; pleasant to look at (not ravishing!); expresses her opinions, even though they are different from my own; good conversationalist."

> "Brains and sincerity—I'm an intellectual fool."

> "Good looks, sincerity. Brains. If she has brains, she then would or should know her place."

Younger men (15 percent of our youngest group compared with 6.5 percent of the oldest) and the more educated (15 percent of college graduates, twice as many as high-school-educated) particularly valued the self-confident woman.

Remember that old TV line, "Round 'em up and head 'em out"?

It was the theme line from a western, "Rawhide." Often an unmarried woman will come into therapy because she is unable to establish successful relationships with men. She has been in a hectic pattern of trying to circulate, meeting as many people as possible, and self-analyzing her interpersonal approaches. Start talking to this woman about herself, rather than about the people she has been seeing, and it becomes apparent to both of you that she lacks a firm idea of who she is, what she wants, and where she's going. In developing her own qualities, she must be introduced to the "Rawhide" principle of therapy, and round up her assets before she heads 'em out. She should stop racing around long enough to pull her act together, to really think about herself, to firm up her center. Sure, she wants men to respond to her as a person, but how can they if she herself doesn't know who that person is? She doesn't have to be extremely accomplished, brilliant, or physically stunning, but she does have to be unique in order for a man to be able to set her apart from the herd. A woman has to convey the attitude that she is different and worth knowing. She should pull together all her strong and interesting points, head them out confidently as a unit, and she'll be as irresistible as a stampede. Self-confidence and the ability to think independently were praised by many of our men:

"A woman who knows who she is and has accepted that. Looks are of some value. . . . Being able to relate to me. Similar interests and drives in many areas. Desire to grow as a person."

"Someone who is aware of their position in life. Most often, though, men want someone to take care of them. I look for someone who is independent."

"Companionship and a solution to alienation and loneliness. All of these qualities including the freedom for her to develop her own interests and direction for self-fulfillment.—Want to marry a mentally healthy partner and would want her to want me in the same way."

"A sense of an intelligent active zest for life—a person who can think for herself with an open mind.—I do prefer a homebody type (not too much)—and I think a lot of men do. Also, a touch of class."

"I think men look for attractive women with ambitions to get along in the world."

"I like most an intelligent woman who is self-assured and independent most of the time. Lack of these is the biggest turn-
off."

"A woman who is warm, understanding and a free spirit. Brains
and sincerity and being a good mother hold a family together."

One out of ten men considered a sense of humor the most important
thing in a long-term relationship. Women are, in general, notoriously
poor joke-tellers. Almost every joke has a butt and is an expression
of hostility. Women are not good joke-tellers because they have been
conditioned to repress open displays of aggression and hostility.
Comediennes, as we mentioned, always direct the hostility back at
themselves, appearing dumb or ineffectual. Wit, as opposed to self-
directed humor, is aimed at others and, like shaving someone with
a straight razor, cutting too deeply can produce hurt and anger,
rather than the desired smooth results.

Men want a woman with a sense of *humor,* not wit. This ensures
that when the relationship is buffeted by something he does that is
inept, ill-advised, or childish, she will not react with anger or distress.
The woman does not have to make herself the butt of the situation,
but neither does she put down the man. The relationship becomes
momentarily comic, but never endangered—the underlying
strength of the union allows the woman to smile at minor mishaps.
Private jokes between a couple must play to the man's strength. A
pair of briefs marked "Home of the Whopper" is funny; a can of
spray-starch at the bedside is not. It's far safer to exaggerate playfully
a man's success in business or in bed than to call attention to his
shortcomings. Joking also allows a couple to fight constructively.
Humor lets them confront their own shortcomings, express aggression, and retreat to an "only-fooling" stance if things get too hot.

Some men felt that sexiness was important in a lifetime partner.
Those subgroups that rated this quality higher than the 11 percent
overall average included blacks (20 percent, twice the number as
whites) and men who had not completed high school, the latter (15
percent) ranking sexiness above intelligence, self-confidence, and a
sense of humor. Sexiness was least important to men who had completed college (8 percent).

Men pointed out that looks and sex appeal were invariably the
initial attraction, and could not be easily discounted:

"A sincere, devoted, understanding woman with good sense
and kind of foxy-looking. Sincerity, good homemaker and good

mother. She must keep up her looks to keep the man stimulated."

"I think that there must first be a physical attraction followed
by an emotional attachment. When it comes to marriage, I
think that an intelligent, self-confident yet sexy and loving
woman is best."

"Smart—good-looking—good sex—NO KIDS."

While there were a number of men who mentioned good looks as a
concern, no one ranked exceptional beauty as a major prerequisite
for a wife. Sexiness encompasses physical appearance and we did not
feel it was necessary to offer beauty as a distinct choice in the objective question about the type of woman most wanted for a long-term
relationship. From the low priority given sexiness in this question
and the secondary consideration accorded to looks in the essay question, we were right in presuming that men would choose a woman
on a basis other than outstanding appearance. In the chapter on
dream girls and other fantasies (Chapter Twelve), our respondents
will discuss further their conceptions of the physical and psychological attributes of the ideal woman.

In sum, the oldest men ranked sincerity and affection slightly
above concern for their needs, and rated self-confidence lowest; this
may be a reflection of old attitudes about male self-sufficiency and
female dependence. Blacks rated sexiness over sincerity, but concern for needs and affection topped their list. Intelligence was valued
second only to concern for needs among those with postgraduate
education, and students ranked it number three, ahead of affection.
Otherwise, the top three were consistent in all subgroups: concern
for needs, sincerity, and affection.

Virtually all women today desire a long-term relationship. Yet they
give the man the exact opposite of what he wants; they gratify his
passions instead of his needs. He, fearing he will be considered a little
boy, accepts the sexual relationship he is subtly offered, for it would
be unmanly to prefer anything else. Women have been led to believe
that, because men today have a variety of potential sexual partners,
they avoid commitment and sincere relationships. As our study has
shown, men still desire marriage as the ideal state, do not think
highly of endless casual affairs, and have never really accepted the
concept of recreational sex for women whom they care about, as we
shall discuss in the next chapter.

# Arms and the Man

While our survey indicates that men value affection more than sex in marriage, the prevailing myth holds that most married men shun displays of affection and that men in general are interested in hugging and kissing only as a prelude to intercourse. One therapist estimates that most of the wives who come to him complain of a lack of romantic expression from their husbands, and another therapist even prescribed six-second daily hugs from one husband, because it was enough 6 P.M. contact to hold the wife until bedtime. Of course, people do not go to therapists unless they have a problem, and it is difficult to gauge how widespread the problem of undemonstrative men really is.

We can see how men have been conditioned against hugging and kissing. While little girls are encouraged to kiss and cuddle, boys are steered into more restricted behavior, such as handshakes. In the preteen years, boys are expected to react with jeers of derision whenever a couple on a movie screen starts grappling with one another instead of with a deadlier adversary. With the discovery of necking, the adolescent boy briefly revises his views, but only until his competitive nature takes the upper hand. Dan Greenburg's nostalgic *Scoring* bore a cover picture of a girl in a prom dress, with targets superimposed on her lips and breasts; the lips were marked "50" and the breasts each "100." Now even a high school senior can shoot for "200" zones.

You couldn't really blame men if they felt hugging and kissing were for kids, not for grown males. But do they feel that way?

*Question 33: How do you feel about hugging and kissing without it leading to sexual intercourse?*

| | |
|---|---|
| Enjoy it, even without sex | 59.1% |
| I have a real need for it | 12.3% |
| It's a routine way of expressing love | 10.9% |
| Find it frustrating unless sex follows | 10.5% |
| I do it mostly to please a woman | 4.8% |
| I rarely do it | 3.2% |
| No answer | 0.2% |

A total of 71 percent find hugging and kissing enjoyable even without subsequent intercourse. Only 19 percent found it frustrating or personally unsatisfying and 11 percent accepted it as a routine sign of affection.

Men over 55 were more likely than those of other ages to regard it as a routine practice or to engage rarely, yet also had the highest percentage (16 percent) who claimed a real need for it. Single men most often reported it to be enjoyable even without subsequent sex (64 percent), but were not as likely as men who were living with or divorced from regular partners to profess a real need for it. Only 44 percent of nonwhites said they enjoyed hugging and kissing even without sex, compared with 61 percent of white males. And 20 percent of black males said they found it frustrating unless sex follows, exactly twice the percentage of white males.

We also asked men to tell us whether there were times when they would like to be hugged and kissed, without it leading to intercourse.

*Essay Question: Under what circumstances would you like to be hugged and kissed without it leading to intercourse? Do you find hugging childish or unmanly, or is it something you crave at times?*

Many men pointed out that hugging and kissing could elicit strongly positive, though not typically sexual, feelings:

"Hugging and kissing under an umbrella, standing in a grassy park in a mild spring rain. It is a different kind of intimate relationship—perhaps more romantic—a feeling of being close/caring without strong sexual connotations.—I do crave this at times, and find it a natural act—not childish/only human."

"I am very physical and utilize contact as a harmless and honest way of expression. I find it very healthy and think too many people are hung up on physical contact."

"Just after having a fight with my wife or when I am feeling low and I need to have her companionship and love. I think hugging is great. It gives me a warm, close feeling."

"I wish I could do it more, because I find there is a need from my wife for us to hug often. I don't consider it childish or unmanly to do it, after all if *it helps my wife it helps me* and I do crave it at times."

"I've very often felt the need to be hugged and touched, but not sexually. Just to smell a woman's hair and feel her breasts against my chest and her breathing on my shoulder makes me feel very happy. Hugging and kissing will also sometimes turn me off. A girl last summer whom I was very open with sexually, we tried various different positions, even out of doors and all sorts of things with enemas, oral sex, etc. I still didn't feel like hugging and kissing her all the time. Hugging is usually an emotional—as opposed to sexual—need and certainly not unmanly although male emotions are played down in the U.S."

Some spoke of hugging and kissing from a variety of different people, not just mates:

"Among close friends and family—sign of affection, open and truthful feelings. There is a need for it in order to communicate properly, to express emotional sensations."

"I think a relationship is very important. It doesn't have to end with intercourse. Someone loving who cares is more important. I enjoy being hugged and kissed any time by a woman who is sincere."

"I love to hug. It's an emotional outlet to show joy to a woman or a man. There is nothing immature about it. Everyone needs warmth whether they admit it or not."

"We all need it—an occasional embrace is good even by men to men."

A few men spoke of actually craving such signs of affection:

"Any circumstance would be just about all right 'cause I really dig hugging and necking. I crave it many times, especially when I'm alone."

"I enjoy being hugged. I crave it at times. Mostly, I crave it to bolster my trust and love."

"When it was not possible to have intercourse. Yes, I crave it sometimes because it's nice to have someone close to you hugging back."

"I am very affectionate and like to be hugged and kissed many times almost anytime but not too crowded places. Something I crave all the time."

There were men who still related the issue of hugging and kissing to sex in some way:

> "I find hugging and kissing to be a great starting point for any new relationship, and it's also an easy lead-in to foreplay and intercourse. I find hugging especially comforting after intercourse, when I can rest my head on my partner's breasts."

> "If I realize that the woman I am with is interested in sex (not turned off) but just doesn't feel ready. Then I hug and kiss."

> "If I did not need satisfaction, I would still like to hug and kiss. Also, I like just being close for a long period before sex. I don't feel it unmanly, and only childish if the woman is."

> "During period we just hug and kiss with a blow job for cause hell, I'm not having *my* period. Hug and kissing is good."

Less than one in 20 insisted that hugging and kissing always lead to intercourse or expressed some negative sentiment:

> "Don't necessarily enjoy hugging; kissing is passé. [It is] not my cup of tea, the ABC's of sex are not hugging, kissing, and intercourse."

> "Find it frustrating. Do it only to support a woman needing support and/or affection."

> "When my wife and I have just experienced something thrilling together. Do not like kissing just for sake of kissing. Feel hugging more expressive than kissing."

> "I usually want hugging and kissing to end with fucking."

> "Do not have desire anymore."

> "I think it's disgusting!"

Moods mentioned by our subjects as leading to a desire to be hugged and kissed were "When I'm blue. . . . when something has happened to me that hurts emotionally . . . needing a 'stroke' . . . when I am down in the dumps about something . . . feeling lonely or depressed . . . particularly when I'm tired . . . when upset . . . case of sickness or pain . . . a need for security and affection, a feeling of being needed

. . . when I am down after a particularly frustrating day at work . . . anytime I feel strong emotions toward her."

Occasions deemed suitable for hugging and kissing were "Welcomes, goodbyes . . . after a business trip, going away . . . celebrations or just being together . . . during friendly gatherings . . . when out on the town and celebrating . . . during menstrual period . . . nonpublic circumstances, not at work . . . after a victory of some sort or perhaps a bitter tragedy . . . only leaving to work, going in and out the door . . . when time is limited, no privacy . . . winning a prize . . . anytime she feels like it . . . promotion or raise . . . when out socially, or after a hard day at the office . . . when greeting and leaving and whenever I feel like it . . . just when my partner wants to say, 'I love you' . . . when there is not enough time for intercourse . . . when wife is unable to respond sexually . . . as part of everyday affection . . . when we are in a place or situation where intercourse is not possible . . . when just messing around . . . when you already been to bed and you are leaving."

People considered appropriate to hug and kiss were "Someone I trust . . . a fairly well-known friend . . . personal friend that does not provoke me sexually . . . any friend for hugging, any women friends for both . . . by my mother . . . by my father . . . sister, mother, or daughter . . . when my buddy Jack comes to town."

It seems apparent from our subjects' responses that men do enjoy hugging and kissing, but that they associate it with an emotional state or experience. They do not engage in it routinely as women tend to, probably because as children extensive physical displays of affection were socially discouraged and ritual kissing of relatives was imposed as an unemotional duty. Adolescent hugging and kissing was passionate or strategically designed to increase passion, never routine.

Women often complain that men are unromantic because they do not routinely give embraces and kisses; but, if a man is feeling calm, contented, and secure, he lacks the emotional excitement at that moment to feel like displaying affection. A woman can motivate him to more frequent physical demonstrations of affection by reaching out to him when he is feeling something—a positive spurt, such as follows victory, success, gain, or recreation, or a low mood, following disappointment, loss, frustration, or fatigue. Men's embraces are generally less frequent than women's, but they are also more spontaneous. Setting a quick change in mood with a gesture of concern, such as bringing him a pillow or a drink, will make him more receptive and demonstrative than if he is in a steady state, emotionally speaking.

One other common complaint from women is that they often have a craving for body contact without sex, but that men always want to proceed to intercourse. Women without direct genital stimulation rarely get all that aroused, whereas erections are fairly easy to provoke in men. Maybe it's his goal-directed thinking again, but give a man an erection and he wants to do something with it. Instead of enjoying the mild exhilaration that early stages of arousal bring, he sees himself at the first station on a familiar route and feels almost obligated to go the rest of the way. It's not hopeless, however; we have seen how men, over the span of one generation, have eschewed rapid orgasm for prolonged intercourse as much to enjoy the pleasurable tension as to please their partners. Unless a man is chronically frustrated from ever reaching orgasm, an erection that never reaches the anticlimactic stage will cause him no distress.

A woman can help condition her man to accepting hugging and kissing as extracoital activity by initiating it when he seems to need it most in a nonsexual way—when he is dejected, tired, or frustrated. Men are least likely to respond sexually at such times and most likely to experience it as a gesture of tenderness and comfort, such as he received from his mother and other solicitous adults when he was a child. Most men do not seem to have much difficulty accepting affection without sex and remaining free of feelings of childishness. Nor should such affection be regarded as purely nonsexual, for the sexual realm encompasses a myriad of experiences, not only those directly related to intercourse. We learn sex as adults, but love as children; regressing to recapture the security that sustained us in our early years is often needed to replenish our capacity to give love as adults.

Being held is the first comfort we receive as infants coming into a cold, threatening world. Throughout our lives, the embrace remains a source of solace and strength, if we only reach out for it.

## Falling Out

If men feel a true need for affection, it would follow that the loss of someone they cared for would affect them deeply. Yet our culture tends to portray women as getting the worst of it when a love affair ends. The torch singers, the soap opera ingenues, and the paperback heroines taking a nonfatal underdose vividly exemplify the devastating effects on a woman when her man is gone. But who could imagine Robert Redford or John Wayne sobbing over a romance gone sour? At best, they might slug down an extra belt at the bar and maybe ask the piano player to render something sad before they sauntered back out into the night.

Ben was nearly 21 when he came into therapy because he was

feeling "uptight and kind of confused." He was having shortness of breath at times, headaches, and his family doctor had detected a moderately elevated blood pressure. In spite of his youth, Ben was already making a good living working on the commodities exchange and supplementing his income with knowledgeable investments. Ben had become engaged a month ago to a girl he had dated steadily for about a year.

Everything seemed to be going well in his life. Ben came to therapy, however, because he had experienced symptoms like the present ones only once before, less than two years previously. He had finally seen a psychiatrist, who related Ben's symptoms to a deteriorating relationship with a girl he had been dating two years. With almost formal syllogistic reasoning, Ben now concluded: "The only time I felt this way before, it was because I was having problems with my girl friend and I wanted to break up. I am having these symptoms now. Therefore there must be a problem with my fiancée." It was only at the end of the first therapy session that Ben mentioned he had called off an engagement party scheduled originally for the subsequent week. Within six months, Ben's symptoms, the engagement, and his therapy were over.

Ben was trying to break an engagement, but was also mourning the loss this would entail; his head was in such a muddle that he would awaken in the morning not knowing for a moment where he was— yet he went on about his business casually until his body rebelled under the suppressed tension. Are most men so out of touch with their feelings? Do they pop up like a kid's bop-bag or the toy "weebles" that wobble but don't fall down? Or are male hearts no more shockproof and shatterproof than female models?

*Question 34: How would you feel when a love affair ends?*

| | |
|---|---|
| A little sad, but adjust easily | 37.3% |
| Quite hurt, avoid women for a while | 21.5% |
| Quite hurt, but quickly seek a new woman | 19.8% |
| Indifferent | 9.5% |
| So depressed my work suffers | 6.0% |
| No answer | 4.6% |
| Close to a mental breakdown | 2.3% |

Bearing in mind that we specified "love affair," and would expect even more drastic responses in the case of a divorce, about 30 percent of the men said they would be so hurt that they would avoid women for a while, that their work would suffer, or that they would be close to a mental breakdown. Over 2 percent said they would be "close to a mental breakdown," a state that we tend to think men practically never approach as a consequence of disappointment in love. About three out of eight felt they would adjust easily and another one in ten claimed they would be indifferent. We can therefore say that more than half of all men would be significantly hurt by the breakup of a romance, though over a third of this group would try to find a new partner quickly.

Men in the youngest age group (26 percent) would most tend to avoid women for a while, as would those who had never been married (28 percent). Men living with a partner, unmarried, said more often (10 percent) than any other group that their work would suffer; divorced/widowed men were next frequent (9 percent) in implicating their work performance.

Five percent of the men who had not completed high school said they would be close to a mental breakdown, more than twice as many as the more educated men. And 4 percent of black men and a staggering 9 percent of "other races" said they would be close to a mental breakdown, compared with 2 percent of whites—although 13 percent of blacks and 18 percent of other races said they would be "indifferent," compared with 9 percent of whites.

We asked men to write about their likely feelings if a love affair broke up, particularly how it would affect various areas of their lives:

*Essay Question: How would you be likely to feel if a love affair of yours broke up? How would it affect your feelings, your work performance, your sex life, and your relationship with women?*

In response to this question more than any other, men shared their particular personal experiences with us:

"Having had a couple of love affairs break up, I am only to comment on my own problems at 'readjustment.' As far as my work performance has been affected, if anything, my work has improved—perhaps due to some form of compensation on my part. As for my relationship with women, I do not hold the entire female sex responsible for an inability for one particular woman and myself being unable to form a more permanent relationship. I do tend to be rather depressed at the termination of a love affair, but I think that depression is anger directed at myself. As for my sex life, if I do happen to meet a potential mate soon after a breakup, I am not one to stand in the way of progress. On the other hand, I do not actively seek out mates for a period of three to four months after a breakup."

"Having been married more than once and having lived with a woman from the time I was 17, each breakup caused different trauma. Sometimes work was affected but normally I replaced a woman with another quickly as I know my own needs and enjoy having a woman care for me."

"When I was younger I was married and really in love, my wife really kicked me in the teeth. I really was broken up. Now if it happened, it would be just another day. Go on to next woman."

"I remain friends with every woman I have ever had a love affair with (except two). Adjustment to new circumstances is just an adjustment, not a trauma."

"It did—it destroyed my feelings—my performance—my sex life—even to the point of impotency—but I still have high hopes because all women are not alike—because through some-one nice I'm getting a new slant on life.—There are still some nice domestic people still left in this world—thank God for that. —Nothing is nicer than a good woman."

"The first broken love affair was devastating emotionally. For a long (two years) time I felt inadequate in all those areas. Now I think I could handle another breakup."

"I've usually been fairly shattered for about a month, but there's also a terrific sense of relief. Breaking up is one of the best parts of getting together."

Some men expected to be sad if they were to have a breakup, but knew their depression would be short-lived:

"A casual affair—not too much disappointment. Someone I loved—would probably affect me totally, but only temporarily. Life is short, and there's not much time to be spent in despair."

"Sad, but optimistic. If it broke up, there was a reason. I feel that things would be better in the future. It would not affect my work but I might be in a state of shock for a while and would take a little time to date again, and get in the swing."

"I would probably be depressed for a short time and I would fall back to relationships with other women who understood me as a friend—in other words—an easy comfortable relationship—

where—my security could be reinforced. My work performance would not be affected—on the contrary—more of my energy would be spent on my work."

A substantial minority claimed they would be philosophical or indifferent:

"Natural progression of a relationship between two people. I hope I would learn from each relationship I would have and have had with each woman to better prepare me for the next fabulous relationship."

"It would all depend on my attachment to the woman and our mutual understanding. If a relationship broke up consciously and with understanding, it wouldn't affect me negatively."

"I would feel bad only if I didn't know why, how or when. But —if we didn't get along, weren't compatible, why continue to make two people unhappy?"

"Love affairs are like tides, they ebb and flow, with highs and lows. When the tide goes out, it will always come back."

"Would not affect me at all. I need more experience."

"Would find another girl. I still have my wife to come home to."

But there were many more men who unashamedly confided that a broken love affair would have profound effects on them:

"It would be devastating to me. I don't go halfway with my relationships. With me, it's all or nothing. I could never handle breakups. I can't even stand to lose a friend, even where no sex is involved. Obviously, if I lost a sex partner (who would also be a friend or wife) it would affect all other aspects of my life."

"I would feel like shit. I would mope around for a while, really feeling sorry for myself. My work performance wouldn't change because it is important but my schoolwork would drop because I couldn't concentrate on reading. I would be thinking of her. Most of these feelings I just listed on this questionnaire are if she broke up with me. I wouldn't care the other way around. I would miss her though."

"Empty, as if part of my self died. I would have to gradually rebuild, change my patterns. My relationship with women would not change, and the same with my work. I don't know about my sex life."

"I would feel very lost for a time, I would be resentful and moody. My work performance would probably drop. I feel I would seek out sex relations with other women but try not to get attached."

"Hurt for a while, wouldn't affect my work performance. I'd probably try a lot of one-night stands for a while then get on a level basis before too long and find another chick to soothe my hurt ego."

"It would affect all of these if I looked at my breakup as a failure experience instead of a growth experience. It would be difficult for me not to look at it as a failure."

"If my love affair broke up, a part of me would never be the same. For my love has given an important part of me—a part that may never be the same."

"I believe I am strong enough to rebound.—I would actively take it out on all women—but I would try to learn from previous mistakes."

Other strong responses elicited were "Would go right down the tube for a while . . . it would really tear me up . . . I am goofed up all around . . . Temporarily out of order . . . return to gay life only . . . I'd be a mess . . . would feel a little weird for a while . . . hurt and emotionally wasted for a time . . . certain scars would remain . . . sad—like a part of my life was over."

Unlike many women, men do have more resources to draw on when a love affair ends. More have productive jobs, advanced studies, and a greater range of social opportunities. Men still approach women more freely than vice versa, and can even turn to prostitutes. We have seen that a broken love affair can nevertheless have profound effects on men.

The depth of a man's reaction to a breakup is difficult to predict, even for a psychiatrist.

The phone rang at 4 A.M. on New Year's Day. It was Sandra, long-time girl friend of Jeff, a divorced college professor in his mid-thirties, calling Jeff's psychiatrist to express her concern over his apparently depressed state. He had brought her home from a New Year's Eve party, telling her they were through. The psychiatrist had never spoken to Sandra before, but felt he knew her well after hearing about her for two years. He told her Jeff was sane enough to handle his own life and could make his own calls for help.

Jeff spent his next session describing his discouragement about his unfulfilling relationship with Sandra—and all women. Intoxicated, he had called not only Sandra after the party, but two other girl friends to break off with them as well. "I had my gun out," Jeff confessed. "I even put it to my head."

Had the therapist underestimated Jeff's suicide potential and blundered in handling Sandra's call as a ploy to enlist the therapist in her own cause? In this case, Jeff's well-known obsessive-compulsive traits, even in a state of intoxication, defended him against an impulsive suicide. "Then, I figured," Jeff went on, "that the earliest I could kill myself would be January eighteenth. I had to get my class's final grades in."

# To Form a More
# Perfect Union

... conjugation without domesticity is not marriage
at all, whereas domesticity without conjugation is still
marriage: in fact it is necessarily the actual condition
of all fertile marriages during a great part of their
duration, and of some marriages during the whole of
it.

—GEORGE BERNARD SHAW, *The Revolutionist's
Handbook*

Shaw knew what he was talking about. He said of his wife, Charlotte,
"As man and wife, we found a relation in which sex had no part. It
ended the old gallantries, flirtations and philanderings for both of us.
Even of these it was the ones that were never consummated that left
the longest and kindliest memories."

In clinical practice it is not uncommon to see marriages that have
been celibate for half a dozen years or more; they are usually not
good marriages, but the partners nevertheless remain together. And
while sex is an important aspect of most marriages, it is rarely the
reason that people marry today. St. Paul gave those who wished to
engage in sex a choice: marriage or hell ("But I say to the unmarried
and to widows, it is good for them if they so remain, even as I. But
if they do not have self-control, let them marry, for it is better to
marry than to burn." —First Corinthians, VII: 8–9). Though few
today would consider themselves morally bound to accept this bibli-
cal Hobson's choice, men do still marry. The marriage rate in the
United States in 1975 was exactly the same as in 1905, despite the
dramatic social changes that had gone between. The divorce rate has

242

increased sixfold over those 70 years, but that has served only to provide believers in matrimony with the chance to test their faith again.

As our question below proved, only 17 percent of the men who had never been married and the same percentage of divorced and widowed men do not want to marry. Even those living with a partner, unmarried, usually see marriage in their future, for only 22 percent said they do not want to marry. Thus about four out of five men currently unwed intend to marry or remarry.

But why do men get married? Perhaps they would automatically answer "love." Well, why *besides* love?

*Question 35: What else besides love would be your main reason for getting married?*

| | |
|---|---|
| Companionship | 47.0% |
| Having a homelife | 24.0% |
| Having children | 14.1% |
| Emotional security | 9.3% |
| Regular sex | 7.6% |
| Don't want to marry | 7.4% |
| No answer | 1.4% |

We have previously found in our survey that men prefer women who relate to them as equals in their sexual encounters (Chapter Three), that men want companionship more than anything else from women (Chapter Eight), and that, in seeking a long-term partner, they value sincerity and a concern for male needs above sexiness, intelligence, and self-confidence (Chapter Nine). It therefore is not surprising at this point that men go on to marry primarily for companionship. The comforts of a homelife, the emotional security of one steady partner, and the convenience of a regular sex life are secondary to the sharing of one's life with someone who cares and is cared for.

Jeff, the divorced college professor we spoke of at the end of the previous chapter, is tall, handsome, intelligent, and accomplished; yet he is haunted by a vision of himself becoming "a lonely old man, living in a cramped furnished room, illuminated by a bare overhanging light bulb." Now 33, Jeff has been in therapy nearly four years, and recently started living with Barbara, a fellow faculty member in her mid-twenties. Recently, the nearly-virgin foreign student who was Jeff's first love while he was still in the process of divorce took the boat back to her homeland; Barbara helped her with her luggage. Jeff also wrote a "Dear John" letter to Sandra, the highly responsive divorcée who is still the best sex partner he has ever known. He has phased the madonna and the prostitute out of his life and is working toward a compromise, though it is not easy. He says of Barbara; "I'm trying to survive thirty-three hours and she's asking if in thirty years we'll be sleeping in the same bed." He foresees "sameness, stability, and boredom in marriage"; yet this picture is less foreboding than that terrible bleak image of the lonely old man he might become.

Genesis tells us God created woman because He felt it was not good for man to be alone. Man is a social animal and most men do not tolerate periods of solitude very well. Few people have Jeff's insight to project themselves far into the future and make a conscious effort to overcome, in the present, their resistance to a committed relationship which poses restrictions and infringements in a world where unrestricted sexual pleasure is readily attainable for any fairly accomplished and attractive young man. Yet, even in the nonintrospective man, there soon comes a point when the loneliness he feels after each casual encounter outweighs the transient fulfillment he has just experienced. In a society that does not offer the support of large family clans, the single man soon suffers pangs of alienation and seeks out the solace of a partner and ultimately a family of his own. Man is a territorial animal, not a member of a nomadic herd, and he craves a set of roots that will give some stability and permanence to his life. If he need answer to no one and can move out tomorrow, he has purchased freedom at the cost of alienation, a price too dear for his basic nature.

Thus, companionship was the main reason for getting married given by every subgroup in our sample. The most highly educated men placed the greatest value on having a wife for a companion: 51 percent of college graduates and 52 percent of those with postgraduate education, compared with 43 percent of high school graduates and 42 percent who did not complete high school. Men over 55 valued companionship most (54 percent), while men in their thirties gave it the lowest rating (44 percent) of any age group. Those living with a partner, unmarried, gave companionship the lowest rating (33 percent) of any subgroup, though it would still be their leading reason for marriage. While white males gave companionship a 48 percent response, blacks valued it highest only 35 percent of the time.

We asked men to tell us their feelings about marriage and to list the pros and cons:

*Essay Question: How do you feel about marriage? Do most men want it? Is it becoming old-fashioned or is it as important as ever? What do you think are its advantages and disadvantages?*

John Adams once said that the only two types of creatures in this world worth anything were those with a commitment and those in need of one. In marriage, one often finds both of Adams's requisites in the same partner:

> "Marriage is an enduring commitment. Growth and improvement occur only through work, struggle, and commitment. It is an important aspect of achieving total mature adulthood. Some are not necessarily cut out for marriage. Yes, most men want marriage, but the media increasingly portray marriage in a negative light in hopes of destroying it. . . . Its advantages, love, commitment, sharing, stability, reliance, trust, growth, shelter (emotional), encouragement, far outweigh cultural maneuver towards free sex, clap, no responsibility, unreliability, and selfish self-indulgence."

> "I love marriage—am married.—Most people don't believe it is as important. I do. Advantages—can truly be free and open—can relax, don't always have to try and impress or work at relationship as hard. Great feeling of companionship.—Cannot find any disadvantages."

> "I want to get married—it is very important to me. It is not old-fashioned. . . . Advantage: mutual commitment of partnership to try to work together. Disadvantage: maybe make a bad choice and have to be legally unbound."

> "It is a sacramental union, a religious covenant. Most men want it, whether they are consciously aware of it or not. It is as important as ever. Advantage: it provides a trusting commitment. Disadvantage: trauma if it ends."

> "A good idea if individuals are compatible; most men probably desire it because of the need for companionship. It still is important, but I feel it is an institution that must evolve with a changing society. Advantages—companionship, opportunity to grow, to get outside of one's self. Disadvantage—loss of individual identity (especially women's)."

> "Marriage can be very good. I prefer the two being one (i.e., not one person domineering) concept, that is, both contributing. A lot of marriages seem to be the man working and the woman laying around most of the time."

"Marriage is becoming less important to me. I am happily married now but if I were divorced tomorrow, I wouldn't mind. The biggest advantage is companionship which at times is the biggest disadvantage."

Only 15 percent of unmarried men gave homelife as the main reason for getting married, but 28 percent of married men gave this as their choice. While 19 percent of men in their twenties selected this, the percentage was up to 27 in men 30–54.

"It fits fine on me. Most young men don't want it until they get tired. Important as ever. [Advantage—] knowing where you can call home. [Disadvantage—] don't get out much anymore."

"I want it but after two divorces I want to be more sure. Probably live with woman for six months first. A woman makes home to come home to."

"Most men don't want it. I believe it may be becoming old-fashioned and not as important. The advantage is a good home-life. The disadvantage is all the responsibility."

"Necessary from a legal standpoint if children are present. Advantages—less uncertainty, solider foundation for homemaking, better for children, retains family as a unit. Disadvantages —no family unit, uncertain financial responsibility, less moral."

"You have taught women," says Don Juan, "to value their own youth, health, shapeliness, and refinement above all things. Well, what place have squalling babies and household cares in this exquisite paradise of the senses and emotions?" Don Juan went on to prophesy: "The day is coming when great nations will find their numbers dwindling from census to census . . . ;" and, with the average American couple having a family of less than two children, that prediction has already come to pass. Contraception, sterilization, and abortion reform have made parenthood a true option rather than an inevitability for most couples, and the woman who formerly spent three decades of her life or more in the raising of small children now devotes only about half a dozen years, if that much, to the exclusive care of offspring. Women have more time to pursue careers and self-development, becoming better companions in the process. Men have likewise deemphasized child rearing as a rationale for marriage; indeed, less than 15 percent of our sample mentioned having children as the prime reason for getting married. Men already married wanted them most (15 percent); the divorced/widowed, probably thinking in terms of remarriage, least (10 percent). Blacks (20 percent) seemed more concerned about children than did whites (14 percent).

Some men did mention children as a motivating force for getting married, and a few saw children as the only justification for marriage as an institution:

"I feel that most men at some period in their life want marriage. It's not becoming old-fashioned, but it is changing. I lived with my wife before we were married and I think that experience helped our marriage immeasurably. We married because we deeply loved each other and wanted to add a permanence to our relationship by getting married and having children. It's great. The advantages of marriage are security, sexual companionship, and the proper atmosphere for the rearing of children. The disadvantages are restricting sex to one partner, the danger of emotional hurt made possible by the closeness and knowledge of another's weaknesses brought about by living together daily."

"Marriage requires a lot of sacrifice between both partners, especially if children are involved. The woman sometimes has the feeling of being a house prisoner and becomes frustrated while the man feels trapped by having to support the family; therefore, it is critical that a woman try to retain employment and the man take on additional household responsibility. I think most men try to make themselves think they don't want marriage when actually a good woman is the *only* thing they want."

"I think marriage in itself is important only if children are involved. I think two people who are in love and want to live together should do so (with or without a marriage license). I see no advantages (unless children) and quite a few disadvantages —partners tend to become possessive."

"I believe marriage is very important as the foundation of the family. Persons not wanting a family should *not* marry. Don't know what most men want, but they seem to want a looser morality. As a family foundation, marriage is great. It provides security and, hopefully, an atmosphere of love for children to relate to. Its main disadvantage is that it is too greatly built up and hence becomes a disappointment."

"I would consider marriage only for the sake of children. My faithfulness is given voluntarily, it is not required or controlled by the civil laws."

"Most of my friends and I want marriage eventually, but would like living with someone first. I think most men want a son, like myself. I want the love and companionship of a wife after I'm on my own. She's someone to talk to, but it's a disadvantage when someone else comes along."

Don Juan protested; "Those who talk most about the blessings of marriage and the constancy of its vows are the very people who declare that if the chain were broken and the prisoners left free to choose, the whole social fabric would fly asunder. You cannot have the argument both ways. If the prisoner is happy, why lock him in? If he is not, why pretend he is?" Nevertheless, one man in ten says that the emotional security involved in a marriage is the most desirable asset.

"The cornerstone of our society. Most men do. It's as important as ever. Its disadvantages are the pressures it exerts on members, especially the male head. Its advantage is its serenity, peace with the world, peace with God."

"Marriage is all right for most men, and men do want to be married. Important as ever. Advantages outweigh the disadvantages because men want security and someone they can turn to."

"I like it!—Have for 32 years. Yes [most want it]. It is as important as ever *but* the timing has changed. Marriages forced by social pressure have diminished but most couples still favor marriage when they are ready for children. Advantage—security. Disadvantage—forced responsibility."

"Like it. Yes [most want it], until after a few years of having it, then most men wish they weren't, but they never tell the mate. Depends on the happiness of the marriage, an advantage may be just peace of mind."

"I look forward to marriage as an expression of love. It is old-fashioned only in the sense that it has existed for a long time, but I doubt that it would ever go out of style. The advantages of marriage lie in the area of a more certain knowledge of the continuance of the relationship, e.g., psychological security."

If sexually active married women, though no less self-indulgent than their active single sisters, are considered nevertheless more virtuous, then virtue, one cynic noted, is but the trade unionism of the married. Today, only a small 7.6 percent of men marry chiefly for regular sex, and the number is even smaller among the never married (4.2 percent) and under 30 (5.9 percent). The percentage increases with advancing age, 11 percent of men over 55 giving regular sex as a prime rationale. Twice as many blacks (14 percent) as whites (7 percent) did or would marry for regular sex.

Only a few men mentioned sex in their answers:

"I feel marriage is very important and that sex should be only among married couples. Most men want it but only after playing around and play around afterward. Advantage because you have a *friend*. And should be part of you."

"I love it. Yes [most men want it]. It is as important as ever. Advantage is you always have sex. Disadvantage is what is yours is hers and what is hers is hers."

"I need marriage—love, companionship, emotional security and regular sex. If it's an 'open marriage' there are few disadvantages because each partner has his/her freedom to grow."

"Most men want it for the security it provides for having a mate on which to perform sexual fantasies. A marriage makes it legal and acceptable."

"Necessary for a family. Not necessary if only fucking is wanted. Most men probably do [want marriage]. Just as important for a family. The main advantage is a ready fuck when needed, unless of course the woman's cunt is as cold as my wife's."

What about the men who did not want to get married? Many felt that just living with a woman was the preferred alternative:

"I don't believe in it. I don't think so [that most want marriage]. I think it is becoming unpopular. If you love someone, live with them. A piece of paper is nothing anymore. I think it has little advantages, but many disadvantages when it comes time to part."

"Don't [want marriage]. I think that most men would like to be married but without the holds that come with being married.

More people would be happier loving and living together than married."

"I think marriage is advisable only when a couple has known each other for more than, say, two or three years and has experienced the ups and downs in life together to make sure their relationship will be eternal."

"Eventually I might want marriage, but not until my income, experience, maturity, and attitude are such that I feel ready. I don't think the need for marriage is stressed as much nowadays by society—other alternatives are becoming increasingly accepted."

"I will probably get married in a year. It is a personal decision between the interested people. Marriage for me, however, is mainly a way to keep my family and peers from treating me (and her) as immoral people."

Several men considered marriage too confining or thought a lifelong commitment was not desirable:

"I think marriage is an anachronistic and impractical institution. No one should be bound to another longer than he/she wants to stay since people change over time."

"Most men who have never been married before want it, but few married or divorced men have anything good to say about it. It is too confining—wife starts to act like your boss after a while."

"Very difficult over the long haul. Yes [most want it]. It's as important as ever only because of limited alternatives. Increased life span makes it difficult to spend 40–50 years faithful to one woman."

"Although I enjoy the companionship of a woman frequently, I do not want to share all of my life with one person."

"I feel marriage is a trap in most instances, women sometimes seem to let themselves go physically after marriage—take their husbands for granted. Advantage could be that the relationship is steady."

And there were a few who blamed women's sexual freedom for their own disinterest in marriage:

"I think marriage is worthless because why buy the cow when you get the milk for free, so most guys I know don't want it. Besides, most chicks I know have made marriage a thing of the past."

"Most men want marriage; this day and age however, I do believe it's becoming old-fashioned. I say this because women are more free with their bodies, morals have gone out the window today, and next to dope, sex is the easiest thing for a single man to get."

"I can do without it. I feel that the idea has run its course and more men feel that they will become prisoners with so many women of varying personalities and lifestyles that may be of interest still on the loose."

"Marriage is an outdated social hang-up. Some men want it, some don't. The only advantage I can see in it is wedding presents and income-tax shelter."

Despite this smattering of misogamists, marriage, our survey has shown, is still a viable institution. Although some social observers have proclaimed informal living-together arrangements as the future replacement for marriage, we have seen in Chapter Three that there are more of these living-togethers who feel that the ideal sex life lies within marriage than who are content with their status quo. We also saw that 70 percent of all men viewed marriage, with or without outside partners, as the ideal sex life. Above, 85 percent of all currently unmarried men indicated they would marry eventually. While living together prior to marriage has increased over the past 30 years, we may interpret it as a period of transition between single life and marriage, rather than the final step for most men in the future. Men want a companion, not only to grow old with, but to enjoy life with, and this implies a degree of stability and even permanence to the relationship; anything that threatens that stability, such as outside partners or lack of commitment will ultimately be rejected, as long as companionship remains man's first priority.

# Greener Pastures

Some grass seems greener than others and some men seem happier than others. Do married men usually cast green, envious looks at the singles? Do singles long for the Elysian fields of marriage?

> *Essay Question: If you are married, would you rather be single, and why? If you are single, would you rather be married, and why?*

Of the single men, 56 percent had no immediate desire to be married and were enjoying their current status, and 44 percent were eager to marry. Among married men, 80 percent were happy with their choice of life-style, but one in five wished they were single again.

Reasons that unmarried men gave for wanting to remain single included love of freedom, unwillingness to assume more responsibility, and their present variety of sexual partners:

"I'm single and hope to remain that way. A marriage certificate seems to smother whatever feelings of freedom you might have."

"Single and content. I am too active in my career to assume the responsibilities of married life."

"At the present I'm satisfied with the way I am. Single!! Because I do, go and there is no bitching from nobody. If there is I tell them to go to hell and keep on pushing and doing my thing."

"Once married but became widower. Would *not* remarry. Enjoy variety of sexual partners without involvement or family responsibility."

"No, because that piece of paper seems to take away a lot from a relationship."

"I am single and would rather stay that way for a while. Quick, early marriages can lead to many problems—financial, emotional, with no advantages that cannot be had outside of marriage."

"At the moment, the demands of my career, which is just starting, make marriage a very dubious prospect. I am able to foresee in the future that I would enjoy being married. Presently I am enjoying life and the challenges of my career but I do feel a lack of continual companionship which I hope marriage, sometime in the future, could provide."

"No.—Marriage ruined a beautiful relationship."

"Flat no, maybe when we get a little wiser."

"No. I'm having too much fun with different women."

Nearly half of the single men were ready to abandon their freedom for the companionship, security, and homelife of marriage—and some were tired of the hunt for sexual partners:

"Single now, but will eventually marry, for companionship and maybe emotional stability."

"I'd like to be married because it is said that two can live as cheap as one and there is more fun with two."

"Yes, because I enjoy having company; someone who I can talk to and listen to deep thoughts."

"I'm separated, getting a divorce, and prefer marriage. I like a companionship-type relationship and want a family."

"Would rather be married with companionship and homelife—single life hectic and unsteady."

"Right now, because my sexual life isn't too great, I would like to be married for the sexual aspect of it."

"I would prefer being married because I find looking for some-one a terrible waste of time."

"Would rather be married but like to act single when right opportunities prevail."

"Sometimes yes, sometimes I want to be settled down and with one person in the same place for a while, then again, other times I'm glad I'm single, free to go where I want, but this feeling is decreasing while the other is increasing."

"Yes, I would rather be married because I'm tired of not having anyone around when I feel lonely. Also it gets monotonous—running around just to have something to do."

"I'm single. I would rather be going with a woman that wants to get married someday and that just loves my company and doesn't expect sex all the time."

Four out of five married men definitely would not have it any other way, for a variety of reasons:

"Married. I enjoy being married although I don't think that the institution of marriage is, in itself, necessary in order for two people, in love, to be happy (or to live together). I think that marriage is important only where children are involved (and only because society places too many burdens upon so-called illegitimate children and their parents). My spouse gives me much pleasure, affection and security—things that are important to me. . . . Marriage itself doesn't affect our relationship (in my opinion), all these things would be present regardless of the license we were given when married."

"I have been married for 15 years (to the same person), and while there are times I'd like to be single, they do not outweigh the good times I have with my wife. It is doubtful that I could ever find anyone who would understand me as well as my wife. In other words, I think I shall remain married to present wife."

"I am married and I like it that way. It gives my life a solid continuity that it would lack being single. The only advantage to single is physical and mental variety and I can have that in marriage."

"No. I have a home and family to come home to. Even when I go out, I have a home to come home to."

"Sometimes I have fantasies about dating or just having an affair, but I realize that what I have in a wife is too important for me to throw it away on a fling."

"Married—getting too lazy to be single."

"Would not want to be single, because my wife is as good a sex partner as I could ever find."

"Would rather be married at this age." (45–54)

"I enjoy closeness of marriage—no fear of disease."

"Not single but a more interesting partner would be better."

"Yes, am married. No, don't want to be single, just like to screw around on my old lady." (He'd cheated with one or two others.)

Every dog has his day, and every married man has had his days of bachelorhood—but not all of them had a crack at it in the swinging seventies. Maybe that's why one in five husbands wonders how it would be to live the life of a single today:

"Sometimes I think it would be nice to be single again so I wouldn't have to worry about all the responsibilities. Also be able to do what I want a lot sooner instead of having to wait a few years when I could afford it for the whole family."

"Only would like to be single because I missed the freedom today's society has in sex. Not as inhibited as we were."

"I enjoy the companionship of marriage, but sometimes I long for the freedom (or irresponsibility) of being single again. I suppose that's natural."

"I would much rather live alone; basically solitary and hate the demands for time, attention entailed by cohabitation with roommate of any sex. Married only to reproduce, and will try to stay away from the kids."

"At the moment, single life sounds awful good. My wife is jealous of my success in business and her every word is against me —my company—my position, etc."

"I would rather be single for I do not love my wife."

"Be single again.—Wife too domineering."

"Yes—single much preferred. Married only for children."

"I'm married and I would rather be single to play the field more."

"Would rather be single: this way I don't 'possess' anyone—nor does anyone possess me."

"I am married. I would rather be single because too much of one woman is a man's key to his grave."

"I am married but would rather be single because you don't have to put up with a bunch of bull."

Our study shows that less than one unmarried man in five does not want to marry, but less than half of these bachelors are dissatisfied with single life. It's like going to heaven—everybody wants to get there, but is in no particular hurry about it. Once married—divorce statistics notwithstanding—most men seem, at any given moment, content to stay there; like heaven, the occasional sense of dullness is preferable to the alternative.

## Old Familiar Places

A reader once wrote to Abigail ("Dear Abby") Van Buren asking, "My husband, who has had a heart attack, asked his doctor if he could have sex. The doctor said only with his wife, because he shouldn't get too excited. Was the doctor serious?" Abby consulted with three cardiologists she knew, but could not get a firm consensus. The first said it depended on the man's relationship with his wife, the second said he had heard that joke in medical school 40 years ago, and the third couldn't stop laughing long enough to respond.

Is marital sex less exciting than premarital and extramarital intercourse? Are single men reluctant to give up sexual variety for fear of being bored by monogamy? Are most married men satisfied with their sex lives?

*Essay Question: Do you feel that married sex gets boring and why? If you are single, how do you picture it? If you are married, what's your sex life like—had it become routine or more enjoyable with time, and why? Did you enjoy sex more before you were married?*

There was just about a true 50–50 split among both the single and married men—actually about a 52 to 48 percent edge for those who believed married sex did not get boring. The single men, of course, based their answers on what they imagined marital sex would be like, while the married and formerly married answered from their own experience. The close correlation between the singles' expectations and the marrieds' experiences leads one to suspect that single men who expect to be bored in marriage create a self-fulfilling prophecy.

Many of the single men who thought marital sex would get boring contended that variety of partners was the only effective preventative against ennui, though some felt other forms of variety might fill the need:

"Single. I would imagine if you did anything with the same person long enough it would become boring. I love meeting people and I like learning from other people and experiences that will help me develop mentally and sexually."

"I am single, and I really can't envision what married sex would be like. I imagine it would grow stale, like anything, unless steps were taken to keep it new—different techniques, etc."

"Single person—I would picture it a bit boring for the average couple. It would depend on the interest and imagination and thought both partners put into sex that would determine what happened. Marriage does not make it boring of itself."

"I think married people let themselves get into a rut—married women get too tired and sex gets boring to them."

"I picture married sex as semi-good. I think that sex before marriage would be more pleasant because you know there isn't any tie. Once you're married, the cat and mouse game is over, thus some of the fun."

"I would imagine married sex becomes boring, especially in older age. Maybe it's not really boring as much as it becomes that much less important. Relationships should not be based totally on sex. In older age, the relationship is strong enough anyhow and sex partially fades out of the picture. I don't really know though, as I'm still single."

"Married sex is boring. You think that you have to perform at least once a week."

"Yes, same old stuff. Won't get married."

Those single men who envisioned marital sex as equal to or better than sex before marriage felt that love added a strong dimension or that more open communication could add to new experiences:

"I would imagine sex might become more stimulating both physically and emotionally because you aren't only having sex with wife but also making love, showing love by having sex."

"It must be based on something deeper than only a physical stimulation. If sexual experiences provide an awakening of the inner self of the participant, it cannot become boring."

"Sex like anything gets boring if you don't put your *all* into it! It depends on you and your partner. If you can't dig it, tell her or him."

"As a single, I picture a married sex life as very satisfying provided that there is total openness between partners and variation in sex—or at least a willingness to experiment."

"I picture it as the perfect way for two people to express their love for each other."

"I am single but I picture married sex as very relaxing and for once legal, with no worry about what mom and dad has to say. As being single, I enjoy sex very much."

"No, if you love someone deeply, sex will always be good and different."

Married men with disappointing sex lives blamed partner's lack of responsiveness, various situational pressures, lack of imagination, and quarreling. They seemed more upset about it than the single men who were discussing theoretical disadvantages of marital sex:

"Yes. Sex gets boring if married because there's always something to interfere, and for one reason or another, excuses are too easily given and 'quickies' seem to be the order of the night. Instead of a little variety and more play.—Sex was more enjoyable as time went by at first, but now it's hit an all-time low.— Yes, I did enjoy sex more as a single man!"

"A female generally makes and breaks a man. And sex is as good as the woman involved.—It gets routine after awhile and a wife goes into what she calls a quickie—because she's either tired or has something bother her—food-money or children problems. Marriage goes——."

"Married sex gets boring because one or more of partners are unwilling to try any different locations, procedures or techniques."

"I'm married—and my sex life isn't very lively! It's not even *routine!* There's no way it could get boring. I don't feel all married sex life can be routine—as long as each partner continually and sincerely attempts to satisfy and help meet the needs and desires of the other."

"Yes it does—same old stuff. I never had sex before marriage. Sex became boring for a while until we got into watching porno films and using a vibrator."

"My wife and I haven't been married a year. Our sex life gets boring in the sense she doesn't have orgasms. That leaves me frustrated quite a bit. I enjoyed sex before marriage more than I do now."

"Sex was more fun and spontaneous when my wife was on the pill. Our sexual activity has decreased now that I use condoms. (My wife stopped using the pill because we both decided it was unhealthy for her, i.e., high blood pressure, etc.)"

"It has become more and more routine. I usually have to wait much longer for sex than I would like. My wife has become more cold and frigid since she became pregnant. I try to make her feel wanted sexually, but she feels she is undesirable."

"I do not feel sex would get boring if you are still in love with your partner. My married sex life is at a standstill for I am not in love with my wife. I feel that if you really love someone, sex becomes a part of living that love."

"Sometimes if a wife doesn't try to do different positions and acts, it gets boring. It has become routine, and that is why I go out with many women."

"Yes. Ex-wife got fat. Very enjoyable with friend I am now living with."

"Plain married sex does get boring. I've been having thoughts of swinging."

"Have no sex with wife for past 13 years. But find my sex pleasure with one woman I've been going with for 12 years on the Q.T."

But for every married man who complained about his sex life, there was at least one who was thoroughly satisfied:

"Married and sex life is becoming more diversified and intense. I enjoy experimentation and satisfying spouse in fantasy."

"I'm married—have been for 10 months. My sex life is great. Frequency of intercourse is a little less than before marriage or early marriage but is more enjoyable, more expressive and more loving and unselfish, with less guilt."

"Not boring. My sex life is great. It had become more routine until I learned to experiment. Two years ago I would have said premarital sex was more enjoyable, but not now."

"Married sex, like everything, has its ups and downs but it has become more enjoyable over the years because of a feeling of closeness that wasn't present during sex as a single man."

"Marital sex for me was not boring. Quite the contrary, it became better with time as inhibitions passed and a deeper intimacy set in. Before marriage, the chase became tiring and enjoyment was dampened by tiredness."

"I'm not married but living with a divorced woman with six kids. Love the sex, love the kids, but hate the responsibility."

"Married. Very active, more enjoyable with time due to partner's liberation from childhood programming."

"Married 38 years and sex life is still great."

"Yes, enjoyed sex before marriage. Married sex is not boring with the right wife. If she is a 'whore' in bed and wants to have a good time, it will not be boring."

It is interesting that, while nearly half of the married men who answered these questions found their sex lives partly or totally unsatisfactory, only about one-fifth said they would rather not be married. Responsiveness and innovation appear to be the wife's best insurance for keeping her husband in the sexually satisfied half.

## No Experience Needed

Is it necessary for a woman to minimize the extent of her experience? Don't most men today feel a woman is entitled to the same freedom of sexual enjoyment that a male is? Wouldn't a man even find a highly experienced woman *more* desirable as a wife, since she would be uninhibited and knowledgeable in giving sexual pleasure? Or is the double standard secretly flourishing with its customary double strength?

*Question 36: What sort of sexual experience would you prefer a wife to have had prior to marriage?*

| | |
|---|---|
| It would not matter | 33.5% |
| No other man except yourself | 32.0% |
| One or a few men she really loved | 20.5% |
| A few casual affairs | 11.5% |
| Many men | 2.2% |
| No answer | 1.0% |

One-third of men today still want to marry a virgin—a woman with no previous sexual partners. More significant, in this era where it is supposedly perfectly acceptable for people to engage freely in sex for the sheer enjoyment of it, only 2 percent of men would want to marry a woman who had engaged in relations with many men.

Of course, one-third did say "It would not matter," but such answers remind us of Dan Greenburg's humorous account of the girl who, when offered a drink, says, "Anything." Offered a gin and tonic, she apologetically asks for vodka and tonic, and then Stolichnaya (a Russian import). People who say "It doesn't matter" go with the choice stuff when it's available, and highly experienced women are apparently not considered high-choice.

Older men were much more likely to value virginity in a wife (51 percent), with sharp drop-offs to 38 percent in the 40–54 age bracket and 27 percent in the thirties. Still, one-quarter of men under 30 want an inexperienced woman, as do 24 percent of those never married. Those in a living-together relationship were most liberal; only 14 percent want to wed an inexperienced woman; divorced/- widowed, highest in disclaiming importance of a woman's past (45 percent "would not matter"), gave virginity a 19 percent priority. Married men wanted an inexperienced wife in a higher percentage (38) than any of the groups not currently married.

Virginity was more sought by high school graduates (39 percent) than college graduates (27 percent). No subgroup topped the 3.2 percent of men living with partner, unmarried, in wanting a woman who had experienced many men, except for the men of "other races" with 5.1 percent. Paradoxically, these men gave virginity a stronger vote (38 percent) than either whites or blacks, possibly reflecting the ethnic diversity of the racial subgroup.

Nearly twice as many men would prefer a partner to have been limited to men she truly loved rather than a few casual affairs.

We also explored men's feelings about how much experience a girl friend or wife should have and whether or not a woman should tell a mate about her past:

> *Essay Question: Should a woman tell a man about her past sex life? Do you want a woman to be experienced, and what kind of experience should she have? How much experience would you want a wife to have?*

Most of the men who wanted to know about a woman's past seemed to have a more liberal attitude towards female experience:

> "If I truly love her, the past matters little. By knowing of her past, I understand her better. The extent of her experience is unimportant, so long as she is open-minded and not naïve to the extent that she cannot relax and enjoy our experiences."

> "Yes, depending on the people involved—I would like to know but it depends on what there is to be told. I prefer a nonvirgin because I'd hate to have to teach someone everything."

> "If a woman and a man are close (close enough to marry), then the woman should tell. A woman's experience doesn't change the way I look at her."

> "A woman should be picked very carefully and once picked should be trusted explicitly as being exactly as she represents herself in one's eyes."

Most men said they did not want to hear a detailed account of their partners' past experiences:

"This depends on the man; personally, I could deal with it. I wouldn't want to know a 'blow by blow' *(pun)* account but if she told me, I'd have to accept it as I've had sex before, also. I wouldn't place much emphasis on my wife's experiences unless perhaps she'd been a prostitute. It's normal for her to have had sex with old boy friends. I did, why can't she?"

"I think that a person's past is his or her own affair and they should not have to discuss it with anyone if they desire not to. As for experience or lack of it, I don't think it makes any difference whether they have experience or not. The only problem or complication I would see is if they didn't have experience and didn't want to learn or had a lot of experience and didn't think they could learn more. Also you could run into trouble if the partner had a compulsion against sex (i.e., it's dirty and only to be performed for procreation)."

"No; what is past should remain so. The past could disillusion a man about the woman he loves. Any woman I am involved with now I prefer her to have *some* experience—I don't need the pretense of innocence at my age. If I were to divorce and marry again, my next wife might be more experienced—a divorcée, perhaps."

"A woman probably should *not* tell her lover or husband about her past sex life. It is really unimportant. Whether I am first or not doesn't matter, so long as I am *last*. Her experience with me is all that counts."

"It's none of his damn business. If she doesn't have some sort of experience, she usually has hang-ups or other things wrong with her."

"Theoretically, yes; practically, no. A little deception is good for the soul."

Many men felt that experience in a woman was desirable, and a few even advocated plenty of it:

"Yes, she's as entitled as a man to have a sexual history! A woman with no sexual history and/or no desire is still in or before puberty, mentally, regarding sex and has very little chance to develop if she's as such.—Yes, experience is best—it shows openness and growth. The question should be quality, not quantity, in terms of sexual experience."

"Fine to be experienced in the entire range of human sexuality. A person who hasn't tried about everything would be probably dull. No need to iterate these experiences to spouse."

"I like a woman who has a fairly large amount of sexual experience but one who is not a braggart about it or considers it something special."

"Yes. I think she should have some experience. If you have had a lot more experience than your wife, difficulties may occur in your sex life."

"It all depends on a lot. I personally have no objection to previous experience in my partner. Hell, I might learn something from her."

W. C. Fields once defined a virgin as "A little girl—about four years old—very ugly." If adult virgins are now as mythological as the unicorns they were allegedly once employed to trap, many men, nevertheless, are seeking or previously sought them:

"I sought a woman who had not been engaged in sexual intercourse prior to marriage. I found her."

"It really doesn't concern me what has happened over the years in her sex life, but I would want a virgin."

"I wanted a virgin wife. Both I and my wife were virgins. P.S. Our sex life in marriage has been *extremely* fulfilling, exciting and adventurous."

"No, the more mystery about her, the more interesting she is. I wouldn't want a young, first wife to be experienced, but if it was the second marriage or at an older age, of course, equal experience would be best."

"At this age she should have experience with a former husband, but when I was young, I wanted to be the first."

"Depends upon couple. I think in a wife, I would want a virgin. In a casual sex partner—experience."

"Never! [talk about past] No [experience], none. I'll teach her everything she needs to know. My wife wouldn't have any!"

"No. No. None. You can learn together—it really doesn't require experience. . . . Any normal human would have romantic encounters but I would prefer that it not include intercourse. It results in more closeness and tends to reduce the idea you should try out sex."

"I have had girl friends tell me of past sexual experiences and it has turned me off. Although I like a sex life for myself, I would prefer a woman who has never had any sexual experiences, especially intercourse, with other men. (A bit male chauvinistic.)"

Some men can accept prior sexual experience in a wife only if she loved—or thought at the time she loved—her partners:

"Only if she really wants [to tell]. A little experience couldn't hurt but it's not necessary. I think if she's been in love with a man and been sexually active, it's fine. But only if she's in love."

"I prefer an experienced woman, ideally one who has had one or more sincere, loving relationships rather than a series of 'one-night-stands.' This would also apply to a potential wife."

"My wife was more experienced than I when we met; at times I am jealous when I think of it, but I accept her former partners on the grounds that she was sincere and they were also, else they wouldn't dare show their face—there was love involved."

Even among men who were not opposed to marrying an experienced woman, many qualified their answers by mentioning she should not have been cheap or promiscuous—and there were even references to our old archetypical acquaintance, the prostitute:

"No [telling about past]—most men couldn't stand it. I want a woman that is experienced and not afraid to tell me what she wants.—Wife—not a whore, but would like her to have moderate experience."

"After we have become intimate enough—yes—sex is not easy and talking and exchanging info is very important.—I wouldn't want my wife to be a whore, but I would not prefer a virgin either."

"It's up to her. Doesn't make any difference to me whether or not she's a virgin—if I'm considering marrying her. If our relationship is not leading to marriage, her past is immaterial. It's okay if my wife hasn't had any experience, as long as she's willing to have premarital sex with me. Would not want my wife to have been very promiscuous."

"A person's past should probably be kept private. Experience is not necessary, however, lack of it should not be from prudishness or lack of imagination. Inexperience in youth should be expected and is desirable. With more age, I would expect more experience. Promiscuity is not necessary or desirable."

"I do not mind experience except if it were gained cheaply without emotional attachment."

"I probably wouldn't marry a hooker—but I would expect my wife to have had prior experience."

"It would matter if she had been doing this for a living."

"No [should not tell]. Yes [experienced], but not a fucking whore, unless I really feel she will become a good wife."

## Almost as Good as New

One man, in response to our question about sexual experience for wives, answered honestly, "It's confusing, I would like her to be experienced, but also a virgin. Though, I'm not a virgin; I can't expect to marry one."

This man has essentially summed up the schizophrenic feelings of the majority of today's men. They want an experienced virgin. Many women tried to satisfy this paradox by engaging in premarital intercourse only with the man designated to be their future husband. In 1953 Kinsey found that 36 per cent of women then in their forties had experienced premarital coitus, and he estimated that half of all women ultimately had sexual intercourse before marriage; of Kinsey's women with premarital experience, 53 percent had limited their intercourse to one partner. In the younger half of Hunt's sample, reported in 1972, over two-thirds of the women had premarital experience, yet 51 percent of these still had been involved with only one partner.

Dr. David Reuben advised his readers in 1969: "There is nothing wrong with funsex. Human beings—and for that matter, all mammals—are provided with penis or vagina and an overwhelming compulsion to use them. There is no reason why they shouldn't, and specifically in a way that will bring them the maximum pleasure." Well, there is no reason, except that, in so doing, the woman will automatically lose any chance of marrying at least half the men in the world. Hunt's 1972 sample found that only 56 percent of men *under 25* felt premarital coitus was acceptable for a female where no strong affection exists, versus 80 percent of them approving if strong affection did exist.

Feminist writer Shulamith Firestone protests the way modern men coerce women into sex by hurling at them a new vocabulary designed for just this purpose (" 'fucked up,' 'ball-breaker,' 'cock-teaser,' 'a real drag' "), only to penalize them later for complying: "Even now many women know what's up and avoid the trap, preferring to be called names rather than be cheated out of the little they can hope for from men (for it is still true that even the hippest want an 'old lady' who is relatively unused)."

What does "relatively unused" mean? This is a dilemma to most men; for the most part, they have gotten around to taking nonvirgins under consideration as long-term love objects and even wives, but there exists in their minds a vague point where the woman crosses the line from respectability into whoredom.

Single women intuitively understand this principle of putting out their favors in limited editions and develop mythological sexual histories, elevating pleasant friendships to deep loves and expurgating minor characters; some women permit themselves to add an additional meaningful relationship to the saga with every few birthdays —unless they edit their ages as well. Fortunately, as we have seen, most men do not want to know—although they will invariably seek some verbal reassurance from the woman that there have not been *that* many. (One recalls the marital fight in the movie, *Carnal Knowledge,* where Ann-Margret protested, "But you wanted to know!" and spouse Art Garfunkel replied in anguish, "But I didn't know there would be so many!")

Some women even adopt a modification of the philosophy used by Nately's whore. Nately, a pilot in Joseph Heller's novel *Catch–22,* was madly in love with an Italian prostitute. She loved Nately deeply in return—so much that she refused to go to bed with him. She reasoned that a love relationship should be special, so if she went to bed with men she cared nothing about, she should do the opposite with Nately. Thus women who would readily have intercourse with a man they have discounted from the start as a potential husband will play the coy virginal role with a man whom they size up as a serious prospect. This is an explosive strategem, for if the man discovers she has been more liberal with others, he feels thoroughly duped; in Tennessee Williams's *A Streetcar Named Desire*, Stanley Kowalski's brutal rape of his sister-in-law occurs only after he learns that, rather than being the virtuous Southern lady she pretended, she had been a whore.

Jeff came into one therapy session very upset. His latest love interest at the time, Ellen, had told him of a sexual experience with a charming foreign seaman she had met in a museum that Sunday. Jeff did not expect complete fidelity from Ellen; she had, after exposure to Jeff's typical profusion of attentions, broken ties with all other current boy friends, only to have Jeff split his attentions again with other women, as he did that Sunday. What infuriated Jeff was that Ellen had tried to reassure him that her interlude was strictly "a physical thing"—the man was charming, but she would never see him again. It amazed Jeff that Ellen expected him to be mollified by her explanation; he could accept her being with a man she loved, or at least liked—but not a total stranger. What was she, some kind of whore?

# Redoubled Standards

It is easy to see why women become vexed. It is not fair, they fume, that men should be comfortable in engaging in what David Reuben cutely calls "funsex" as well as "love-sex," but expect women to abstain from sex for the sheer pleasure of it. If men feel no guilt about having sex without commitment, why should women?

What women fail to understand—and most men fail to admit—is that men have considerable reservations about casual sexual activity. Women tend to see men as accepting sex in a matter-of-fact way, an innocent pleasure in life about which they feel no more compunction than in eating a meal. Yet, the strong adolescent sex drive and the incest taboos compel every male to start his sex life in an atmosphere of guilt. Almost all teen-aged boys masturbate, an activity fraught with guilt because of social prohibitions and, more importantly, the unconscious incest fantasies that accompany it. Defense against incest taboos likewise compels him to set up the prostitute-madonna dichotomy, focusing his early sexual fantasies on partners that are unmaternal and, therefore, bad.

Women tend to equate the man's sexual philosophy with the lust of his penis, not the logic of his head. As powerful as the penis is in its demands, the head is in control most of the time. Immediately after a casual sexual encounter, the exhausted, refractory penis leaves the head in sole command, with some misgivings about what it has just been part of ("Enjoyed no sooner but despised straight"—Shakespeare). There is not just a double standard between men and women, there is a double standard within men themselves, that of lust for a prostitute coexisting with love for a woman. Man's mythology depicts himself not as a two-headed creature, but as a horned monster; the penis represented by a thrusting, hard, insensitive appendage—the horn or horns of the devil, the satyr, the minotaur—and the ultimate fantasy, the unicorn, a combination of virtue and lust, beauty and strength, that finally ceases its struggles in the arms of a virgin.

The "groovy chick" who proclaims an uninhibited enjoyment of sex without emotional ties will never lack for male companionship, but Ms. Firestone warns of such women, "Eventually they are forced to acknowledge the old-wives' truth: a fair and generous woman is (at best) respected, but seldom loved." Such a woman is regarded by men, not with respect, but with terror. Men know that even the most bawdy and licentious of male libertines are sharply limited in their orgasmic potential by the physical limitations of the penis; the new myth of the multiorgasmic woman with unlimited capacity for sexual enjoyment raises the specter of an insatiable woman whom the man could never hope to satisfy, one who would quickly wear away the potent horn of the unicorn and cap him with the impotent horns of the cuckold. (The Italians call a cuckold *"cornuto,"* literally, "the horned one.") The insatiable woman is another deep-seated denizen of the male unconscious, and we will return to examine her further in the chapter on male fantasies.

Midge Decter writes of a "new chastity": "The freedom not to be sexy is the freedom not to be free when one does not wish to be, or, to put it the other way around, to enjoy a publicly approved, sanctioned right to be chaste." While men may not publicly approve chastity, Ms. Decter may be surprised to find how many silently sanction it in their minds. If the prostitute still exists in the imaginations of men to be condemned, the madonna still exists to be venerated. Men use prostitutes; they marry madonnas. The woman who intends to marry should espouse a philosophy of sexual activity only in the context of love, even if she has her own internal double standard, as most men have.

Men, in their general acceptance of nonvirgins as wives and their willingness to live in blissful ignorance of their partners' past, are content to let any motivated woman assume the veil of near-chastity, as long as she renounces the credo of hedonism which was preached to her by ardent bachelors. She may be enshrined in the vestal temple of matrimony even if she is not a virgin—after all, mother wasn't one, either.

# The Fallen Madonna

According to an obsolete joke, a bride, having just consummated the marriage, sighed blissfully, "You're a wonderful lover!" The groom thereupon slapped the astonished woman across the face, exclaiming, "That's for knowing the difference!"

According to Hunt's 1972 study, 81 percent of married women under the age of 25 had engaged in premarital coitus, nearly twice the percentage reported for that age group by Kinsey two decades earlier. Yet, in both studies, of the women with premarital experience, only about half had ever been involved with men other than their fiancés indicating that while the incidence of premarital intercourse has markedly increased, many nonvirginal brides have adhered to the traditional standard of monogamy.

Many men will shun a woman who has had experience with other men, fearing she will be less faithful after marriage should their sex life prove unsatisfactory at some point. Throughout the centuries, an unfaithful wife has been the source of not only personal unhappiness but also of social scorn for the wronged husband. A victimized wife may elicit sympathy, but a cuckold is assumed to be too unmanly a lover to satisfy a woman and is an object of ridicule. Incidentally, "cuckold" is a term that pertains only to husbands of adulteresses; there is no analogous term for women. Men—consciously or unconsciously—fear that a highly experienced wife will compare them unfavorably with past lovers and desert them.

As Marcello Mastroianni demonstrated in the film *Divorce, Italian Style,* some cultures permit a wronged husband to kill a cheating wife with virtual impunity under the "unwritten law," acknowledging the gravity of the insult to the male ego. Yet, many men's first reaction to learning of a wife's infidelity is not rage but disbelief. Dr. Rebecca Liswood writes; "Often, too, a husband will refuse to believe that his wife is having intercourse with another man. It is curious that he can believe that she has been necking and petting but refuses to accept the fact that she has actually had intercourse." Curious, perhaps, but not unexpected. Marriage elevates most women to madonna status in the eyes of their husbands. While the need to deny an act that impugns the husband's potency as a man is a major factor in the disbelief, the equation of wife with mother also plays a role; on the conscious level, mother is viewed as being forever faithful to father, and on an unconscious level, as loving only the son. This sudden transformation from madonna to prostitute may be too overwhelming to confront even in the face of the clearest evidence.

Harry, a young computer operator, was married to a woman who left him with their children four or five nights a week while she went out for recreation "with the girls." Though she openly berated Harry for being a terrible lover and husband, when his psychiatrist suggested she might be seeing other men, Harry's reaction was "I thought he was a quack!" Shortly thereafter, Harry dreamed of his wife as a prostitute; his unconscious mind forced upon him the realization his conscious would not accept.

While wives may occasionally seem oblivious to men's obvious infidelities, they are generally more preoccupied with the possibility of such philandering before it becomes an actuality. Husbands, however, rarely give a thought to the possibility of being cheated on. The women's suspicions are an indictment of male lust and perfidy; the men's suspicions would painfully reflect on male inadequacy and impotence. The cheating man can break a woman's heart; the cheating woman can destroy a man's spirit.

## Groomed for Marriage

"My first marriage failed. There, I guess (since I must assume at least *part* of the blame), I wasn't a good husband. I wanted sex, she didn't. I wanted kids, she didn't. I liked to buy her clothes, she didn't wear them, because she wouldn't go out with me, and was angry when I went out to club functions, etc. I cheated on her, but only after two years of being celibate. I didn't drink to excess, and I didn't shoot dope or gamble. I got tired of arguing about silly things, and got tired of being a 'father figure,' so I left and filed for divorce. Now I'm a statistic —would I be a good husband? I don't know; quite honestly, the idea scares the hell out of me. So did combat—and I guess I made a good soldier—I made it. I'd like to think I'd make a good husband/father/sex partner. It's partly up to the woman, I think; she can make or break her man."

This frank response from a divorced man in his thirties came in answer to our question about what were the qualities of a good husband. After reading men's views on what they wanted in a wife, we wanted to present, at least briefly, the other half of the bridal pact, what the ideal woman should expect in return:

> *Essay Question: What are the qualities that make a good husband—being a good provider, sensitivity, being a good parent, a good lover? What's most important? Are you or would you be a good husband, and why?*

One cynic replied; " 'Good' husband (or wife)—a feature or plateau of the human condition that has not yet been achieved." But most others felt that the required qualities could not only be defined, but also attained. Being a good provider, which includes a sense of responsibility, seemed to be the most important quality, according to our subjects:

> "A good husband, first, is a good provider. Second, a good *partner* and lover. But most, considerate and understanding. Also, should divide his time between work and home, with his family."

> "I feel all these qualities make a good husband; however, change provider to 'producer,' or doing something 'useful' to self for enrichment. I feel I would be a good husband due to family training and my egalitarian approach to male-female relationships."

> "A good provider; hard worker shows the interest of a man. If a woman wants a good husband, she'd better get one that's a good worker. I feel I'm as good a husband as can be. I work hard, honest, decent lover at times. What else could anyone else want?"

> "Good provider, sensitivity, good lover. Most important is good provider. I would be a lousy husband because I detest obligations to others."

> "It seems as though a good husband is one who cannot be sexually aggressive. A wife expects a good husband to be a good provider, a good father, but not a good lover. If you want sex —in a meaningful manner—you must seek a mistress."

A man cannot provide for his wife's emotional needs unless he is able to perceive them. Many men chose sensitivity and understanding:

"A good husband is a good provider, a friend, a man, a good lover, and a good parent. Most important above all is that he has to be sensitive to his wife's wants, needs, desires, and let her know that she is the most important person in the world. I am a good husband because I feel that I am that type of person. That was the way I was raised by my parents, who gave me a happy childhood."

"The most important is sensitivity toward others. Especially for the man to realize that the woman has to have a feeling of serving some meaningful existence other than wife and lover."

"Striving to remain sincerely honest and keeping the 'lines' of communication *open!* (At all times.)"

"Being a good listener is very important in being a good husband, you really pick up a lot of 'positive' or 'negative' vibrations. If you listen, everything else comes more easily."

"Yes, listen and consider gently and affirmatively with explanation when necessary—didactic nature. Love is reconsidering all and accepting what can't be changed without giving up what is correct in your thoughts."

"The husband must be good at all of his roles. Yes, I feel I am a good partner because I have been through a bad marriage and I understand what it is like to be hurt and let down by a partner."

"I would not be a good husband because I am extremely difficult to live with. I force people to do things by my emotional instability."

At the start of the fourteenth century, Dante Alighieri concluded his *Divine Comedy* with a reference to "the Love which moves the sun and the other stars," and, at the dawning of the Age of Aquarius 650 years later, the chorus of *Hair* sang of love that will steer the stars. Many of our men felt that love keeps marriages moving, too:

"I would be a good husband because I would always be striving to make the woman feel like she is the most precious thing that I could possess and cherish."

"I am a good husband. I am a good sexual partner and an understanding friend. I give my wife the freedom to make her future for herself."

"A good husband provides love, protection, and understanding. He also allows his wife the freedom of having her own opinions and wishes. I think I would make a good husband because I can understand the need for loving and receiving love."

"Being a good husband, I believe, would be to put everything you have into a marriage, in all areas. A chain is only as strong as its weakest link. Not only putting everything you have and are now, but can work on becoming. This is for both partners, and love makes it all worth it."

"I would probably not be a good husband because I am too intense, and need a very soothing and understanding and affectionate mate. I am honest, open, and like to give as well as receive much affection and caressing."

"Being honest. I never have 'cheated' on my wife because we know about all of each other's affairs."

White Sox pitcher Ed Cicotte, confessing his sellout to gamblers in the 1919 World Series, proclaimed, "I did it for the wife and kiddies." He was barred from baseball anyway, but several of our subjects agreed that the interests of a good husband's family should come first:

"The quality that makes a good husband is loving the wife and children so much that one would not want to do anything to hurt them and to make them as happy as possible."

"Being a good husband is showing your family that you love them, not trying to be a dictator."

"Being a good parent.—I would not be a good husband—like to drink and run around too much."

It would seem, then, that most men have the knowledge of what makes a good husband, desire marriage, and are eager to build and sustain successful lifetime unions. Why, then, to add a discordant note, were there over 1,000,000 divorces in 1975, the highest number and rate per 1,000 population in the nation's history?

It isn't a lack of faith in marriage, for even the most embittered divorced men dream of making a successful new attempt, as this unhappy respondent indicates:

"I am divorced—but not my doing. My ex-wife committed adultery. This is an unforgivable sin. I honestly feel if I married again and was fortunate to have a good wife ('true') that I would be more than just a good provider and lover and parent. There would not be anything I wouldn't do for her within my financial means and physical means. But women today don't care about being *good* wives anymore. As matter of fact, they wouldn't make a good patch on a lady's ass. If I may be so bold and put it into today's vernacular, they are just 'cunts.'

"If you are a lady—I apologize.

"If you are a man—I think you will agree.

"If you are a fairy—God help you."

Do men really understand what women want? In Shaw's play *Getting Married*, after a long evening's discussion on the nature of matrimony, Mrs. George says, "Hm! Like most men, you think you know everything a woman wants, don't you? But the thing one wants most has nothing to do with marriage at all." Turning to a young clergyman, she adds, "Perhaps Anthony here has a glimmering of it. Eh, Anthony?"

He responds, "Christian fellowship?"

"You call it that, do you?" she says.

"What do you call it?" he asks. She does not get to answer.

Companionship, concern for another's needs, respect for individuality, the golden rule—call it what you will. The key to a successful marriage probably lies not in establishing a balance between a man and a woman, but between two people of equal worth.

# The Other Women

They are right; for man to man so oft unjust,
    Is always so to women; one sole bond
Awaits them, treachery is all their trust.

—BYRON, "Juan and Haidee"

The clinical coordinator enters the office of the medical director of the mental health clinic and announces, "We've got a small problem."

He nods expectantly. The clinic handles routinely 3,000 visits a month, all dealing with problems, few of them small.

"You know that woman sent over from the emergency room this morning who took an overdose because she learned her husband was having an affair?" she says. "Well, now her husband's in the waiting room having a nervous breakdown, and his girl friend's holding his hand. Shall I have the wife wait in the conference room so she doesn't see them?"

"You're right," affirms the director. "While a spontaneous encounter group might conceivably be therapeutic, let's not risk it on a busy morning." While the cool and competent coordinator maneuvers patients from room to room like characters in a French bedroom farce, the director makes a mental note to write a dissenting letter to the next noted psychoanalyst who claims that extramarital affairs are therapeutic and ultimately strengthen marriages.

Cheating is one of the most unpleasant things a psychiatrist has to deal with, especially when the wronged partner is aware of the situation. We all know the "right" approach—stay calm, don't walk out, don't do anything impulsive, realize that both partners are at fault (you can imagine how the victimized spouse feels about *that* one), and analyze the unconscious factors, because it isn't as purely sexual as it looks. Yet, the rage and pain in the betrayed one create an atmosphere of such tension that it is nearly impossible for either partner to remain cool and objective, and the honest therapist will be thinking, "If I were in his or her shoes, I'd probably want to kill my spouse, too."

We will be talking about *cheating*. It seems discussions by experts about "infidelity" invariably begin with pedantic quotes from Webster and discourses on how saying malicious things about a spouse or failure to give emotional support also constitutes infidelity. Discussions on extramarital sexual activity involve nit-picking analyses of "open marriages," wife-swapping, and group sex. "Cheating" is a nice, honest word. It has three implications, all of which apply to our concept of the act. First (and the last defined in the dictionary) is sexual unfaithfulness; quibblers like to ask whether or not friendships with those of the opposite sex, letters, gifts, joking, and flirtation are not also cheating—they may be effective warm-ups, but playing with fire won't get you convicted for arson. Second is the involvement of deceit; if a husband says he is coming home late because he wants to have intercourse with his secretary or tells his wife he will be patronizing a good hooker in Chicago, and she has no objections, this is not cheating. Third is the intentional violation of rules; this definition usually applies to games and sports, but is just as valid in marriage and other committed relationships. Many—if not most—extramarital affairs are conducted without the partner's knowledge, so that no direct lies are ever told; however, the standard marital compact is understood to mandate an exclusive sexual relationship with the spouse, and unless there has been an agreement to the contrary, the errant partner is breaking rules.

So, we used the word "cheating" even though it is somewhat pejorative and implies wrongdoing because only the individual can determine the nature of the contract between partners and how well it has been honored. Since our survey comprised unmarried males, including those living with partners, as well as married, "extramarital sex" would not have been an appropriate term of inquiry. We extended cheating to include "steady girl friend," and had to rely on the judgment of our respondents regarding whether sexual fidelity was a definite commitment in such relationships, enough so to warrant the appellation of cheating. It is conceivable that some married men who were faithful to their wives answered "yes" to the question about actually cheating because they had cheated on a girl friend prior to marriage; however, since in only one of the written answers did a man specify that he had cheated on a girl friend, but not a wife, it seems reasonable to assume that married men answered the question in terms of their wives, and others in terms of ex-wives or girl friends. Ultimately, we were more interested in a man's attitude toward commitment and sexual fidelity than to extramarital activities to date.

## Outside Interests

"Men wander, women weep," laments lyricist-singer Dory Previn. Well, according to Kinsey, *half* of men wander. Kinsey seemed to have had more difficulty gathering data on infidelity than on masturbation and bestiality, but nevertheless drew the inexact conclusion that "about half of all the married males have intercourse with women other than their wives, at some time while they are married."

In 1972 George and Nena O'Neill's book *Open Marriage* was a best-seller; since that time, there have been innumerable books and articles extolling or, at least, exploring, the concept of a variety of partners beyond marriage. Since Kinsey wrote his 1948 study, there has been an increase in premarital intercourse, a decrease in sexual inhibitions, and a rise in the divorce rate. We would naturally expect cheating—or, at least, extramarital sexual activity—to be on the rise. But is it? What of the unmarried couples living together: are men in such relationships as faithful as husbands? Did divorced men reach their solitary state because they were less faithful than their still-married brothers?

*Question 37: Have you ever cheated on your wife or steady girl friend?*

| | |
|---|---|
| No | 49.5% |
| Yes, with one or two others | 28.5% |
| Yes, with many different women | 13.0% |
| Yes, with partner's knowledge and consent | 5.5% |
| Never had a wife or steady girl friend | 2.8% |
| No answer | 1.1% |

Despite the revolutionary changes in premarital freedom during the past 30 years, half the men are still honoring commitments to wives or steady girl friends. Adjusting for the 3.9 percent who either did not answer or had never had a steady girl friend or wife, 51 percent of men, including the unmarried, had never cheated in a relationship.

Married men were equally faithful. Only 43 percent had been

involved in extramarital sexual activity, and 4 percent had engaged with their partners' consent and knowledge. Less than half as many had cheated with many different women (13 percent) as had with only one or two outside partners (26 percent).

The divorced men (this group also includes widowers, who are outnumbered by the divorced, 6 to 1) had cheated in 61 percent of the cases, though 9 percent had their partners' consent.

Men living with partners to whom they were not married seemed less committed to a monogamous ideal, because approximately 66 percent, or two-thirds, admitted to cheating, 10 percent with partners' approval.

(The above percentages were adjusted slightly to correct for those who did not answer or said they never had a wife or steady girl friend.)

Of the 90 percent of single men who had experience with steady girl friends, about 43 percent had never cheated and 8 percent had done so with partner's consent.

Hunt's 1972 study reported that 41 percent of married and divorced white men had ever engaged in extramarital coitus. Our own figures, which include 10 percent nonwhite men, show that 45 percent of combined married, divorced, and widowed men have had extramarital sex and, as indicated earlier, 43 percent of the married. Whereas Kinsey estimated that 50 percent of married men would eventually cheat, he found no more than 37 percent in any of his 5-year age brackets currently involved in infidelity. As discussed further below, it seems more appropriate to compare our data with Kinsey's actual findings than with his subjective projected estimate. If we examine our sample by age brackets, we note a definite increase in cheating among younger men.

Comparing the men in our sample by age, we found a great difference between those over 55 and those under. Discounting all the men who said they never had a wife or steady girl friend, we found that 50 percent of men in the age brackets between 30 and 54, and 52 per cent below 30, had cheated, but only 36 percent of men at least 55 years old, despite their longer period of opportunity, had been unfaithful. The percentage of men who had never been married in the 40–54 and the 55–65 age bracket was identical, so we cannot assume the difference was due to a greater amount of cheating on girl friends, as opposed to wives, in the 40–54 group. While only 3 percent of men over 40 had never been married, 8 percent of those in their thirties and 52 percent of those under 30 had never been married.

We can compare our incidence of men who had cheated at various ages with those surveyed by Hunt in 1972. Hunt's figures are for married men only, though, as we have just indicated, 92 percent of our sample in their thirties and 97 percent over 40 have been married. Also, 9 percent of our men under 30 who had never been married were living with a partner, as were 2 percent of bachelors in their thirties and 1 percent of men over 40 who had never been married.

| *Hunt (Married/divorced males who ever had extramarital coitus)* | | *Our Study (All males who ever cheated on wife, girl friend)* | |
|---|---|---|---|
| *Age* | *% of men* | *Age* | *% of men* |
| Under 25 | 32 | | |
| 25–34 | 41 | 18–29 | 52 |
| 35–44 | 47 | 30–39 | 50 |
| 45–54 | 38 | 40–54 | 50 |
| 55 and over | 43 | 55–65 | 36 |

Hunt attributes the low figure (38 percent) for his 40–54 cohort on a probable statistical error due to the smallness of the sample. He also says his figures would have been slightly higher if he had included black males, which he omitted in the above report so that his study would coincide with Kinsey's.

Our figures do include nonwhite males who, indeed, show a higher rate of cheating. Correcting for the 4 percent who never had wives or steady girl friends and who did not answer, 72 percent of black males admitted to having cheated, as opposed to 47 percent of white males.

Kinsey's 1948 study found only 27 to 37 percent of males in each of his 5-year age brackets admitting to current extramarital coitus. Yet everyone quotes his estimate of 50 percent, which is not based on objective data at all but on his equivocal statement that begins: "On the basis of these active data, and allowing for the cover-up that has been involved, it is probably safe to suggest . . ." If the men in our 55–65 age bracket had been surveyed by Kinsey in 1948 at the age of 25–35, they probably would have reported, according to his figures, a 28 percent incidence of extramarital intercourse. Given Hunt's contention that two-thirds of married men who cheat will do so in the first 5 years of marriage, our 36 percent figure for these oldsters seems quite plausible, despite Kinsey's prediction that half would eventually be unfaithful. Kinsey was making the reasonable assumption that, since the males he surveyed were admitting current extramarital intercourse, there would be, in any given age bracket, those males who had once had extramarital partners but were no longer involved with any. Yet, his oldest age groups were almost as actively involved in extramarital sex as the ones in their thirties, who had the highest active incidence; so it seems safe to say that cheating is not so much a phase some men go through as a general way of life for those who engage in it.

## With Malice Aforethought

Premeditation does not always precede infidelity, nor does cheating inevitably follow wishful thinking; however, it would seem that the man who leaves the door open to possibility will permit easy entry when temptation comes knocking.

No one can predict how many men will ultimately cheat. If we know their attitudes, however, we can obtain a fair estimate of how many are likely to cheat. Kinsey says that in a study by Terman in 1938, 72 percent of the men admitted they wished on occasion to have extramarital intercourse, and 10 years later, Kinsey again found about three-quarters of his sample of similar mind. Wishing is not the same as intention; more important than "Would you like to?" is "Would you—and when?"

Do men today expect to be faithful to their wives and steady girl friends, or is monogamy passé? Would they do it only if their relationship went sour, if the temptation was great, or do it just for the sheer pleasure of it?

*Question 38: What is your attitude towards cheating on your wife or steady girl friend?*

| | |
|---|---|
| Would never become involved with anyone else | 33.6% |
| Would cheat only if affair was brief and casual | 17.9% |
| Would cheat only if relationship with regular partner was bad | 17.2% |
| Would cheat only if away from partner for a long period | 13.0% |
| Would cheat to have different sexual partners regardless of wife or girl friend | 11.7% |
| Would cheat only if I fell in love | 7.0% |
| No answer | 1.5% |

While only one-third of the men feel they would never become involved with anyone else, less than one man in eight would expect to cheat simply because he believes a man should have variety.

Of course, if we consider the 17 percent who said they would cheat only if the relationship was bad to be basically monogamous, our percentage of potential philanderers is back down to that old 50 percent of Kinsey's. The prospect of a brief and casual affair seems to pose the biggest threat to fidelity, apparently because the risk of detection is so low—a better solution to having your cake and eating it, too, than Cookie Monster could devise. Only 7 percent said they would cheat only if they fell in love, which would indicate that men, married or otherwise, do not fantasize about some great and special romance better than their current lot. Men seem to want affairs for variety, adventure, and to fill a void created by an absent or unloving wife, but not to replace their current partner as a primary love object.

We do see a very definite trend toward infidelity among the younger men today. While 47 percent of men over 55 said they would never cheat, only about 30 percent of men under 40 voiced this sentiment. And 38 percent of married men vowed perpetual fidelity, but only 19 percent of unmarried men living with partners felt this way. This living-together group was highest in advocating routine extramarital affairs, with 20 percent, whereas only 10 percent of married males espoused such liberality.

Of men who had never been married, 27 percent—about one-fourth—would enter marriage with dreams of unwavering commitment, and 15 percent expect to have outside partners regardless of mitigating factors. Divorced/widowed men were nearly identical in these responses to the never-married, in spite of their greater age, though more of the divorced group said they would cheat only if their prime relationship was bad and more of the never-married advocated brief and casual affairs.

Nonwhites said they would never cheat in only 22 percent of cases, compared with 35 percent of thoroughly monogamous whites. Almost twice as many black males as white said they would cheat to have different sexual partnerships. Men of "other races" said in 16 percent of cases they would cheat only if in love, a romanticized sentiment not often found among whites (7 percent) or blacks (6 percent).

Kinsey said men of lower educational levels are less faithful, particularly in their very early years. We did not find this to be true either in actual occurrence of cheating or in attitude. In fact, 37 percent of high school graduates and 34 percent of those with even less education said they would never be unfaithful, compared with 32 percent of college graduates. The men with higher educations did show more preference for brief and casual affairs, while the most poorly educated would be more prone to indiscriminate activity.

# Taking the Bait

Shaw's John Tanner, M.I.R.C. (Member of the Idle Rich Class) once wrote: "Virtue consists, not in abstaining from vice, but in not desiring it."

By that standard, few men are truly virtuous. Even the faithful are generally like the extremely scrupulous politician who spent several minutes politely and graciously declining some shady offers from a constituent, and then suddenly flew into a violent rage and practically hurled the solicitor from his office. When a perplexed aide asked what had triggered the uncharacteristic outburst, the politician explained, "He was getting too near my price."

Every man has his Achilles' heel, and if it is not strictly true that time wounds all heels, a little knowledge about male vulnerability on a wife's part may ensure that temptation will ultimately take to *its* heels, not *his*.

What circumstances would lead to a flip alibi like "The devil made me do it!"? Is it the hot tomato on the outside or the cold fish at home that whets a man's appetite for a dilly of a dalliance?

*Question 39: What would be most likely to tempt you to cheat?*

| | |
|---|---|
| Poor sex at home | 26.7% |
| Exceptionally attractive woman | 24.8% |
| Fighting at home | 18.4% |
| Would not be tempted | 15.5% |
| A woman who understands me better | 10.8% |
| Available woman at work | 8.2% |
| No answer | 2.2% |

And so, a few more of the hard-core faithful bite the dust—from the 51 percent who had never cheated to the 34 percent who would never cheat to the 15.5 percent who would not even be tempted!

For those men who saw themselves capable of being tempted, slightly over half of those provocations would come from inside the home, as a result of poor sex or fighting.

Men over 55 saw themselves as far less vulnerable to temptation; 29 percent said they would not be tempted, just about twice the average percentage of invulnerable men under 55. While this may reflect a decline in sexual interest for this age group, the attitude seems quite in line with the lower actual incidence of cheating and the commitment to fidelity that we have seen in men of that generation.

Married men cited poor sex at home as the prime inducement to cheat (32 percent), while the various unmarried subgroups felt an exceptionally attractive woman would be the biggest threat. Divorced/widowed men, however, gave the *femme fatale* less than a 1 percent edge over poor sex at home, while those who had never married (14 percent) and those living with partners (18 percent) ranked poor sex at home as considerably less probable, perhaps having been more blessed themselves with satisfactory sex lives.

Men under 30 gave exceptionally attractive women the highest rating (33 percent), but men over 30 all chose poor sex, averaging 31 percent. High-school-educated men saw poor sex at home as the biggest threat, whereas college-educated men gave a slight edge to a very attractive woman. Students gave attractiveness an exceptionally high 40 percent preference and picked "a woman who understands me better" as their second choice, the only group to rate it higher than fourth among the five suggested temptations.

If a wife sees that her man has a good sex life, which, in turn, should induce him to keep any fighting limited to daylight skirmishes, she will have half the field defended against invasion by temptation. The "exceptionally attractive woman" is more a fantasy than a threat (wouldn't Robert Redford tempt *you*, ma'am?)—unless things get really bad at home, in which cases Gravel Gertie could look like a rock star. If you understand your man well, no woman could possibly understand him better. By now you probably understand that a good sex life for most men means not just passive compliance, but true responsiveness—and, if a wife is not satisfied herself, she should show enough concern with their relationship to communicate and experiment toward mutual gratification.

Finally, a word about the "available woman at work": as our respondents have indicated, the "office wife" rarely poses a threat to the original. Businesses tend to take on the psychological structure of families, and if attraction develops from proximity, it suffers from familiarity and the taboos imposed by the gossipers who are as much a part of any office as the telephones, and twice as busy. If a man is dissatisfied at home or must boost his ego through a relationship wherein he is clearly the boss, he will risk or even welcome a questionable reputation among his coworkers; but if he is secure in his own love life, availability will, in itself, pose no temptation. He will then emulate with equal imperviousness, but hopefully less cruelty, the character who replied to a girl who said, "I'm free tonight," with "Fine, honey, keep your prices down."

# True Confessions

Whether at the card table or the conference table, men universally despise the man who cheats another. When women and sex are involved, the gravity of the matter takes on a far lighter tone. Not only did half our sample admit to cheating on their wives and steady girl friends, but they were willing to write frankly about their experiences and feelings:

*Essay Question: Have you ever thought about cheating on your wife or girl friend? Did you, and under what circumstances? What conditions might tempt you to cheat?*

Poor sex or fighting with the partner was the most frequently cited reason among those who had actually cheated:

"I have cheated on my wife. It was due to lack of interest on her part, and a similar lack on her [other woman's] husband's part and being good friends, one thing led to another, etc."

"Yes [thought about it]. Yes [cheated]. Poor communication at home. Puritan hang-ups. Has changed both, now enjoy each other."

"Yes, and I have. During a bad time emotionally and sexually with girl friend. And under the influence of alcohol and marijuana and an aggressive girl while my girl friend was asleep in the next room. Very exciting!"

"I've usually been honest with my girl friend(s). If I've told my girl friend I've cheated then it's usually a sign that we're not satisfying each other. I've had some purely physical affairs, but I've decided not to tell her because they mean nothing in our relationship."

"Yes! [Thought about it.] Yes, after arguments or after being turned down for sex at home. Argument, indifference, especially nagging."

"Unpleasant home conditions has made me cheat several times."

"I cheated on my ex-wife near the end of our marriage. The love (if there was any to begin with) was gone, sex with my ex-wife wasn't satisfying. I had a casual affair with a business associate."

"After the fox!" is a cry not limited to English hunters with hounds, seeking the prize of a fox's tail. Many monogamous marriages go to the dogs when a man spies an attractive vixen:

"Yes, I have cheated. Circumstances differed. Usually the woman was exceptionally attractive or aggressive or someone I have known during or before my current relationship."

"Yes. I have, but only if the other girl was better-looking. Perhaps because of peer pressure, going out with the guys to pick up different girls."

"Yes. Have done several times, when I met someone new who turned me on."

"I've cheated, simply because I wanted to screw the other person badly. I felt a little guilty, but it passed."

Some psychiatrists believe otherwise-rational compulsive thieves should not be held legally responsible because they suffer from an "irresistible impulse." Other psychiatrists counter this with the "policeman-at-the-elbow" argument—even the most compulsive kleptomaniac will not steal if a policeman is watching. When there is virtually no chance of getting caught, impulses seem to become, in many situations, "irresistible":

"Yes, when the opportunity strongly presented itself. My regular partner had no way of knowing so I felt like it—purely physical."

"Yes, I did, a brief affair, and I would do it again under similar conditions—brief, no strings, remain friendly."

"Yes, several times. It just seems to happen. Privacy and conditions right, I'd probably do it again."

"Yes, I have when out drinking and met a willing girl. [Be tempted by] same condition."

"Yes [thought about it]. Yes, one time. Out of curiosity, availability, attractiveness and sympathy."

"Sure! Had affair with girl at work. Convenience of affair tempts me."

"I don't think about cheating on my wife. It just happens. Usually I'm tempted at work."

Pinocchio was another fellow who got into trouble when there were no strings attached, though when he attempted to lie, it was as plain as the nose on his face. Like many men, Pinocchio had difficulty especially when far from home and conscience:

"Yes, I've had. Away from partner for extended periods, little emotional satisfaction, a feeling for independence, but felt guilty afterward. Felt I've hurt someone."

"Yes. I have 'cheated' once during a long trip away for 1-½ months. [Would be tempted by] exceptionally interesting woman, whether physically attractive or not."

"Yes, when I was away at school and my girl friend was at home. Alcohol makes me more aggressive and lessens my conscience. [Tempted by] peer group pressure."

Many men rationalize cheating by applying philosophical terms to it —others just enjoy it:

"All the time—best of both worlds. Exhilarated living on the wild side. As long as ignorance is bliss. Has to be a worthwhile experience as long as it brings a high or euphoria from mundane-existential existence."

"Yes [thought about it]. Yes [did it] and under the pretense of self actualization. So perhaps it should not be considered 'cheating.'"

"I have cheated only as desired and encountered a homosexual experience."

"Yes, I have. For no other reason but to enjoy sex with that woman. I don't feel cheating is a good word. I think other relationships help keep people together where boredom is a large reason for many split-ups."

"Brother, you can't go to jail for what you're thinking" went a

carefree lyric in *The Most Happy Fella*. Many of our respondents pleaded "not guilty" to cheating, but as for thinking about
it, it was *nolo contendere*:

"Yes, I thought of cheating on my lady friend (and permanent
roommate) just the other day; but I weighed the consequences
and decided that *I* would be the 'loser' in such an affair. If the
occasion arose out-of-town, I would participate."

"Yes, I've thought about it, but the chance has never arisen. If
I was out of town—and horny, and my girl friend wasn't there
I would screw some other female if I would never see her
again."

"Yes, I have thought about cheating. This, in my case, is caused
by high sexual desire. I need some variation in my sexual partner every once in a while—but not often. I would hope my
wife-to-be could understand—but I doubt it."

"Yes. At this point (five years), I have not made a serious effort
to cheat or even an attempt. Because of long work hours, and
time spent with children, freedom for cheating is limited. The
circumstance would either be spontaneous (not preplanned) or
getting serious about another woman (which is not beyond com-
prehension)."

"I have thought about it but never have. My life-style at home
with my wife would have to be both mentally and sexually bad
and I would have to like my new partner very much."

"Yes—have not. Would need to be a 'ship in the night' affair—
e.g., conference out of town."

"I have thought about cheating. I never have yet. If I could
do it without my wife finding out. Or anybody else finding
out."

When the saints go marching in, here's a few who will probably be
in that number:

"Cheating implies a secrecy and in my relationship I would not
consider this. I give and take honesty and openness. There is no
marital problem that cannot (or should not) be discussed. I
would have a relationship with another woman only if my mari-

tal relationship had come to an end or if my wife and I had discussed the situation and decided to separate."

"I am now married 2 years 4 months and can honestly say I haven't thought about cheating; I might be tempted only if my home situation became totally sour and no peace was left between us."

"I would not cheat! Circumstances might influence me to leave my wife, but I have no desire to attempt to fake reality or acquire the guilt inherent in cheating."

"Why should I have to as long as she lives up to my expectations? Cheating would not be necessary unless a breakdown in the marriage occurs."

"Yes, but always the thought of ensuing guilt for broken moral values has prevented cheating. If my wife stops caring and stopped trying to satisfy my needs, then . . ."

"No—would prefer divorce to cheating—it only complicates."

"The opportunity may have arisen but dismissed it at once. No, I have never cheated on my wife. Excessive drinking might tempt me to cheat, otherwise no."

"I may have thought about it, but realize I've got a great marriage and sex partner and couldn't ruin my life or hers by doing something so demoralizing."

"No, I have never thought of cheating on my wife. [Would be tempted] if I found that my wife was cheating or she was dead."

Like the diplomatic cowpoke who said to his opponent, "No offense, but the top card of that deck looks a mite dusty," some people want to avoid the word "cheating":

"You both should look at it with an open mind. Cheating is the wrong word."

"The term 'cheating' I find absurd and have not had to apply it—all my relationships have been upfront—though not all have been met with reciprocity."

"I didn't cheat on my ex-wife but I have several girl friends now, and we have an understanding on sharing sex. Would not cheat on next wife unless *very unusual* circumstances. Will end marriage *immediately* when communication stops."

"I do not like the term cheating, it implies that I am doing something wrong. If I was sexually attracted to another woman, and her to me, there is no reason why we shouldn't sleep together..My partner is free to do likewise."

When Cleopatra's political adversary, Pothinus, asks about her relationship with Caesar, "But how can you be sure that he does not love you as men love women?" she replies simply, "Because I cannot make him jealous. I have tried."

Jealousy is usually condemned as egocentric or neurotic by the experts, but it's still a rare man, south of the polar regions, who is willing to share his wife or lover. Only 10 percent of unmarried men living with partners said they had engaged in affairs with their mates' knowledge and consent, nevertheless reflecting a greater tendency toward open relationships than in people involved in conventional marriages. And a smaller 4 percent of our married men still living with their wives had a history of affairs under advise-and-consent principles. The divorced men living alone were more than twice as high as the still-married in having had affairs with partners' knowledge and consent.

In our overview on cheating, we see a definite increase, although more than half the married men are still remaining faithful. The most striking finding is the jump in infidelity from one-third in men over 55 to one-half or more in men under 55. (Again, we are talking about men who have ever cheated, not just those currently cheating.) Cheating seems to have deleterious effects on marital stability, for divorced men have a much higher incidence of cheating than those currently married, although poor sex and quarreling at home are the main reasons given for cheating by men over 30, and it is difficult in the divorced to distinguish between cause and effect where cheating and domestic turmoil coexist. Only about one-quarter of men who have never been married would enter marriage with the firm commitment of never cheating, though only 15 percent are determined to have outside partners regardless of marital satisfaction. About one man in six sees himself as beyond temptation. Our society is still a long way from prevalent "open relationships," since only 6 percent of our sample have engaged in outside activity with their partners' consent, and even the liberal living-togethers show 10 percent. Since 52 percent of men under 30 have already cheated, we can anticipate their extramarital experience will increase somewhat with time, but, learning from Kinsey's difficulty with overprojection, it seems safe to say that 40 percent of married men will remain faithful for the foreseeable future, despite increasingly liberal attitudes in our society.

## Double Allegiance

Not all affairs are short and simple; some are as long and complex as a 5–4 Supreme Court decision on obscenity standards. For example, Charlie's situation was as hectic as a Marx Brothers comedy—although nobody was doing much laughing.

Charlie was in his mid-thirties when his wife Judy learned about a complex affair he had been carrying on for 4 years. Judy was 6 years younger than Charlie and married him after she finished high school. Both were virgins when they wed; Judy was always an adequate sexual partner, often taking the initiative in intercourse, and had borne two children. Lola, the other woman, was Judy's age. She had worked as a secretary for Charlie in a business he shared with two partners, one his wife's brother. Charlie found Lola more physically attractive than his wife, more sexually responsive, and apparently more emotionally dependent on him. When the business failed, in spite of his loss of several thousand dollars, Charlie set up Lola, a divorcée, and her two children in an apartment.

Then began Charlie's frantic double life. He got a job as a forklift operator, but told his wife he also had a second job in the evenings and a third job on Saturdays. Lola was working, but Charlie gave her one-quarter of his weekly take-home pay. When he got through work at 5:00, Charlie would go home to Lola. At 1:30 A.M., he would arise from bed and drive home to his wife, leaving from there to go back to his one job. Saturdays would be spent with Lola under the pretense of working the third job, and Sundays would be spent with his wife. Lola's neighbors regarded Charlie as a devoted spouse and family man.

Though the wife is generally the last to know (because she doesn't want to know), a husband with enough guilt or weariness will eventually force the knowledge upon her. Thus, after 4 years, Judy found in Charlie's wallet pictures of Lola and her children, along with a receipt for a gift of jewelry. Judy confronted Charlie and demanded he choose between them. For several weeks, Charlie would spend a couple of days with one, only to shuttle to the other. Lola, victim of a fatherless childhood and a marriage to an abusive alcoholic, begged

Charlie to stay with her, professing her deep love and need for him. While Charlie's parents and in-laws pleaded on Judy's behalf, Judy herself would stoically say, "Do what you want," and continue to run the household with her usual efficiency.

Judy's reaction was undoubtedly not what Charlie had counted on. Instead of telling him she needed him and loved him as much as Lola did, she took her characteristically stolid stance; he could not fault her for saying "Do what you want" (which he obviously would), but he didn't know what he wanted. He knew all along that Judy was more faithful, efficient, and a better mother; he wanted to see if she would try to match Lola's attractions, which were dependency and desire.

The thing that really made Lola irresistible was her responsiveness in bed. She was always game for sex (even, during her liaison with Charlie, with other partners) and engaged vigorously and vociferously. She made Charlie, who had previously had intercourse with only one dutiful woman, feel a sense of self-esteem as a man which he had never dreamed possible. Charlie was not only a victim of a prostitute-madonna split, he became a commuter on the prostitute-madonna shuttle. He really wanted to be satisfied by one woman—it would have been cheaper and less fatiguing—but he couldn't find all his requirements in either one. There was enough genuine communication and child-raising experience in Lola for her to claim a bit of madonna blue blood, but her philandering and relegation of her children to secondary status qualified her in Charlie's mind as a scarlet-stained prostitute. Yet Judy, already the barely approachable madonna, became even more saintly and self-sacrificing under Charlie's brutal continued involvement with Lola; and if the mistress seemed woefully inadequate in madonna traits, Judy had none of the prostitute's.

Lola probably would have won out, except for a curious quirk of circumstance through which her greatest asset—her sexual responsiveness—became her downfall. Judy's brother, who had been campaigning for her along with the other relatives, broke down and told Charlie that he himself had been carrying on with Lola, their mutual former secretary. Charlie could not believe it, but when his brother-in-law described in detail Lola's unique bedroom performances, the shuttle ground to a halt. Lola was pure prostitute—and Judy had a husband with only one job, but considerably more pay.

While our survey indicates that far more men prefer brief, uncomplicated cheating episodes, preferably far from home, there are exceptions such as Charlie. Poor sex at home is a major cause of cheating and for the man with no premarital experience with other partners, satisfactory sex may suddenly become highly unsatisfactory when he becomes exposed to an aggressive and passionate woman. Younger and more inexperienced men are more vulnerable to attractive women and are not as able to view them in perspective against the assets of their long-term partners. The wife of such a man must be a creature of sufficient variety to prevent his extra marital forays in search of something more in a woman.

# Kiss and Tell

In Shaw's *Don Juan in Hell,* when the virtuous Dona Ana finds herself in hell and protests her unexpected assignment there, having always sincerely repented her sins and confessed more than she really committed, Don Juan admonishes, "Ah, that is perhaps as bad as confessing too little."

Most therapists agree that confessions of infidelity may bring relief to the guilty party, but rarely benefit the offended partner or the marriage. Brief and casual affairs are rarely confessed; if they are, it is more out of hostility than concern towards the partner. It may be a husband's way of saying to a wife who seems sexually disinterested that he is, indeed, attractive to women, so the fault in their sagging sex life is clearly hers. Sometimes a husband will place his wife in a bind where she loses either way: if she becomes angry or hurt, he berates her for being so unsympathetic to his difficult and heartfelt confession, and threatens to withhold future indiscretions if she persists in her immature attitude; but if she receives his words calmly and with understanding, he views her benign reaction as license to transgress further.

Some husbands, however, are motivated by a threatened loss of love. They reason, "My wife loves me. But, since she doesn't know what I've done, she doesn't know the *real* me. The man she loves is a fiction. I can't feel truly loved under these circumstances."

A wife will rarely learn of an affair without her husband's conscious or unconscious cooperation. He may force her to make the ultimate confrontation by leaving a blatant trail of clues but waiting for her to broach the subject. The wife must be emotionally ready not to make any ultimatums or demands she cannot withdraw from, such as "Get out and don't ever come back!" or "If you ever see that woman again, it means a divorce!" On the other hand, she should convey her feelings of distress and anger, both for her own emotional well-being and to underscore how seriously she regards the breach of trust. The woman who goes into a marriage with the attitude that all husbands cheat is likely to find that her own spouse conforms to her expectations, for people communicate messages in many subtle and unconscious ways. The wife who expects cheating feels that she herself or any woman could never be adequate enough to satisfy all of a man's needs, so she never really attempts to and chooses a man who will not make such a demand.

It is difficult for a woman when she feels most angry to make the effort to improve her relationship with a cheating husband. Still, the often-heated discourse that follows the discovery of infidelity may be the first meaningful communication between a couple in years. In the midst of their differences, the couple will see themselves as distinct individuals and can use this perception as a way to become reacquainted. Time alone together is important, even if the affair has put a strain on the relationship. "Regard" is derived from "to look at"; unless two people take the time and trouble to really look at one another, there can be no truly valid concern.

While the sexual relationship seems to precipitate most affairs, it is the esteem the man derives from the act that has more profound ramifications than the physical gratification. The experienced prostitute can please a man physically, but he knows she regards him as a satisfied customer, not a satisfying lover. The woman who feels or shows delight in a man's lovemaking sets his brain aglow with pride and happiness long after his genital sensations have petered out. The man who knows he has a wife with whom he can share his sexual needs, inadequacies, fantasies, and moods, and who expects the same from her has little incentive to seek an outside partner where he can wind up feeling only less emotionally gratified, not more. On the other hand, the married man whose sex life is uninspired and routine can pursue the dream of a woman who will reflect through her regard the self-image of a competent, virile lover to which practically all men aspire.

## The Dashing Don Juan

"Then the lady, who had been happy and idle enough before, became anxious, preoccupied with me, always intriguing, conspiring, pursuing, watching, waiting, bent wholly on making sure of her prey: I being the prey, you understand. . . . I ran away from it. I ran away from it very often: in fact I became famous for running away from it." This is Don Juan speaking, of course. We have quoted Shaw's hero in hell several times before and now finally give him the spotlight for himself. It is important to think of Don Juan not only in terms of his conquests, but also in his quick departures to new fields; he is a hit-and-run type, who scores his hits, then runs.

Don Juan and his descendants are basically insecure men. That George Bernard Shaw could portray this Oedipal quest with such psychological accuracy in 1903, before Freud had formulated his major theories in *Three Essays on Sexuality,* is a striking example of how artists intuitively grasp basic truths before the methodical behavioral scientists. From his unique vantage point in hell, Shaw's dashing lover can conduct a postmortem examination of his life freed from the passions of his body; he comes to understand his unrealistic idealization of women, his inevitable disillusionment, and his terror of being depended on, rather than getting his own dependency needs met. He finds the path to heaven by accepting the sexual drive as a powerful and purposeful force, without the fantasies and glamour with which the poets and dreamers endow it. He becomes a puritan—not a Victorian prude, who rejects sex or secretly relishes it as lascivious recreation—but one who respects sex as a potent component of an ordered universe, something beyond man's full understanding, often out of his full control, but essential to his ultimate happiness and survival.

The Don Juans on earth, unfortunately, usually fail to resolve their hang-ups through philosophy or other means. Psychiatrists write about the Don Juan's basic feelings of sexual inadequacy, leading them to seek new women in order to validate again and again that they can satisfy a woman. This is true, up to a point, but it fails to explain why a man would repeatedly risk failure and discount the approval of many women in the hope of adding one more to his growing list. The insatiable thirst for confirmation of manhood is only half of the story. The other half is the idealization of the woman, the unconscious quest for the perfect mother, followed by disillusionment and retreat.

The woman who succumbs to the Don Juan is left gasping in his wake. Here he has been relentlessly pursuing her, flattering her, telling her how much he desires her; they have genuinely enjoyed each other's company and been physically compatible. Just as she believes she has found her great love in life, he's gone—no quarrel, no crisis, no rival—he's just gone. Try to pin him down, and he'll say something about freedom or not being ready to make a commitment or not believing in traditional values; if his cant sounds unconvincing, it's because he himself cannot verbalize his unconscious motivation, to flee the responsibilities inherent in an adult relationship and continue his search for a doting mother. Some Don Juans do marry, and then cheat like a man with a deck of aces; the wife becomes a functional, but not ideal, mother who cannot give him the unqualified admiration his narcissistic ego craves—so the search goes on.

A woman should beware the man who besieges her with traditional romantic sentiments and alternately puts down monogamy, marriage, and commitment. If a man wants to take time out for a few years to formulate his goals and philosophy, this is understandable, but he should not then take fanciful flight into pleas for love and devotion from the woman he will struggle against tomorrow.

Don Juan's descendant rails: "If we try to go where you do not want us to go there is no law to prevent us; but when we take the first step your breasts are under our foot as it descends; your bodies are under our wheels when we start. No woman shall ever enslave me in that way." Rather than doing without women, he moves from one to another before any claim can be made on him, before his frailties are discovered.

The man with low self-esteem is the one most likely to present himself as the suave, competent lover, knowing he can make an exit before he is unmasked. Thus, the man who reaches 40, or 50, or 60, and feels old, unaccomplished, sexually declining, or unappreciated at home may go questing for a gullible woman who will believe in the man behind the mask. These quixotic dons are not run-of-the-mill neurotics like their younger counterparts who have never matured; they are men in retreat, making a last stand against the vicissitudes of age and loss. These errant knights will usually gladly give up the wearisome quest for a maid who will be dazzled by their armor and panoply for a wife who can help them value again the man underneath the trappings.

## Harem-Scarum

*Higamus, hogamus,*
Woman's monogamous.
*Hogamus, higamus,*
Man is polygamous.

This bit of doggerel with its chauvinist pig latin was recited by one of the characters in *The Marriage-Go-Round*, a play about a middle-aged married professor whose voluptuous young houseguest asked him to be a sperm donor for her desired child, without the troublesome intervention of an artificial insemination laboratory.

Are men naturally more polygamous than women? Are they more inclined to desire several mates at the same time? Are they naturally more promiscuous, taking and discarding mates with little discrimination and lack of emotional involvement? The key word here is "naturally." It is doubtful anyone would dispute that men engage more frequently in extramarital intercourse than women. Kinsey estimated the incidence of extramarital involvement for married women at some time in their life to be 26 percent, against twice that for males. Most therapists gauge the prevalence of affairs for married women to lie between 25 and 50 percent, and for men between 40 and 55 percent. Theodore Rubin inexplicably says, "I've seen the recent surveys that indicate that only about one-fifth of all married men in the United States commit adultery," which indicates he has not yet caught up in his reading to Hunt's 1972 study. Hunt has the best data on married women, showing that 12 to 24 percent of wives have been unfaithful at some point, the percentage being higher among the youngest women in the sample; Hunt feels Kinsey's estimate of 26 percent was inordinately high because of the unrepresentative ratio of divorced women under 45 to still-married women of the same age—more than eight times the incidence in the United States population at the time of the Kinsey study. By rebalancing Kinsey's data to correct for this sampling error, Hunt calculated a more accurate estimate of female extramarital experience in 1953 to be 20 percent, the same as Hunt's own figures.

So, at least from the data on married people, men seem to be involved more than twice as much with other partners as are women. Since every heterosexual encounter usually involves one woman to one man, does this mean that women take on twice as many partners? Prostitutes will skew the data, assuming some married men cheat only with them, but we must also remember that unmarried partners do not show up in the above figures, and affairs between married men and single women are far more common than between wives and bachelors. After these considerations, there is no doubt that more men than women continue after marriage to have a variety of sexual partners.

In the preceding chapter, we discussed the impact of the unfaithful wife upon a man. The question of fidelity, with the decline of premarital virginity, has assumed more complexity for the woman herself. Since many women do not regard their husbands as the only men to whom they can ever give their bodies, past experience having already refuted this, marital fidelity requires a different rationale. They must now redefine their orientation to sex and commitment, either by seeing marriage as a situation distinct from all previous experience, or by reformulating their individual philosophies in an independent, introspective manner, unable as they are to rely on the traditional moral maxims and prohibitions. If sexual freedom has become more than ever before a matter under women's voluntary control, so too has fidelity.

Some feminists claim that women are not more promiscuous simply because they have been conditioned to suppress their normal sexual appetites. Others, such as Midge Decter, argue that women do not possess men's genital lust and, when a young girl is told to accede to her own sexual wishes, she has no criteria by which to guide herself. Even the adventurous Erica Jong remarked in a *Playboy* interview that men said they envied attractive women in the way they could go out and get sex any time they wanted, and could not seem to understand that women did not desire sex that way.

We are not speaking here of women's capacity for sexual gratification, which, with their multiorgasmic potential, may far exceed that of men. Nor are we talking about a woman's ability to be intensely attracted to and fantasize about an intriguing man she first sees. But the female genital response always follows a conscious intellectual process, whereas men may experience instantaneous genital arousal. While pornographic books abound with descriptions of women who look hungrily at a man and find their panties suddenly drenched with vaginal "passion juices," the fact is that even the most eager woman usually requires adequate physical stimulation to become physiologically ready to achieve orgasm through intercourse.

Traditionally, since the woman's head was involved in the encounter before her genitals, she drew the defensive assignment, putting off the amorous male until she knew him better, drawing his conscious processes into play before he was allowed to arouse her physical components. Today a woman still accedes or withdraws on a conscious basis; she may give herself out of love, philosophical conviction, desire to please, desire to control, or even to avoid an argument, but rarely out of sheer lust. Again, once involved in the act, her passion may be more uninhibited than his, but it does not naturally precede the act, as in the case of a man. Thus, she can choose to yield herself indiscriminately, but she does not desire indiscriminately.

The second factor that makes men more promiscuous is not biological, but psychological; yet it is so common to all men in their course of development that we may term it "natural." This is, again, the tendency to need and seek out both "good" and "bad" women. Basically, this, too, stems from male lust, the repressed sexual excitation the pubertal boy feels towards his mother, which causes him to repudiate good, maternal women and seek out the "bad," where he feels no guilt. While girls may harbor erotic feelings toward their fathers, these are more easily denied because of the lack of damning evidence such as an erection constitutes in the case of the boy. The male is more prone to masturbation with accompanying sexual fantasies that must be focused on distinctly unmaternal females. Furthermore, since the father enters the life of both boy and girl as a love object much later than the mother, and never becomes as important for primary dependency needs, the children assign the mother the role of preserving the chastity she preaches to them, and father may be perceived as a sexually frustrated, but not virginal male. While a virgin mother may be highly desirable, an asexual father would be impotent as a lover, so women do not seek out such males as lovers the way men seek madonnas.

It is the boy, who in his rivalry with the father, is most likely to mock him as impotent; the circus clown with his drooping hat, the baggy pants he cannot fill, bald head, and fumbling mannerisms is a caricature of the impotent old father. The girl may want the father to desire her and may carry this over into fantasies of satyric pursuers and swashbuckling rapists, but she resists for fear of competing with mother and losing the needed nurturing. Since women do not need two distinct types of men in their lives, the virtuous and the profane, they are more easily monogamous.

*Must* men be promiscuous? No, for even with marginal use of his intellect, man can curb his indiscriminate lust. Woman used to ensure this by holding the line against lust until the male brain could catch up. Now, the man must be responsible for his sexual initiatives, for if women endlessly comply, he will be doomed to an eternity of unmaternal prostitutes and never find the caring madonna who will truly meet his needs. If lust is unchecked, all chance for love will be destroyed.

Women are subject to temptation as well. Curiosity, need for physical closeness, praise from a man, and boredom may motivate affairs for them, just as for men. However, their immunity to spontaneous physical arousal and their freedom from the prostitute-madonna complex make them far less "naturally" promiscuous. But man's "nature" includes will as well as passion:

"Our moral sense! And is that not a passion?" declares Don Juan's descendant. "If it were not a passion—if it were not the mightiest of the passions, all the other passions would sweep it away like a leaf before a hurricane. It is the birth of that passion that turns a child into a man."

Many cheating men are still emotional children. The birth of the moral passion is overdue, but may yet occur with a little midwifery from a mature and loving woman.

# Dream Girls

DONA ANA: I daresay you all want to marry lovely incarnations of music and painting and poetry. Well, you can't have them, because they don't exist. If flesh and blood is not good enough for you, you must go without: that's all. Women have to put up with flesh-and-blood husbands—and little enough of that, too, sometimes; and you will have to put up with flesh-and-blood wives.

—GEORGE BERNARD SHAW, *Man and Superman*

In 1907, in a paper on creative writing, Sigmund Freud wrote of a discovery that now does not seem very impressive—the fact that people have daydreams or fantasies. It took the new science of psychoanalysis to get people to discuss something that was never then talked about in polite company, the worlds of fantasy that people construct for themselves and idle away time in visiting. Children are very open about their fantasies, for most of their pretending deals with what they would do if they were grown-up and therefore represents commendable ambition. Adult fantasies, however, reflect a return to the child's world or the ambitions that lie beyond the potential of the dreamer; thus, adult fantasies are often a source of shame. Freud said that the creative artist was a surrogate dreamer for society; through his skill, he wove fantasies that people could enjoy without experiencing the guilt that would be involved if they constructed the daydreams themselves.

Much of our sex lives are highly involved with fantasy. Many fantasies, like dreams, seem bizarre and uncharacteristic of everyday behavior, but this does not make them pathological. Just as this book has dealt throughout with normal sexuality, so, too, will this chapter be dealing with the fantasies of average men.

In almost all males, masturbation precedes intercourse by a considerable period of time. Masturbation is almost always accompanied by fantasies of sexual activity involving a partner, this fantasy providing the ongoing stimulation for sexual excitation and orgasm; while a man can become excited through physical stimulation alone, only very socially withdrawn males are ever likely to give a fantasy-free masturbatory history. Boys may also have the sort of romantic fantasies we typically associate with girls, of being in love with a beautiful, loving woman who will share his life and dreams. Because the prostitute-madonna split is strongest in adolescence, the partner in such daydreams may be excluded entirely from the masturbatory fantasies, which involve a bawdier, sensual type of woman unfit for consideration as a romantic love object. Teen-aged girls invariably have romantic fantasies before they engage (if ever) in masturbation, and have a far easier time integrating the two types of fantasy.

While men practically always fantasize during masturbation, they do so far less frequently during intercourse, for the obvious reason that they have a real partner who does not have to be supplied in imagination. People's minds are rarely blank, but a true fantasy involves imagining something that is not actually going on or that you cannot perceive through your senses at the time. Men who "think about" their partner during intercourse might be merely attentive to her presence and reactions; however, if they are trying to imagine what she is experiencing, thinking about parts of her body they cannot actually see at the moment, or returning in memory to a particularly exciting experience they have had with that partner in the past, they are then really fantasizing. Men's fantasies are generally simpler than those of women. The easy accessibility of stories and photographs specifically designed to provide sexual titillation (sometimes called 'one-handed' magazines) has made it unnecessary for this generation of men to develop their creative skills. Most men masturbate with the aim of reaching orgasm as quickly as possible and, while they may delay their orgasms in intercourse, they have only themselves to please in masturbation. Adult males who masturbate usually do so not because they want to get aroused, but because lack of regular sexual activity or stimulation in the absence of a regular partner has made them already aroused; so again, they do not require complex fantasies to provide the excitement they already feel. Boys develop the habit of masturbating quickly because their activities are generally carried out in family bathrooms where prolonged stays will cause suspicion, as well as possible inconvenience on the part of others.

About 20 years ago Felicia Saunders captured America's imagination with the theme from the movie *Moulin Rouge,* a song that asked

"Where Is Your Heart?" The lyric described the worry and wondering a woman felt with her lover and asked if when they kissed, he closed his eyes, pretending she was someone else. The thing that bothers a woman most about a man's fantasies is the nagging concern that she might not even be in them.

What do men fantasize about mostly during sexual activity? How often are they thinking about someone else? Is their usual sex life exciting enough, or do they dream of more exotic situations?

*Question 40: What sort of thoughts do you have during intercourse or masturbation?*

| | |
|---|---|
| About partner you're currently involved with | 64.0% |
| About a person other than current partner | 11.0% |
| Recalling a past sexual experience | 11.0% |
| No thoughts | 9.1% |
| About group sex or other unusual sexual experiences | 4.5% |
| Sadistic or masochistic ideas | 2.2% |
| No answer | 1.4% |

It will probably be reassuring to women to learn that about two-thirds of men are preoccupied with their current partners. Married men (64 percent) gave this answer just as often as the others, although, at 12 percent, they were slightly higher than men not living with wives in fantasizing about *other* partners.

College-educated men seemed to have richer fantasy lives, since about 8 percent said they had no fantasies compared to approximately 12 percent of men who did not go beyond high school. Similarly, professional men (6 percent) and students (7 percent) were least likely to report "no thoughts," while the retired/unemployed were highest (15 percent) in disavowing fantasies.

The oldest age group reported "no thoughts" in 17 percent of the case, about twice as often as men under 55. This group over 55 also had the lowest frequency of fantasies about outside partners—6 percent—compared to 11 or 12 percent in the other age brackets.

Non-white males were less prone to fantasize; 13 percent of them reporting no thoughts, against 9 percent of whites. However, their fantasies were more likely to be unconventional, with 4 percent of blacks and 7 percent of "other races" reporting sadistic or masochistic ideas, compared to 2 percent of whites. Also, the nonwhites said they thought about group sex or other unusual sexual experiences in 7 percent of the cases, as did only 4 percent of white males.

# Such Stuff as Dreams Are Made On

Women's fantasies often read like erotic novels, as evidenced by books such as Nancy Friday's *My Secret Garden* and *Forbidden Flowers*. Men do not cultivate their fantasies as carefully; as youngsters, their problem is not to coax their sexual drives into bloom, but, like weeds, to keep them under control. We suspect that the men who did have involved fantasies were reluctant to reveal them, and we did get such answers as: "Too personal . . . can't answer question without lying—insufficient data . . . uninformed in this area . . . don't remember . . . N.C. . . . classified information . . . I'll have to think about this one."

What was the question that provoked more evasive responses than the Watergate hearings? What was the question that men shied away from after discussing oral sex, impotence, and cheating?

*Essay Question: What are your favorite sexual fantasies during masturbation? Do you think about famous sex symbols, about far-out sexy things, or about your usual sex partner? Do you ever fantasize during intercourse, and what about?*

Although only 11 percent of our sample said on the computerized questionnaire that they thought about a person other than their current partner, a far larger percentage of those giving a written response spoke of fantasies involving other women in answer to this query. The multiple-choice question mentioned intercourse first, while the essay question referred first to masturbation, so perhaps men concentrated on their reactions during intercourse when 64 percent checked "partner currently involved with." Many of the reported fantasies involving women other than a wife or regular partner did not pertain to specific women, but to anonymous desirable imaginary females:

"When I masturbate, I usually think about girls seducing me. These girls are usually older experienced women and are so used to having sex that they can pay attention to your satisfaction, rather than thinking about their own orgasms or satisfying themselves. Sex symbols do not turn me on at all; I usually think that they have no sexual organs. I usually am turned on by magazines like *Penthouse, Gallery, Hustler*. The pictures that easily produce an erection are those of women in very natural unself-conscious poses, and the women are usually *not* endowed with silicone breasts, pink vulva lips and combed pubic hair. I often think of anal sex. One of the first girls I had sex with did not want to lose her virginity, so I had my first orgasm *in* a woman in her anus. I often masturbate imagining this with my prevailing girl friend who doesn't want it."

"Pretty blondes with shapely rears, spread apart with all sex organs exposed. Never any fantasies about my usual sex partner. Yes [during intercourse], more often about someone that I know or have seen recently."

"Fantasies—walking up to a fox chick, asking her to go to bed with a consent, no strings attached. During sex with wife, I am totally wrapped up in her love and sex."

"I like porno films and sometimes think about the sexy women in them, or put myself in the man's place. Never about my sex partner."

"I do not fantasize during sexual encounters with my wife. My fantasies at other times have to do with situations and actions of a generalized visible partner rather than specific people."

"I think about sexy, very pretty women, nude. I fantasize about my sexual partner's nude body during intercourse."

"Yes—other partners, what youth would have been like had I not been a virgin when married."

"Being with an extremely well-built woman."

Women today seem to be very tolerant of husbands or steady mates who warm up their libidos by thumbing through male-oriented magazines. These girls are merely paper tigresses, but when a man begins fantasizing about flesh-and-blood women in the immediate vicinity, there is always the danger that one of them might actually get into the game:

"My favorite fantasy is making love with women I know on a daily basis who I would never have a chance to enjoy. Oral sex is a thing with me—an ego trip of another woman who one would never suspect to enjoy such things. During intercourse with my wife, I have thought of past relationships or someone else I would enjoy making love with."

"I fantasize mostly on a girl I've wanted or one which was very pretty. Usually these girls are uninterested in me. This is due to lack in personality when you first meet."

"I just keep repeating the name of the woman I used to go with. I fantasize about her all the time."

"Within the past couple of years, I decided that masturbation was 'wrong,' even though I understand that it's considered healthy. During intercourse, often fantasize about a gal whom I'd rather be with, because I'm not totally interested in my present partner."

"Only about different women who I would like to have sex with. And usually will within about 6 months. I just put my mind to it."

"Fantasize before, during, and after both masturbation and intercourse. Masturbate whenever I need to relax—think of any woman I know or imagine—not any stars. Intercourse—always about another woman unless a new experience. Variety is the key."

"Making love to sisters-in-law. Yes [during intercourse], fantasize about different partners and positions."

"Making it with a Farrah Fawcett or some other sex symbol. [During intercourse], once in a while. When I'm not with my usual partner."

"Raquel Welch, Marilyn Monroe."

"Getting a 'special' from Linda Lovelace."

Walter de la Mare wrote: "Memory—that strange deceiver!/Who can trust her? How believe her . . . ." Perhaps it is memory's unreliability that makes men return to past pleasures in the midst of present ones, as a few of our respondents do:

"A past experience which was outstanding. [Think about] far-out sexy things. I fantasize about one of my ex-lovers who is the best sex partner I ever had and who is also in my heart."

"Fantasize about past sexual experiences before I got married.

Pin-ups in girlie magazines or women that have encouraged me but I didn't pursue."

"To be making love to a long-ago love, who is now married."

"Old sex encounters. Yes [during intercourse], things I've heard or read that I'd like to try."

"My fantasies during masturbation are recalling pleasurable moments of past experiences, or substituting another woman into those scenes. (Always someone I personally know.) No fantasies occur during intercourse."

How far is "far-out"? The bible says that King Solomon had 700 wives and 300 concubines; it also says he was wise, so we assume he never engaged more than one at a time in bed. In fantasy, however, there is a place for folly:

"I think about my usual sexual partner and some about past partners. I sometimes fantasize about my past partners being all together at once and exciting me."

"Being in bed with two women is my most common fantasy. Movie starlets and Playmates of the month are unrealistic silicone dolls."

"I sometimes think about sex with two women at the same time or about two women having sex together."

"Having some girl sit on my cock (fucking) and having oral sex with another female—other times, just about my female. Most of time, I just concentrate on what is going on."

"I fantasize about having intercourse with six women at one time!"

Men have been known to say, "The worst sex I ever had was still pretty good." Some men fantasize about it's being even better than it usually is, however:

"Making a woman have an orgasm she can't handle and hold me like never before, and during orgasm having oral sex with me."

"First of all, I guess I am in the minority, but I do not masturbate. I sometimes fantasize that intercourse is going to be more intense than it actually is. Never about another woman."

"Boobs, famous sex symbols or less famous sex symbols. Having a bigger penis."

"Large penises and oral sex."

"That it will never stop."

Dan Greenburg recently wrote in *Playboy:* "I suppose that going into an S/M store to buy chain shackles in the seventies is equivalent to going into a drugstore for a box of condoms in the fifties." Well, maybe so, but the few who admitted to fantasies of domination and control were restrained in their comments:

"I think of different ways of having control over the woman I am having sex with such as 'B&D.'"

"[During masturbation] attractive woman that I find more perfect than my wife (i.e., anatomy). [During intercourse] not usually, unless it's to convince myself that I'm sexually dominating her."

"I have sadomasochistic fantasies."

"Rape. No [fantasies during intercourse]."

Since a fantasy is the product of imagination, it should not be unimaginative. Here are a few of the more original ones:

"Only masturbation fantasies would be of a woman masturbating to give herself more pleasure and heightened orgasm. [During intercourse] I just think of the pleasure I'm giving the woman I'm with."

"Oral and anal intercourse with my wife."

"Having a beautiful woman with me. I think about sex symbols or my sex partner. I have fantasized about being in a different environment with my partner."

"Two women making love."

"I think about my wife nude—and about having anal sex."

"Having sex with another partner, male/female. More times male than female. Do not fantasize during intercourse, because it is happening!"

"[During masturbation] a nude woman on a satin bed. Yes [during intercourse], another partner."

"I think about a favorite partner. I fantasize about floating during intercourse."

"Yes. I enjoy dog style. Fantasize I'm a big black dog."

Considering they were in the majority, we got few detailed answers from the men who thought about their current partners. This is because the thoughts were rarely true fantasies and focused on actual events that were happening or had recently occurred:

"Most of the time I think about my usual sex partner, but occasionally I will fantasize about some girl I have met or seen during the day or perhaps a week."

"Wouldn't masturbate in the first place. If I need to be relieved myself, my wife would feel free enough to help me climax without intercourse. Yes [fantasize during intercourse] about how many different ways me and my wife could do it."

"I mostly think about my partner; making her feel sexy."

"My thoughts are involved with the person I am with, only."

"Just give it all I've got and enjoy the relationship I've got with my wife."

"I fantasize about how great the relationship is with my partner and what I can do to make her happy. I concentrate my thoughts on the fabulous feelings we are experiencing."

In the play *A Thousand Clowns,* when the unconventional hero was told by his angry girl friend to return to reality, he replied, "Only as a tourist!" Some down-to-earth men, however, rarely leave it:

"No famous sex symbols since 16 years old! Usually don't [masturbate] anymore—basically have the urges covered by love relationships. Don't fantasize during intercourse either since about 19 years."

"No favorite fantasies. I love my sex, my demands are quite high, I love lovemaking, my wife fulfills all my desires, she had a good teacher."

"Fantasies consist more of 'far-out sexy things' than about famous sex symbols. Intercourse is too 'attention grabbing' to allow for fantasy."

"Never fantasize. I believe in total reality."

"About taking care of the business at present."

"I have always had good woman; mother thumb and her four daughters don't cut it. Fantasy is just that—fantasy; reality is what counts."

## Fantastic Lovers

Claudia's dream really upset her; she dreamed she was having an affair with another man. So, guilt-ridden, she told her husband about it and the man involved—Tonto. "How did he take it?" her therapist asked. "He thought it was funny," she said.

The therapist thought it was funny, too, but he and Claudia both realized the dream wasn't all as innocent as it seemed. Claudia was far too moralistic to dream, let alone fantasize, about an affair with a real man, even one whom she didn't know. The Lone Ranger would have been fairly safe—no one even has seen what he looks like with his mask off; but to be *extra* cautious, Claudia displaced the fantasy one step farther to the *faithful* Indian companion: a remote man of another race, one who is never seen with a woman.

Like Freud, Claudia was surprised to learn that other people have fantasies, too. After Kevin, her husband, proved so accepting of her brave confession, she asked him if he ever fantasized about other women. Kevin admitted to an occasional erotic thought about Barbara Eden. Kevin, like Claudia, was also displacing his fantasies to a remote, unreal figure. Not only is Barbara Eden an inaccessible Hollywood actress, but she portrays a completely implausible character on her television show, a genie who can disappear at will, change size, live for centuries, and work all sorts of magic. While Miss Eden's physical attractions are very real, by relating to the character she portrays, Kevin could dispel any lingering guilt, because the genie is so obviously unreal.

Husbands and wives are often encouraged to share their sexual fantasies with one another. This is generally a good idea, for it often leads to discovery of mutually acceptable ideas for adding variety to their sex lives, and even the discussion itself can be erotically stimulating. The advantage of a long-term committed sexual relationship is precisely that the partners can get to know each other's preferences and idiosyncrasies far better than any casual partner; the sexually inhibited wife who insists on a lackluster, routine pattern of lovemaking is like a player who leaves the strongest piece on the board unmoved or the highest card unplayed. However, when it comes to turning fantasies face-up, beware of revealing faces other than the partner's own which crop up in sexual reveries—it can lead to accusations of two-faced duplicity and doubling your jeopardy rather than your fun.

Fantasizing about someone other than the spouse or regular partner is not really the same as fantasizing about cheating. We have seen that two-thirds of men believe they are not totally invulnerable to the prospect of cheating, and yet not much more than one in ten has erotic fantasies about other women, and many of these involve improbable partners such as magazine models and film stars or even totally imaginary people. The girl in the sexual fantasy is a throwback to the adolescent masturbatory fantasy, the forbidden, highly sensual prostitute who existed only for the purpose of sexual gratification. It is difficult for some men to see their wives (just as they could not see their mothers) in such a role, so they may have to rely on images of their first real or fantasized erotic objects to intensify their sexual arousal.

The wife will usually not be aware of her husband's secret fantasies, but if she should find out (and some men confess them when wishing to punish the wife), does she have to accept them as an immutable fact of their particular sex life? No, she may be able to displace her imaginary rivals by helping her husband to see her, without guilt, in the role of the uninhibited "prostitute." Note that several of our respondents reported that they fantasized about their wives engaging in oral or anal intercourse or various sexual positions, or exhibiting her nude body. Here, they converted their customary love objects into more exciting sexual objects by imagining them engaging in forms of erotic activity thought somewhat taboo or, at least, less conventional. We suspect most of these men rarely were able to get their wives to engage in the kind of variety that so stimulated them in fantasy. Visual stimulation is also far more important to men than women, as evidenced by the success of the profusion of erotic pictorial publications—when publishers tried to cash in on a similar market among liberated women, the chief buyers of the nude male layouts were male homosexuals. Darkness, bedcovers, and most sexual positions deny a man the sight of his partner's body during intercourse, and many try to retain an image in memory.

What of men like the respondent who kept repeating the name of a girl he had loved many years ago? Or the married men who fantasized about women they encountered in their everyday life? Such men are more likely to be dissatisfied with their marriages, since they are dwelling on partners who are not the clearly unattainable fantasy figures that other men use to build or release sexual tension. The fish that got away was always the best one, and the girl a man did not quite marry is easy to imagine as the ageless perfect mate; in most affairs, partners rarely have to put up with each other at their worst, so the mutual admiration that builds self-esteem is constructed on an incomplete foundation and rarely weathers the assaults of time, except in fantasy.

Fantasies involving theoretically accessible people are vicarious affairs and, if the women involved do not dominate the man's interests or eclipse his feelings toward his wife, are certainly preferable to actual affairs and may even revitalize his sexual prowess. Some therapists believe that occasional extramarital affairs can be beneficial to a marriage by increasing the sexual interest and performance of a man, who will then bring this renewed vigor back to a stagnant marriage. What the experts never explain is why the man, having found such satisfaction elsewhere, would bother to come back to an unrewarding marriage. The older man who fears his potency is declining or who actually experiences impotence through anxiety is likely to find the problem aggravated, not ameliorated, by attempting intercourse with a strange partner—unless the new partner is extremely supportive and his wife very unsympathetic. Again, how such an experience is supposed to make him want to return from the flush of victory to the scene of his previous defeats is incomprehensible. If the mistress who exists in fantasy keeps him motivated only for sexual activity, he will not experience failure with his wife, and she remains the ultimate recipient of his lovemaking. Again, a real embrace is a better trophy than a kiss blown into the air from a fantasy, so a wife who provides ongoing motivation and rewards may soon obviate the need for imaginary cheerleaders.

# Beyond Wildest Dreams

As far as his treatment of women, there was no nicer guy than Jeff. After his divorce in his early thirties, he developed relationships with several women. Unlike many other men, Jeff never foisted himself sexually upon a woman; he would take her out to dinner, engage in deep conversation for hours afterward, maybe even play his guitar for her, and go to bed with her only if she seemed to really desire him (which she invariably did). Nor was Jeff the possessive type; he didn't expect to be the only man in a woman's life—it generally happened that after a few weeks of consistent exposure to Jeff's sincere attentions and devoted concern, the woman began turning away other men so that Jeff would have as much of her time as he wanted. Then, Jeff would become aware of shortcomings in the relationship, decide he was seeing too much of her, and find a more attractive woman. After this happened several times, Jeff's therapist wondered aloud if Jeff might not be harboring certain feelings of hostility toward women. Jeff, a psychologically sophisticated sort, could certainly see why this would be suspected; but, try as he might, he honestly did not feel any conscious resentment or anger towards women. Finally, the therapist asked Jeff what he thought about when he masturbated.

"I rarely do it," Jeff said, "but the fantasy is always the same. I'm having intercourse with an attractive girl I barely know. When I'm finished, I look down at her with a feeling of contempt and say, 'That's all you're good for!' "

The masturbatory fantasy, if it can be expressed, often reflects the core attitudes and conflicts about sex. The fantasy may be brought to intercourse to fulfill emotional needs that the act with a particular partner cannot fill. According to Hunt, 72 percent of young husbands still masturbate, 50 percent above Kinsey's figures 25 years earlier, and with a frequency four times as great as that reported by Kinsey. The median frequency for husbands under 35 is about twice a month; while this may be dependent to some extent on the unavailability of the wife as a sexual partner, for reasons of menstruation, illness, or pregnancy, the fact that more husbands now masturbate and more frequently since Kinsey's time, in spite of women's increased acceptance and enjoyment of intercourse and willingness to participate in noncoital sexual activity, would indicate that men are freer from guilt to follow their natural inclinations.

Both Kinsey and Hunt found that about 86 percent of single men under the age of 24 masturbated; however, Hunt found, 25 years after Kinsey, that far fewer single men stopped masturbating but rather, did so more frequently than in Kinsey's time as they entered their thirties. It is ironic that it was the Women's Liberation Movement which was highly instrumental in stressing the importance of masturbation, especially for women who had difficulty in achieving orgasm. With the increased preoccupation with the clitoris as the physiological center for orgasm, many writers extolled the superiority of masturbation over intercourse as a source of female gratification, and the lesbian wing of the movement swooped on this approach to advocate eliminating men from women's sex lives altogether. Eminent sex therapists, such as Masters and Johnson and Helen Singer Kaplan, encouraged female patients who had never reached orgasms with partners to seek orgasm first through masturbatory techniques.

This wide acceptance of female masturbation seemed to encourage males, whose prohibitions against masturbation generally are derived directly or indirectly from their mothers, to regard their own masturbatory activities with less guilt. Not all men can accept it, of course. Harry came into one session and literally sobbed, "Do you know what I did last week? I masturbated—just like a little boy! If I had acted like a man, I could have gone down to the bar and picked up some woman. What's wrong with me?"

To the therapist, it seemed that it would be far healthier for Harry to relieve his tension in a solitary act rather than engaging another human being in an impersonal act. If the woman were a true whore, it would further strengthen Harry's convictions that all women were prostitutes; he had married and divorced three wives who were flagrant cheaters. If he had justified the pickup by pretending a romantic interest, he likely would have talked both the woman and himself into another stormy affair, such as he had just ended, or a fourth disastrous marriage. Not many men, fortunately, have Harry's incredible propensity for ill-fated liaisons, but the man who completely rejects masturbation as immature is bound to treat women, at least some of the time, as mere lust objects—i.e., prostitutes. A vagina is an ideal receptacle for a penis in need of sexual release, as one tends to get every few days; however, vaginas are inevitably attached to entire women, possessing brains and feelings—some liberated women oblige by not bringing their feelings to the encounter, which tends to leave a man, postorgasm, with Jeff's postmasturbatory sentiment: "That's all you're good for."

The married man, faced with an unenthusiastic wife, may prefer masturbation rather than confront the most threatening turn-off for today's man, the unresponsive woman; or, the truly empathetic husband who is guilt-free about masturbating might honestly feel it would be insensitive to press a tired or ill wife just for the sake of his own gratification. Or he may have a psychological need to be alone with his fantasies.

The most common "far-out" fantasies—group sex, extraordinarily prolonged sex, and sadomasochism—have a common theme of domination and control. They reassure the man who questions his adequacy. Group sex fantasies rarely involve other men, as a real "orgy" would, but only two or more women. The fantasizer feels he is so competent that he can satisfy not only one woman, but several at once.

Men often fantasize about having larger penises. Despite the reams of advice written by experts that penis size has nothing whatever to do with satisfying a woman (we must bear in mind that the average expert probably has an average penis and may be prejudiced), many males have never accepted this and feel that length is the yardstick of a man's true measure. Men know that, despite the writings of experts who point out that large breasts represent accumulations of fat, do not contain more mammary glandular tissue, do not reflect femininity or sexuality, and are only modified sweat glands anyhow, the amply endowed woman still beats the competition nearly every time—if men so size up women, why should not women do the same? Masters and Johnson's detailed description (contemptuously called by Shere Hite "a Rube Goldberg model") of how the penis exerts traction indirectly on the clitoral hood by moving the engorged labia suggests that a thick penis might actually be more effective in producing orgasm in a woman—this might have led to men's swapping their rulers for tape measures, but did nothing to alleviate their preoccupation with measurements. Even if he is content with standard operating equipment, the man may dream of being able to prolong intercourse for hours, inducing his partner to one cataclysmic orgasm after the other until her brain is numbed with ecstasy and she is convinced he is the most desirable lover she could possibly wish.

Sadomasochistic fantasies are obviously related to ideas of control and domination. While only 2.2 percent of our sample reported S-M fantasies (and, in another question, 1.2 percent wanted to try more of such activity), other investigators have reported considerably higher figures, especially among younger groups. In Hunt's 1972 study, 18 percent of men under 35 had experienced fantasies of rape while masturbating, 6.2 percent of that age group had experienced pleasure from inflicting pain, and 10.3 percent of all single males had experienced sexual pleasure from inflicting pain. In *Playboy*'s 1976 college campus poll, 3 percent of males reported trying and enjoying master-slave role-playing and being tied up in sexual activity, while another 2 percent had enjoyed inflicting or receiving pain during sex. More significant, 19 percent said they would like to try the role playing and 18 percent were willing to try bondage.

Since we are dealing primarily with fantasy here, we can rule out the mildest and most common types of pain inflicted in sexual activity, the biting, scratching or otherwise rough behavior incidentally, accidentally or purposefully inflicted during passionate lovemaking. Bondage and role playing do not usually involve pain; Alex Comfort's section on bondage in *Joy of Sex,* with its emphasis on soft tying material, careful positioning, time limits, and precautions, would encourage only a long-suffering masochistic "master" to attempt such pseudo-sadistic endeavors. In such activities, the aim is ostensibly to intensify the orgasm of the restrained partner, hardly a cruel pastime.

Altruism notwithstanding, the bound female has always figured prominently in preadolescent male fantasies. The cover illustrations on any comic-book rack will portray in ample quantity young women tied, chained, pinioned, or otherwise restrained while being threatened by whatever savages, jungle beasts, space aliens, or criminals are appropriate to the type of comic book the bound heroine is a routine part of. Wonder Woman can be effectively bound only by her own golden lasso, but since she conveniently carries it on her belt, it is the handiest thing available to her foes, and she manages to get into a bind at least once an issue. Nor do boys always outgrow this fascination; Hera was the queen of all the Greek goddesses, but you hardly ever see a painting or statue of her, whereas a nobody like Andromeda, whose only claim to fame was being chained naked to a rock, inspired more paintings and statues than Farrah Fawcett-Majors did posters.

Some psychoanalysts say the bound female represents the boy's mother. He denies her sexual interest in father by picturing her as held in the sexual relationship against her will. When the boy dreams of rescuing schoolmarms from outlaws or damsels from dragons, the villain is dear old dad; the hero rides off quickly before the Oedipal fantasy gets too out of hand.

In the *Playboy* cartoon or the adult *S-M* fantasy, the hero picks up where the villain left off, and the juvenile bondage fantasy progresses to the adult rape fantasy. Rape as a crime is violent and aggressive rather than erotic; but in the typical rape fantasy, hostility is not as much the motivating factor as is fear, the dread of competing openly in a free market, and of trying to win a woman's love given voluntarily. The man may have fantasies in which he is participating in or even merely watching a gang rape, identifying with men he sees as more powerful and masculine than himself. In most rape fantasies, as in the pornographic books and movies, the female victim struggles virtuously, but ultimately has a tremendous orgasm as a result of the rape, a very improbable happening in real life; in the fantasy, she may beg her assaulter to continue or fall in love with him. The woman's initial resistance is crucial, however—it affirms the madonna's repudiation of sex from other men, and once the rapist has demonstrated his exceptional capabilities, the woman is now forevermore his spiritual captive, knowing no other man could begin to satisfy her as well.

In one "underground novel" from the Victorian era, the hero not only restrains and has his way with the virgin of his dreams, but enlists her help into repeating the adventure with two subsequent nonvirgins; one, however, proves to have been deflowered by scoundrels who drugged her, and the other is a young widow whose husband died within weeks of their marriage, so in the fantasy, even nonvirgins must be practically virgins. As the hero incites them to implausible levels of lust, the madonnas become prostitutes, the two ancient fantasy images fusing into one woman. The hero's last two victims are actually a mother and daughter pair, a hefty but still voluptuous matron and an innocent maiden, both resistant, and both finally succumbing, as the hero triumphs over even the Victorian sexual mother who inspired the prostitute-madonna complex to begin with.

In the preadolescent bondage fantasy, the hero wins the woman's love by freeing her from an evil captor, but he cannot accept the physical rewards of that love. In the adult rape fantasy, the hero is now the captor, but he nevertheless wins the woman's love by freeing her from the sexual inhibitions that checked her orgasms; he proves himself the superlover.

Do not assume that, in S-M fantasies, men are always the dominant ones. Many men not only picture themselves as the ones in bondage, but many pay prostitutes high fees to help them act out these fantasies. At the 1976 annual meeting of the American Psychiatric Association, Doctors Janus and Bess reported on a study involving 52 high-class call girls and madams, whose clientele consisted chiefly of politicians and powerful executives. These prominent men tended to prefer flagellation, bondage and humiliation—the opposite of the role their daily life demanded. We might speculate that the inability of these men to assert themselves in the sexual sphere makes them channel their aggressive drives into business and political activities as a compensation mechanism. Prostitutes who specialize in "B&D" (bondage and discipline) usually do not even engage in sexual relations with their high-paying customers. Paradoxically, the prostitute becomes the punitive madonna, punishing the man for his sexual desires and withholding gratification.

According to Hunt, there are always twice as many females engaging in masochistic sexual roles as in sadistic ones, while in males, the sadistic predominates, two-to-one. However, Hunt found that nearly as many young men fantasize about being forced to have sex as about forcing a partner; nearly one-quarter of women under 35 fantasize about rape while masturbating, but only 3 percent see themselves in the role of a rapist. Young men who fantasize about being raped and dominated by women do so not only to escape the guilt they may feel about sex, but also to feel that their bodies are admired and craved by women the way that men feel desire. Feminists claim that rape fantasies debase women, but many females report, on the contrary, a feeling of exhilaration while fantasizing about how their bodies are driving one or more men into a frenzy of lust. Some men are weary of being the satyric pursuers, not knowing whether a woman really wants sex with them, or is merely trying to placate them; they delight in fantasies about being a highly desired object of female lust.

When S-M fantasies and bedroom games enter the darker areas of painful bondage, flagellation, and other infliction of pain, the male frustration at handling a conventional give-and-take love affair spills into more overt hostility, particularly in fantasies. Couples who actually engage in bedroom beating (it's respectable enough for Alex Comfort to give pointers in *The Joy of Sex* and for specialty shops to stock whips and paddles which, according to one owner, average secretaries rush to buy as Valentine's Day gifts) are more likely into sublimated guilt than frank hostility, with the more masochistic partner not only receiving, but calling the shots. We shall not attempt to evaluate the detailed anatomical lessons written by experts who discuss the common roots of the posterior femoral cutaneous nerve, the perineal nerve, and the dorsal nerve of the clitoris whereby blows to the buttocks transmit impulses, etc.—there are obviously more direct routes to clitoral stimulation. But fantasies begin to be threatening when the violence outweighs the sex. We could accept a villain's attempting to split Pearl White in half with a buzz saw or the natives stringing up Fay Wray as a human sacrifice because we understood the censors would not let them indulge in the nice, healthy sexual activity they would have preferred. Now, when the violence persists and overshadows the sexual expression that is openly permitted on screen, we are far more disquieted by films such as *Clockwork Orange* and *Straw Dogs* than the innocent mayhem of the thirties or even the primarily sexual excesses of *The Story of O* or *Belle de Jour*.

It is a dangerous mistake to suppose that true sadism and sexual cruelty spring entirely from repressive societies. Boredom is also a stimulus to such excesses. Frustration arises when people engage in sexual activity with an air of detachment, where one partner has not the slightest inkling of the other's thoughts or feelings; the infliction of pain or discomfort would at least force the recipient to acknowledge the presence of the other, to respond in some meaningful way, to care about what is happening. Aggression and sexual behavior are closely linked in animals, for males must vie with others to win females, and females must often select mates by fending off undesirable ones. It is folly to think that evolution has freed us completely of the old neural interactions. S-M fantasies and bedroom games are not necessarily pathological and may be exciting, but as society becomes increasingly bored with "freedom" and turns to ever-new experimentation, dangerous borders are passed without notice.

The use of children in pornographic films and books is already widespread enough to cause national concern. There are the underground "snuff" films, which allegedly show women actually being mutilated and killed; while it is believed these films are fakes, their chief appeal lies in the uncertainty of what one is witnessing. How far could things possibly go? We can always recall the Roman Empire where the arena of the Colosseum was the scene of preadolescent girls raped by apes, men castrated, and wild dogs tearing apart a prostitute and her partner in the midst of a sex demonstration; the horror of the Colosseum was not that such things occurred, but that they were eagerly enjoyed by the general populace, the mob as well as the distinguished writers, Petronius, Suetonius, Martial, and others whose vivid eyewitness accounts survive them. At the end of the line of the most brutal sexual excesses one finds not ultimate revulsion and rebellion, but boredom, spiritual death. Thus Marcus Aurelius said of the Roman games: "I wouldn't mind the games being brutal and degrading if only they weren't so damned monotonous."

This grim little digression has a point. Fantasy and novelty can be the lifeblood of a sexual relationship, but they can never substitute fully for feelings of love, security, and purpose within a relationship. Fantasy, like sex itself, is a powerful force and should never be taken lightly; his fantasy probably brings us closer to the real person than all his conscious philosophies and goals. Men can never completely escape their fantasies, but neither must they allow the fantasies to enslave them. Fantasy must be the flame that illuminates a world of realistic satisfactions, not one that consumes that reality and leaves ashes where there once was hope.

# The Woman to Beat

Jeff, our now-familiar patient, never seemed satisfied. The wife he divorced had been a petite, attractive but unimposing brunette. His first serious love after her was a pretty, devoted foreign student, whom he ultimately deserted for a well-built, highly responsive divorcée. Still his eyes wandered and he kept imagining himself with what he termed a "really strong" woman. When asked to define "strong," he spoke of a tall girl, long, blonde hair, spectacular figure —formidable, perhaps, but not "strong" in its usual sense. It seems that Jeff was always pitting in his imagination the current love of his life against some ideal who he felt to be still beyond his worth, but whom he was nearing with each woman he wooed, won, and discarded. "Did you ever have a dream girl?" his thera- pist asked. "Someone who had all the qualifications you could pos- sibly want in a woman, someone you fantasized about being in love with?" And Jeff would always say, "No, I don't think so—no one really definite."

Unsatisfied, his therapist would repeat the question every few months. Then, after Jeff had been in therapy for well over a year, he gave a different answer to the old question: "Well, I don't know if you'd really consider it having a dream girl. There was this blonde I used to imagine . . . her name was Susan. . . ."

The therapist sighed. "She has a name? You're not sure whether you had a dream girl, and you gave her a *name*?"

Susan had been with Jeff since the age of 8. He recalled showing a picture of a model on a calendar to a little girl and saying, "That's my girl friend." Jeff did not recall where the name came from; Susan was the name of one of the neighborhood mothers, any of whom would have been perceived as preferable to his own unaffectionate and complaining mother. Long before puberty, he was having fanta- sies of meeting this adult woman in hallways and clutching her in truly erotic embraces. Susan was his sidekick in his most cherished fantasies, being an intrepid FBI agent wielding a deadly pistol. Years later, as a college professor, Jeff would secretly pack his target pistol under his jacket and yearn to be a policeman. Susan had been almost forgotten, but his eyes would not stop wandering until he either found her or consciously renounced her.

Wives and sweethearts often look with envy at the pinup girls and television stars their men ogle; these are the women they feel they could never hope to beat, and the love of their men is secure only because these models of physical perfection are in short supply and beyond the reach of the average working man. These pinups, or their similar predecessors, were the objects of the man's first juvenile sexual fantasies, their images the sole mute witnesses to his masturbatory sins. They, for all their sweet smiles and wholesome attitudes, are the "prostitutes" that cater to the fantasies unable to find vent in real objects.

Wives and sweethearts are rarely aware of a far more powerful rival, the dream girl. The pinup prostitute is the imagined first sex object, but the dream girl is the first love object. As the teen-aged boy grows too big to seek counsel and direct affection from his mother, while he is still too insecure and immature to find emotional support in a female peer, he fantasizes a girl who is sweetheart, confidante, companion, and partner—essentially a young madonna to complement his paper prostitutes. While the dream girl, as his true love, is envisioned to be the male's sex partner, the erotic components are minimized; sex acts with the dream girl tend to be dispassionate, aesthetic visions, as opposed to graphic masturbatory fantasies. The dream girl is rarely perceived as a threat, as the woman to beat, by someone who seeks to win a man's love—but if he seems vaguely dissatisfied, if he has the uneasy sensation that the relationship is not quite right, or if he casts an apprehensive eye at every female passerby, beware the dream girl. A loving woman might successfully battle flesh-and-blood threats to her relationship, but taking on the dream girl is like shadowboxing. Nobody ever beat a shadow, even a delicate feminine one—but shedding some light on it might dispel the threat.

*Essay Question: Have you ever had a "dream girl"? What is she or what was she like?*

One commonly expressed idea was that the dream girl functioned as a partner and ally. The man was no longer alone but, with her, was part of an effective team:

"Physically—attractive, slim, well-proportioned. I am more concerned with the overall effect than in being a breast man or a leg man or whatever. She should be intelligent, self-confident, able and willing to keep up with current affairs. She should be compassionate—someone I can express fears to, try out ideas on and expect a tactful 'it stinks' if, indeed, it does. She should be good at cooking, keeping house and running a home, yet be a good hostess and an excellent date. Being perfectly realistic— no woman can be all things, but that would be my dream world. Any woman who meets the intelligence criteria wouldn't be happy as a housewife. But most important—my dream girl has to have an attitude that allows her to go into harness, if necessary. Not under me but with me; i.e., partners in good or bad times."

"Very loving, intelligent, sexy, doing everything together, and having a good time when together."

"Yes, she's a Puerto Rican girl, my age, very intelligent, interested in just one man, very attractive, loves children and her work, and is interested in my ways just as I am hers."

"Good build, fairly attractive, one who would want to share everything possible, one who has an attitude of *we*, not I or you. So we could seek a pleasurable enjoyable life in all things and activities, *lovingly.*"

"A good-looking girl I could be sure loved me as much as I loved her."

Love follows acceptance and acceptance requires understanding. Many men dreamed of a woman who understood them well and cared about them and for their needs:

"My dream girl is a beautiful woman—clean at all times, good in bed and good wife. Also that enjoys me and understands me under any circumstance."

"A woman who fully understands me, knows how to take my moods, so that in turn it would probably help me to understand hers and other people's moods better."

"Someone who realizes that, despite the lifelong propaganda, no one person can ever be all things to a mate, and makes allowances for that."

"She was nice and very humorous to be with. Had a good personality and was understanding to your feelings."

"Tall, thin, nice breasts, nice ass, pretty, loving, active sex partner. Independent, but able to make me feel needed."

"Yes, she was 42"–30"–42," very caring and kind to mostly everyone."

Some men wanted a little of everything:

> "My dream girl would be intelligent, have a nice figure and took care of it properly, should be fun-loving and tried to make as much out of life as she could in the amount of time she is allotted on earth."

> "Assuming 'had' does not have a sexual connotation, yes. She is intelligent, fun to be with, honest and open, not the slightest bit bitchy, and good-looking."

> " 'Dream girls,' like dreams, lack depth and exist only in the mind. My ideal woman would be intelligent, assertive, sincere, warm, beautiful, and sexy."

> "Blonde, blue eyes, intelligent, good cook and good sex partner. Be willing to work and have kids, at least two kids."

> "Intelligent, confident, independent, pretty, and rich."

> "Contains all the best features of previous girl friends."

For some, the qualifications were chiefly physical:

> "Yes. When I was younger mostly. Now and then at present. Usually the 'dream girls' stem from the movies and television. She would fit my requirements as to color of eyes brown or black, height short 5'2" to 5'5" (I'm 5'7 ½" tall). Large breast (not too large—about a 36" or 38"). Flat stomach and thin waistline and shapely legs."

> "Medium height, dark complexion, cute face and trim body, adventurous, likes sex, an outdoors person and my equal in some things, worse in some, others, so that she could help in case I had trouble with something and I could help her in her weak areas."

> "My dream girl is not necessarily the woman that I would like to live with. Blonde, blue eyes, well-proportioned, short and outgoing. 'All-American cheerleader type.' "

> "She would be nice, long hair, good head on her shoulders, close companion. Probably foreign. Half Japanese or something."

There were men who did not mention looks at all—or even said their dream girls were not necessarily beautiful:

"Yes. She's a woman who can accept me for what I am and can live with my mistakes, a woman who has some direction and can do things without being asked or told; she doesn't have to be beautiful, just someone who makes an effort at understanding me equal to the effort I make understanding her."

"Someone with plain old common sense—doesn't have to be beautiful because beauty is only skin deep. It's what's underneath all the makeup that counts."

"Physically attractive (that does not necessarily mean beautiful), intelligence commensurate with my own, a quick wit and a penchant for laughter. Must love adventure in the very broad sense of the word. I suppose that the implication is that we love each other; that is, that there is an emotional attachment. There must be some mutual recreational activities but also the opportunity to be free, open, and independent."

"Very attractive in a plain way. Like the commercial of the 'healthy look.' Very loving and compassionate; very outgoing and energetic. Willing to love me for myself."

"Sure, I think everyone has. It's the type of girl who you always get along with and have the same basic ideas. She has to be easy to talk to. She didn't have to have sex unless she wanted to and I never got mad if she didn't."

"Yes, she's the one you wish you had. Everything to help and make you succeed as a success man."

"She is a girl that combines with my personality and tastes so perfectly that the result is like one new person."

For some men, the dream girl was a woman they had actually known, or at least worshiped from afar:

"There is a 'dream girl' who is the object of many fantasies. She is a beautiful blonde woman (about 10 years older than myself) who lives across the street from my parents. I have, in my mind, bestowed all the qualities of an ideal woman on her. I don't think I ever want to really meet her because it would inevitably burst my balloon. I don't think any woman could have all the right qualities I imagine her having—intelligence, beauty, affection, and self-confidence."

"Yes. I had a crush on the next-door neighbor and took her out a couple of times but never really got to know her due to the fact that she became very interested in someone else. Looked like a replica of the Be-good-to-yourself Tab blonde."

"She was a divorcée, mid-thirties, who was only interested in a good time."

"My dream girl was a high school acquaintance—she was a prom queen."

"I had a dream girl and found her and had her for myself but then lost her to another man."

"She's sexy, intelligent, loving, and married to someone else."

To psychiatrists, a screen memory is one that is recalled in place of a more forbidden one, but to many men, a screen memory is finding your dream girl in a movie or a TV show:

"Yes, I have had a 'dream girl'—I believe all men have had one, at one time in their life! So do all women have 'dream men.' Mine was ideal—she was a replica of former screen star Dolores Del Rio . . . one of the most beautiful and alluring women in the world and on the screen!"

"Farrah Fawcett. But I realize that she is impossible. And I am very much in love with the woman I live with. She is everything I've ever dreamed of."

"The girl in *King Kong*, old and new version."

"Ann Corio, truly a sex symbol."

"Marilyn Monroe and Ingrid Bergman, and a voice like Ella Fitzgerald."

"It was Kim Novak—'point of interest:' My wife is nothing like her but I got a better deal."

"Linda Darnell (dead movie star)."

Farrah Fawcett-Majors was the most mentioned (though her name was spelled correctly only once, with the hyphen omitted). Raquel Welch, Sophia Loren, and Pam Grier got the only other nominations.
A few men married their dream girls:

"I guess I'm one of the few who can say I'm now married to that 'dream girl'—she's everything that woman can mean to a man —beautiful, sexy, loving, intelligent, considerate, kind, understanding, efficient, needs love, gives love, etc."

"Yes—I'm married to her. She loves sex as much as I do. The two of us worked side by side to build our own home. She is a wonderful cook and mother."

"My dream girl is the girl I live with. She is intelligent, has a good personality and enjoys sex with me. She shares many of my goals and interests."

"I married her 30 years ago. The mind of a wizard, the face of an angel, the patience of Job and the body of a prostitute."

"Yes. She was loving, giving, caring, interested in my needs, and then the honeymoon was over."

Not all men dream:

"Since all women are basically different, it's difficult to find a dream girl. Also, I wouldn't bother putting such a consideration like that on anyone. Once you classify someone as a dream girl, then you become dissatisfied with everyone else instead of accepting everyone as individuals. That is discrimination in the very broadest sense of the word and I'm against that. I prefer all my women to be independent individuals."

"I don't need idealized conceptions of women. Real-life women are far more diverse and interesting than anything I can dream up."

"Only as a child—'Utopia,' which is impossible now that I have matured."

"Zilch. Adolescent and immature thinking. For mindless individuals only."

"No. There's too many 'real' ones out there to keep me occupied."

"I don't think there is such a thing."

No two men have quite the same dream. If hell is, as Don Juan says, "the home of the unreal and of the seekers for happiness," then marriages may be made in heaven, but dream girls are fabricated elsewhere:

"Well built and not a brain in her head."

"Yes. She was perfect but has no face."

"One well endowed with everything—looks and tits."

"Yes. Fantasy. ½ earth-½ spiritual."

"Yes.—Unattainable—like the white-knight-on-a-horse routine."

"Yes—beautiful and a nymph."

"An 18-year-old virgin nymphomaniac whose father owns a liquor store."

## Enchantresses and Nymphs

There was a sizable group of men who dreamed of a girl who was always ready to please them sexually and otherwise, who lived her life with the sole purpose of serving them. It was the "Dream of Jeannie" fantasy, the affectionate, beautiful slave with the power to make every wish come true. This theme has been repeated with variations on several TV shows; before Barbara Eden's highly successful *Arabian Nights* fantasy, there was Elizabeth Montgomery's "Bewitched" marriage, the old "Topper" series in which Anne Jeffries played a seductive ghost, and a short-lived affair in which statuesque Julie Newmar played a robot. The comedy in these plots stems either from the women's inability to deliver the happiness their powers promise, or, more likely, the bumbling male's shyness and lack of sophistication which prevent him from capitalizing on his incredible opportunities.

The nymphomaniac is the female counterpart to the myth of the satyr, the sexually insatiable man. The more experts write on the female potential for multiple orgasms, the desirability of uncommitted sex for women, and the advantages of wide experience in sexual partners, the more the nymphomaniac emerges from the subconscious recesses of male minds as a living horror. It has often puzzled social scientists why so many women should have difficulty reaching orgasm; some have postulated, in all seriousness, that primitive man killed off women who had a high sexual drive, leaving only the less responsive women to reproduce; this had to be done for the good of civilization, for the sexually insatiable woman would neither work the fields nor care for the family, but would prowl around in an endless quest for men to gratify her.

Men know that, no matter how much they enjoy sex, they have their limits. They cannot have endless orgasms or even infinitely repeated erections. Women, they have been told, have no such limitations. As in the classical experiment wherein electrodes were imbedded in a rat's hypothalamic pleasure centers of the brain whereupon the rat disdained food and sleep to keep pushing the lever that delivered current through those wires, the woman is envisioned as engaging in an endless sexual revelry, wearing out one male after another in the process of feeding her insatiable lust. Men are aware that some prostitutes can accommodate literally dozens of men a night; men forget that prostitutes virtually never have orgasms with their customers and are not the ecstatically happy creatures our folklore sometimes pictures them to be. The application of the term "whore" to the rare cases of actual nymphomania is a poor choice, for the nymphomaniac truly desires sex, while the whore rarely derives pleasure from her means of livelihood. Like the Don Juans, nymphomaniacs are driven by neurotic needs to prove their desirability or to obtain the illusion of parental affection and concern, not by an uninhibited delight in intercourse and orgasm. Still, men fantasize and dread a creature whom they could never satisfy and who will abandon them when their potency fails under her unmeetable demands.

Why then do many men say they prefer aggressive, highly responsive women? The key here is that such a woman must be totally committed to them, through marriage or other compact. They can accept such a woman only as a one-night stand (prostitute) or as a wife who has progressed from near-virgin to nymph under the man's expert tutelage. He cannot really accept her on any sort of intermediate relationship because he feels he must constantly prove himself and will ultimately lose her on account of the biological inequities between the limited male and the limitless female.

The enchantress is a recurrent myth in our literature; women like Circe and Morgan le Fay were highly attractive to the men they ultimately enslaved. The idea behind the myth is that the woman who has full control over her powers (for sexual gratification) is extremely alluring to men, but will finally rob them of their potency and reduce them to lowly beasts. Only if such a woman is under man's total domination, as in the genie fantasy, can he accept the fully sexual woman. The goodness and unselfish care of the madonna then become fused with the sensuality of the prostitute to give him, in fantasy at least, the best of both.

Here is that fantasy, expressed in the words of our respondents:

"Everyone has at some time [had a 'dream girl']. What is better than dreaming about a beautiful, curvy sexy girl, a gal that would go to bed with you anytime."

"A couple have come close. One was 5' tall, 80–90 lbs., very sexy and always horny, and an outgoing, very active person. Another was 5'4" tall, 110–115 lbs., a beautiful woman and very sexy dancer, who liked to spend a lot of time with me doing what I wanted to do."

"Yes—tall blonde or redhead—sexy-looking figure who wanted to do everything I asked her to—not just sex. She never expressed her opinions."

"Beautiful—sensuous, intelligent and thought a lot more of my needs than her own."

"My dream girl is the right girl for me. The one that can take care of me in all ways."

"Yes! A Greek girl that lived only to please me in all aspects of the life we had. Sexually, socially, a raving beauty, but the fortunes of war caused a separation that could not be rejoined."

"She likes *me* more than anything else."

"Yes, one who knows how to please me, likes the outdoors and is not inhibited."

"She'd do anything I wanted."

"37–24–36. Light brown hair. There at the snap of the fingers."

"Good-looking—not great, smart, sincere and dedicated to me. Very loving."

"Yes. A quiet sort of girl with a sharp mind and wants to please me all the time. She tells me how she loves me and wants me and acts really mature. She talks problems out and doesn't blow up."

"My 'dream girl' was composed of two women. Sexually uninhibited and very loving."

"A dream girl would be warm, intelligent, kind and sincere about herself. She could be either a sweet, coy thing or a harlot, as her mood changes. She would also give great head."

"She was sweet, kind, considerate and giving. But she was also strong, somewhat independent. She was innocent in her actions but experienced and enjoyed lovemaking."

"One hell of a nymphomaniac."

"It'd have to be a beautiful slave."

"Dream girls—36–24–36. Blond—5'6", cute, affectionate, a cook in the kitchen and a whore in the bedroom!"

## The Saintly Prostitute

"Composed of two women. Sexually uninhibited and very loving." . . . "a sweet coy thing or a harlot" . . . "a cook in the kitchen and a whore in the bedroom" . . . again and again that theme of madonna and prostitute repeats itself. In search of the roots of the male myth, we stumble repeatedly against this most ancient of female myths.

Men worship virgins. Back in ancient times, the Greeks had six major goddesses, and half of them (Artemis, Athene, and Hestia) were virgins, though Hestia, as goddess of the hearth, was certainly entitled to a husband. The three nonvirgins were compelled to give up their chastity by virtue of their occupations. Aphrodite, as goddess of love, could scarcely have remained virginal, though she was handicapped in her pursuits by having the ugliest god on Olympus as a husband. Demeter, as goddess of the earth and fertility, likewise could not stay sterile, though half her affairs were rapes by horses and bulls. Hera, as wife of the chief, Zeus, fulfilled her wifely duties, but renewed her virginity once a year by bathing in the magic spring, Canathus. Virginity has been "in" for over 3,000 years and will not become passé until men can wholeheartedly accept their mothers as sexual beings truly enjoying intercourse with fathers; since men would have to accept this in a spirit of maturity at the immature age of 4 or 5, it is unlikely that the sexual revolution now or subsequent periods of enlightenment will ever dethrone the madonna.

But since men must ultimately confront the fact that their mothers were not virgins when they gave birth and since men do not want to despise their mothers as prostitutes, they often turn to a hybrid myth, one that attempts to reconcile the split—that of the prostitute with the heart of gold. Classical and popular literature abounds with these women of ill repute who are truly good and lovable: Sonia in Dostoevsky's *Crime and Punishment;* Melina Mercouri's Ilya in *Never on Sunday;* Broadway's *Irma la Douce;* and "Gunsmoke" 's Miss Kitty (TV costar James Arness caused the producers much embarrassment by saying in an interview what he thought was obvious —"Why, Kitty's a tramp"—not realizing the viewers' psychological need to deny how a saloon girl in the West made her living). The saintly prostitute is man's way of forgiving mother, of rationalizing her sexual history as a harsh and undesired necessity or a repented crime.

The most curious example of man's psychological need for the saintly prostitute is the myth of Mary Magdalene. Even the most devout Bible reader will tell you that she, Christ's most devoted follower, was a prostitute or adulteress who repented her past sins— and there is absolutely no evidence for this in the Scriptures; some church authorities even identify her as a patrician woman of fine breeding, possibly a cousin of Christ. While Luke says she was one of certain women "who had been cured of evil spirits and infirmities," possession by devils was not necessarily related to sin, and was the explanation given for disturbed emotional behavior. There is a preceding account in Luke's gospel of a nameless woman "sinner" who was forgiven by Christ, but there is no justification for assuming this woman was Mary Magdalene, as nearly everyone does.

Significantly, in the new creed that was to replace all the old myths —at the foot of the cross, one of the most influential symbols in man's history, we find a madonna and a prostitute.

# Appendix:
# The Survey

A total of 4,066 men answered our questionnaire. Their homes were located in the following cities and regions:

*NORTHEAST*—1,330 men
New York—Bronx, Queens, Massapequa, Spring Valley, Nanuet, Binghamton, Poughkeepsie, Johnson City, and Dutchess County
New Jersey—Newark and Woodbridge
Massachusetts—Brockton and Framingham
*NORTH CENTRAL*—1,025 men
Ohio—Cincinnati, Kenwood, Dillionville, Hyde Park, Dayton, Fairborn, and Harris Township
Illinois—Chicago, Rosemont, Glen Ellyn, and Palatine
Missouri—Kansas City, St. Louis, and Independence
Wisconsin—Menominee
*SOUTH*—812 men
Washington, D.C.
Maryland—Bowie and College Park
Kentucky—Louisville
Florida—West Palm Beach
Texas—Dallas, Fort Worth, and Irving
Indiana—Clarksville
Georgia—Sumter County
*WEST*—837 men
California—Los Angeles, San Francisco, and Van Nuys
Colorado—Denver
Washington—Seattle
Oregon—Deschutes County
Montana—Great Falls
[62 respondents did not answer the multiple-choice question re-

331

garding the section of the United States in which they lived, probably because of difficulty ascertaining to which region their state
belonged; therefore, the figures given above total 4,004 instead of
4,066]

Comparing our study of 4,066 men with 1970 U.S. Bureau of Census figures, the latest available, we were gratified to see how closely
the percentages in our sample approximated census data regarding
household status, income, type of employment, age, and other
parameters.

| Current Household Status | U.S. Census | Our Study |
|---|---|---|
| Married, living with wife | 70.0% | 64.9% |
| Never married, living alone or with parents and relatives | 20.8% | 18.8% |
| Divorced or separated, alone | 6.6% | 5.8% |
| Widowed, living alone | 2.6% | 0.9% |

Note that the U.S. Census provides no data on unmarried people
living together. We felt that men living with a partner to whom they
were not married should be considered as a special class, rather than
be grouped with the single, divorced, or widowed. And we found
that 6.9 percent of the men we surveyed fell into that category. It
is probable that many such couples reported themselves as married
to census takers. Since our percentages in the above table total only
90.4, the addition of these "living-togethers" to the married column
would bring our figures even closer to those of the Census Bureau.
Only 2.8 percent of our sample reported their household status as
"other," possibly reflecting a shared home with a partner of the same
sex (although we did not qualify "living with adult partner" with
regard to sex), living with a friend, or communal arrangements.

For the purpose of analyzing responses to other questions, we
broke down our sample into four categories of household status:
married, living with wife; never married, living without partner (included those living alone and living with parents or relatives); living
with partner, unmarried (included those never married, widowed,
and divorced or separated currently living with an adult partner);
and divorced or widowed, living alone.

| Total Household Income, Before Taxes | U.S. Census | Our Study |
|---|---|---|
| Under $8,000 | 24.6% | 13.3% |
| $8,000 to $9,999 | 8.6% | 8.6% |
| $10,000 to $14,999 | 22.3% | 29.0% |
| $15,000 to $24,999 | 30.4% | 31.3% |
| $25,000 and over | 14.1% | 17.2% |

The major discrepancy between the above tables is in the groups earning under $8,000. Since seven years have elapsed since the last census, inflation probably accounts for much of the difference. Earning power predictably increased—just as buying power predictably decreased.

| Type of Job Held | U.S. Census All men from age 14 | U.S. Census Men 25–64 years | Our Study |
|---|---|---|---|
| Professional | 10.9% | 22.8% | 25.3% |
| Managerial | 10.0% | 20.0% | 16.2% |
| Other white collar | 9.4% | 14.7% | 12.9% |
| Blue collar | 36.0% | 39.9% | 17.9% |
| Nonworking (retired, unemployed, student) | 22.4% | | 18.2% |

Note that the table of U.S. Census figures for men aged 25 to 64 gives percentages of *employed* men. If the nonworking men were included, all percentages would be correspondingly decreased. In any case, our sample seems to overrepresent professionals and underrepresent blue-collar workers. Job categories were self-defined by the respondents, so that an aspiring artist working as a dishwasher might consider himself a professional rather than a blue-collar worker. While we tend to identify professionals as high-income earners, 34 percent of our professionals reported gross incomes under $15,000, as did 31 percent of those defining themselves as managerial. These two classes did lead the high income group, which included 30 percent of professionals and 27 percent of managerial workers. Among employed men, more professionals (6.1 percent) reported incomes under $8,000 than did nonmanagerial white collars (4.0 percent); blue collars led the low-income group with a barely higher 7.7 percent. Thus, job classification was not strictly related to income.

| Section of the United States | U.S. Census | Our Study |
|---|---|---|
| Northeast | 23.8% | 32.7% |
| North Central | 27.9% | 25.2% |
| South | 30.9% | 20.0% |
| West | 17.4% | 20.6% |

Our research firm considered Washington, D.C., Maryland, and Indiana as South territory. The men themselves probably checked "Northeast" or, in the case of Indiana, "North Central" on the computerized questionnaire. If they did revert to the Civil War battle lines, we don't blame them. We still had fair representation from all areas.

| Age | U.S. Census | Our Study |
|---|---|---|
| 18–19 | 5.7% | 6.3% |
| 20–29 | 25.1% | 31.7% |
| 30–39 | 18.2% | 22.8% |
| 40–44 | 7.9% | 7.9% |
| 45–54 | 16.7% | 20.2% |
| 55–64 | 13.5% | 8.9% |
| 65 and over | 12.9% | 1.7% |

The census figures show percentages by age for adult men. Our figures are similar, except that our study did not include men over 65; thus we would expect our percentages to be somewhat higher than census numbers for each age bracket under 65 to compensate. This was not true for the older men and, despite an annual national birthrate 60 percent above the death rate, which leads to a younger population, our sample was slightly younger than the overall population, but fairly close.

| Racial Background | U.S. Census | Our Study |
|---|---|---|
| White | 89.1% | 87.5% |
| Black | 9.4% | 5.9% |
| Other | 1.5% | 3.4% |

Our sample closely approximated the national population with respect to white and nonwhite men. Whereas the Census Bureau reports a racial category for each person, 3.2 percent of our sample did not answer this question. We suspect most of these were nonwhite because brown-skinned people simply cannot categorize themselves easily. A Puerto Rican might describe himself as "white," "black," or "other." Since questions about race have either been eliminated or designated with qualifying statements on employment forms and other documents in an effort to prevent racial discrimination, many nonwhites automatically refuse to answer questions about racial background. Men who classified themselves as belonging to "other" races might include Orientals, Hispanics (Puerto Ricans, Mexicans, Dominicans) and various other islanders. Their replies sometimes coincided with the blacks, but often were at variance where blacks and whites agreed. The only generalization we can make about this mixed group is that their heritage, unlike that of the American Negro, includes predominant foreign elements, whether Asiatic or European modified by mixing with native Indian groups.

| Total Amount of Schooling | U.S. Census | Our Study |
|---|---|---|
| Less than grammar school graduate | 10.3% | 0.8% |
| Grammar school graduate | 8.6% | 1.0% |
| Less than high school graduate | 15.4% | 5.9% |
| High School Graduate | 34.3% | 25.5% |
| Some College | 15.7% | 36.2% |
| College Graduate | 8.9% | 15.8% |
| Some Postgraduate | 6.9% | 6.0% |
| Postgraduate Degree(s) | [no data] | 7.1% |

It was in the schooling area that our survey was the most biased. As with any study involving written questionnaires, we could not include illiterates and were bound to miss the poverty cultures. We nevertheless had representation from those with less than high school diplomas (7.7 percent) and high school graduates (26 percent), though the graduate students (6.0 percent) and those with postgraduate degrees (7.1 percent) were slightly overrepresented. Our biases, however, were slight compared to Shere Hite's study of female sexuality, where, of the 952 women on whom she obtained educational data, only 19 percent had failed to attend college and 21 percent had postgraduate schooling or degrees—even more striking when one considers that more than twice as many men as women attend graduate school according to 1974 census figures.

We can comfort ourselves, as Morton Hunt does, with the statement by sociologist Ira Reiss that "one can fault [Kinsey] on the level of not having a random sample of the nation, but using that yardstick we would throw out almost all sociological research."

For purposes of analyzing responses to questions, we grouped all men who failed to complete high school under the category "less than high school graduate." These constituted 7.7 percent of our sample and often showed attitudes that were markedly different from the more educated men. The men with graduate school degrees and those still working toward them were likewise grouped together as "some/completed postgraduate." Attitudes of high school graduates, those still in college or with college education short of degrees, and college graduates were reported separately.

Because of space limitations on the data-processing sheets, certain other categories, usually those involving small samples, were grouped under a single heading. Besides those involving schooling and marital status, already discussed, we grouped those men earning under $8,000 yearly (13 percent) with those making $8,000 to $9,999 (8.6 percent) for a single low-income group designated "under $10,-000." In the age brackets, the 18- and 19-year-olds (6.3 percent) were included with the 20–29 group (32 percent); the 40–44 (7.9 percent) and 45–54 (20 percent) were considered as a single middle-aged group; and the 65-year-olds (1.7 percent) were absorbed by the 8.9 percent in the 55–64 range. Thus, we had four age groups: 18–29, 30–39, 40–54, and 55–65.

Finally, in the occupational groups, we combined the retired (3.1 percent), the unemployed (3.5 percent) and "other" (6.8 percent) into a single category. This was a curious group and difficult to make interpretations about; the unemployed were generally young and the retired were generally old, so that 38 percent of the entire subgroup fell into the 18–29 year bracket, 16 percent for 30–39, 23 percent for 40–54, and 23 percent for 55–65. Necessity bred this hybrid, whose men tended to give responses of a conservative, passive nature, perhaps reflective of their enforced or voluntary inactivity. We were glad we resisted temptation and left students standing as an independent category, for they showed views that often differed significantly from most of the other subjects, views that may predict the changing attitudes of men in years to come.

# The Tables

# Q. 1 WHAT IS YOUR CURRENT HOUSEHOLD STATUS?

TABLE 1

Values shown as count / percent.

| | TOTAL | INCOME: UNDER $10000 | $10-14999 | $15-24999 | $25000 & OVER | EDUCATION: LESS THAN H.S. GRAD | HIGH SCHL GRAD | SOME COLLEGE | COLLEGE GRAD | SOME COMPL POST GRAD | OCCUPATION: PRO-FESS STDN. | MANA-GER-IAL | OTHER WHITE COLLR | BLUE COLLR | RET'D UNEMP OTHER | STU-DENT |
|---|---|---|---|---|---|---|---|---|---|---|---|---|---|---|---|---|
| TOTAL RESPONDENTS | 4066 / 100.0 | 889 / 100.0 | 1178 / 100.0 | 1271 / 100.0 | 698 / 100.0 | 311 / 100.0 | 1038 / 100.0 | 1472 / 100.0 | 643 / 100.0 | 533 / 100.0 | 1028 / 100.0 | 658 / 100.0 | 523 / 100.0 | 729 / 100.0 | 544 / 100.0 | 472 / 100.0 |
| MARRIED, LIVING WITH WIFE | 2639 / 64.9 | 336 / 37.8 | 779 / 66.1 | 984 / 77.4 | 526 / 75.4 | 225 / 72.3 | 743 / 71.6 | 835 / 56.7 | 406 / 63.1 | 386 / 72.4 | 750 / 73.0 | 509 / 77.4 | 364 / 69.6 | 519 / 71.2 | 341 / 62.7 | 107 / 22.7 |
| NEVER MARRIED, LIVING ALONE | 349 / 8.6 | 171 / 19.2 | 102 / 8.7 | 54 / 4.2 | 19 / 2.7 | 15 / 4.8 | 40 / 3.9 | 160 / 10.9 | 77 / 12.0 | 50 / 9.4 | 80 / 7.8 | 31 / 4.7 | 51 / 9.8 | 38 / 5.2 | 28 / 5.1 | 107 / 22.7 |
| NEVER MARRIED, LIVING WITH PARENTS OR RELATIVES | 414 / 10.2 | 171 / 19.2 | 72 / 6.1 | 83 / 6.5 | 79 / 11.3 | 20 / 6.4 | 78 / 7.5 | 234 / 15.9 | 57 / 8.9 | 16 / 3.0 | 50 / 4.9 | 24 / 3.6 | 27 / 5.2 | 68 / 9.3 | 57 / 10.5 | 159 / 33.7 |
| NEVER MARRIED, LIVING WITH ADULT PARTNER | 170 / 4.2 | 76 / 8.5 | 50 / 4.2 | 28 / 2.2 | 15 / 2.1 | 6 / 1.9 | 39 / 3.8 | 73 / 5.0 | 30 / 4.7 | 21 / 3.9 | 38 / 3.7 | 22 / 3.3 | 22 / 4.2 | 27 / 3.7 | 21 / 3.9 | 36 / 7.6 |
| DIVORCED OR SEPARATED, LIVING WITHOUT ADULT PARTNER | 235 / 5.8 | 49 / 5.5 | 84 / 7.1 | 65 / 5.1 | 36 / 5.2 | 22 / 7.1 | 61 / 5.9 | 74 / 5.0 | 34 / 5.3 | 39 / 7.3 | 68 / 6.6 | 42 / 6.4 | 32 / 6.1 | 38 / 5.2 | 37 / 6.8 | 10 / 2.1 |
| DIVORCED OR SEPARATED, LIVING WITH ADULT PARTNER | 98 / 2.4 | 22 / 2.5 | 44 / 3.7 | 24 / 1.9 | 8 / 1.1 | 9 / 2.9 | 32 / 3.1 | 31 / 2.1 | 16 / 2.5 | 10 / 1.9 | 23 / 2.2 | 19 / 2.9 | 11 / 2.1 | 22 / 3.0 | 15 / 2.8 | 4 / .8 |
| WIDOWED, LIVING ALONE | 36 / .9 | 7 / .8 | 15 / 1.3 | 11 / .9 | 3 / .4 | 3 / 1.0 | 17 / 1.6 | 11 / .7 | 4 / .6 | 1 / .2 | 4 / .4 | 3 / .5 | 6 / 1.1 | 7 / 1.0 | 15 / 2.8 | 1 / .2 |
| WIDOWED, LIVING WITH ADULT PARTNER | 12 / .3 | 2 / .2 | 4 / .3 | 4 / .3 | 2 / .3 | 2 / .6 | 5 / .5 | 4 / .3 | | | | 2 / .3 | 1 / .2 | 1 / .2 | 7 / 1.3 | 1 / .2 |
| OTHER | 112 / 2.8 | 55 / 6.2 | 28 / 2.4 | 18 / 1.4 | 9 / 1.3 | 9 / 2.9 | 22 / 2.1 | 50 / 3.4 | 19 / 3.0 | 10 / 1.9 | 15 / 1.5 | 6 / .9 | 9 / 1.7 | 10 / 1.4 | 23 / 4.2 | 46 / 9.7 |
| NO ANSWER | 1 / * | | | | 1 / .1 | | 1 / .1 | 1 / .1 | | | | | | | | 1 / .2 |
| SIGMA | 4066 / 100.1 | 889 / 99.9 | 1178 / 99.9 | 1271 / 99.9 | 698 / 99.9 | 311 / 99.9 | 1038 / 100.1 | 1472 / 100.0 | 643 / 100.1 | 533 / 100.0 | 1028 / 100.1 | 658 / 100.0 | 523 / 100.0 | 729 / 100.0 | 544 / 100.1 | 472 / 99.9 |

* LESS THAN 0.05 PERCENT

TABLE 1

Q. 1 WHAT IS YOUR CURRENT HOUSEHOLD STATUS?

| | TOTAL | MARITAL STATUS — MARR'D LIVING WITH WIFE | MARITAL STATUS — NEVER MARR'D LIVING W/O PARTNR | MARITAL STATUS — LIVING WITH UN-MARR'D PARTNR | MARITAL STATUS — DIVRCE WIDOWD OR LIVING ALONE | AGE — 18-29 | AGE — 30-39 | AGE — 40-54 | AGE — 55-65 | RACE — WHITE | RACE — BLACK | RACE — OTHER |
|---|---|---|---|---|---|---|---|---|---|---|---|---|
| TOTAL RESPONDENTS | 4066 / 100.0 | 2639 / 100.0 | 763 / 100.0 | 280 / 100.0 | 383 / 100.0 | 1547 / 100.0 | 927 / 100.0 | 1143 / 100.0 | 432 / 100.0 | 3559 / 100.0 | 240 / 100.0 | 138 / 100.0 |
| MARRIED,LIVING WITH WIFE | 2639 / 64.9 | 2639 / 100.0 | | | | 556 / 35.9 | 726 / 78.3 | 966 / 84.5 | 381 / 88.2 | 2313 / 65.0 | 156 / 65.0 | 84 / 60.9 |
| NEVER MARRIED,LIVING ALONE | 349 / 8.6 | | 349 / 45.7 | | | 282 / 18.2 | 42 / 4.5 | 15 / 1.3 | 7 / 1.6 | 295 / 8.3 | 20 / 8.3 | 20 / 14.5 |
| NEVER MARRIED,LIVING WITH PARENTS OR RELATIVES | 414 / 10.2 | | 414 / 54.3 | | | 383 / 24.8 | 13 / 1.4 | 13 / 1.1 | 3 / .7 | 375 / 10.5 | 22 / 9.2 | 8 / 5.8 |
| NEVER MARRIED,LIVING WITH ADULT PARTNER | 170 / 4.2 | | | 170 / 60.7 | | 134 / 8.7 | 20 / 2.2 | 12 / 1.0 | 3 / .7 | 149 / 4.2 | 10 / 4.2 | 9 / 6.5 |
| DIVORCED OR SEPARATED, LIVING WITHOUT ADULT PARTNER | 235 / 5.8 | | | | 235 / 61.4 | 73 / 4.7 | 76 / 8.2 | 78 / 6.8 | 8 / 1.9 | 207 / 5.8 | 12 / 5.0 | 4 / 2.9 |
| DIVORCED OR SEPARATED, LIVING WITH ADULT PARTNER | 98 / 2.4 | | | 98 / 35.0 | | 35 / 2.3 | 32 / 3.5 | 24 / 2.1 | 6 / 1.4 | 87 / 2.4 | 5 / 2.1 | 3 / 2.2 |
| WIDOWED,LIVING ALONE | 36 / .9 | | | | 36 / 9.4 | 5 / .3 | 1 / .1 | 16 / 1.4 | 14 / 3.2 | 33 / .9 | 2 / .8 | |
| WIDOWED, LIVING WITH ADULT PARTNER | 12 / .3 | | | 12 / 4.3 | | 2 / .1 | 1 / .1 | 3 / .3 | 6 / 1.4 | 9 / .3 | | 2 / 1.4 |
| OTHER | 112 / 2.8 | | | | 112 / 29.2 | 76 / 4.9 | 16 / 1.7 | 16 / 1.4 | 4 / .9 | 90 / 2.5 | 13 / 5.4 | 8 / 5.8 |
| NO ANSWER | 1 / * | | | | | 1 / .1 | | | | 1 / * | | |
| SIGMA | 4066 / 100.1 | 2639 / 100.0 | 763 / 100.0 | 280 / 100.0 | 383 / 100.0 | 1547 / 100.0 | 927 / 100.0 | 1143 / 99.9 | 432 / 100.0 | 3559 / 99.9 | 240 / 100.0 | 138 / 100.0 |

* LESS THAN 0.05 PERCENT

TABLE 2

Q. 2 HOW DO YOU FEEL ABOUT SEX?

| | TOTAL | MARITAL STATUS | | | | | AGE | | | | RACE | | |
|---|---|---|---|---|---|---|---|---|---|---|---|---|---|
| | | MARR'D LIVING WITH WIFE | NEVER MARR'D LIVING WITH PARTNR | LIVING WITH PARTNR UN-MARR'D W/O | LIVING PARTNR MARR'D | DIVRCE OR WIDOWD LIVING ALDNE | 18-29 | 30-39 | 40-54 | 55-65 | WHITE | BLACK | OTHER |
| TOTAL RESPONDENTS | 4066 100.0 | 2639 100.0 | 763 100.0 | 280 100.0 | | 383 100.0 | 1547 100.0 | 927 100.0 | 1143 100.0 | 432 100.0 | 3559 100.0 | 240 100.0 | 138 100.0 |
| IT'S THE MOST IMPORTANT PLEASURE IN LIFE | 805 19.8 | 538 20.4 | 136 17.8 | 67 23.9 | | 64 16.7 | 302 19.5 | 175 18.9 | 243 21.3 | 81 18.8 | 661 18.6 | 69 28.8 | 38 27.5 |
| NOT THE MOST, BUT A VERY IMPORTANT PLEASURE | 2488 61.2 | 1645 62.3 | 451 59.1 | 151 53.9 | | 240 62.7 | 934 60.4 | 622 67.1 | 682 59.7 | 243 56.3 | 2261 63.5 | 99 41.3 | 66 47.8 |
| IT'S IMPORTANT ONLY AS A MEANS OF EXPRESSING LOVE | 465 11.4 | 285 10.8 | 107 14.0 | 34 12.1 | | 39 10.2 | 209 13.5 | 73 7.9 | 132 11.5 | 47 10.9 | 396 11.1 | 32 13.3 | 21 15.2 |
| IT'S STRICTLY A PHYSICAL PLEASURE | 171 4.2 | 105 4.0 | 29 3.8 | 15 5.4 | | 22 5.7 | 50 3.2 | 32 3.5 | 58 5.1 | 30 6.9 | 132 3.7 | 22 9.2 | 7 5.1 |
| IT'S SOMETHING YOU HAVE TO DO | 29 .7 | 14 .5 | 6 .8 | 5 1.8 | | 4 1.0 | 14 .9 | 3 .3 | 7 .6 | 5 1.2 | 21 .6 | 2 .8 | 5 3.6 |
| IT'S NOT VERY IMPORTANT TO ME | 56 1.4 | 29 1.1 | 14 1.8 | 3 1.1 | | 10 2.6 | 16 1.0 | 7 .8 | 11 1.0 | 20 4.6 | 45 1.3 | 6 2.5 | |
| OTHER THINGS ARE MORE IMPORTANT, SUCH AS BUSINESS OR HOBBIES | 71 1.7 | 35 1.3 | 23 3.0 | 4 1.4 | | 9 2.3 | 37 2.4 | 14 1.5 | 9 .8 | 11 2.5 | 59 1.7 | 7 2.9 | 2 1.4 |
| NO ANSWER | 20 .5 | 12 .5 | 5 .7 | 2 .7 | | 1 .3 | 5 .3 | 4 .4 | 9 .8 | 2 .5 | 16 .4 | 3 1.3 | |
| SIGMA | 4105 100.9 | 2663 100.9 | 771 101.0 | 281 100.3 | | 389 101.5 | 1567 101.2 | 930 100.4 | 1151 100.8 | 439 101.7 | 3591 100.9 | 240 100.1 | 139 100.6 |

TABLE 2

# Q. 2 HOW DO YOU FEEL ABOUT SEX?

| | TOTAL | INCOME | | | | EDUCATION | | | | | OCCUPATION | | | | | |
|---|---|---|---|---|---|---|---|---|---|---|---|---|---|---|---|---|
| | | UNDER $10000 | $10-14999 | $15-24999 | $25000 & OVER | LESS THAN H.S. GRAD | HIGH SCHL GRAD | SOME COLLEGE | COL-LEGE GRAD | SOME/COMPL POST GRAD | PRO-FES-SION | MANA-GER-IAL | OTHER WHITE COLLR | BLUE COLLR | RET'D/UNEMP OTHER | STU-DENT |
| TOTAL RESPONDENTS | 4066 / 100.0 | 889 / 100.0 | 1178 / 100.0 | 1271 / 100.0 | 698 / 100.0 | 311 / 100.0 | 1038 / 100.0 | 1472 / 100.0 | 643 / 100.0 | 533 / 100.0 | 1028 / 100.0 | 658 / 100.0 | 523 / 100.0 | 729 / 100.0 | 544 / 100.0 | 472 / 100.0 |
| IT'S THE MOST IMPORTANT PLEASURE IN LIFE | 805 / 19.8 | 178 / 20.0 | 259 / 22.0 | 219 / 17.2 | 144 / 20.6 | 92 / 29.6 | 223 / 21.5 | 275 / 18.7 | 112 / 17.4 | 89 / 16.7 | 205 / 19.9 | 121 / 18.4 | 100 / 19.1 | 168 / 23.0 | 120 / 22.1 | 67 / 14.2 |
| NOT THE MOST, BUT A VERY IMPORTANT PLEASURE | 2488 / 61.2 | 512 / 57.6 | 689 / 58.5 | 839 / 66.0 | 433 / 62.0 | 149 / 47.9 | 585 / 56.4 | 937 / 63.7 | 415 / 64.5 | 360 / 67.5 | 662 / 64.4 | 435 / 66.1 | 327 / 62.5 | 423 / 58.0 | 272 / 50.0 | 297 / 62.9 |
| IT'S IMPORTANT ONLY AS A MEANS OF EXPRESSING LOVE | 465 / 11.4 | 113 / 12.7 | 143 / 12.1 | 126 / 9.9 | 75 / 10.7 | 42 / 13.5 | 134 / 12.9 | 163 / 11.1 | 61 / 9.5 | 55 / 10.3 | 104 / 10.1 | 63 / 9.6 | 63 / 12.0 | 74 / 10.2 | 79 / 14.5 | 66 / 14.0 |
| IT'S STRICTLY A PHYSICAL PLEASURE | 171 / 4.2 | 47 / 5.3 | 50 / 4.2 | 44 / 3.5 | 29 / 4.2 | 17 / 5.5 | 56 / 5.4 | 49 / 3.3 | 31 / 4.8 | 16 / 3.0 | 30 / 2.9 | 26 / 4.0 | 14 / 2.7 | 40 / 5.5 | 39 / 7.2 | 20 / 4.2 |
| IT'S SOMETHING YOU HAVE TO DO | 29 / .7 | 10 / 1.1 | 7 / .6 | 7 / .6 | 5 / .7 | 8 / 2.6 | 3 / .3 | 11 / .7 | 5 / .8 | 2 / .4 | 5 / .5 | 4 / .6 | 5 / 1.0 | 1 / .1 | 9 / 1.7 | 5 / 1.1 |
| IT'S NOT VERY IMPORTANT TO ME | 56 / 1.4 | 16 / 1.8 | 16 / 1.4 | 18 / 1.4 | 4 / .6 | 6 / 1.9 | 18 / 1.7 | 16 / 1.1 | 8 / 1.2 | 4 / .8 | 7 / .7 | 4 / .6 | 6 / 1.1 | 13 / 1.8 | 14 / 2.6 | 8 / 1.7 |
| OTHER THINGS ARE MORE IMPORTANT, SUCH AS BUSINESS OR HOBBIES | 71 / 1.7 | 23 / 2.6 | 18 / 1.5 | 20 / 1.6 | 10 / 1.4 | 4 / 1.3 | 20 / 1.9 | 26 / 1.8 | 10 / 1.6 | 10 / 1.9 | 15 / 1.5 | 8 / 1.2 | 9 / 1.7 | 10 / 1.4 | 15 / 2.8 | 12 / 2.5 |
| NO ANSWER | 20 / .5 | 3 / .3 | 6 / .5 | 6 / .5 | 5 / .7 | | 8 / .8 | 7 / .5 | 4 / .6 | 1 / .2 | 5 / .5 | 1 / .2 | 4 / .8 | 5 / .7 | 3 / .6 | 1 / .2 |
| SIGMA | 4105 / 100.9 | 902 / 101.4 | 1188 / 100.8 | 1279 / 100.7 | 705 / 100.9 | 318 / 102.3 | 1047 / 100.9 | 1484 / 100.9 | 646 / 100.4 | 537 / 100.8 | 1033 / 100.5 | 662 / 100.7 | 528 / 100.9 | 734 / 100.7 | 551 / 101.5 | 476 / 100.8 |

Q. 3 HOW DO YOU FEEL ABOUT HUGGING AND KISSING WITHOUT IT LEADING TO SEXUAL INTERCOURSE?

TABLE 3

| | TOTAL | MARITAL STATUS | | | | AGE | | | | RACE | | |
|---|---|---|---|---|---|---|---|---|---|---|---|---|
| | | MARR'D LIVING WITH WIFE | NEVER MARR'D LIVING W/O PARTNR | MARR'D WITH UN-MARR'D PARTNR | DIVRCE OR WIDOWD LIVING ALONE | 18-29 | 30-39 | 40-54 | 55-65 | WHITE | BLACK | OTHER |
| TOTAL RESPONDENTS | 4066 100.0 | 2639 100.0 | 763 100.0 | 280 100.0 | 383 100.0 | 1547 100.0 | 927 100.0 | 1143 100.0 | 432 100.0 | 3559 100.0 | 240 100.0 | 138 100.0 |
| I HAVE A REAL NEED FOR IT | 502 12.3 | 358 13.6 | 68 8.9 | 27 9.6 | 49 12.8 | 168 10.9 | 118 12.7 | 146 12.8 | 67 15.5 | 426 12.0 | 30 12.5 | 26 18.8 |
| ENJOY IT, EVEN WITHOUT SEX | 2401 59.1 | 1522 57.7 | 488 64.0 | 162 57.9 | 228 59.5 | 974 63.0 | 535 57.7 | 671 58.7 | 216 50.0 | 2170 61.0 | 106 44.2 | 62 44.9 |
| FIND IT FRUSTRATING UNLESS SEX FOLLOWS | 428 10.5 | 269 10.2 | 83 10.9 | 35 12.5 | 41 10.7 | 152 9.8 | 114 12.3 | 119 10.4 | 36 8.3 | 348 9.8 | 47 19.6 | 12 8.7 |
| I DO IT MOSTLY TO PLEASE A WOMAN | 195 4.8 | 131 5.0 | 28 3.7 | 21 7.5 | 15 3.9 | 62 4.0 | 53 5.7 | 55 4.8 | 25 5.8 | 165 4.6 | 15 6.3 | 12 8.7 |
| IT'S A ROUTINE WAY OF EXPRESSING LOVE | 443 10.9 | 296 11.2 | 83 10.9 | 27 9.6 | 37 9.7 | 159 10.3 | 82 8.8 | 129 11.3 | 71 16.4 | 372 10.5 | 34 14.2 | 17 12.3 |
| I RARELY DO IT | 132 3.2 | 83 3.1 | 21 2.8 | 9 3.2 | 19 5.0 | 42 2.7 | 30 3.2 | 36 3.1 | 23 5.3 | 102 2.9 | 14 5.8 | 11 8.0 |
| NO ANSWER | 8 .2 | 7 .3 | 1 .1 | | | 3 .2 | 3 .3 | 1 .1 | 1 .2 | 6 .2 | | |
| SIGMA | 4109 101.0 | 2666 101.1 | 772 101.3 | 281 100.3 | 389 101.6 | 1560 100.9 | 935 100.7 | 1157 101.2 | 439 101.5 | 3589 101.0 | 246 102.6 | 140 101.4 |

Q. 3 HOW DO YOU FEEL ABOUT HUGGING AND KISSING WITHOUT IT LEADING TO SEXUAL INTERCOURSE?

TABLE 3

| | TOTAL | INCOME | | | | EDUCATION | | | | | OCCUPATION | | | | | |
|---|---|---|---|---|---|---|---|---|---|---|---|---|---|---|---|---|
| | | UNDER $10000 | $10-14999 | $15-24999 | $25000 & OVER | LESS THAN H.S. GRAD | HIGH SCHL GRAD | SOME COLLEGE | COL-LEGE GRAD | SOME/COMPL POST GRAD | PRO-FES-SION. | MANA-GER-IAL | OTHER WHITE COLLR | BLUE COLLR | RET'D, UNEMP, OTHER | STU-DENT |
| TOTAL RESPONDENTS | 4066 100.0 | 889 100.0 | 1178 100.0 | 1271 100.0 | 698 100.0 | 311 100.0 | 1038 100.0 | 1472 100.0 | 643 100.0 | 533 100.0 | 1028 100.0 | 658 100.0 | 523 100.0 | 729 100.0 | 544 100.0 | 472 100.0 |
| I HAVE A REAL NEED FOR IT | 502 12.3 | 101 11.4 | 149 12.6 | 163 12.8 | 84 12.0 | 40 12.9 | 131 12.6 | 155 10.5 | 90 14.0 | 71 13.3 | 137 13.3 | 83 12.6 | 69 13.2 | 91 12.5 | 57 10.5 | 47 10.0 |
| ENJOY IT, EVEN WITH-OUT SEX | 2401 59.1 | 517 58.2 | 676 57.4 | 761 59.9 | 433 62.0 | 152 48.9 | 556 53.6 | 929 63.1 | 395 61.4 | 331 62.1 | 635 61.8 | 400 60.8 | 308 58.9 | 406 55.7 | 285 52.4 | 299 63.3 |
| FIND IT FRUSTRATING UNLESS SEX FOLLOWS | 428 10.5 | 109 12.3 | 129 11.0 | 121 9.5 | 62 8.9 | 41 13.2 | 128 12.3 | 139 9.4 | 59 9.2 | 55 10.3 | 100 9.7 | 68 10.3 | 49 9.4 | 87 11.9 | 74 13.6 | 39 8.3 |
| I DO IT MOSTLY TO PLEASE A WOMAN | 195 4.8 | 44 4.9 | 48 4.1 | 66 5.2 | 36 5.2 | 19 6.1 | 49 4.7 | 64 4.3 | 31 4.8 | 30 5.6 | 51 5.0 | 40 6.1 | 23 4.4 | 33 4.5 | 26 4.8 | 17 3.6 |
| IT'S A ROUTINE WAY OF EXPRESSING LOVE | 443 10.9 | 100 11.2 | 139 11.8 | 129 10.1 | 72 10.3 | 52 16.7 | 138 13.3 | 151 10.3 | 58 9.0 | 38 7.1 | 91 8.9 | 54 8.2 | 65 12.4 | 85 11.7 | 79 14.5 | 57 12.1 |
| I RARELY DO IT | 132 3.2 | 33 3.7 | 41 3.5 | 36 2.8 | 21 3.0 | 10 3.2 | 47 4.5 | 44 3.0 | 14 2.2 | 13 2.4 | 22 2.1 | 19 2.9 | 15 2.9 | 30 4.1 | 24 4.4 | 16 3.4 |
| NO ANSWER | 8 .2 | 1 .1 | 3 .3 | 2 .2 | 2 .3 | 1 .3 | 2 .2 | 3 .2 | 2 .2 | 3 .3 | 3 .3 | 1 .2 | 3 .3 | 2 .3 | 2 .4 | |
| SIGMA | 4109 101.0 | 905 101.8 | 1185 100.7 | 1278 100.5 | 710 101.7 | 315 101.3 | 1051 101.2 | 1485 100.8 | 648 100.8 | 538 100.8 | 1039 101.1 | 665 101.1 | 529 101.2 | 734 100.7 | 547 100.6 | 475 100.7 |

Q. 4 WHAT SEXUAL ACTIVITY GIVES YOU THE MOST PLEASURE DURING FOREPLAY?

TABLE 4

| | TOTAL | MARITAL STATUS | | | | AGE | | | | RACE | | |
|---|---|---|---|---|---|---|---|---|---|---|---|---|
| | | MARR'D LIVING WITH WIFE | NEVER MARR'D LIVING W/O PARTNR | MARR'D LIVING WITH UN-MARR'D PARTNR | DIVRCE OR WIDOWD LIVING ALONE | 18-29 | 30-39 | 40-54 | 55-65 | WHITE | BLACK | OTHER |
| TOTAL RESPONDENTS | 4066 100.0 | 2639 100.0 | 763 100.0 | 280 100.0 | 383 100.0 | 1547 100.0 | 927 100.0 | 1143 100.0 | 432 100.0 | 3559 100.0 | 240 100.0 | 138 100.0 |
| LOOKING AT PARTNER'S NUDE BODY | 430 10.6 | 291 11.0 | 70 9.2 | 28 10.0 | 41 10.7 | 156 10.1 | 84 9.1 | 126 11.0 | 58 13.4 | 347 9.7 | 28 11.7 | 28 20.3 |
| TOUCHING AND SUCKING BREASTS | 903 22.2 | 660 25.0 | 123 16.1 | 48 17.1 | 72 18.8 | 271 17.5 | 198 21.4 | 313 27.4 | 114 26.4 | 762 21.4 | 57 23.8 | 42 30.4 |
| KISSING AND CARESSING | 1502 36.9 | 927 35.1 | 318 41.7 | 96 34.3 | 160 41.8 | 554 35.8 | 336 36.2 | 433 37.9 | 174 40.3 | 1322 37.1 | 86 35.8 | 49 35.5 |
| TOUCHING FEMALE GENITAL AREA (SEX ORGANS) | 776 19.1 | 528 20.0 | 128 16.8 | 50 17.9 | 70 18.3 | 277 17.9 | 192 20.7 | 228 19.9 | 76 17.6 | 650 18.3 | 63 26.3 | 31 22.5 |
| ORAL SEX | 1077 26.5 | 655 24.8 | 193 25.3 | 108 38.6 | 120 31.3 | 484 31.3 | 289 31.2 | 252 22.0 | 46 10.6 | 984 27.6 | 43 17.9 | 26 18.8 |
| DON'T LIKE FOREPLAY | 64 1.6 | 42 1.6 | 12 1.6 | 3 1.1 | 7 1.8 | 22 1.4 | 7 .8 | 22 1.9 | 13 3.0 | 49 1.4 | 8 3.3 | 6 4.3 |
| NO ANSWER | 34 .8 | 21 .8 | 9 1.2 | 1 .4 | 3 .8 | 11 .7 | 8 .9 | 9 .8 | 5 1.2 | 24 .7 | 1 .4 | 1 .7 |
| SIGMA | 4786 117.7 | 3124 118.3 | 853 111.9 | 334 119.4 | 473 123.5 | 1775 114.7 | 1114 120.3 | 1383 120.9 | 486 112.5 | 4138 116.2 | 286 119.2 | 183 132.5 |

TABLE 4

Q. 4 WHAT SEXUAL ACTIVITY GIVES YOU THE MOST PLEASURE DURING FOREPLAY?

| | TOTAL | INCOME | | | | EDUCATION | | | | | OCCUPATION | | | | | |
| --- | --- | --- | --- | --- | --- | --- | --- | --- | --- | --- | --- | --- | --- | --- | --- | --- |
| | | UNDER $10000 | $10-14999 | $15-24999 | $25000 & OVER | LESS THAN H.S. GRAD | HIGH SCHL GRAD. | SOME COLLEGE | COLLEGE GRAD | SOME/ COMPL POST GRAD. | PRO-FESSION. | MANA-GER-IAL | OTHER WHITE COLLR | BLUE COLLR | RET'D, UNEMP, OTHER | STU-DENT |
| TOTAL RESPONDENTS | 4066 100.0 | 889 100.0 | 1178 100.0 | 1271 100.0 | 698 100.0 | 311 100.0 | 1038 100.0 | 1472 100.0 | 643 100.0 | 533 100.0 | 1028 100.0 | 658 100.0 | 523 100.0 | 729 100.0 | 544 100.0 | 472 100.0 |
| LOOKING AT PARTNER'S NUDE BODY | 430 10.6 | 100 11.2 | 136 11.5 | 129 10.1 | 58 8.3 | 40 12.9 | 124 11.9 | 146 9.9 | 60 9.3 | 46 8.6 | 111 10.8 | 60 9.1 | 62 11.9 | 67 9.2 | 68 12.5 | 37 7.8 |
| TOUCHING AND SUCKING BREASTS | 903 22.2 | 176 19.8 | 269 22.8 | 284 22.3 | 166 23.8 | 86 27.7 | 248 23.9 | 305 20.7 | 123 19.1 | 123 23.1 | 216 21.0 | 163 24.8 | 113 21.6 | 160 21.9 | 128 23.5 | 88 18.6 |
| KISSING AND CARESS-ING | 1502 36.9 | 361 40.6 | 428 36.3 | 465 36.6 | 238 34.1 | 100 32.2 | 398 38.3 | 532 36.1 | 246 38.3 | 197 37.0 | 363 35.3 | 228 34.7 | 214 40.9 | 258 35.4 | 210 38.6 | 176 37.3 |
| TOUCHING FEMALE GENITAL AREA (SEX ORGANS) | 776 19.1 | 169 19.0 | 232 19.7 | 239 18.8 | 130 18.6 | 61 19.6 | 198 19.1 | 298 20.2 | 110 17.1 | 93 17.4 | 191 18.6 | 135 20.5 | 99 18.9 | 121 16.6 | 114 21.0 | 90 19.1 |
| ORAL SEX | 1077 26.5 | 226 25.4 | 297 25.2 | 338 26.6 | 207 29.7 | 61 19.6 | 249 24.0 | 430 29.2 | 173 26.9 | 147 27.6 | 315 30.6 | 169 25.7 | 116 22.2 | 198 27.2 | 104 19.1 | 132 28.0 |
| DON'T LIKE FOREPLAY | 64 1.6 | 14 1.6 | 18 1.5 | 20 1.6 | 12 1.7 | 7 2.3 | 20 1.9 | 19 1.3 | 10 1.6 | 7 1.3 | 13 1.3 | 8 1.2 | 3 .6 | 12 1.6 | 17 3.1 | 9 1.9 |
| NO ANSWER | 34 .8 | 8 .9 | 14 1.2 | 7 .6 | 4 .6 | 2 .6 | 10 1.0 | 15 1.0 | 4 .6 | 1 .2 | 5 .5 | 3 .5 | 3 .6 | 10 1.4 | 5 .9 | 3 .6 |
| SIGMA | 4786 117.7 | 1054 118.5 | 1394 118.2 | 1482 116.6 | 815 116.8 | 357 114.9 | 1247 120.1 | 1745 118.4 | 726 112.9 | 614 115.2 | 1214 118.1 | 766 116.5 | 610 116.7 | 826 113.3 | 646 118.7 | 535 113.3 |

Q. 5 HOW HAVE YOUR FEELINGS ABOUT SEX CHANGED OVER THE PAST FIVE YEARS?                                                                 TABLE 5

| | TOTAL | MARITAL STATUS | | | | AGE | | | | RACE | | |
|---|---|---|---|---|---|---|---|---|---|---|---|---|
| | | MARR'D LIVING WITH WIFE | NEVER MARR'D LIVING W/O PARTNR | LIVING WITH PARTNR UN-MARR'D | DIVRCE OR WIDOWD LIVING ALONE | 18-29 | 30-39 | 40-54 | 55-65 | WHITE | BLACK | OTHER |
| TOTAL RESPONDENTS | 4066 100.0 | 2639 100.0 | 763 100.0 | 280 100.0 | 383 100.0 | 1547 100.0 | 927 100.0 | 1143 100.0 | 432 100.0 | 3559 100.0 | 240 100.0 | 138 100.0 |
| NOT AT ALL | 1059 26.0 | 773 29.3 | 153 20.1 | 56 20.0 | 77 20.1 | 308 19.9 | 217 23.4 | 368 32.2 | 161 37.3 | 908 25.5 | 73 30.4 | 35 25.4 |
| FIND SEX MORE ENJOY-ABLE THAN EVER | 1637 40.3 | 1043 39.5 | 317 41.5 | 116 41.4 | 160 41.8 | 654 42.3 | 413 44.6 | 435 38.1 | 130 30.1 | 1450 40.7 | 91 37.9 | 51 37.0 |
| FIND IT LESS ENJOY-ABLE | 186 4.6 | 134 5.1 | 14 1.8 | 16 5.7 | 22 5.7 | 39 2.5 | 32 3.5 | 63 5.5 | 52 12.0 | 167 4.7 | 8 3.3 | 4 2.9 |
| VARY MY SEX PRACTICES MORE | 437 10.7 | 269 10.2 | 88 11.5 | 38 13.6 | 42 11.0 | 195 12.6 | 115 12.4 | 102 8.9 | 24 5.6 | 396 11.1 | 22 9.2 | 12 8.7 |
| SEX SEEMS MORE ROUTINE | 265 6.5 | 196 7.4 | 39 5.1 | 12 4.3 | 18 4.7 | 85 5.5 | 59 6.4 | 75 6.6 | 43 10.0 | 224 6.3 | 17 7.1 | 12 8.7 |
| HAVE CHANGED ATTITUDE, WANT TO EXPERIMENT MORE | 540 13.3 | 265 10.0 | 155 20.3 | 50 17.9 | 70 18.3 | 288 18.6 | 111 12.0 | 113 9.9 | 26 6.0 | 472 13.3 | 30 12.5 | 28 20.3 |
| NO ANSWER | 24 .6 | 9 .3 | 11 1.4 | 2 .7 | 2 .5 | 11 .7 | 4 .4 | 6 .5 | 1 .2 | 16 .4 | 1 .4 | 1 .7 |
| SIGMA | 4148 102.0 | 2669 101.8 | 777 101.7 | 290 103.6 | 391 102.1 | 1580 102.1 | 951 102.7 | 1162 101.7 | 437 101.2 | 3633 102.0 | 242 100.8 | 143 103.7 |

Q. 5 HOW HAVE YOUR FEELINGS ABOUT SEX CHANGED OVER THE PAST FIVE YEARS?

TABLE 5

| | TOTAL | INCOME | | | | EDUCATION | | | | | OCCUPATION | | | | | |
|---|---|---|---|---|---|---|---|---|---|---|---|---|---|---|---|---|
| | | UNDER $10000 | $10-14999 | $15-24999 | $25000 & OVER | LESS THAN H.S. GRAD | HIGH SCHL GRAD | SOME COL-LEGE | COL-LEGE GRAD | SOME/COMPL POST GRAD | PRO-FES-SION | MANA-GER-IAL | OTHER WHITE COLLR | BLUE COLLR | RET'D/UNEMP OTHER | STU-DENT |
| TOTAL RESPONDENTS | 4066 100.0 | 889 100.0 | 1178 100.0 | 1271 100.0 | 698 100.0 | 311 100.0 | 1038 100.0 | 1472 100.0 | 643 100.0 | 533 100.0 | 1028 100.0 | 658 100.0 | 523 100.0 | 729 100.0 | 544 100.0 | 472 100.0 |
| NOT AT ALL | 1059 26.0 | 202 22.7 | 292 24.8 | 359 28.2 | 200 28.7 | 98 31.5 | 287 27.6 | 355 24.1 | 161 25.0 | 137 25.7 | 272 26.5 | 190 28.9 | 152 29.1 | 191 26.2 | 150 27.6 | 80 16.9 |
| FIND SEX MORE ENJOY-ABLE THAN EVER | 1637 40.3 | 367 41.3 | 487 41.3 | 514 40.4 | 253 36.2 | 108 34.7 | 428 41.2 | 599 40.7 | 255 39.7 | 217 40.7 | 426 41.4 | 267 40.6 | 215 41.1 | 282 38.7 | 216 39.7 | 178 37.7 |
| FIND IT LESS ENJOY-ABLE | 186 4.6 | 33 3.7 | 62 5.3 | 57 4.5 | 33 4.7 | 26 8.4 | 55 5.3 | 52 3.5 | 27 4.2 | 23 4.3 | 42 4.1 | 33 5.0 | 26 5.0 | 39 5.3 | 36 6.6 | 8 1.7 |
| VARY MY SEX PRACTICES MORE | 437 10.7 | 88 9.9 | 131 11.1 | 139 10.9 | 77 11.0 | 29 9.3 | 90 8.7 | 174 11.8 | 64 10.0 | 77 14.4 | 135 13.1 | 74 11.2 | 46 8.8 | 66 9.1 | 45 8.3 | 61 12.9 |
| SEX SEEMS MORE ROUTINE | 265 6.5 | 51 5.7 | 76 6.5 | 79 6.2 | 58 8.3 | 24 7.7 | 67 6.5 | 82 5.6 | 42 6.5 | 45 8.4 | 54 5.3 | 51 7.8 | 39 7.5 | 47 6.4 | 37 6.8 | 34 7.2 |
| HAVE CHANGED ATTITUDE, WANT TO EXPERIMENT MORE | 540 13.3 | 170 19.1 | 140 11.9 | 137 10.8 | 90 12.9 | 31 10.0 | 121 11.7 | 227 15.4 | 100 15.6 | 56 10.5 | 126 12.3 | 52 7.9 | 48 9.2 | 107 14.7 | 66 12.1 | 115 24.4 |
| NO ANSWER | 24 .6 | 4 .4 | 12 1.0 | 4 .3 | 3 .4 | 1 .3 | 6 .6 | 10 .7 | 4 .6 | 5 .5 | 5 .5 | 1 .2 | 2 .4 | 5 .7 | 4 .7 | 5 1.1 |
| SIGMA | 4148 102.0 | 915 102.8 | 1200 101.9 | 1289 101.3 | 714 102.2 | 317 101.9 | 1054 101.6 | 1499 101.8 | 653 101.6 | 555 104.0 | 1060 103.2 | 668 101.6 | 528 101.1 | 737 101.1 | 554 101.8 | 481 101.9 |

TABLE 6

Q. 6 WHAT COULD YOUR PARTNER DO TO MAKE YOU MORE EXCITED?

| | TOTAL | MARITAL STATUS | | | | AGE | | | | RACE | | |
|---|---|---|---|---|---|---|---|---|---|---|---|---|
| | | MARR'D LIVING WITH WIFE | NEVER MARR'D LIVING W/O PARTNR | LIVING WITH UN- MARR'D PARTNR | DIVRCE WIDOWD OR LIVING ALONE | 18-29 | 30-39 | 40-54 | 55-65 | WHITE | BLACK | OTHER |
| TOTAL RESPONDENTS | 4066 100.0 | 2639 100.0 | 763 100.0 | 280 100.0 | 383 100.0 | 1547 100.0 | 927 100.0 | 1143 100.0 | 432 100.0 | 3559 100.0 | 240 100.0 | 138 100.0 |
| DISPLAY NUDE BODY MORE | 456 11.2 | 299 11.3 | 86 11.3 | 23 8.2 | 48 12.5 | 157 10.1 | 81 8.7 | 154 13.5 | 59 13.7 | 396 11.1 | 26 10.8 | 14 10.1 |
| WEAR SEXY LINGERIE | 638 15.7 | 423 16.0 | 115 15.1 | 44 15.7 | 56 14.6 | 237 15.3 | 146 15.7 | 187 16.4 | 64 14.8 | 550 15.5 | 33 13.8 | 26 18.8 |
| TOUCH PENIS MORE | 723 17.8 | 490 18.6 | 128 16.8 | 46 16.4 | 59 15.4 | 240 15.5 | 165 17.8 | 225 19.7 | 89 20.6 | 607 17.1 | 49 20.4 | 38 27.5 |
| USE MORE ORAL SEX | 990 24.3 | 645 24.4 | 163 21.4 | 81 28.9 | 100 26.1 | 374 24.2 | 258 27.8 | 276 24.1 | 77 17.8 | 874 24.6 | 54 22.5 | 34 24.6 |
| BE MORE ACTIVE DURING SEX | 1399 34.4 | 852 32.3 | 298 39.1 | 96 34.3 | 153 39.9 | 604 39.0 | 303 32.7 | 362 31.7 | 126 29.2 | 1239 34.8 | 73 30.4 | 52 37.7 |
| USE EXCITING WORDS | 273 6.7 | 170 6.4 | 46 6.0 | 25 8.9 | 32 8.4 | 99 6.4 | 61 6.6 | 77 6.7 | 35 8.1 | 229 6.4 | 22 9.2 | 14 10.1 |
| NO ANSWER | 124 3.0 | 82 3.1 | 23 3.0 | 11 3.9 | 8 2.1 | 35 2.3 | 28 3.0 | 40 3.5 | 17 3.9 | 108 3.0 | 7 2.9 | |
| SIGMA | 4603 113.1 | 2961 112.1 | 859 112.7 | 326 116.3 | 456 119.0 | 1746 112.8 | 1042 112.3 | 1321 115.6 | 467 108.1 | 4003 112.5 | 264 110.0 | 178 128.8 |

Q. 6 WHAT COULD YOUR PARTNER DO TO MAKE YOU MORE EXCITED?

TABLE 6

| | TOTAL | INCOME | | | | EDUCATION | | | | | OCCUPATION | | | | | |
|---|---|---|---|---|---|---|---|---|---|---|---|---|---|---|---|---|
| | | UNDER $10000 | $10-14999 | $15-24999 | $25000 & OVER | LESS THAN H.S. GRAD | HIGH SCHL GRAD | SOME COLLEGE | COLLEGE GRAD | SOME/COMPL POST GRAD | PRO/FES-SION. | MANA-GER-IAL | OTHER WHITE COLLR | BLUE COLLR | RET'D, UNEMP, OTHER | STU-DENT |
| TOTAL RESPONDENTS | 4066 / 100.0 | 889 / 100.0 | 1178 / 100.0 | 1271 / 100.0 | 698 / 100.0 | 311 / 100.0 | 1038 / 100.0 | 1472 / 100.0 | 643 / 100.0 | 533 / 100.0 | 1028 / 100.0 | 658 / 100.0 | 523 / 100.0 | 729 / 100.0 | 544 / 100.0 | 472 / 100.0 |
| DISPLAY NUDE BODY MORE | 456 / 11.2 | 96 / 10.8 | 126 / 10.7 | 156 / 12.3 | 72 / 10.3 | 43 / 13.8 | 123 / 11.8 | 160 / 10.9 | 75 / 11.7 | 43 / 8.1 | 113 / 11.0 | 68 / 10.3 | 65 / 12.4 | 70 / 9.6 | 71 / 13.1 | 48 / 10.2 |
| WEAR SEXY LINGERIE | 638 / 15.7 | 149 / 16.8 | 186 / 15.8 | 195 / 15.3 | 100 / 14.3 | 57 / 18.3 | 166 / 16.0 | 224 / 15.2 | 111 / 17.3 | 67 / 12.6 | 176 / 17.1 | 98 / 14.9 | 81 / 15.5 | 117 / 16.0 | 80 / 14.7 | 62 / 13.1 |
| TOUCH PENIS MORE | 723 / 17.8 | 160 / 18.0 | 213 / 18.1 | 220 / 17.3 | 124 / 17.8 | 58 / 18.6 | 203 / 19.6 | 252 / 17.1 | 107 / 16.6 | 86 / 16.1 | 157 / 15.3 | 126 / 19.1 | 105 / 20.1 | 121 / 16.6 | 117 / 21.5 | 70 / 14.8 |
| USE MORE ORAL SEX | 990 / 24.3 | 190 / 21.4 | 294 / 25.0 | 310 / 24.4 | 188 / 26.9 | 71 / 22.8 | 245 / 23.6 | 374 / 25.4 | 141 / 21.9 | 145 / 27.2 | 278 / 27.0 | 157 / 23.9 | 115 / 22.0 | 203 / 27.8 | 119 / 21.9 | 85 / 18.0 |
| BE MORE ACTIVE DURING SEX | 1399 / 34.4 | 338 / 38.0 | 384 / 32.6 | 430 / 33.8 | 237 / 34.0 | 107 / 34.4 | 319 / 30.7 | 537 / 36.5 | 226 / 35.1 | 190 / 35.6 | 348 / 33.9 | 246 / 37.4 | 169 / 32.3 | 231 / 31.7 | 162 / 29.8 | 199 / 42.2 |
| USE EXCITING WORDS | 273 / 6.7 | 57 / 6.4 | 94 / 8.0 | 78 / 6.1 | 38 / 5.4 | 16 / 5.1 | 65 / 6.3 | 108 / 7.3 | 41 / 6.4 | 38 / 7.1 | 65 / 6.3 | 40 / 6.1 | 34 / 6.5 | 43 / 5.9 | 48 / 8.8 | 32 / 6.8 |
| NO ANSWER | 124 / 3.0 | 23 / 2.6 | 35 / 3.0 | 41 / 3.2 | 23 / 3.3 | 11 / 3.5 | 39 / 3.8 | 36 / 2.4 | 12 / 1.9 | 23 / 4.3 | 37 / 3.6 | 16 / 2.4 | 15 / 2.9 | 19 / 2.6 | 22 / 4.0 | 9 / 1.9 |
| SIGMA | 4603 / 113.1 | 1013 / 114.0 | 1332 / 113.2 | 1430 / 112.4 | 782 / 112.0 | 363 / 116.5 | 1160 / 111.8 | 1691 / 114.8 | 713 / 110.9 | 592 / 111.0 | 1174 / 114.2 | 751 / 114.1 | 584 / 111.7 | 804 / 110.2 | 619 / 113.8 | 505 / 107.0 |

Q. 7 WHAT DO YOU CONSIDER THE IDEAL SEX LIFE FOR YOURSELF?

TABLE 7

| | TOTAL | MARITAL STATUS | | | | AGE | | | | RACE | | |
|---|---|---|---|---|---|---|---|---|---|---|---|---|
| | | MARR'D LIVING WITH WIFE | NEVER MARR'D LIVING W/O PARTNR | LIVING WITH PARTNR UN-MARR'D | DIVRCE OR WIDOWD LIVING ALONE | 18-29 | 30-39 | 40-54 | 55-65 | WHITE | BLACK | OTHER |
| TOTAL RESPONDENTS | 4066 100.0 | 2639 100.0 | 763 100.0 | 280 100.0 | 383 100.0 | 1547 100.0 | 927 100.0 | 1143 100.0 | 432 100.0 | 3559 100.0 | 240 100.0 | 138 100.0 |
| MARRIAGE, WIFE BEING ONLY SEX PARTNER | 2054 50.5 | 1621 61.4 | 242 31.7 | 72 25.7 | 119 31.1 | 617 39.9 | 472 50.9 | 664 58.1 | 292 67.6 | 1836 51.6 | 93 38.8 | 50 36.2 |
| MARRIAGE, WITH OUT-SIDE SEXUAL ACTIVITY | 811 19.9 | 693 26.3 | 67 8.8 | 27 9.6 | 24 6.3 | 240 15.5 | 238 25.7 | 256 22.4 | 75 17.4 | 708 19.9 | 60 25.0 | 23 16.7 |
| LIVING WITH ONE FEMALE PARTNER, UNMARRIED | 433 10.6 | 107 4.1 | 156 20.4 | 87 31.1 | 83 21.7 | 261 16.9 | 75 8.1 | 78 6.8 | 18 4.2 | 374 10.5 | 27 11.3 | 22 15.9 |
| A FEW REGULAR PARTNERS | 377 9.3 | 123 4.7 | 132 17.3 | 52 18.6 | 70 18.3 | 202 13.1 | 76 8.2 | 77 6.7 | 22 5.1 | 334 9.4 | 21 8.8 | 14 10.1 |
| MANY CASUAL PARTNERS | 255 6.3 | 80 3.0 | 101 13.2 | 31 11.1 | 42 11.0 | 152 9.8 | 44 4.7 | 38 3.3 | 18 4.2 | 204 5.7 | 22 9.2 | 20 14.5 |
| ONE FEMALE PARTNER, BUT LIVING SEPARATELY | 166 4.1 | 40 1.5 | 67 8.8 | 15 5.4 | 44 11.5 | 84 5.4 | 32 3.5 | 38 3.3 | 10 2.3 | 134 3.8 | 17 7.1 | 10 7.2 |
| NO ANSWER | 44 1.1 | 25 .9 | 12 1.6 | 3 1.1 | 4 1.0 | 14 .9 | 9 1.0 | 14 1.2 | 5 1.2 | 35 1.0 | 1 .4 | 1 .7 |
| SIGMA | 4140 101.8 | 2689 101.9 | 777 101.8 | 287 102.6 | 386 100.9 | 1570 101.5 | 946 102.1 | 1165 101.8 | 440 102.0 | 3625 101.9 | 241 100.6 | 140 101.3 |

Q. 8 WHAT TYPE OF WOMAN WOULD YOU MOST WANT FOR A LONG-TERM RELATIONSHIP?

TABLE 8

| | TOTAL | INCOME UNDER $10000 | INCOME $10-14999 | INCOME $15-24999 | INCOME $25000 & OVER | EDU LESS THAN H.S. GRAD | EDU HIGH SCHL GRAD | EDU SOME COLLEGE | EDU COL-LEGE GRAD | EDU SOME/COMPL POST GRAD | OCC PRO-FES-SION | OCC MANA-GER-IAL | OCC OTHER WHITE COLLR | OCC BLUE COLLR | OCC RET'D, UNEMP, OTHER | OCC STU-DENT |
|---|---|---|---|---|---|---|---|---|---|---|---|---|---|---|---|---|
| TOTAL RESPONDENTS | 4066 / 100.0 | 889 / 100.0 | 1178 / 100.0 | 1271 / 100.0 | 698 / 100.0 | 311 / 100.0 | 1038 / 100.0 | 1472 / 100.0 | 643 / 100.0 | 533 / 100.0 | 1028 / 100.0 | 658 / 100.0 | 523 / 100.0 | 729 / 100.0 | 544 / 100.0 | 472 / 100.0 |
| A SEXY WOMAN | 451 / 11.1 | 120 / 13.5 | 128 / 10.9 | 128 / 10.1 | 67 / 9.6 | 47 / 15.1 | 138 / 13.3 | 158 / 10.7 | 50 / 7.8 | 45 / 8.4 | 113 / 11.0 | 53 / 8.1 | 48 / 9.2 | 89 / 12.2 | 79 / 14.5 | 44 / 9.3 |
| AN INTELLIGENT WOMAN | 653 / 16.1 | 166 / 18.7 | 164 / 13.9 | 188 / 14.8 | 129 / 18.5 | 34 / 10.9 | 108 / 10.4 | 249 / 16.9 | 117 / 18.2 | 129 / 24.2 | 180 / 17.5 | 103 / 15.7 | 72 / 13.8 | 87 / 11.9 | 85 / 15.6 | 100 / 21.2 |
| A SELF-CONFIDENT WOMAN | 496 / 12.2 | 121 / 13.6 | 139 / 11.8 | 138 / 10.9 | 93 / 13.3 | 25 / 8.0 | 77 / 7.4 | 203 / 13.8 | 101 / 15.7 | 81 / 15.2 | 142 / 13.8 | 69 / 10.5 | 52 / 9.9 | 91 / 12.5 | 54 / 9.9 | 63 / 13.3 |
| A SINCERE WOMAN | 934 / 23.0 | 190 / 21.4 | 269 / 22.8 | 314 / 24.7 | 153 / 21.9 | 63 / 20.3 | 244 / 23.5 | 338 / 23.0 | 160 / 24.9 | 110 / 20.6 | 221 / 21.5 | 159 / 24.2 | 125 / 23.9 | 164 / 22.5 | 117 / 21.5 | 105 / 22.2 |
| A WOMAN WITH A GOOD SENSE OF HUMOR | 420 / 10.3 | 108 / 12.1 | 111 / 9.4 | 123 / 9.7 | 73 / 10.5 | 40 / 12.9 | 96 / 9.2 | 150 / 10.2 | 59 / 9.2 | 66 / 12.4 | 120 / 11.7 | 53 / 8.1 | 44 / 8.4 | 66 / 9.1 | 69 / 12.7 | 50 / 10.6 |
| AN AFFECTIONATE WOMAN | 846 / 20.8 | 187 / 21.0 | 231 / 19.6 | 283 / 22.3 | 137 / 19.6 | 68 / 21.9 | 231 / 22.3 | 310 / 21.1 | 118 / 18.4 | 101 / 18.9 | 197 / 19.2 | 147 / 22.3 | 107 / 20.5 | 165 / 22.6 | 129 / 23.7 | 72 / 15.3 |
| A WOMAN WITH A CONCERN FOR MY NEEDS | 1153 / 28.4 | 256 / 28.8 | 322 / 27.3 | 374 / 29.4 | 191 / 27.4 | 94 / 30.2 | 295 / 28.4 | 448 / 30.4 | 150 / 23.3 | 144 / 27.0 | 312 / 30.4 | 184 / 28.0 | 154 / 29.4 | 196 / 26.9 | 137 / 25.2 | 131 / 27.8 |
| NO ANSWER | 34 / .8 | 9 / 1.0 | 11 / .9 | 7 / .6 | 5 / .7 | 5 / 1.6 | 10 / 1.0 | 9 / .6 | 3 / .5 | 3 / .6 | 7 / .7 | 1 / .2 | 1 / .2 | 7 / 1.0 | 6 / 1.1 | 8 / 1.7 |
| SIGMA | 4987 / 122.7 | 1157 / 130.1 | 1375 / 116.6 | 1555 / 122.5 | 848 / 121.5 | 376 / 120.9 | 1199 / 115.5 | 1865 / 126.7 | 758 / 118.0 | 679 / 127.3 | 1292 / 125.8 | 769 / 117.1 | 603 / 115.3 | 865 / 118.7 | 676 / 124.2 | 573 / 121.4 |

Q. 9 WHAT TYPE OF WOMAN MAKES YOU FEEL MOST NERVOUS?

TABLE 9

| | TOTAL | MARITAL STATUS | | | | AGE | | | | RACE | | |
|---|---|---|---|---|---|---|---|---|---|---|---|---|
| | | MARR'D LIVING WITH WIFE | NEVER MARR'D LIVING W/O PARTNR | LIVING WITH UN-MARR'D PARTNR | DIVRCE OR WIDOWD LIVING ALONE | 18-29 | 30-39 | 40-54 | 55-65 | WHITE | BLACK | OTHER |
| TOTAL RESPONDENTS | 4066 100.0 | 2639 100.0 | 763 100.0 | 280 100.0 | 383 100.0 | 1547 100.0 | 927 100.0 | 1143 100.0 | 432 100.0 | 3559 100.0 | 240 100.0 | 138 100.0 |
| VERY INTELLIGENT WOMAN | 871 21.4 | 621 23.5 | 135 17.7 | 45 16.1 | 70 18.3 | 287 18.6 | 202 21.8 | 280 24.5 | 98 22.7 | 745 20.9 | 64 26.7 | 32 23.2 |
| WOMAN WITH HIGH PAY-ING JOB | 367 9.0 | 256 9.7 | 54 7.1 | 19 6.8 | 38 9.9 | 114 7.4 | 84 9.1 | 112 9.8 | 56 13.0 | 320 9.0 | 18 7.5 | 15 10.9 |
| BEAUTIFUL WOMAN | 1006 24.7 | 635 24.1 | 196 25.7 | 73 26.1 | 102 26.6 | 408 26.4 | 236 25.5 | 273 23.9 | 83 19.2 | 901 25.3 | 56 23.3 | 29 21.0 |
| WOMAN WITH MUCH SEXUAL EXPERIENCE | 516 12.7 | 303 11.5 | 134 17.6 | 31 11.1 | 48 12.5 | 222 14.4 | 91 9.8 | 138 12.1 | 65 15.0 | 451 12.7 | 38 15.8 | 13 9.4 |
| WEALTHY WOMAN | 477 11.7 | 298 11.3 | 104 13.6 | 34 12.1 | 41 10.7 | 196 12.7 | 119 12.8 | 121 10.6 | 40 9.3 | 431 12.1 | 16 6.7 | 14 10.1 |
| VIRGIN | 570 14.0 | 324 12.3 | 113 14.8 | 56 20.0 | 77 20.1 | 238 15.4 | 135 14.6 | 142 12.4 | 51 11.8 | 476 13.4 | 45 18.8 | 27 19.6 |
| NO ANSWER | 340 8.4 | 250 9.5 | 43 5.6 | 26 9.3 | 20 5.2 | 108 7.0 | 73 7.9 | 112 9.8 | 43 10.0 | 301 8.5 | 14 5.8 | 11 8.0 |
| SIGMA | 4147 101.9 | 2687 101.9 | 779 102.1 | 284 101.5 | 396 103.3 | 1573 101.9 | 940 101.5 | 1178 103.1 | 436 101.0 | 3625 101.9 | 251 104.6 | 141 102.2 |

Q. 9 WHAT TYPE OF WOMAN MAKES YOU FEEL MOST NERVOUS?

TABLE 9

| | TOTAL | INCOME | | | | EDUCATION | | | | | OCCUPATION | | | | | |
|---|---|---|---|---|---|---|---|---|---|---|---|---|---|---|---|---|
| | | UNDER $10000 | $10-14999 | $15-24999 | $25000 & OVER | LESS THAN H.S. GRAD. | HIGH SCHL GRAD. | SOME COLLEGE | COLLEGE GRAD | SOME/ COMPL POST GRAD. | PRO- FES- SION. | MANA- GER- IAL | OTHER WHITE COLLR | BLUE COLLR | RET'D, UNEMP, OTHER | STU- DENT |
| TOTAL RESPONDENTS | 4066 100.0 | 889 100.0 | 1178 100.0 | 1271 100.0 | 698 100.0 | 311 100.0 | 1038 100.0 | 1472 100.0 | 643 100.0 | 533 100.0 | 1028 100.0 | 658 100.0 | 523 100.0 | 729 100.0 | 544 100.0 | 472 100.0 |
| VERY INTELLIGENT WOMAN | 871 21.4 | 201 22.6 | 270 22.9 | 269 21.2 | 125 17.9 | 109 35.0 | 292 28.1 | 279 19.0 | 111 17.3 | 62 11.6 | 187 18.2 | 130 19.8 | 114 21.8 | 208 28.5 | 130 23.9 | 83 17.6 |
| WOMAN WITH HIGH PAY- ING JOB | 367 9.0 | 69 7.8 | 118 10.0 | 119 9.4 | 59 8.5 | 25 8.0 | 97 9.3 | 124 8.4 | 67 10.4 | 46 8.6 | 84 8.2 | 60 9.1 | 70 13.4 | 65 8.9 | 47 8.6 | 29 6.1 |
| BEAUTIFUL WOMAN | 1006 24.7 | 228 25.6 | 294 25.0 | 315 24.8 | 161 23.1 | 66 21.2 | 240 23.1 | 382 26.0 | 168 26.1 | 139 26.1 | 238 23.2 | 168 25.5 | 130 24.9 | 175 24.0 | 135 24.8 | 134 28.4 |
| WOMAN WITH MUCH SEXUAL EXPERIENCE | 516 12.7 | 130 14.6 | 148 12.6 | 153 12.0 | 82 11.7 | 39 12.5 | 132 12.7 | 198 13.5 | 74 11.5 | 67 12.6 | 113 11.0 | 79 12.0 | 67 12.8 | 85 11.7 | 71 13.1 | 84 17.8 |
| WEALTHY WOMAN | 477 11.7 | 109 12.3 | 134 11.4 | 142 11.2 | 90 12.9 | 30 9.6 | 96 9.2 | 175 11.9 | 90 14.0 | 74 13.9 | 141 13.7 | 80 12.2 | 60 11.5 | 75 10.3 | 56 10.3 | 56 11.9 |
| VIRGIN | 570 14.0 | 121 13.6 | 164 13.9 | 179 14.1 | 99 14.2 | 27 8.7 | 133 12.8 | 227 15.4 | 84 13.1 | 86 16.1 | 167 16.2 | 98 14.9 | 52 9.9 | 88 12.1 | 76 14.0 | 69 14.6 |
| NO ANSWER | 340 8.4 | 59 6.6 | 77 6.5 | 113 8.9 | 88 12.6 | 25 8.0 | 69 6.6 | 118 8.0 | 59 9.2 | 62 11.6 | 116 11.3 | 58 8.8 | 33 6.3 | 47 6.4 | 44 8.1 | 23 4.9 |
| SIGMA | 4147 101.9 | 917 103.1 | 1205 102.3 | 1290 101.6 | 704 100.9 | 321 103.0 | 1059 101.8 | 1503 102.2 | 653 101.6 | 536 100.5 | 1046 101.8 | 673 102.3 | 526 100.6 | 743 101.9 | 559 102.8 | 478 101.3 |

TABLE 10

Q. 10 HOW DO YOU USUALLY FEEL AFTER CLIMAXING?

| | TOTAL | MARITAL STATUS | | | | AGE | | | | RACE | | |
|---|---|---|---|---|---|---|---|---|---|---|---|---|
| | | MARR'D LIVING WITH WIFE | NEVER MARR'D LIVING W/O PARTNR | MARR'D LIVING WITH UN-MARR'D PARTNR | DIVRCE OR WIDOWD LIVING ALONE | 18-29 | 30-39 | 40-54 | 55-65 | WHITE | BLACK | OTHER |
| TOTAL RESPONDENTS | 4066 100.0 | 2639 100.0 | 763 100.0 | 280 100.0 | 383 100.0 | 1547 100.0 | 927 100.0 | 1143 100.0 | 432 100.0 | 3559 100.0 | 240 100.0 | 138 100.0 |
| VERY LOVING | 973 23.9 | 605 22.9 | 190 24.9 | 66 23.6 | 112 29.2 | 372 24.0 | 198 21.4 | 281 24.6 | 113 26.2 | 808 22.7 | 89 37.1 | 40 29.0 |
| VERY DROWSY | 631 15.5 | 467 17.7 | 79 10.4 | 33 11.8 | 52 13.6 | 194 12.5 | 133 14.3 | 206 18.0 | 94 21.8 | 542 15.2 | 37 15.4 | 22 15.9 |
| SOMEWHAT DEPRESSED | 90 2.2 | 50 1.9 | 29 3.8 | 3 1.1 | 8 2.1 | 41 2.7 | 13 1.4 | 19 1.7 | 17 3.9 | 74 2.1 | 6 2.5 | 7 5.1 |
| SOMEWHAT GUILTY | 61 1.5 | 30 1.1 | 18 2.4 | 5 1.8 | 8 2.1 | 31 2.0 | 10 1.1 | 14 1.2 | 5 1.2 | 46 1.3 | 8 3.3 | 6 4.3 |
| EXHILARATED/HIGH | 647 15.9 | 352 13.3 | 171 22.4 | 63 22.5 | 60 15.7 | 330 21.3 | 152 16.4 | 136 11.9 | 27 6.3 | 565 15.9 | 45 18.8 | 25 18.1 |
| CONTENT | 1839 45.2 | 1247 47.3 | 301 39.4 | 125 44.6 | 166 43.3 | 633 40.9 | 463 49.9 | 542 47.4 | 196 45.4 | 1667 46.8 | 74 30.8 | 44 31.9 |
| NO ANSWER | 27 .7 | 12 .5 | 14 1.8 | 1 .3 | 1 .3 | 12 .8 | 3 .3 | 10 .9 | 1 .2 | 24 .7 | | |
| SIGMA | 4268 104.9 | 2763 104.7 | 802 105.1 | 295 105.4 | 407 106.3 | 1613 104.2 | 972 104.8 | 1208 105.7 | 453 105.0 | 3726 104.7 | 259 107.9 | 144 104.3 |

Q. 10 HOW DO YOU USUALLY FEEL AFTER CLIMAXING?

TABLE 10

| | TOTAL | INCOME | | | | EDUCATION | | | | | OCCUPATION | | | | | |
|---|---|---|---|---|---|---|---|---|---|---|---|---|---|---|---|---|
| | | UNDER $10000 | $10-14999 | $15-24999 | $25000 & OVER | LESS THAN H.S. GRAD | HIGH SCHL GRAD | SOME COL-LEGE | COL-LEGE GRAD | SOME/COMPL POST GRAD | PRO-FES-SION. | MANA-GER-IAL | OTHER WHITE COLLR | BLUE COLLR | RET'D, UNEMP, OTHER | STU-DENT |
| TOTAL RESPONDENTS | 4066 100.0 | 889 100.0 | 1178 100.0 | 1271 100.0 | 698 100.0 | 311 100.0 | 1038 100.0 | 1472 100.0 | 643 100.0 | 533 100.0 | 1028 100.0 | 658 100.0 | 523 100.0 | 729 100.0 | 544 100.0 | 472 100.0 |
| VERY LOVING | 973 23.9 | 243 27.3 | 280 23.8 | 267 21.0 | 169 24.2 | 91 29.3 | 264 25.4 | 321 21.8 | 159 24.7 | 111 20.8 | 242 23.5 | 128 19.5 | 111 21.2 | 172 23.6 | 159 29.2 | 119 25.2 |
| VERY DROWSY | 631 15.5 | 110 12.4 | 189 16.0 | 217 17.1 | 111 15.9 | 51 16.4 | 171 16.5 | 225 15.3 | 89 13.8 | 83 15.6 | 141 13.7 | 116 17.6 | 98 18.7 | 126 17.3 | 82 15.1 | 53 11.2 |
| SOMEWHAT DEPRESSED | 90 2.2 | 34 3.8 | 19 1.6 | 19 1.5 | 18 2.6 | 8 2.6 | 18 1.7 | 25 1.7 | 19 3.0 | 18 3.4 | 23 2.2 | 17 2.6 | 7 1.3 | 13 1.8 | 11 2.0 | 16 3.4 |
| SOMEWHAT GUILTY | 61 1.5 | 22 2.5 | 23 2.0 | 12 .9 | 4 .6 | 10 3.2 | 20 1.9 | 17 1.2 | 8 1.2 | 6 1.1 | 11 1.1 | 9 1.4 | 10 1.9 | 11 1.5 | 10 1.8 | 8 1.7 |
| EXHILARATED/HIGH | 647 15.9 | 170 19.1 | 187 15.9 | 193 15.2 | 93 13.3 | 38 12.2 | 136 13.1 | 266 18.1 | 104 16.2 | 90 16.9 | 168 16.3 | 93 14.1 | 65 12.4 | 113 15.5 | 98 18.0 | 90 19.1 |
| CONTENT | 1839 45.2 | 357 40.2 | 521 44.2 | 613 48.2 | 340 48.7 | 126 40.5 | 471 45.4 | 678 46.1 | 289 44.9 | 250 46.9 | 499 48.5 | 322 48.9 | 245 46.8 | 315 43.2 | 209 38.4 | 196 41.5 |
| NO ANSWER | 27 .7 | 6 .7 | 9 .8 | 8 .6 | 2 .3 | 5 1.6 | 5 .5 | 8 .5 | 4 .6 | 2 .4 | 6 .6 | 3 .6 | 3 .6 | 6 .8 | 3 .6 | 4 .8 |
| SIGMA | 4268 104.9 | 942 106.0 | 1228 104.3 | 1329 104.5 | 737 105.6 | 329 105.8 | 1085 104.5 | 1540 104.7 | 672 104.4 | 560 105.1 | 1090 105.9 | 685 104.1 | 539 102.9 | 756 103.7 | 572 105.1 | 486 102.9 |

TABLE 11

Q. 11 DO YOU DELIBERATELY TRY TO DELAY YOUR ORGASM AND FOR HOW LONG?

| | TOTAL | MARITAL STATUS | | | | AGE | | | | RACE | | |
|---|---|---|---|---|---|---|---|---|---|---|---|---|
| | | MARR'D LIVING WITH WIFE | NEVER MARR'D LIVING W/O PARTNR | LIVING WITH PARTNR UN-MARR'D | DIVRCE OR WIDOWD LIVING ALONE | 18-29 | 30-39 | 40-54 | 55-65 | WHITE | BLACK | OTHER |
| TOTAL RESPONDENTS | 4066 100.0 | 2639 100.0 | 763 100.0 | 280 100.0 | 383 100.0 | 1547 100.0 | 927 100.0 | 1143 100.0 | 432 100.0 | 3559 100.0 | 240 100.0 | 138 100.0 |
| NO, DON'T TRY | 598 14.7 | 359 13.6 | 133 17.4 | 44 15.7 | 62 16.2 | 226 14.6 | 106 11.4 | 163 14.3 | 100 23.1 | 492 13.8 | 56 23.3 | 21 15.2 |
| YES, UP TO 5 MIN-UTES | 218 5.4 | 161 6.1 | 34 4.5 | 9 3.2 | 14 3.7 | 66 4.3 | 48 5.2 | 62 5.4 | 41 9.5 | 188 5.3 | 13 5.4 | 7 5.1 |
| YES, UNTIL PARTNER HAS ORGASM | 1277 31.4 | 898 34.0 | 191 25.0 | 80 28.6 | 107 27.9 | 446 28.8 | 337 36.4 | 353 30.9 | 136 31.5 | 1148 32.3 | 50 20.8 | 44 31.9 |
| YES, UNTIL PARTNER SEEMS SATISFIED | 959 23.6 | 602 22.8 | 172 22.5 | 77 27.5 | 108 28.2 | 372 24.0 | 220 23.7 | 283 24.8 | 82 19.0 | 840 23.6 | 61 25.4 | 30 21.7 |
| YES, AS LONG AS POSSIBLE | 1009 24.8 | 629 23.8 | 207 27.1 | 74 26.4 | 99 25.8 | 425 27.5 | 220 23.7 | 292 25.5 | 68 15.7 | 890 25.0 | 60 25.0 | 33 23.9 |
| NO EXPERIENCE IN INTERCOURSE | 48 1.2 | 12 .5 | 29 3.8 | 1 .4 | 6 1.6 | 36 2.3 | 1 .1 | 7 .6 | 4 .9 | 43 1.2 | 2 .8 | 3 2.2 |
| NO ANSWER | 22 .5 | 12 .5 | 5 .7 | 4 1.4 | 1 .3 | 4 .3 | 5 .5 | 5 .4 | 5 1.2 | 15 .4 | 2 .8 | 1 .7 |
| SIGMA | 4131 101.6 | 2673 101.3 | 771 101.0 | 289 103.2 | 397 103.7 | 1575 101.8 | 937 101.0 | 1165 101.9 | 436 100.9 | 3616 101.6 | 244 101.5 | 139 100.7 |

Q. 11 DO YOU DELIBERATELY TRY TO DELAY YOUR ORGASM AND FOR HOW LONG?

TABLE 11

| | TOTAL | INCOME UNDER $10000 | INCOME $10-14999 | INCOME $15-24999 | INCOME $25000 & OVER | EDU LESS THAN H.S. GRAD | HIGH SCHL GRAD | SOME COLLEGE | COL-LEGE GRAD | SOME/COMPL POST GRAD | PRO-FES-SION. | MANA-GER-IAL | OTHER WHITE COLLR | BLUE COLLR | RET'D, UNEMP, OTHER | STU-DENT |
|---|---|---|---|---|---|---|---|---|---|---|---|---|---|---|---|---|
| TOTAL RESPONDENTS | 4066 / 100.0 | 889 / 100.0 | 1178 / 100.0 | 1271 / 100.0 | 698 / 100.0 | 311 / 100.0 | 1038 / 100.0 | 1472 / 100.0 | 643 / 100.0 | 533 / 100.0 | 1028 / 100.0 | 658 / 100.0 | 523 / 100.0 | 729 / 100.0 | 544 / 100.0 | 472 / 100.0 |
| NO, DON'T TRY | 598 / 14.7 | 150 / 16.9 | 184 / 15.6 | 174 / 13.7 | 84 / 12.0 | 62 / 19.9 | 187 / 18.0 | 194 / 13.2 | 86 / 13.4 | 53 / 9.9 | 119 / 11.6 | 82 / 12.5 | 75 / 14.3 | 119 / 16.3 | 108 / 19.9 | 74 / 15.7 |
| YES, UP TO 5 MIN-UTES | 218 / 5.4 | 40 / 4.5 | 75 / 6.4 | 62 / 4.9 | 39 / 5.6 | 26 / 8.4 | 57 / 5.5 | 70 / 4.8 | 33 / 5.1 | 28 / 5.3 | 52 / 5.1 | 38 / 5.8 | 39 / 7.5 | 38 / 5.2 | 25 / 4.6 | 23 / 4.9 |
| YES, UNTIL PARTNER HAS ORGASM | 1277 / 31.4 | 245 / 27.6 | 348 / 29.5 | 435 / 34.2 | 240 / 34.4 | 90 / 28.9 | 305 / 29.4 | 473 / 32.1 | 203 / 31.6 | 184 / 34.5 | 374 / 36.4 | 209 / 31.8 | 168 / 32.1 | 196 / 26.9 | 161 / 29.6 | 128 / 27.1 |
| YES, UNTIL PARTNER SEEMS SATISFIED | 959 / 23.6 | 209 / 23.5 | 271 / 23.0 | 305 / 24.0 | 170 / 24.4 | 75 / 24.1 | 234 / 22.5 | 345 / 23.4 | 156 / 24.3 | 133 / 25.0 | 252 / 24.5 | 169 / 25.7 | 117 / 22.4 | 181 / 24.8 | 103 / 18.9 | 104 / 22.0 |
| YES, AS LONG AS POSSIBLE | 1009 / 24.8 | 240 / 27.0 | 295 / 25.0 | 300 / 23.6 | 168 / 24.1 | 60 / 19.3 | 254 / 24.5 | 378 / 25.7 | 169 / 26.3 | 135 / 25.3 | 237 / 23.1 | 160 / 24.3 | 129 / 24.7 | 194 / 26.6 | 142 / 26.1 | 131 / 27.8 |
| NO EXPERIENCE IN INTERCOURSE | 48 / 1.2 | 21 / 2.4 | 10 / .8 | 12 / .9 | 4 / .6 | 2 / .6 | 11 / 1.1 | 26 / 1.8 | 5 / .8 | 4 / .8 | 4 / .4 | 3 / .5 | 3 / .6 | 6 / .8 | 12 / 2.2 | 16 / 3.4 |
| NO ANSWER | 22 / .5 | 2 / .2 | 8 / .7 | 6 / .5 | 3 / .4 | 1 / .3 | 3 / .3 | 9 / .6 | 4 / .6 | 1 / .2 | 4 / .4 | 3 / .5 | 1 / .2 | 4 / .5 | 3 / .6 | 2 / .4 |
| SIGMA | 4131 / 101.6 | 907 / 102.1 | 1191 / 101.0 | 1294 / 101.8 | 708 / 101.5 | 316 / 101.5 | 1051 / 101.3 | 1495 / 101.6 | 656 / 102.1 | 538 / 101.0 | 1042 / 101.5 | 664 / 101.1 | 532 / 101.8 | 738 / 101.1 | 554 / 101.9 | 478 / 101.3 |

TABLE 12

Q. 12 IDEALLY, HOW OFTEN WOULD YOU WANT INTERCOURSE?

| | TOTAL | MARITAL STATUS | | | | AGE | | | | RACE | | |
|---|---|---|---|---|---|---|---|---|---|---|---|---|
| | | MARR'D LIVING WITH WIFE | NEVER MARR'D LIVING W/O PARTNR | MARR'D LIVING WITH UN-MARR'D PARTNR | DIVRCE OR WIDOWD LIVING ALONE | 18-29 | 30-39 | 40-54 | 55-65 | WHITE | BLACK | OTHER |
| TOTAL RESPONDENTS | 4066 100.0 | 2639 100.0 | 763 100.0 | 280 100.0 | 383 100.0 | 1547 100.0 | 927 100.0 | 1143 100.0 | 432 100.0 | 3559 100.0 | 240 100.0 | 138 100.0 |
| MORE THAN ONCE A DAY | 531 13.1 | 259 9.8 | 136 17.8 | 64 22.9 | 71 18.5 | 291 18.8 | 122 13.2 | 95 8.3 | 21 4.9 | 439 12.3 | 47 19.6 | 28 20.3 |
| 5 TO 7 TIMES A WEEK | 1029 25.3 | 587 22.2 | 252 33.0 | 82 29.3 | 108 28.2 | 504 32.6 | 249 26.9 | 225 19.7 | 48 11.1 | 919 25.8 | 58 24.2 | 27 19.6 |
| 3 TO 4 TIMES A WEEK | 1408 34.6 | 975 36.9 | 222 29.1 | 85 30.4 | 126 32.9 | 502 32.4 | 387 41.7 | 421 36.8 | 96 22.2 | 1255 35.3 | 72 30.0 | 46 33.3 |
| 1 TO 2 TIMES A WEEK | 738 18.2 | 569 21.6 | 95 12.5 | 26 9.3 | 48 12.5 | 162 10.5 | 137 14.8 | 290 25.4 | 146 33.8 | 652 18.3 | 36 15.0 | 21 15.2 |
| 2 TO 3 TIMES A MONTH | 240 5.9 | 177 6.7 | 34 4.5 | 11 3.9 | 18 4.7 | 57 3.7 | 18 1.9 | 80 7.0 | 83 19.2 | 199 5.6 | 15 6.3 | 11 8.0 |
| ONCE A MONTH OR LESS | 70 1.7 | 49 1.9 | 9 1.2 | 3 1.1 | 9 2.3 | 12 .8 | 4 .4 | 19 1.7 | 32 7.4 | 57 1.6 | 7 2.9 | 1 .7 |
| NEVER | 17 .4 | 6 .2 | 7 .9 | 2 .7 | 2 .5 | 6 .4 | 3 .3 | 5 .4 | 3 .7 | 13 .4 | 2 .8 | 2 1.4 |
| NO ANSWER | 33 .8 | 17 .6 | 8 1.0 | 7 2.5 | 1 .3 | 13 .8 | 7 .8 | 8 .7 | 3 .7 | 25 .7 | 3 1.3 | 2 1.4 |
| SIGMA | 4066 100.0 | 2639 99.9 | 763 100.0 | 280 100.1 | 383 99.9 | 1547 100.0 | 927 100.0 | 1143 100.0 | 432 100.0 | 3559 100.0 | 240 100.1 | 138 99.9 |

Q. 12 IDEALLY, HOW OFTEN WOULD YOU WANT INTERCOURSE?

TABLE 12

| | TOTAL | INCOME | | | | EDUCATION | | | | | OCCUPATION | | | | | |
|---|---|---|---|---|---|---|---|---|---|---|---|---|---|---|---|---|
| | | UNDER $10000 | $10-14999 | $15-24999 | $25000 & OVER | LESS THAN H.S. GRAD | HIGH SCHL GRAD. | SOME COL-LEGE | COL-LEGE GRAD | SOME/ COMPL POST GRAD. | PRO-FES-SION. | MANA-GER-IAL | OTHER WHITE COLLR | BLUE COLLR | RET'D, UNEMP, OTHER | STU-DENT |
| TOTAL RESPONDENTS | 4066 100.0 | 889 100.0 | 1178 100.0 | 1271 100.0 | 698 100.0 | 311 100.0 | 1038 100.0 | 1472 100.0 | 643 100.0 | 533 100.0 | 1028 100.0 | 658 100.0 | 523 100.0 | 729 100.0 | 544 100.0 | 472 100.0 |
| MORE THAN ONCE A DAY | 531 13.1 | 172 19.3 | 150 12.7 | 126 9.9 | 75 10.7 | 43 13.8 | 132 12.7 | 219 14.9 | 72 11.2 | 57 10.7 | 166 16.1 | 55 8.4 | 53 10.1 | 76 10.4 | 91 16.7 | 75 15.9 |
| 5 TO 7 TIMES A WEEK | 1029 25.3 | 249 28.0 | 299 25.4 | 299 23.5 | 179 25.6 | 69 22.2 | 240 23.1 | 400 27.2 | 179 27.8 | 126 23.6 | 258 25.1 | 139 21.1 | 127 24.3 | 195 26.7 | 137 25.2 | 143 30.3 |
| 3 TO 4 TIMES A WEEK | 1408 34.6 | 265 29.8 | 407 34.6 | 504 39.7 | 224 32.1 | 94 30.2 | 349 33.6 | 515 35.0 | 226 35.1 | 203 38.1 | 353 34.3 | 274 41.6 | 188 35.9 | 265 36.4 | 142 26.1 | 150 31.8 |
| 1 TO 2 TIMES A WEEK | 738 18.2 | 117 13.2 | 207 17.6 | 248 19.5 | 160 22.9 | 63 20.3 | 197 19.0 | 232 15.8 | 122 19.0 | 111 20.8 | 183 17.8 | 134 20.4 | 114 21.8 | 128 17.6 | 94 17.3 | 70 14.8 |
| 2 TO 3 TIMES A MONTH | 240 5.9 | 53 6.0 | 80 6.8 | 67 5.3 | 39 5.6 | 29 9.3 | 84 8.1 | 70 4.8 | 31 4.8 | 21 3.9 | 43 4.2 | 41 6.2 | 26 5.0 | 47 6.4 | 54 9.9 | 22 4.7 |
| ONCE A MONTH OR LESS | 70 1.7 | 16 1.8 | 21 1.8 | 14 1.1 | 17 2.4 | 7 2.3 | 26 2.5 | 18 1.2 | 6 .9 | 9 1.7 | 13 1.3 | 9 1.4 | 12 2.3 | 11 1.5 | 15 2.8 | 6 1.3 |
| NEVER | 17 .4 | 5 .6 | 3 .3 | 7 .6 | 2 .3 | 4 1.3 | 3 .3 | 5 .3 | 1 .2 | 4 .8 | 4 .4 | 2 .3 | | 1 .1 | 7 1.3 | 3 .6 |
| NO ANSWER | 33 .8 | 12 1.3 | 11 .9 | 6 .5 | 2 .3 | 2 .6 | 7 .7 | 13 .9 | 6 .9 | 2 .4 | 8 .8 | 4 .6 | 3 .6 | 6 .8 | 4 .7 | 3 .6 |
| SIGMA | 4066 100.0 | 889 100.0 | 1178 100.1 | 1271 100.1 | 698 99.9 | 311 100.0 | 1038 100.0 | 1472 100.1 | 643 99.9 | 533 100.0 | 1028 100.0 | 658 100.0 | 523 100.0 | 729 99.9 | 544 100.0 | 472 100.0 |

Q. 13 WHAT ELSE BESIDES LOVE WOULD BE YOUR MAIN REASON FOR GETTING MARRIED?

TABLE 13

| | TOTAL | MARITAL STATUS | | | | AGE | | | | RACE | | |
|---|---|---|---|---|---|---|---|---|---|---|---|---|
| | | MARR'D LIVING WITH WIFE | NEVER MARR'D LIVING W/O PARTNR | MARR'D LIVING WITH PARTNR UN-MARR'D | DIVRCE WIDOWD LIVING ALONE | 18-29 | 30-39 | 40-54 | 55-65 | WHITE | BLACK | OTHER |
| TOTAL RESPONDENTS | 4066 100.0 | 2639 100.0 | 763 100.0 | 280 100.0 | 383 100.0 | 1547 100.0 | 927 100.0 | 1143 100.0 | 432 100.0 | 3559 100.0 | 240 100.0 | 138 100.0 |
| COMPANIONSHIP | 1913 47.0 | 1304 49.4 | 351 46.0 | 93 33.2 | 164 42.8 | 711 46.0 | 412 44.4 | 553 48.4 | 231 53.5 | 1715 48.2 | 84 35.0 | 57 41.3 |
| REGULAR SEX | 311 7.6 | 225 8.5 | 32 4.2 | 23 8.2 | 31 8.1 | 92 5.9 | 66 7.1 | 104 9.1 | 49 11.3 | 249 7.0 | 34 14.2 | 12 8.7 |
| HAVING CHILDREN | 575 14.1 | 402 15.2 | 94 12.3 | 40 14.3 | 39 10.2 | 207 13.4 | 145 15.6 | 160 14.0 | 58 13.4 | 487 13.7 | 48 20.0 | 21 15.2 |
| HAVING A HOMELIFE | 976 24.0 | 743 28.2 | 113 14.8 | 49 17.5 | 71 18.5 | 300 19.4 | 253 27.3 | 315 27.6 | 102 23.6 | 837 23.5 | 69 28.8 | 36 26.1 |
| EMOTIONAL SECURITY | 379 9.3 | 233 8.8 | 79 10.4 | 34 12.1 | 33 8.6 | 166 10.7 | 89 9.6 | 94 8.2 | 26 6.0 | 344 9.7 | 15 6.3 | 11 8.0 |
| DON'T WANT TO MARRY | 300 7.4 | 43 1.6 | 131 17.2 | 61 21.8 | 65 17.0 | 193 12.5 | 51 5.5 | 41 3.6 | 15 3.5 | 259 7.3 | 14 5.8 | 17 12.3 |
| NO ANSWER | 56 1.4 | 27 1.0 | 15 2.0 | 5 1.8 | 9 2.3 | 18 1.2 | 20 2.2 | 9 .8 | 7 1.6 | 42 1.2 | 5 2.1 | 3 2.2 |
| SIGMA | 4510 110.8 | 2977 112.7 | 815 106.9 | 305 108.9 | 412 107.5 | 1687 109.1 | 1036 111.7 | 1276 111.7 | 488 112.9 | 3933 110.6 | 269 112.2 | 157 113.8 |

Q. 13 WHAT ELSE BESIDES LOVE WOULD BE YOUR MAIN REASON FOR GETTING MARRIED?

TABLE 13

| | TOTAL | INCOME | | | | EDUCATION | | | | | OCCUPATION | | | | | |
| --- | --- | --- | --- | --- | --- | --- | --- | --- | --- | --- | --- | --- | --- | --- | --- | --- |
| | | UNDER $10000 | $10-14999 | $15-24999 | $25000 & OVER | LESS THAN H.S. GRAD | HIGH SCHL GRAD. | SOME COLLEGE | COLLEGE GRAD | SOME/COMPL POST GRAD. | PRO-FES-SION. | MANA-GER-IAL | OTHER WHITE COLLR | BLUE COLLR | RET'D/UNEMP, OTHER | STU-DENT |
| TOTAL RESPONDENTS | 4066 100.0 | 889 100.0 | 1178 100.0 | 1271 100.0 | 698 100.0 | 311 100.0 | 1038 100.0 | 1472 100.0 | 643 100.0 | 533 100.0 | 1028 100.0 | 658 100.0 | 523 100.0 | 729 100.0 | 544 100.0 | 472 100.0 |
| COMPANIONSHIP | 1913 47.0 | 413 46.5 | 535 45.4 | 622 48.9 | 330 47.3 | 130 41.8 | 449 43.3 | 700 47.6 | 327 50.9 | 277 52.0 | 498 48.4 | 320 48.6 | 261 49.9 | 317 43.5 | 228 41.9 | 231 48.9 |
| REGULAR SEX | 311 7.6 | 62 7.0 | 99 8.4 | 92 7.2 | 57 8.2 | 32 10.3 | 91 8.8 | 108 7.3 | 38 5.9 | 35 6.6 | 72 7.0 | 39 5.9 | 51 9.8 | 68 9.3 | 44 8.1 | 25 5.3 |
| HAVING CHILDREN | 575 14.1 | 118 13.3 | 162 13.8 | 184 14.5 | 104 14.9 | 43 13.8 | 151 14.5 | 220 14.9 | 73 11.4 | 73 13.7 | 160 15.6 | 93 14.1 | 62 11.9 | 90 12.3 | 96 17.6 | 57 12.1 |
| HAVING A HOMELIFE | 976 24.0 | 189 21.3 | 289 24.5 | 314 24.7 | 177 25.4 | 84 27.0 | 278 26.8 | 331 22.5 | 139 21.6 | 115 21.6 | 237 23.1 | 173 26.3 | 134 25.6 | 180 24.7 | 137 25.2 | 84 17.8 |
| EMOTIONAL SECURITY | 379 9.3 | 82 9.2 | 109 9.3 | 115 9.0 | 69 9.9 | 22 7.1 | 82 7.9 | 142 9.6 | 78 12.1 | 50 9.4 | 107 10.4 | 53 8.1 | 49 9.4 | 74 10.2 | 34 6.3 | 54 11.4 |
| DON'T WANT TO MARRY | 300 7.4 | 101 11.4 | 91 7.7 | 70 5.5 | 36 5.2 | 22 7.1 | 80 7.7 | 123 8.4 | 42 6.5 | 32 6.0 | 56 5.4 | 33 5.0 | 27 5.2 | 57 7.8 | 54 9.9 | 62 13.1 |
| NO ANSWER | 56 1.4 | 13 1.5 | 16 1.4 | 13 1.0 | 12 1.7 | 8 2.6 | 12 1.2 | 21 1.4 | 4 .6 | 7 1.3 | 22 2.1 | 6 .9 | 5 1.0 | 7 1.0 | 8 1.5 | 3 .6 |
| SIGMA | 4510 110.8 | 978 110.2 | 1301 110.5 | 1410 110.8 | 785 112.6 | 341 109.7 | 1143 110.2 | 1645 111.7 | 701 109.0 | 589 110.6 | 1152 112.0 | 717 108.9 | 589 112.8 | 793 108.8 | 601 110.5 | 516 109.2 |

Q. 14 WHO SHOULD TAKE RESPONSIBILITY FOR BIRTH CONTROL?

TABLE 14

| | TOTAL | MARITAL STATUS | | | | AGE | | | | RACE | | |
|---|---|---|---|---|---|---|---|---|---|---|---|---|
| | | MARR'D LIVING WITH WIFE | NEVER MARR'D LIVING W/O PARTNR | MARR'D LIVING WITH UN-MARR'D PARTNR | DIVRCE OR WIDOWD LIVING ALONE | 18-29 | 30-39 | 40-54 | 55-65 | WHITE | BLACK | OTHER |
| TOTAL RESPONDENTS | 4066 100.0 | 2639 100.0 | 763 100.0 | 280 100.0 | 383 100.0 | 1547 100.0 | 927 100.0 | 1143 100.0 | 432 100.0 | 3559 100.0 | 240 100.0 | 138 100.0 |
| WOMAN SHOULD TAKE THE SOLE RESPONSIBILITY | 799 19.7 | 516 19.6 | 126 16.5 | 67 23.9 | 90 23.5 | 271 17.5 | 185 20.0 | 246 21.5 | 93 21.5 | 664 18.7 | 71 29.6 | 29 21.0 |
| MEN SHOULD USE PROTECTION (CONDOMS) | 245 6.0 | 208 7.9 | 16 2.1 | 5 1.8 | 16 4.2 | 55 3.6 | 46 5.0 | 92 8.0 | 51 11.8 | 210 5.9 | 14 5.8 | 9 6.5 |
| PREFERABLE FOR WOMAN TO BE RESPONSIBLE, BUT MEN SHOULD HAVE PROTECTION READY | 1461 35.9 | 898 34.0 | 294 38.5 | 117 41.8 | 151 39.4 | 595 38.5 | 328 35.4 | 410 35.9 | 125 28.9 | 1332 37.4 | 55 22.9 | 32 23.2 |
| BOTH SHOULD USE PROTECTION METHODS | 1308 32.2 | 836 31.7 | 291 38.1 | 70 25.0 | 111 29.0 | 544 35.2 | 335 36.1 | 312 27.3 | 115 26.6 | 1164 32.7 | 68 28.3 | 51 37.0 |
| WITHDRAWAL METHOD SHOULD BE USED | 59 1.5 | 42 1.6 | 8 1.0 | 4 1.4 | 5 1.3 | 22 1.4 | 4 .4 | 21 1.8 | 11 2.5 | 41 1.2 | 9 3.8 | 6 4.3 |
| NO BIRTH CONTROL MEASURES SHOULD BE TAKEN | 166 4.1 | 117 4.4 | 22 2.9 | 13 4.6 | 14 3.7 | 58 3.7 | 25 2.7 | 49 4.3 | 32 7.4 | 129 3.6 | 19 7.9 | 11 8.0 |
| NO ANSWER | 58 1.4 | 37 1.4 | 10 1.3 | 6 2.1 | 5 1.3 | 16 1.0 | 7 .8 | 24 2.1 | 7 1.6 | 44 1.2 | 5 2.1 | 2 1.4 |
| SIGMA | 4096 100.8 | 2654 100.6 | 767 100.4 | 282 100.6 | 392 102.4 | 1561 100.9 | 930 100.4 | 1154 100.9 | 434 100.3 | 3584 100.7 | 241 100.4 | 140 101.4 |

TABLE 14

Q. 14 WHO SHOULD TAKE RESPONSIBILITY FOR BIRTH CONTROL?

|  | TOTAL | INCOME | | | | EDUCATION | | | | | OCCUPATION | | | | | |
|---|---|---|---|---|---|---|---|---|---|---|---|---|---|---|---|---|
|  |  | UNDER $10000 | $10-14999 | $15-24999 | $25000 & OVER | LESS THAN H.S. GRAD. | HIGH SCHL GRAD. | SOME COLLEGE | COLLEGE GRAD | SOME/COMPL POST GRAD. | PRO-FESSION. | MANA-GER-IAL | OTHER WHITE COLLR | BLUE COLLR | RET'D, UNEMP, OTHER | STU-DENT |
| TOTAL RESPONDENTS | 4066 / 100.0 | 889 / 100.0 | 1178 / 100.0 | 1271 / 100.0 | 698 / 100.0 | 311 / 100.0 | 1038 / 100.0 | 1472 / 100.0 | 643 / 100.0 | 533 / 100.0 | 1028 / 100.0 | 658 / 100.0 | 523 / 100.0 | 729 / 100.0 | 544 / 100.0 | 472 / 100.0 |
| WOMAN SHOULD TAKE THE SOLE RESPONSIBILITY | 799 / 19.7 | 186 / 20.9 | 242 / 20.5 | 224 / 17.6 | 141 / 20.2 | 80 / 25.7 | 244 / 23.5 | 255 / 17.3 | 122 / 19.0 | 85 / 15.9 | 203 / 19.7 | 121 / 18.4 | 101 / 19.3 | 158 / 21.7 | 122 / 22.4 | 73 / 15.5 |
| MEN SHOULD USE PROTECTION (CONDOMS) | 245 / 6.0 | 35 / 3.9 | 80 / 6.8 | 83 / 6.5 | 43 / 6.2 | 30 / 9.6 | 77 / 7.4 | 76 / 5.2 | 30 / 4.7 | 29 / 5.4 | 65 / 6.3 | 40 / 6.1 | 33 / 6.3 | 47 / 6.4 | 42 / 7.7 | 13 / 2.8 |
| PREFERABLE FOR WOMAN TO BE RESPONSIBLE, BUT MEN SHOULD HAVE PROTECTION READY | 1461 / 35.9 | 312 / 35.1 | 417 / 35.4 | 451 / 35.5 | 272 / 39.0 | 87 / 28.0 | 342 / 32.9 | 580 / 39.4 | 229 / 35.6 | 202 / 37.9 | 380 / 37.0 | 266 / 40.4 | 193 / 36.9 | 235 / 32.2 | 176 / 32.4 | 174 / 36.9 |
| BOTH SHOULD USE PROTECTION METHODS | 1308 / 32.2 | 298 / 33.5 | 356 / 30.2 | 434 / 34.1 | 212 / 30.4 | 78 / 25.1 | 292 / 28.1 | 477 / 32.4 | 235 / 36.5 | 202 / 37.9 | 331 / 32.2 | 195 / 29.6 | 170 / 32.5 | 234 / 32.1 | 144 / 26.5 | 193 / 40.9 |
| WITHDRAWAL METHOD SHOULD BE USED | 59 / 1.5 | 14 / 1.6 | 19 / 1.6 | 15 / 1.2 | 10 / 1.4 | 14 / 4.5 | 20 / 1.9 | 14 / 1.0 | 4 / .6 | 5 / .9 | 12 / 1.2 | 7 / 1.1 | 5 / 1.0 | 14 / 1.9 | 16 / 2.9 | 3 / .6 |
| NO BIRTH CONTROL MEASURES SHOULD BE TAKEN | 166 / 4.1 | 42 / 4.7 | 53 / 4.5 | 54 / 4.2 | 17 / 2.4 | 22 / 7.1 | 52 / 5.0 | 60 / 4.1 | 20 / 3.1 | 9 / 1.7 | 34 / 3.3 | 22 / 3.3 | 19 / 3.6 | 36 / 4.9 | 39 / 7.2 | 14 / 3.0 |
| NO ANSWER | 58 / 1.4 | 11 / 1.2 | 18 / 1.5 | 18 / 1.4 | 8 / 1.1 | 5 / 1.6 | 19 / 1.8 | 19 / 1.3 | 7 / 1.1 | 3 / .6 | 11 / 1.1 | 11 / 1.7 | 5 / 1.0 | 10 / 1.4 | 11 / 2.0 | 2 / .4 |
| SIGMA | 4096 / 100.8 | 898 / 100.9 | 1185 / 100.5 | 1279 / 100.5 | 703 / 100.7 | 316 / 101.6 | 1046 / 100.6 | 1481 / 100.7 | 647 / 100.6 | 535 / 100.3 | 1036 / 100.8 | 662 / 100.6 | 526 / 100.6 | 734 / 100.6 | 550 / 101.1 | 472 / 100.1 |

Q. 15 WHAT SORT OF THOUGHTS DO YOU HAVE DURING INTERCOURSE OR MASTURBATION?

TABLE 15

| | TOTAL | MARITAL STATUS | | | | AGE | | | | RACE | | |
|---|---|---|---|---|---|---|---|---|---|---|---|---|
| | | MARR'D LIVING WITH WIFE | NEVER MARR'D LIVING W/O PARTNR | MARR'D LIVING WITH PARTNR UN-MARR'D | DIVRCE OR WIDOWD LIVING ALONE | 18-29 | 30-39 | 40-54 | 55-65 | WHITE | BLACK | OTHER |
| TOTAL RESPONDENTS | 4066 100.0 | 2639 100.0 | 763 100.0 | 280 100.0 | 383 100.0 | 1547 100.0 | 927 100.0 | 1143 100.0 | 432 100.0 | 3559 100.0 | 240 100.0 | 138 100.0 |
| ABOUT PARTNER YOU'RE CURRENTLY INVOLVED WITH | 2603 64.0 | 1684 63.8 | 503 65.9 | 175 62.5 | 241 62.9 | 1004 64.9 | 586 63.2 | 739 64.7 | 261 60.4 | 2328 65.4 | 131 54.6 | 67 48.6 |
| ABOUT A PERSON OTHER THAN CURRENT PARTNER | 448 11.0 | 320 12.1 | 64 8.4 | 27 9.6 | 37 9.7 | 178 11.5 | 114 12.3 | 129 11.3 | 27 6.3 | 397 11.2 | 25 10.4 | 14 10.1 |
| RECALLING A PAST SEXUAL EXPERIENCE | 449 11.0 | 278 10.5 | 90 11.8 | 33 11.8 | 48 12.5 | 175 11.3 | 106 11.4 | 123 10.8 | 45 10.4 | 394 11.1 | 23 9.6 | 20 14.5 |
| SADISTIC OR MASOCHISTIC IDEAS | 88 2.2 | 52 2.0 | 15 2.0 | 10 3.6 | 11 2.9 | 34 2.2 | 15 1.6 | 25 2.2 | 14 3.2 | 65 1.8 | 10 4.2 | 9 6.5 |
| ABOUT GROUP SEX OR OTHER UNUSUAL SEXUAL EXPERIENCES | 181 4.5 | 108 4.1 | 35 4.6 | 15 5.4 | 22 5.7 | 73 4.7 | 52 5.6 | 39 3.4 | 16 3.7 | 148 4.2 | 17 7.1 | 10 7.2 |
| NO THOUGHTS | 368 9.1 | 257 9.7 | 56 7.3 | 17 6.1 | 38 9.9 | 111 7.2 | 79 8.5 | 106 9.3 | 72 16.7 | 302 8.5 | 32 13.3 | 19 13.8 |
| NO ANSWER | 57 1.4 | 31 1.2 | 15 2.0 | 6 2.1 | 5 1.3 | 20 1.3 | 11 1.2 | 14 1.2 | 8 1.9 | 43 1.2 | 5 2.1 | 2 1.4 |
| SIGMA | 4194 103.2 | 2730 103.4 | 778 102.0 | 283 101.1 | 402 104.9 | 1595 103.1 | 963 103.8 | 1175 102.9 | 443 102.6 | 3677 103.4 | 243 101.3 | 141 102.1 |

Q. 15 WHAT SORT OF THOUGHTS DO YOU HAVE DURING INTERCOURSE OR MASTURBATION?

TABLE 15

| | TOTAL | INCOME | | | | EDUCATION | | | | | OCCUPATION | | | | | |
| --- | --- | --- | --- | --- | --- | --- | --- | --- | --- | --- | --- | --- | --- | --- | --- | --- |
| | | UNDER $10000 | $10-14999 | $15-24999 | $25000 & OVER | LESS THAN H.S. GRAD | HIGH SCHL GRAD. | SOME COL-LEGE | COL-LEGE GRAD | SOME/ COMPL POST GRAD. | PRO-FES-SION. | MANA-GER-IAL | OTHER WHITE COLLR | BLUE COLLR | RET'D, UNEMP, OTHER | STU-DENT |
| TOTAL RESPONDENTS | 4066 100.0 | 889 100.0 | 1178 100.0 | 1271 100.0 | 698 100.0 | 311 100.0 | 1038 100.0 | 1472 100.0 | 643 100.0 | 533 100.0 | 1028 100.0 | 658 100.0 | 523 100.0 | 729 100.0 | 544 100.0 | 472 100.0 |
| ABOUT PARTNER YOU'RE CURRENTLY INVOLVED WITH | 2603 64.0 | 565 63.6 | 740 62.8 | 825 64.9 | 457 65.5 | 181 58.2 | 645 62.1 | 983 66.8 | 409 63.6 | 338 63.4 | 689 67.0 | 412 62.6 | 338 64.6 | 452 62.0 | 325 59.7 | 309 65.5 |
| ABOUT A PERSON OTHER THAN CURRENT PARTNER | 448 11.0 | 98 11.0 | 126 10.7 | 145 11.4 | 77 11.0 | 33 10.6 | 87 8.4 | 165 11.2 | 85 13.2 | 72 13.5 | 131 12.7 | 80 12.2 | 49 9.4 | 78 10.7 | 46 8.5 | 55 11.7 |
| RECALLING A PAST SEXUAL EXPERIENCE | 449 11.0 | 109 12.3 | 135 11.5 | 130 10.2 | 72 10.3 | 39 12.5 | 109 10.5 | 153 10.4 | 75 11.7 | 69 12.9 | 105 10.2 | 82 12.5 | 57 10.9 | 83 11.4 | 54 9.9 | 57 12.1 |
| SADISTIC OR MASOCHISTIC IDEAS | 88 2.2 | 14 1.6 | 39 3.3 | 20 1.6 | 14 2.0 | 6 1.9 | 31 3.0 | 29 2.0 | 7 1.1 | 14 2.6 | 20 1.9 | 11 1.7 | 18 3.4 | 16 2.2 | 15 2.8 | 5 1.1 |
| ABOUT GROUP SEX OR OTHER UNUSUAL SEXUAL EXPERIENCES | 181 4.5 | 39 4.4 | 55 4.7 | 45 3.5 | 39 5.6 | 14 4.5 | 47 4.5 | 72 4.9 | 23 3.6 | 23 4.3 | 47 4.6 | 19 2.9 | 28 5.4 | 34 4.7 | 29 5.3 | 20 4.2 |
| NO THOUGHTS | 368 9.1 | 80 9.0 | 107 9.1 | 123 9.7 | 55 7.9 | 38 12.2 | 124 11.9 | 109 7.4 | 44 6.8 | 47 8.8 | 64 6.2 | 66 10.0 | 43 8.2 | 70 9.6 | 79 14.5 | 34 7.2 |
| NO ANSWER | 57 1.4 | 8 .9 | 17 1.4 | 17 1.3 | 10 1.4 | 5 1.6 | 8 .8 | 22 1.5 | 13 2.0 | 2 .4 | 15 1.5 | 7 1.1 | 3 .6 | 11 1.5 | 11 2.0 | 4 .8 |
| SIGMA | 4194 103.2 | 913 102.8 | 1219 103.5 | 1305 102.6 | 724 103.7 | 316 101.5 | 1051 101.2 | 1533 104.2 | 656 102.0 | 565 105.9 | 1071 104.1 | 677 103.0 | 536 102.5 | 744 102.1 | 559 102.7 | 484 102.6 |

Q. 16 DO YOU TELL THE WOMAN YOU HAVE SEX WITH WHAT YOU'D LIKE HER TO DO?

TABLE 16

| | TOTAL | MARITAL STATUS | | | | | AGE | | | | RACE | | |
|---|---|---|---|---|---|---|---|---|---|---|---|---|---|
| | | MARR'D LIVING WITH WIFE | NEVER MARR'D LIVING W/O_ PARTNR | MARR'D WITH UN- MARR'D PARTNR | LIVING WITH PARTNR | DIVRCE OR WIDOWD LIVING ALONE | 18-29 | 30-39 | 40-54 | 55-65 | WHITE | BLACK | OTHER |
| TOTAL RESPONDENTS | 4066 100.0 | 2639 100.0 | 763 100.0 | 280 100.0 | | 383 100.0 | 1547 100.0 | 927 100.0 | 1143 100.0 | 432 100.0 | 3559 100.0 | 240 100.0 | 138 100.0 |
| NO, I JUST DO WHAT I ENJOY | 796 19.6 | 555 21.0 | 132 17.3 | 43 15.4 | | 66 17.2 | 265 17.1 | 171 18.4 | 236 20.6 | 121 28.0 | 666 18.7 | 67 27.9 | 31 22.5 |
| NO, I'D BE TOO INHIBITED OR EMBARRASSED | 124 3.0 | 77 2.9 | 29 3.8 | 3 1.1 | | 15 3.9 | 49 3.2 | 16 1.7 | 39 3.4 | 20 4.6 | 111 3.1 | 4 1.7 | 2 1.4 |
| NO, I DO WHAT SHE SEEMS TO ENJOY | 1027 25.3 | 727 27.5 | 182 23.9 | 48 17.1 | | 70 18.3 | 315 20.4 | 241 26.0 | 331 29.0 | 137 31.7 | 903 25.4 | 58 24.2 | 30 21.7 |
| ONLY AFTER CONSIDER- ABLE EXPERIENCE TOGETHER | 644 15.8 | 347 13.1 | 154 20.2 | 57 20.4 | | 86 22.5 | 285 18.4 | 140 15.1 | 166 14.5 | 48 11.1 | 573 16.1 | 30 12.5 | 23 16.7 |
| YES, DISCUSS IT AS WE HAVE SEX | 1137 28.0 | 740 28.0 | 189 24.8 | 91 32.5 | | 116 30.3 | 464 30.0 | 281 30.3 | 305 26.7 | 84 19.4 | 1024 28.8 | 50 20.8 | 36 26.1 |
| YES, TALK ABOUT IT BEFORE WE START OR AFTER WE FINISH | 370 9.1 | 217 8.2 | 76 10.0 | 35 12.5 | | 42 11.0 | 177 11.4 | 84 9.1 | 89 7.8 | 20 4.6 | 315 8.9 | 33 13.8 | 15 10.9 |
| NO ANSWER | 43 1.1 | 20 .8 | 14 1.8 | 6 2.1 | | 3 .8 | 14 .9 | 11 1.2 | 7 .6 | 7 1.6 | 35 1.0 | 2 .8 | 1 .7 |
| SIGMA | 4141 101.9 | 2683 101.5 | 776 101.8 | 283 101.1 | | 398 104.0 | 1569 101.4 | 944 101.8 | 1173 102.6 | 437 101.0 | 3627 102.0 | 244 101.7 | 138 100.0 |

TABLE 16

**Q. 16 DO YOU TELL THE WOMAN YOU HAVE SEX WITH WHAT YOU'D LIKE HER TO DO?**

Values shown as count (top) and percent (bottom).

| | TOTAL | INCOME: UNDER $10000 | $10-14999 | $15-24999 | $25000 & OVER | EDUCATION: LESS THAN H.S. GRAD | HIGH SCHL GRAD | SOME COLLEGE | COLLEGE GRAD | SOME/COMPL POST GRAD | OCCUPATION: PROFESSION. | MANAGERIAL | OTHER WHITE COLLR | BLUE COLLR | RET'D/UNEMP/OTHER | STUDENT |
|---|---|---|---|---|---|---|---|---|---|---|---|---|---|---|---|---|
| TOTAL RESPONDENTS | 4066 / 100.0 | 889 / 100.0 | 1178 / 100.0 | 1271 / 100.0 | 698 / 100.0 | 311 / 100.0 | 1038 / 100.0 | 1472 / 100.0 | 643 / 100.0 | 533 / 100.0 | 1028 / 100.0 | 658 / 100.0 | 523 / 100.0 | 729 / 100.0 | 544 / 100.0 | 472 / 100.0 |
| NO, I JUST DO WHAT I ENJOY | 796 / 19.6 | 181 / 20.4 | 250 / 21.2 | 239 / 18.8 | 121 / 17.3 | 100 / 32.2 | 250 / 24.1 | 246 / 16.7 | 105 / 16.3 | 80 / 15.0 | 182 / 17.7 | 125 / 19.0 | 101 / 19.3 | 162 / 22.2 | 136 / 25.0 | 70 / 14.8 |
| NO, I'D BE TOO INHIBITED OR EMBARRASSED | 124 / 3.0 | 23 / 2.6 | 52 / 4.4 | 34 / 2.7 | 15 / 2.1 | 12 / 3.9 | 35 / 3.4 | 47 / 3.2 | 19 / 3.0 | 11 / 2.1 | 26 / 2.5 | 13 / 2.0 | 17 / 3.3 | 27 / 3.7 | 24 / 4.4 | 17 / 3.6 |
| NO, I DO WHAT SHE SEEMS TO ENJOY | 1027 / 25.3 | 188 / 21.1 | 281 / 23.9 | 366 / 28.8 | 185 / 26.5 | 82 / 26.4 | 294 / 28.3 | 365 / 24.8 | 151 / 23.5 | 119 / 22.3 | 250 / 24.3 | 195 / 29.6 | 150 / 28.7 | 182 / 25.0 | 130 / 23.9 | 98 / 20.8 |
| ONLY AFTER CONSIDERABLE EXPERIENCE TOGETHER | 644 / 15.8 | 156 / 17.5 | 179 / 15.2 | 188 / 14.8 | 113 / 16.2 | 35 / 11.3 | 129 / 12.4 | 250 / 17.0 | 115 / 17.9 | 104 / 19.5 | 161 / 15.7 | 114 / 17.3 | 80 / 15.3 | 98 / 13.4 | 68 / 12.5 | 101 / 21.4 |
| YES, DISCUSS IT AS WE HAVE SEX | 1137 / 28.0 | 250 / 28.1 | 324 / 27.5 | 342 / 26.9 | 214 / 30.7 | 59 / 19.0 | 243 / 23.4 | 434 / 29.5 | 200 / 31.1 | 182 / 34.1 | 335 / 32.6 | 163 / 24.8 | 140 / 26.8 | 185 / 25.4 | 139 / 25.6 | 137 / 29.0 |
| YES, TALK ABOUT IT BEFORE WE START OR AFTER WE FINISH | 370 / 9.1 | 97 / 10.9 | 103 / 8.7 | 113 / 8.9 | 56 / 8.0 | 26 / 8.4 | 93 / 9.0 | 145 / 9.9 | 58 / 9.0 | 39 / 7.3 | 83 / 8.1 | 54 / 8.2 | 45 / 8.6 | 75 / 10.3 | 52 / 9.6 | 50 / 10.6 |
| NO ANSWER | 43 / 1.1 | 6 / .7 | 13 / 1.1 | 13 / 1.0 | 8 / 1.1 | 4 / 1.3 | 8 / .8 | 17 / 1.2 | 6 / .9 | 4 / .8 | 8 / .8 | 8 / 1.2 | 3 / .6 | 7 / 1.0 | 5 / .9 | 6 / 1.3 |
| SIGMA | 4141 / 101.9 | 901 / 101.3 | 1202 / 102.0 | 1295 / 101.9 | 712 / 101.9 | 318 / 102.5 | 1052 / 101.4 | 1504 / 102.3 | 654 / 101.7 | 539 / 101.1 | 1045 / 101.7 | 672 / 102.1 | 536 / 102.6 | 736 / 101.0 | 554 / 101.9 | 479 / 101.5 |

TABLE 17

**Q. 17 HOW DO YOU FEEL ABOUT STIMULATING A WOMAN'S SEXUAL ORGANS WITH YOUR MOUTH?**

| | TOTAL | MARITAL STATUS | | | | AGE | | | | RACE | | |
| --- | --- | --- | --- | --- | --- | --- | --- | --- | --- | --- | --- | --- |
| | | MARR'D LIVING WITH WIFE | NEVER MARR'D LIVING W/O PARTNR | MARR'D LIVING WITH UN-MARR'D PARTNR | DIVRCE WIDOWD OR LIVING ALONE | 18-29 | 30-39 | 40-54 | 55-65 | WHITE | BLACK | OTHER |
| TOTAL RESPONDENTS | 4066 100.0 | 2639 100.0 | 763 100.0 | 280 100.0 | 383 100.0 | 1547 100.0 | 927 100.0 | 1143 100.0 | 432 100.0 | 3559 100.0 | 240 100.0 | 138 100.0 |
| ENJOY IT | 2216 54.5 | 1397 52.9 | 405 53.1 | 185 66.1 | 228 59.5 | 961 62.1 | 579 62.5 | 525 45.9 | 141 32.6 | 2020 56.8 | 72 30.0 | 66 47.8 |
| DON'T MIND IT, BUT DO IT MOSTLY TO PLEASE THE WOMAN | 916 22.5 | 549 20.8 | 212 27.8 | 66 23.6 | 89 23.2 | 367 23.7 | 202 21.8 | 280 24.5 | 65 15.0 | 795 22.3 | 54 22.5 | 35 25.4 |
| FIND IT BORING OR UNPLEASANT | 116 2.9 | 78 3.0 | 23 3.0 | 2 .7 | 13 3.4 | 42 2.7 | 21 2.3 | 37 3.2 | 15 3.5 | 94 2.6 | 11 4.6 | 5 3.6 |
| DON'T DO IT | 612 15.1 | 460 17.4 | 94 12.3 | 19 6.8 | 39 10.2 | 140 9.0 | 96 10.4 | 230 20.1 | 145 33.6 | 490 13.8 | 78 32.5 | 25 18.1 |
| THINK IT'S UNNATURAL | 197 4.8 | 150 5.7 | 24 3.1 | 4 1.4 | 19 5.0 | 33 2.1 | 27 2.9 | 71 6.2 | 65 15.0 | 153 4.3 | 26 10.8 | 7 5.1 |
| NO ANSWER | 38 .9 | 23 .9 | 11 1.4 | 4 1.4 | | 10 .6 | 7 .8 | 11 1.0 | 7 1.6 | 31 .9 | 2 .8 | 1 .7 |
| SIGMA | 4095 100.7 | 2657 100.7 | 769 100.7 | 280 100.0 | 388 101.3 | 1553 100.2 | 932 100.7 | 1154 100.9 | 438 101.3 | 3583 100.7 | 243 101.2 | 139 100.7 |

Q. 17 HOW DO YOU FEEL ABOUT STIMULATING A WOMAN'S SEXUAL ORGANS WITH YOUR MOUTH?

TABLE 17

| | TOTAL | INCOME | | | | EDUCATION | | | | | OCCUPATION | | | | | |
| --- | --- | --- | --- | --- | --- | --- | --- | --- | --- | --- | --- | --- | --- | --- | --- | --- |
| | | UNDER $10000 | $10-14999 | $15-24999 | $25000 & OVER | LESS THAN H.S. GRAD | HIGH SCHL GRAD | SOME COLLEGE | COL-LEGE GRAD | SOME/COMPL POST GRAD | PRO-FESSION | MANA-GER-IAL | OTHER WHITE COLLR | BLUE COLLR | RET'D, UNEMP, OTHER | STU-DENT |
| TOTAL RESPONDENTS | 4066 100.0 | 889 100.0 | 1178 100.0 | 1271 100.0 | 698 100.0 | 311 100.0 | 1038 100.0 | 1472 100.0 | 643 100.0 | 533 100.0 | 1028 100.0 | 658 100.0 | 523 100.0 | 729 100.0 | 544 100.0 | 472 100.0 |
| ENJOY IT | 2216 54.5 | 479 53.9 | 645 54.8 | 682 53.7 | 392 56.2 | 145 46.6 | 499 48.1 | 852 57.9 | 380 59.1 | 305 57.2 | 613 59.6 | 360 54.7 | 262 50.1 | 396 54.3 | 259 47.6 | 257 54.4 |
| DON'T MIND IT, BUT DO IT MOSTLY TO PLEASE THE WOMAN | 916 22.5 | 214 24.1 | 239 20.3 | 300 23.6 | 158 22.6 | 59 19.0 | 242 23.3 | 334 22.7 | 146 22.7 | 123 23.1 | 212 20.6 | 159 24.2 | 122 23.3 | 165 22.6 | 114 21.0 | 121 25.6 |
| FIND IT BORING OR UNPLEASANT | 116 2.9 | 19 2.1 | 36 3.1 | 40 3.1 | 21 3.0 | 11 3.5 | 25 2.4 | 39 2.6 | 16 2.5 | 22 4.1 | 32 3.1 | 23 3.5 | 20 3.8 | 20 2.7 | 9 1.7 | 9 1.9 |
| DON'T DO IT | 612 15.1 | 137 15.4 | 194 16.5 | 179 14.1 | 98 14.0 | 69 22.2 | 196 18.9 | 194 13.2 | 79 12.3 | 63 11.8 | 128 12.5 | 85 12.9 | 82 15.7 | 116 15.9 | 119 21.9 | 69 14.6 |
| THINK IT'S UNNATURAL | 197 4.8 | 40 4.5 | 58 4.9 | 68 5.4 | 30 4.3 | 27 8.7 | 73 7.0 | 49 3.3 | 21 3.3 | 19 3.6 | 44 4.3 | 25 3.8 | 35 6.7 | 30 4.1 | 46 8.5 | 12 2.5 |
| NO ANSWER | 38 .9 | 6 .7 | 11 .9 | 10 .8 | 7 1.0 | 4 1.3 | 7 .7 | 13 .9 | 6 .9 | 2 .4 | 8 .8 | 7 1.1 | 4 .8 | 6 .8 | 3 .6 | 5 1.1 |
| SIGMA | 4095 100.7 | 895 100.7 | 1183 100.5 | 1279 100.7 | 706 101.1 | 315 101.3 | 1042 100.4 | 1481 100.6 | 648 100.8 | 534 100.2 | 1037 100.9 | 659 100.2 | 525 100.4 | 733 100.4 | 550 101.3 | 473 100.1 |

TABLE 18

Q. 18 WHAT WOULD YOU MOST LIKE TO DO MORE OFTEN?

| | TOTAL | MARITAL STATUS | | | | AGE | | | | RACE | | |
|---|---|---|---|---|---|---|---|---|---|---|---|---|
| | | MARR'D LIVING WITH WIFE | NEVER MARR'D LIVING W/O PARTNR | MARR'D LIVING WITH PARTNR UN-MARR'D | DIVRCE OR WIDOWD LIVING ALONE | 18-29 | 30-39 | 40-54 | 55-65 | WHITE | BLACK | OTHER |
| TOTAL RESPONDENTS | 4066 100.0 | 2639 100.0 | 763 100.0 | 280 100.0 | 383 100.0 | 1547 100.0 | 927 100.0 | 1143 100.0 | 432 100.0 | 3559 100.0 | 240 100.0 | 138 100.0 |
| ORAL SEX | 877 21.6 | 581 22.0 | 158 20.7 | 59 21.1 | 79 20.6 | 346 22.4 | 205 22.1 | 247 21.6 | 75 17.4 | 783 22.0 | 41 17.1 | 26 18.8 |
| DIFFERENT SEXUAL POSITIONS | 2216 54.5 | 1448 54.9 | 415 54.4 | 140 50.0 | 213 55.6 | 860 55.6 | 528 57.0 | 610 53.4 | 211 48.8 | 1943 54.6 | 125 52.1 | 83 60.1 |
| ANAL SEX | 169 4.2 | 110 4.2 | 23 3.0 | 14 5.0 | 22 5.7 | 58 3.7 | 41 4.4 | 48 4.2 | 20 4.6 | 140 3.9 | 18 7.5 | 3 2.2 |
| SADO-MASOCHISTIC ACTIVITY | 47 1.2 | 29 1.1 | 5 .7 | 5 1.8 | 8 2.1 | 21 1.4 | 10 1.1 | 12 1.0 | 4 .9 | 32 .9 | 9 3.8 | 5 3.6 |
| SEX WITH MORE THAN ONE WOMAN AT A TIME | 430 10.6 | 245 9.3 | 104 13.6 | 35 12.5 | 45 11.7 | 209 13.5 | 97 10.5 | 103 9.0 | 19 4.4 | 373 10.5 | 27 11.3 | 16 11.6 |
| HOMOSEXUAL ACTIVITY | 67 1.6 | 22 .8 | 23 3.0 | 16 5.7 | 6 1.6 | 37 2.4 | 13 1.4 | 16 1.4 | 1 .2 | 57 1.6 | 5 2.1 | 4 2.9 |
| NONE | 443 10.9 | 311 11.8 | 73 9.6 | 21 7.5 | 38 9.9 | 110 7.1 | 88 9.5 | 145 12.7 | 98 22.7 | 388 10.9 | 29 12.1 | 9 6.5 |
| NO ANSWER | 61 1.5 | 46 1.7 | 8 1.0 | 5 1.8 | 2 .5 | 12 .8 | 13 1.4 | 17 1.5 | 16 3.7 | 47 1.3 | 6 2.5 | 3 2.2 |
| SIGMA | 4310 106.1 | 2792 105.8 | 809 106.0 | 295 105.4 | 413 107.7 | 1653 106.9 | 995 107.4 | 1198 104.8 | 444 102.7 | 3763 105.7 | 260 108.5 | 149 107.9 |

TABLE 18

**Q. 18 WHAT WOULD YOU MOST LIKE TO DO MORE OFTEN?**

| | TOTAL | INCOME | | | | EDUCATION | | | | | OCCUPATION | | | | | |
| --- | --- | --- | --- | --- | --- | --- | --- | --- | --- | --- | --- | --- | --- | --- | --- | --- |
| | | UNDER $10000 | $10-14999 | $15-24999 | $25000 & OVER | LESS THAN H.S. GRAD | HIGH SCHL GRAD. | SOME COL-LEGE | COL-LEGE GRAD | SOME/COMPL POST GRAD. | PRO-FES-SION. | MANA-GER-IAL | OTHER WHITE COLLR | BLUE COLLR | RET'D/UNEMP/OTHER | STU-DENT |
| TOTAL RESPONDENTS | 4066 / 100.0 | 889 / 100.0 | 1178 / 100.0 | 1271 / 100.0 | 698 / 100.0 | 311 / 100.0 | 1038 / 100.0 | 1472 / 100.0 | 643 / 100.0 | 533 / 100.0 | 1028 / 100.0 | 658 / 100.0 | 523 / 100.0 | 729 / 100.0 | 544 / 100.0 | 472 / 100.0 |
| ORAL SEX | 877 / 21.6 | 177 / 19.9 | 243 / 20.6 | 288 / 22.7 | 161 / 23.1 | 72 / 23.2 | 218 / 21.0 | 320 / 21.7 | 146 / 22.7 | 106 / 19.9 | 241 / 23.4 | 152 / 23.1 | 107 / 20.5 | 178 / 24.4 | 91 / 16.7 | 73 / 15.5 |
| DIFFERENT SEXUAL POSITIONS | 2216 / 54.5 | 485 / 54.6 | 638 / 54.2 | 704 / 55.4 | 374 / 53.6 | 168 / 54.0 | 587 / 56.6 | 798 / 54.2 | 350 / 54.4 | 280 / 52.5 | 559 / 54.4 | 353 / 53.6 | 306 / 58.5 | 379 / 52.0 | 289 / 53.1 | 274 / 58.1 |
| ANAL SEX | 169 / 4.2 | 34 / 3.8 | 58 / 4.9 | 51 / 4.0 | 26 / 3.7 | 15 / 4.8 | 35 / 3.4 | 60 / 4.1 | 32 / 5.0 | 21 / 3.9 | 42 / 4.1 | 25 / 3.8 | 22 / 4.2 | 28 / 3.8 | 25 / 4.6 | 19 / 4.0 |
| SADO-MASOCHISTIC ACTIVITY | 47 / 1.2 | 12 / 1.3 | 20 / 1.7 | 12 / .9 | 3 / .4 | 7 / 2.3 | 14 / 1.3 | 18 / 1.2 | 3 / .5 | 5 / .9 | 8 / .8 | 6 / .9 | 11 / 2.1 | 10 / 1.4 | 4 / .7 | 6 / 1.3 |
| SEX WITH MORE THAN ONE WOMAN AT A TIME | 430 / 10.6 | 101 / 11.4 | 122 / 10.4 | 122 / 9.6 | 79 / 11.3 | 27 / 8.7 | 94 / 9.1 | 184 / 12.5 | 65 / 10.1 | 53 / 9.9 | 115 / 11.2 | 63 / 9.6 | 44 / 8.4 | 72 / 9.9 | 55 / 10.1 | 64 / 13.6 |
| HOMOSEXUAL ACTIVITY | 67 / 1.6 | 17 / 1.9 | 22 / 1.9 | 19 / 1.5 | 9 / 1.3 | 6 / 1.9 | 12 / 1.2 | 27 / 1.8 | 7 / 1.1 | 14 / 2.6 | 17 / 1.7 | 8 / 1.2 | 8 / 1.5 | 6 / .8 | 9 / 1.7 | 14 / 3.0 |
| NONE | 443 / 10.9 | 103 / 11.6 | 123 / 10.4 | 128 / 10.1 | 86 / 12.3 | 32 / 10.3 | 111 / 10.7 | 154 / 10.5 | 64 / 10.0 | 72 / 13.5 | 102 / 9.9 | 68 / 10.3 | 52 / 9.9 | 72 / 9.9 | 90 / 16.5 | 46 / 9.7 |
| NO ANSWER | 61 / 1.5 | 12 / 1.3 | 11 / .9 | 22 / 1.7 | 12 / 1.7 | 6 / 1.9 | 12 / 1.2 | 22 / 1.5 | 6 / .9 | 7 / 1.3 | 18 / 1.8 | 10 / 1.5 | 5 / 1.0 | 10 / 1.4 | 9 / 1.7 | 3 / .6 |
| SIGMA | 4310 / 106.1 | 941 / 105.8 | 1237 / 105.0 | 1346 / 105.9 | 750 / 107.4 | 333 / 107.1 | 1083 / 104.5 | 1583 / 107.5 | 673 / 104.7 | 558 / 104.5 | 1102 / 107.3 | 685 / 104.0 | 555 / 106.1 | 755 / 103.6 | 572 / 105.1 | 499 / 105.8 |

Q. 19 WHEN DOES A SEX ACT END?

TABLE 19

| | TOTAL | MARITAL STATUS | | | | AGE | | | | RACE | | |
|---|---|---|---|---|---|---|---|---|---|---|---|---|
| | | MARR'D LIVING WITH WIFE | NEVER MARR'D LIVING W/O PARTNR | MARR'D LIVING WITH UN-PARTNR | LIVING WITH PARTNR MARR'D DIVRCE OR WIDOWD LIVING ALONE | 18-29 | 30-39 | 40-54 | 55-65 | WHITE | BLACK | OTHER |
| TOTAL RESPONDENTS | 4066 100.0 | 2639 100.0 | 763 100.0 | 280 100.0 | 383 100.0 | 1547 100.0 | 927 100.0 | 1143 100.0 | 432 100.0 | 3559 100.0 | 240 100.0 | 138 100.0 |
| WHEN I HAVE ONE ORGASM | 739 18.2 | 591 22.4 | 65 8.5 | 35 12.5 | 48 12.5 | 179 11.6 | 156 16.8 | 273 23.9 | 127 29.4 | 639 18.0 | 50 20.8 | 23 16.7 |
| WHEN I HAVE MORE THAN ONE ORGASM | 209 5.1 | 110 4.2 | 66 8.7 | 13 4.6 | 20 5.2 | 105 6.8 | 43 4.6 | 47 4.1 | 13 3.0 | 170 4.8 | 23 9.6 | 11 8.0 |
| WHEN THE WOMAN HAS AN ORGASM | 211 5.2 | 167 6.3 | 19 2.5 | 5 1.8 | 20 5.2 | 51 3.3 | 42 4.5 | 74 6.5 | 42 9.7 | 183 5.1 | 8 3.3 | 7 5.1 |
| WHEN THE WOMAN HAS MORE THAN ONE ORGASM | 203 5.0 | 123 4.7 | 35 4.6 | 24 8.6 | 20 5.2 | 81 5.2 | 41 4.4 | 56 4.9 | 22 5.1 | 165 4.6 | 20 8.3 | 9 6.5 |
| WHEN WE BOTH HAVE AN ORGASM | 1663 40.9 | 1159 43.9 | 250 32.8 | 109 38.9 | 145 37.9 | 587 37.9 | 428 46.2 | 493 43.1 | 151 35.0 | 1502 42.2 | 72 30.0 | 43 31.2 |
| WHEN THE WOMAN WANTS TO STOP | 718 17.7 | 376 14.2 | 199 26.1 | 60 21.4 | 83 21.7 | 362 23.4 | 160 17.3 | 147 12.9 | 48 11.1 | 633 17.8 | 42 17.5 | 28 20.3 |
| WHEN I WANT TO STOP | 440 10.8 | 193 7.3 | 151 19.8 | 44 15.7 | 52 13.6 | 245 15.8 | 74 8.0 | 82 7.2 | 38 8.8 | 375 10.5 | 30 12.5 | 20 14.5 |
| NO ANSWER | 53 1.3 | 20 .8 | 17 2.2 | 5 1.8 | 11 2.9 | 28 1.8 | 12 1.3 | 8 .7 | 2 .5 | 45 1.3 | 3 1.3 | 1 .7 |
| SIGMA | 4236 104.2 | 2739 103.8 | 802 105.2 | 295 105.3 | 399 104.2 | 1638 105.8 | 956 103.1 | 1180 103.3 | 443 102.6 | 3712 104.3 | 248 103.3 | 142 103.0 |

TABLE 19

# Q. 19 WHEN DOES A SEX ACT END?

| | TOTAL | INCOME | | | | EDUCATION | | | | | OCCUPATION | | | | | |
|---|---|---|---|---|---|---|---|---|---|---|---|---|---|---|---|---|
| | | UNDER $10000 | $10-14999 | $15-24999 | $25000 & OVER | LESS THAN H.S. GRAD | HIGH SCHL GRAD | SOME COL-LEGE | COL-LEGE GRAD | SOME/ COMPL POST GRAD | PRO-FES-SION.IAL | MANA-GER-IAL | OTHER WHITE COLLR | BLUE COLLR | RET'D/ UNEMP/ OTHER | STU-DENT |
| TOTAL RESPONDENTS | 4066 100.0 | 889 100.0 | 1178 100.0 | 1271 100.0 | 698 100.0 | 311 100.0 | 1038 100.0 | 1472 100.0 | 643 100.0 | 533 100.0 | 1028 100.0 | 658 100.0 | 523 100.0 | 729 100.0 | 544 100.0 | 472 100.0 |
| WHEN I HAVE ONE ORGASM | 739 18.2 | 129 14.5 | 237 20.1 | 241 19.0 | 128 18.3 | 82 26.4 | 212 20.4 | 214 14.5 | 111 17.3 | 105 19.7 | 166 16.1 | 134 20.4 | 117 22.4 | 145 19.9 | 108 19.9 | 53 11.2 |
| WHEN I HAVE MORE THAN ONE ORGASM | 209 5.1 | 51 5.7 | 68 5.8 | 50 3.9 | 38 5.4 | 22 7.1 | 50 4.8 | 78 5.3 | 30 4.7 | 25 4.7 | 62 6.0 | 22 3.3 | 25 4.8 | 42 5.8 | 27 5.0 | 26 5.5 |
| WHEN THE WOMAN HAS AN ORGASM | 211 5.2 | 23 2.6 | 79 6.7 | 62 4.9 | 44 6.3 | 16 5.1 | 63 6.1 | 80 5.4 | 22 3.4 | 25 4.7 | 52 5.1 | 40 6.1 | 38 7.3 | 42 5.8 | 21 3.9 | 12 2.5 |
| WHEN THE WOMAN HAS MORE THAN ONE ORGASM | 203 5.0 | 53 6.0 | 51 4.3 | 63 5.0 | 33 4.7 | 18 5.8 | 55 5.3 | 73 5.0 | 22 3.4 | 30 5.6 | 62 6.0 | 26 4.0 | 22 4.2 | 40 5.5 | 23 4.2 | 24 5.1 |
| WHEN WE BOTH HAVE AN ORGASM | 1663 40.9 | 324 36.4 | 444 37.7 | 577 45.4 | 311 44.6 | 105 33.8 | 418 40.3 | 595 40.4 | 298 46.3 | 223 41.8 | 453 44.1 | 280 42.6 | 232 44.4 | 277 38.0 | 223 41.0 | 154 32.6 |
| WHEN THE WOMAN WANTS TO STOP | 718 17.7 | 209 23.5 | 199 16.9 | 199 15.7 | 106 15.2 | 49 15.8 | 149 14.4 | 305 20.7 | 106 16.5 | 99 18.6 | 163 15.9 | 114 17.3 | 61 11.7 | 121 16.6 | 98 18.0 | 128 27.1 |
| WHEN I WANT TO STOP | 440 10.8 | 139 15.6 | 125 10.6 | 114 9.0 | 56 8.0 | 30 9.6 | 109 10.5 | 184 12.5 | 67 10.4 | 39 7.3 | 89 8.7 | 47 7.1 | 46 8.8 | 87 11.9 | 68 12.5 | 86 18.2 |
| NO ANSWER | 53 1.3 | 14 1.6 | 12 1.0 | 16 1.3 | 6 .9 | 3 1.0 | 7 .7 | 23 1.6 | 8 1.2 | 6 1.1 | 14 1.4 | 8 1.2 | 4 .8 | 4 .5 | 5 .9 | 10 2.1 |
| SIGMA | 4236 104.2 | 942 105.9 | 1215 103.1 | 1322 104.2 | 722 103.4 | 325 104.6 | 1063 102.5 | 1552 105.4 | 664 103.2 | 552 103.5 | 1061 103.3 | 671 102.0 | 545 104.4 | 758 104.0 | 573 105.4 | 493 104.3 |

Q. 20 WHAT PERCENT OF THE TIME DOES YOUR PARTNER HAVE AN ORGASM DURING INTERCOURSE?

TABLE 20

| | TOTAL | MARITAL STATUS | | | | AGE | | | | RACE | | |
|---|---|---|---|---|---|---|---|---|---|---|---|---|
| | | MARR'D LIVING WITH WIFE | NEVER MARR'D LIVING W/O PARTNR | LIVING WITH PARTNR UN-MARR'D | DIVRCE WIDOWD OR LIVING ALONE | 18-29 | 30-39 | 40-54 | 55-65 | WHITE | BLACK | OTHER |
| TOTAL RESPONDENTS | 4066 100.0 | 2639 100.0 | 763 100.0 | 280 100.0 | 383 100.0 | 1547 100.0 | 927 100.0 | 1143 100.0 | 432 100.0 | 3559 100.0 | 240 100.0 | 138 100.0 |
| 0 TO 9% | 183 4.5 | 127 4.8 | 33 4.3 | 8 2.9 | 15 3.9 | 60 3.9 | 40 4.3 | 56 4.9 | 27 6.3 | 158 4.4 | 9 3.8 | 9 6.5 |
| 10 TO 19% | 132 3.2 | 94 3.6 | 22 2.9 | 6 2.1 | 10 2.6 | 41 2.7 | 26 2.8 | 46 4.0 | 18 4.2 | 112 3.1 | 9 3.8 | 5 3.6 |
| 20 TO 29% | 133 3.3 | 85 3.2 | 31 4.1 | 11 3.9 | 6 1.6 | 52 3.4 | 34 3.7 | 34 3.0 | 13 3.0 | 109 3.1 | 13 5.4 | 7 5.1 |
| 30 TO 39% | 174 4.3 | 122 4.6 | 27 3.5 | 9 3.2 | 16 4.2 | 63 4.1 | 33 3.6 | 50 4.4 | 28 6.5 | 147 4.1 | 17 7.1 | 5 3.6 |
| 40 TO 49% | 206 5.1 | 151 5.7 | 31 4.1 | 11 3.9 | 13 3.4 | 65 4.2 | 44 4.7 | 73 6.4 | 23 5.3 | 176 4.9 | 14 5.8 | 6 4.3 |
| 50 TO 59% | 397 9.8 | 259 9.8 | 72 9.4 | 27 9.6 | 39 10.2 | 145 9.4 | 81 8.7 | 121 10.6 | 49 11.3 | 345 9.7 | 30 12.5 | 9 6.5 |
| 60 TO 69% | 225 5.5 | 135 5.1 | 62 8.1 | 15 5.4 | 13 3.4 | 98 6.3 | 50 5.4 | 60 5.2 | 17 3.9 | 203 5.7 | 9 3.8 | 7 5.1 |
| 70 TO 79% | 405 10.0 | 242 9.2 | 82 10.7 | 37 13.2 | 44 11.5 | 167 10.8 | 99 10.7 | 102 8.9 | 36 8.3 | 366 10.3 | 13 5.4 | 11 8.0 |
| 80 TO 89% | 425 10.5 | 289 11.0 | 64 8.4 | 34 12.1 | 38 9.9 | 162 10.5 | 118 12.7 | 112 9.8 | 32 7.4 | 376 10.6 | 21 8.8 | 15 10.9 |
| 90% OR MORE | 1212 29.8 | 823 31.2 | 172 22.5 | 86 30.7 | 130 33.9 | 447 28.9 | 289 31.2 | 359 31.4 | 111 25.7 | 1084 30.5 | 58 24.2 | 39 28.3 |
| I'M NOT SURE WHEN SHE HAS AN ORGASM | 529 13.0 | 291 11.0 | 150 19.7 | 34 12.1 | 54 14.1 | 229 14.8 | 106 11.4 | 119 10.4 | 72 16.7 | 444 12.5 | 46 19.2 | 24 17.4 |
| NO ANSWER | 45 1.1 | 21 .8 | 17 2.2 | 2 .7 | 5 1.3 | 18 1.2 | 7 .8 | 11 1.0 | 6 1.4 | 39 1.1 | 1 .4 | 1 .7 |
| SIGMA | 4066 100.1 | 2639 100.0 | 763 99.9 | 280 99.8 | 383 100.0 | 1547 100.2 | 927 100.2 | 1143 100.0 | 432 100.0 | 3559 100.0 | 240 100.2 | 138 100.0 |

Q. 20 WHAT PERCENT OF THE TIME DOES YOUR PARTNER HAVE AN ORGASM DURING INTERCOURSE?

TABLE 20

| | TOTAL | INCOME | | | | EDUCATION | | | | | OCCUPATION | | | | | |
|---|---|---|---|---|---|---|---|---|---|---|---|---|---|---|---|---|
| | | UNDER $10000 | $10-14999 | $15-24999 | $25000 & OVER | LESS THAN H.S. GRAD | HIGH SCHL GRAD | SOME COL-LEGE | COL-LEGE GRAD | SOME/ COMPL POST GRAD. | PRO-FES-SION. | MANA-GER-IAL | OTHER WHITE COLLR | BLUE COLLR | RET'D, UNEMP, OTHER | STU-DENT |
| TOTAL RESPONDENTS | 4066 / 100.0 | 889 / 100.0 | 1178 / 100.0 | 1271 / 100.0 | 698 / 100.0 | 311 / 100.0 | 1038 / 100.0 | 1472 / 100.0 | 643 / 100.0 | 533 / 100.0 | 1028 / 100.0 | 658 / 100.0 | 523 / 100.0 | 729 / 100.0 | 544 / 100.0 | 472 / 100.0 |
| 0 TO 9% | 183 / 4.5 | 44 / 4.9 | 54 / 4.6 | 53 / 4.2 | 29 / 4.2 | 27 / 8.7 | 54 / 5.2 | 50 / 3.4 | 23 / 3.6 | 28 / 5.3 | 44 / 4.3 | 27 / 4.1 | 24 / 4.6 | 39 / 5.3 | 25 / 4.6 | 17 / 3.6 |
| 10 TO 19% | 132 / 3.2 | 34 / 3.8 | 39 / 3.3 | 32 / 2.5 | 27 / 3.9 | 19 / 6.1 | 31 / 3.0 | 44 / 3.0 | 18 / 2.8 | 20 / 3.8 | 31 / 3.0 | 26 / 4.0 | 23 / 4.4 | 11 / 1.5 | 22 / 4.0 | 16 / 3.4 |
| 20 TO 29% | 133 / 3.3 | 26 / 2.9 | 49 / 4.2 | 38 / 3.0 | 20 / 2.9 | 11 / 3.5 | 47 / 4.5 | 42 / 2.9 | 16 / 2.5 | 15 / 2.8 | 29 / 2.8 | 20 / 3.0 | 16 / 3.1 | 27 / 3.7 | 24 / 4.4 | 14 / 3.0 |
| 30 TO 39% | 174 / 4.3 | 34 / 3.8 | 54 / 4.6 | 53 / 4.2 | 33 / 4.7 | 16 / 5.1 | 50 / 4.8 | 55 / 3.7 | 31 / 4.8 | 20 / 3.8 | 43 / 4.2 | 30 / 4.6 | 26 / 5.0 | 28 / 3.8 | 26 / 4.8 | 15 / 3.2 |
| 40 TO 49% | 206 / 5.1 | 46 / 5.2 | 65 / 5.5 | 65 / 5.1 | 30 / 4.3 | 18 / 5.8 | 53 / 5.1 | 78 / 5.3 | 26 / 4.0 | 25 / 4.7 | 50 / 4.9 | 37 / 5.6 | 21 / 4.0 | 46 / 6.3 | 27 / 5.0 | 21 / 4.4 |
| 50 TO 59% | 397 / 9.8 | 79 / 8.9 | 113 / 9.6 | 129 / 10.1 | 74 / 10.6 | 28 / 9.0 | 99 / 9.5 | 151 / 10.3 | 67 / 10.4 | 44 / 8.3 | 101 / 9.8 | 69 / 10.5 | 45 / 8.6 | 73 / 10.0 | 53 / 9.7 | 43 / 9.1 |
| 60 TO 69% | 225 / 5.5 | 51 / 5.7 | 59 / 5.0 | 68 / 5.4 | 45 / 6.4 | 17 / 5.5 | 48 / 4.6 | 84 / 5.7 | 44 / 6.8 | 29 / 5.4 | 59 / 5.7 | 44 / 6.7 | 30 / 5.7 | 33 / 4.5 | 31 / 5.7 | 25 / 5.3 |
| 70 TO 79% | 405 / 10.0 | 92 / 10.3 | 118 / 10.0 | 139 / 10.9 | 55 / 7.9 | 18 / 5.8 | 99 / 9.5 | 163 / 11.1 | 64 / 10.0 | 57 / 10.7 | 105 / 10.2 | 73 / 11.1 | 57 / 10.9 | 64 / 8.8 | 47 / 8.6 | 50 / 10.6 |
| 80 TO 89% | 425 / 10.5 | 75 / 8.4 | 138 / 11.7 | 140 / 11.0 | 70 / 10.0 | 23 / 7.4 | 121 / 11.7 | 141 / 9.6 | 78 / 12.1 | 59 / 11.1 | 111 / 10.8 | 70 / 10.6 | 70 / 13.4 | 88 / 12.1 | 40 / 7.4 | 35 / 7.4 |
| 90% OR MORE | 1212 / 29.8 | 217 / 24.4 | 321 / 27.2 | 407 / 32.0 | 258 / 37.0 | 85 / 27.3 | 280 / 27.0 | 458 / 31.1 | 189 / 29.4 | 175 / 32.8 | 368 / 35.8 | 196 / 29.8 | 149 / 28.5 | 206 / 28.3 | 147 / 27.0 | 116 / 24.6 |
| I'M NOT SURE WHEN SHE HAS AN ORGASM | 529 / 13.0 | 176 / 19.8 | 154 / 13.1 | 139 / 10.9 | 53 / 7.6 | 45 / 14.5 | 147 / 14.2 | 188 / 12.8 | 82 / 12.8 | 57 / 10.7 | 79 / 7.7 | 61 / 9.3 | 56 / 10.7 | 108 / 14.8 | 95 / 17.5 | 113 / 23.9 |
| NO ANSWER | 45 / 1.1 | 15 / 1.7 | 14 / 1.2 | 8 / .6 | 4 / .6 | 4 / 1.3 | 9 / .9 | 18 / 1.2 | 5 / .8 | 4 / .8 | 8 / .8 | 5 / .8 | 6 / 1.1 | 6 / .8 | 7 / 1.3 | 7 / 1.5 |
| SIGMA | 4066 / 100.1 | 889 / 99.8 | 1178 / 100.0 | 1271 / 99.9 | 698 / 100.1 | 311 / 100.0 | 1038 / 100.1 | 1472 / 100.1 | 643 / 100.0 | 533 / 100.2 | 1028 / 100.1 | 658 / 100.1 | 523 / 100.0 | 729 / 99.9 | 544 / 100.0 | 472 / 100.0 |

Q. 21 WHAT MOST IRRITATES YOU DURING SEX?

TABLE 21

|  | TOTAL | MARITAL STATUS | | | | AGE | | | | RACE | | |
|---|---|---|---|---|---|---|---|---|---|---|---|---|
|  |  | MARR'D LIVING WITH WIFE | NEVER MARR'D LIVING W/O PARTNR | LIVING WITH PARTNR UN-MARR'D | DIVRCE OR WIDOWD LIVING ALONE | 18-29 | 30-39 | 40-54 | 55-65 | WHITE | BLACK | OTHER |
| TOTAL RESPONDENTS | 4066 100.0 | 2639 100.0 | 763 100.0 | 280 100.0 | 383 100.0 | 1547 100.0 | 927 100.0 | 1143 100.0 | 432 100.0 | 3559 100.0 | 240 100.0 | 138 100.0 |
| IF THE WOMAN MADE THE FIRST ADVANCE | 113 2.8 | 80 3.0 | 20 2.6 | 4 1.4 | 9 2.3 | 44 2.8 | 22 2.4 | 24 2.1 | 22 5.1 | 82 2.3 | 19 7.9 | 4 2.9 |
| IF THE WOMAN SEEMS COLD OR DISINTEREST- ED | 2445 60.1 | 1600 60.6 | 457 59.9 | 160 57.1 | 227 59.3 | 952 61.5 | 580 62.6 | 684 59.8 | 223 51.6 | 2195 61.7 | 114 47.5 | 76 55.1 |
| IF THE WOMAN MAKES DEMANDS | 200 4.9 | 132 5.0 | 38 5.0 | 10 3.6 | 20 5.2 | 66 4.3 | 41 4.4 | 66 5.8 | 27 6.3 | 169 4.7 | 19 7.9 | 6 4.3 |
| IF THE WOMAN IS "TOO EASY" (SEEMS PROMIS- CUOUS) | 194 4.8 | 85 3.2 | 69 9.0 | 17 6.1 | 23 6.0 | 97 6.3 | 28 3.0 | 44 3.8 | 23 5.3 | 146 4.1 | 23 9.6 | 17 12.3 |
| IF THE WOMAN CRITICIZES YOU | 469 11.5 | 308 11.7 | 84 11.0 | 29 10.4 | 48 12.5 | 161 10.4 | 103 11.1 | 146 12.8 | 54 12.5 | 408 11.5 | 35 14.6 | 12 8.7 |
| I NEVER GET IRRITAT- ED | 675 16.6 | 447 16.9 | 109 14.3 | 58 20.7 | 61 15.9 | 239 15.4 | 162 17.5 | 187 16.4 | 86 19.9 | 585 16.4 | 40 16.7 | 24 17.4 |
| NO ANSWER | 38 .9 | 21 .8 | 11 1.4 | 4 1.4 | 2 .5 | 12 .8 | 10 1.1 | 10 .9 | 3 .7 | 28 .8 | 1 .4 | 1 .7 |
| SIGMA | 4134 101.6 | 2673 101.2 | 788 103.2 | 282 100.7 | 390 101.7 | 1571 101.5 | 946 102.1 | 1161 101.6 | 438 101.4 | 3613 101.5 | 251 104.6 | 140 101.4 |

Q. 21 WHAT MOST IRRITATES YOU DURING SEX?

TABLE 21

| | TOTAL | INCOME | | | | EDUCATION | | | | | OCCUPATION | | | | | |
| --- | --- | --- | --- | --- | --- | --- | --- | --- | --- | --- | --- | --- | --- | --- | --- | --- |
| | | UNDER $10000 | $10-14999 | $15-24999 | $25000 & OVER | LESS THAN H.S. GRAD | HIGH SCHL GRAD. | SOME COLLEGE | COLLEGE GRAD. | SOME/COMPL POST GRAD. | PRO-FES-SION. | MANA-GER-IAL | OTHER WHITE COLLR | BLUE COLLR | RET'D/UNEMP/OTHER | STU-DENT |
| TOTAL RESPONDENTS | 4066 100.0 | 889 100.0 | 1178 100.0 | 1271 100.0 | 698 100.0 | 311 100.0 | 1038 100.0 | 1472 100.0 | 643 100.0 | 533 100.0 | 1028 100.0 | 658 100.0 | 523 100.0 | 729 100.0 | 544 100.0 | 472 100.0 |
| IF THE WOMAN MADE THE FIRST ADVANCE | 113 2.8 | 33 3.7 | 47 4.0 | 23 1.8 | 9 1.3 | 28 9.0 | 36 3.5 | 23 1.6 | 19 3.0 | 4 .8 | 19 1.8 | 17 2.6 | 17 3.3 | 22 3.0 | 24 4.4 | 12 2.5 |
| IF THE WOMAN SEEMS COLD OR DISINTEREST-ED | 2445 60.1 | 516 58.0 | 667 56.6 | 808 63.6 | 437 62.6 | 150 48.2 | 598 57.6 | 904 61.4 | 409 63.6 | 344 64.5 | 644 62.6 | 404 61.4 | 295 56.4 | 446 61.2 | 293 53.9 | 301 63.8 |
| IF THE WOMAN MAKES DEMANDS | 200 4.9 | 39 4.4 | 77 6.5 | 51 4.0 | 33 4.7 | 19 6.1 | 56 5.4 | 71 4.8 | 27 4.2 | 25 4.7 | 44 4.3 | 31 4.7 | 36 6.9 | 39 5.3 | 26 4.8 | 20 4.2 |
| IF THE WOMAN IS "TOO EASY" (SEEMS PROMIS-CUOUS) | 194 4.8 | 64 7.2 | 67 5.7 | 37 2.9 | 23 3.3 | 16 5.1 | 53 5.1 | 79 5.4 | 20 3.1 | 18 3.4 | 43 4.2 | 21 3.2 | 23 4.4 | 31 4.3 | 36 6.6 | 32 6.8 |
| IF THE WOMAN CRITICIZES YOU | 469 11.5 | 95 10.7 | 145 12.3 | 155 12.2 | 70 10.0 | 41 13.2 | 130 12.5 | 163 11.1 | 58 9.0 | 67 12.6 | 106 10.3 | 76 11.6 | 73 14.0 | 91 12.5 | 62 11.4 | 43 9.1 |
| I NEVER GET IRRITAT-ED | 675 16.6 | 156 17.5 | 181 15.4 | 207 16.3 | 128 18.3 | 58 18.6 | 167 16.1 | 254 17.3 | 112 17.4 | 77 14.4 | 184 17.9 | 103 15.7 | 85 16.3 | 100 13.7 | 114 21.0 | 69 14.6 |
| NO ANSWER | 38 .9 | 8 .9 | 11 .9 | 8 .6 | 8 1.1 | 5 1.6 | 8 .8 | 9 .6 | 4 .6 | 6 1.1 | 6 .6 | 10 1.5 | 3 .6 | 3 .5 | 2 .4 | 4 .8 |
| SIGMA | 4134 101.6 | 911 102.4 | 1195 101.4 | 1289 101.4 | 708 101.3 | 317 101.8 | 1048 101.0 | 1503 102.2 | 649 100.9 | 541 101.5 | 1046 101.7 | 662 100.7 | 532 101.9 | 733 100.5 | 557 102.5 | 481 101.8 |

Q. 22 WHEN ARE YOU LIKELY TO BE SO "TURNED OFF" YOU CAN'T COMPLETE A SEX ACT?

TABLE 22

| | TOTAL | MARITAL STATUS | | | | AGE | | | | RACE | | |
|---|---|---|---|---|---|---|---|---|---|---|---|---|
| | | MARR'D LIVING WITH WIFE | NEVER MARR'D LIVING W/O PARTNR | LIVING WITH PARTNR UN-MARR'D | DIVRCE OR WIDOWD LIVING ALONE | 18-29 | 30-39 | 40-54 | 55-65 | WHITE | BLACK | OTHER |
| TOTAL RESPONDENTS | 4066 100.0 | 2639 100.0 | 763 100.0 | 280 100.0 | 383 100.0 | 1547 100.0 | 927 100.0 | 1143 100.0 | 432 100.0 | 3559 100.0 | 240 100.0 | 138 100.0 |
| IF IT'S THE FIRST TIME WITH THAT WOMAN | 124 3.0 | 58 2.2 | 39 5.1 | 7 2.5 | 20 5.2 | 62 4.0 | 19 2.0 | 29 2.5 | 13 3.0 | 96 2.7 | 14 5.8 | 10 7.2 |
| IF YOU'VE BEEN QUARRELLING | 739 18.2 | 528 20.0 | 97 12.7 | 55 19.6 | 59 15.4 | 245 15.8 | 164 17.7 | 232 20.3 | 95 22.0 | 648 18.2 | 43 17.9 | 21 15.2 |
| IF THE WOMAN SEEMS UNRESPONSIVE | 1853 45.6 | 1229 46.6 | 345 45.2 | 103 36.8 | 176 46.0 | 703 45.4 | 432 46.6 | 527 46.1 | 185 42.8 | 1665 46.8 | 84 35.0 | 52 37.7 |
| IF THE WOMAN TRIES TO CONTROL THINGS | 195 4.8 | 127 4.8 | 35 4.6 | 10 3.6 | 23 6.0 | 58 3.7 | 39 4.2 | 70 6.1 | 26 6.0 | 152 4.3 | 24 10.0 | 12 8.7 |
| IF THE WOMAN SEEMS PHYSICALLY UNATTRACTIVE | 507 12.5 | 249 9.4 | 149 19.5 | 48 17.1 | 61 15.9 | 259 16.7 | 115 12.4 | 95 8.3 | 37 8.6 | 448 12.6 | 29 12.1 | 20 14.5 |
| I NEVER GET "TURNED OFF" | 660 16.2 | 452 17.1 | 101 13.2 | 55 19.6 | 51 13.3 | 228 14.7 | 168 18.1 | 189 16.5 | 74 17.1 | 564 15.8 | 48 20.0 | 25 18.1 |
| NO ANSWER | 67 1.6 | 37 1.4 | 18 2.4 | 7 2.5 | 5 1.3 | 24 1.6 | 12 1.3 | 19 1.7 | 9 2.1 | 55 1.5 | 3 1.3 | 1 .7 |
| SIGMA | 4145 101.9 | 2680 101.5 | 784 102.7 | 285 101.7 | 395 103.1 | 1579 101.9 | 949 102.3 | 1161 101.5 | 439 101.6 | 3628 101.9 | 245 102.1 | 141 102.1 |

TABLE 22

Q. 22 WHEN ARE YOU LIKELY TO BE SO "TURNED OFF" YOU CAN'T COMPLETE A SEX ACT?

| | TOTAL | INCOME UNDER $10000 | INCOME $10-14999 | INCOME $15-24999 | INCOME $25000 & OVER | EDUC. LESS THAN HIGH SCHL GRAD | EDUC. HIGH SCHL GRAD | EDUC. SOME COLLEGE | EDUC. COLLEGE GRAD | EDUC. SOME/COMPL POST GRAD | OCC. PROFESSION | OCC. MANAGERIAL | OCC. OTHER WHITE COLLR | OCC. BLUE COLLR | OCC. RET'D, UNEMP, OTHER | OCC. STUDENT |
|---|---|---|---|---|---|---|---|---|---|---|---|---|---|---|---|---|
| TOTAL RESPONDENTS | 4066 / 100.0 | 889 / 100.0 | 1178 / 100.0 | 1271 / 100.0 | 698 / 100.0 | 311 / 100.0 | 1038 / 100.0 | 1472 / 100.0 | 643 / 100.0 | 533 / 100.0 | 1028 / 100.0 | 658 / 100.0 | 523 / 100.0 | 729 / 100.0 | 544 / 100.0 | 472 / 100.0 |
| IF IT'S THE FIRST TIME WITH THAT WOMAN | 124 / 3.0 | 42 / 4.7 | 37 / 3.1 | 29 / 2.3 | 15 / 2.1 | 18 / 5.8 | 34 / 3.3 | 41 / 2.8 | 17 / 2.6 | 11 / 2.1 | 23 / 2.2 | 22 / 3.3 | 7 / 1.3 | 21 / 2.9 | 22 / 4.0 | 24 / 5.1 |
| IF YOU'VE BEEN QUARRELLING | 739 / 18.2 | 139 / 15.6 | 217 / 18.4 | 255 / 20.1 | 123 / 17.6 | 52 / 16.7 | 179 / 17.2 | 252 / 17.1 | 125 / 19.4 | 113 / 21.2 | 215 / 20.9 | 138 / 21.0 | 91 / 17.4 | 117 / 16.0 | 89 / 16.4 | 63 / 13.3 |
| IF THE WOMAN SEEMS UNRESPONSIVE | 1853 / 45.6 | 398 / 44.8 | 524 / 44.5 | 597 / 47.0 | 320 / 45.8 | 126 / 40.5 | 444 / 42.8 | 692 / 47.0 | 307 / 47.7 | 252 / 47.3 | 458 / 44.6 | 320 / 48.6 | 262 / 50.1 | 330 / 45.3 | 204 / 37.5 | 223 / 47.2 |
| IF THE WOMAN TRIES TO CONTROL THINGS | 195 / 4.8 | 40 / 4.5 | 72 / 6.1 | 48 / 3.8 | 34 / 4.9 | 22 / 7.1 | 52 / 5.0 | 67 / 4.6 | 26 / 4.0 | 25 / 4.7 | 52 / 5.1 | 19 / 2.9 | 31 / 5.9 | 42 / 5.8 | 29 / 5.3 | 18 / 3.8 |
| IF THE WOMAN SEEMS PHYSICALLY UNATTRACTIVE | 507 / 12.5 | 122 / 13.7 | 139 / 11.8 | 149 / 11.7 | 95 / 13.6 | 32 / 10.3 | 110 / 10.6 | 210 / 14.3 | 89 / 13.8 | 62 / 11.6 | 116 / 11.3 | 67 / 10.2 | 64 / 12.2 | 97 / 13.3 | 60 / 11.0 | 90 / 19.1 |
| I NEVER GET "TURNED OFF" | 660 / 16.2 | 158 / 17.8 | 187 / 15.9 | 199 / 15.7 | 110 / 15.8 | 63 / 20.3 | 212 / 20.4 | 223 / 15.1 | 84 / 13.1 | 71 / 13.3 | 161 / 15.7 | 88 / 13.4 | 76 / 14.5 | 121 / 16.6 | 146 / 26.8 | 58 / 12.3 |
| NO ANSWER | 67 / 1.6 | 15 / 1.7 | 18 / 1.5 | 20 / 1.6 | 11 / 1.6 | 8 / 2.6 | 13 / 1.3 | 23 / 1.6 | 10 / 1.6 | 7 / 1.3 | 15 / 1.5 | 11 / 1.7 | 5 / 1.0 | 13 / 1.8 | 6 / 1.1 | 7 / 1.5 |
| SIGMA | 4145 / 101.9 | 914 / 102.8 | 1194 / 101.3 | 1297 / 102.2 | 708 / 101.4 | 321 / 103.3 | 1044 / 100.6 | 1508 / 102.5 | 658 / 102.2 | 541 / 101.5 | 1040 / 101.3 | 665 / 101.1 | 536 / 102.4 | 741 / 101.7 | 556 / 102.1 | 483 / 102.3 |

Q. 23 WITH WHAT TYPE OF PARTNER DO YOU USUALLY ENGAGE IN SEX?

TABLE 23

| | TOTAL | MARITAL STATUS | | | | AGE | | | | RACE | | |
|---|---|---|---|---|---|---|---|---|---|---|---|---|
| | | MARR'D LIVING WITH WIFE | NEVER MARR'D LIVING W/O PARTNR | LIVING WITH UN- MARR'D PARTNR | DIVRCE OR WIDOWD LIVING ALONE | 18-29 | 30-39 | 40-54 | 55-65 | WHITE | BLACK | OTHER |
| TOTAL RESPONDENTS | 4066 100.0 | 2639 100.0 | 763 100.0 | 280 100.0 | 383 100.0 | 1547 100.0 | 927 100.0 | 1143 100.0 | 432 100.0 | 3559 100.0 | 240 100.0 | 138 100.0 |
| WOMEN ONLY | 3799 93.4 | 2519 95.5 | 686 89.9 | 240 85.7 | 353 92.2 | 1434 92.7 | 883 95.3 | 1066 93.3 | 404 93.5 | 3360 94.4 | 207 86.3 | 119 86.2 |
| MEN ONLY | 51 1.3 | 20 .8 | 9 1.2 | 13 4.6 | 9 2.3 | 21 1.4 | 10 1.1 | 17 1.5 | 3 .7 | 39 1.1 | 6 2.5 | 5 3.6 |
| WOMEN AND MEN | 125 3.1 | 58 2.2 | 32 4.2 | 24 8.6 | 11 2.9 | 54 3.5 | 17 1.8 | 41 3.6 | 12 2.8 | 91 2.6 | 22 9.2 | 7 5.1 |
| NO SEXUAL EXPERIENCE | 48 1.2 | 14 .5 | 26 3.4 | 2 .7 | 6 1.6 | 28 1.8 | 4 .4 | 8 .7 | 8 1.9 | 39 1.1 | 2 .8 | 6 4.3 |
| NO ANSWER | 43 1.1 | 28 1.1 | 10 1.3 | 1 .4 | 4 1.0 | 10 .6 | 13 1.4 | 11 1.0 | 5 1.2 | 30 .8 | 3 1.3 | 1 .7 |
| SIGMA | 4066 100.1 | 2639 100.1 | 763 100.0 | 280 100.0 | 383 100.0 | 1547 100.0 | 927 100.0 | 1143 100.1 | 432 100.1 | 3559 100.0 | 240 100.1 | 138 99.9 |

Q. 23 WITH WHAT TYPE OF PARTNER DO YOU USUALLY ENGAGE IN SEX?

TABLE 23

| | TOTAL | INCOME | | | | EDUCATION | | | | | OCCUPATION | | | | | |
|---|---|---|---|---|---|---|---|---|---|---|---|---|---|---|---|---|
| | | UNDER $10000 | $10-14999 | $15-24999 | $25000 & OVER | LESS THAN H.S. GRAD. | HIGH SCHL GRAD. | SOME COL-LEGE | COL-LEGE GRAD | SOME/ COMPL POST GRAD. | PRO-FES-SION. | MANA-GER-IAL | OTHER WHITE COLLR | BLUE COLLR | RET'D, UNEMP, OTHER | STU-DENT |
| TOTAL RESPONDENTS | 4066 100.0 | 889 100.0 | 1178 100.0 | 1271 100.0 | 698 100.0 | 311 100.0 | 1038 100.1 | 1472 100.0 | 643 100.0 | 533 100.0 | 1028 100.1 | 658 100.0 | 523 100.0 | 729 100.0 | 544 100.0 | 472 100.0 |
| WOMEN ONLY | 3799 93.4 | 813 91.5 | 1094 92.9 | 1195 94.0 | 673 96.4 | 274 88.1 | 975 93.9 | 1377 93.5 | 620 96.4 | 493 92.5 | 965 93.9 | 627 95.3 | 490 93.7 | 685 94.0 | 498 91.5 | 436 92.4 |
| MEN ONLY | 51 1.3 | 12 1.3 | 19 1.6 | 15 1.2 | 4 .6 | 9 2.9 | 13 1.3 | 14 1.0 | 5 .8 | 10 1.9 | 14 1.4 | 7 1.1 | 8 1.5 | 8 1.1 | 9 1.7 | 4 .8 |
| WOMEN AND MEN | 125 3.1 | 39 4.4 | 39 3.3 | 34 2.7 | 13 1.9 | 13 4.2 | 29 2.8 | 47 3.2 | 13 2.0 | 21 3.9 | 31 3.0 | 18 2.7 | 16 3.1 | 23 3.2 | 19 3.5 | 16 3.4 |
| NO SEXUAL EXPERIENCE | 48 1.2 | 18 2.0 | 16 1.4 | 10 .8 | 4 .6 | 6 1.9 | 8 .8 | 26 1.8 | 3 .5 | 5 .9 | 7 .7 | 5 1.0 | 5 1.0 | 6 .8 | 12 2.2 | 15 3.2 |
| NO ANSWER | 43 1.1 | 7 .8 | 10 .8 | 17 1.3 | 4 .6 | 9 2.9 | 13 1.3 | 8 .5 | 2 .3 | 4 .8 | 11 1.1 | 6 .9 | 4 .8 | 4 1.0 | 6 1.1 | 1 .2 |
| SIGMA | 4066 100.1 | 889 100.0 | 1178 100.0 | 1271 100.0 | 698 100.1 | 311 100.0 | 1038 100.1 | 1472 100.0 | 643 100.0 | 533 100.0 | 1028 100.1 | 658 100.0 | 523 100.1 | 729 100.1 | 544 100.0 | 472 100.0 |

Q. 24 HOW DO YOU FEEL ABOUT HAVING INTERCOURSE DURING PARTNER'S PERIOD?

TABLE 24

| | TOTAL | MARITAL STATUS | | | | AGE | | | | RACE | | |
|---|---|---|---|---|---|---|---|---|---|---|---|---|
| | | MARR'D LIVING WITH WIFE | NEVER MARR'D LIVING W/O PARTNR | MARR'D LIVING WITH UN-MARR'D PARTNR | DIVRCE OR WIDOWD LIVING ALONE | 18-29 | 30-39 | 40-54 | 55-65 | WHITE | BLACK | OTHER |
| TOTAL RESPONDENTS | 4066 100.0 | 2639 100.0 | 763 100.0 | 280 100.0 | 383 100.0 | 1547 100.0 | 927 100.0 | 1143 100.0 | 432 100.0 | 3559 100.0 | 240 100.0 | 138 100.0 |
| ENJOY SEX AS MUCH | 1275 31.4 | 753 28.5 | 231 30.3 | 127 45.4 | 164 42.8 | 591 38.2 | 333 35.9 | 260 22.7 | 86 19.9 | 1145 32.2 | 58 24.2 | 38 27.5 |
| HAVE SEX, BUT DO NOT ENJOY IT AS MUCH | 535 13.2 | 344 13.0 | 91 11.9 | 39 13.9 | 61 15.9 | 208 13.4 | 134 14.5 | 156 13.6 | 34 7.9 | 485 13.6 | 22 9.2 | 18 13.0 |
| HAVE SEX ONLY TO PLEASE PARTNER | 205 5.0 | 123 4.7 | 51 6.7 | 10 3.6 | 21 5.5 | 82 5.3 | 41 4.4 | 63 5.5 | 18 4.2 | 166 4.7 | 19 7.9 | 11 8.0 |
| DO NOT HAVE INTER-COURSE, BUT ENGAGE IN OTHER SEX PLAY | 786 19.3 | 471 17.8 | 206 27.0 | 56 20.0 | 52 13.6 | 331 21.4 | 182 19.6 | 220 19.2 | 52 12.0 | 682 19.2 | 47 19.6 | 28 20.3 |
| LIMIT CONTACT TO HUGGING, KISSING | 769 18.9 | 572 21.7 | 109 14.3 | 32 11.4 | 56 14.6 | 231 14.9 | 149 16.1 | 271 23.7 | 116 26.9 | 672 18.9 | 53 22.1 | 21 15.2 |
| AVOID PARTNER PHYSICALLY | 449 11.0 | 353 13.4 | 59 7.7 | 12 4.3 | 25 6.5 | 83 5.4 | 81 8.7 | 167 14.6 | 118 27.3 | 377 10.6 | 40 16.7 | 19 13.8 |
| NO ANSWER | 72 1.8 | 37 1.4 | 23 3.0 | 5 1.8 | 7 1.8 | 33 2.1 | 10 1.1 | 13 1.1 | 11 2.5 | 52 1.5 | 3 1.3 | 5 3.6 |
| SIGMA | 4091 100.6 | 2653 100.5 | 770 100.9 | 281 100.4 | 386 100.7 | 1559 100.7 | 930 100.3 | 1150 100.4 | 435 100.7 | 3579 100.7 | 242 101.0 | 140 101.4 |

Q. 24 HOW DO YOU FEEL ABOUT HAVING INTERCOURSE DURING PARTNER'S PERIOD?

TABLE 24

| | TOTAL | INCOME | | | | EDUCATION | | | | | OCCUPATION | | | | | |
|---|---|---|---|---|---|---|---|---|---|---|---|---|---|---|---|---|
| | | UNDER $10000 | $10-14999 | $15-24999 | $25000 & OVER | LESS THAN H.S. GRAD | HIGH SCHL GRAD | SOME COLLEGE | COLLEGE GRAD | SOME/COMPL POST GRAD | PROFESSION | MANAGERIAL | OTHER WHITE COLLR | BLUE COLLR | RET'D, UNEMP, OTHER | STUDENT |
| TOTAL RESPONDENTS | 4066 / 100.0 | 889 / 100.0 | 1178 / 100.0 | 1271 / 100.0 | 698 / 100.0 | 311 / 100.0 | 1038 / 100.0 | 1472 / 100.0 | 643 / 100.0 | 533 / 100.0 | 1028 / 100.0 | 658 / 100.0 | 523 / 100.0 | 729 / 100.0 | 544 / 100.0 | 472 / 100.0 |
| ENJOY SEX AS MUCH | 1275 / 31.4 | 320 / 36.0 | 361 / 30.6 | 372 / 29.3 | 208 / 29.8 | 73 / 23.5 | 294 / 28.3 | 494 / 33.6 | 208 / 32.3 | 188 / 35.3 | 347 / 33.8 | 178 / 27.1 | 139 / 26.6 | 231 / 31.7 | 175 / 32.2 | 166 / 35.2 |
| HAVE SEX, BUT DO NOT ENJOY IT AS MUCH | 535 / 13.2 | 122 / 13.7 | 155 / 13.2 | 160 / 12.6 | 95 / 13.6 | 38 / 12.2 | 112 / 10.8 | 193 / 13.1 | 90 / 14.0 | 93 / 17.4 | 140 / 13.6 | 96 / 14.6 | 80 / 15.3 | 77 / 10.6 | 59 / 10.8 | 66 / 14.0 |
| HAVE SEX ONLY TO PLEASE PARTNER | 205 / 5.0 | 53 / 6.0 | 68 / 5.8 | 51 / 4.0 | 32 / 4.6 | 24 / 7.7 | 50 / 4.8 | 81 / 5.5 | 31 / 4.8 | 16 / 3.0 | 42 / 4.1 | 42 / 6.4 | 30 / 5.7 | 44 / 6.0 | 23 / 4.2 | 21 / 4.4 |
| DO NOT HAVE INTERCOURSE, BUT ENGAGE IN OTHER SEX PLAY | 786 / 19.3 | 177 / 19.9 | 206 / 17.5 | 251 / 19.7 | 150 / 21.5 | 49 / 15.8 | 200 / 19.3 | 290 / 19.7 | 127 / 19.8 | 106 / 19.9 | 202 / 19.6 | 135 / 20.5 | 108 / 20.7 | 130 / 17.8 | 82 / 15.1 | 108 / 22.9 |
| LIMIT CONTACT TO HUGGING, KISSING | 769 / 18.9 | 121 / 13.6 | 231 / 19.6 | 267 / 21.0 | 145 / 20.8 | 55 / 17.7 | 229 / 22.1 | 264 / 17.9 | 122 / 19.0 | 86 / 16.1 | 192 / 18.7 | 132 / 20.1 | 106 / 20.3 | 135 / 18.5 | 112 / 20.6 | 73 / 15.5 |
| AVOID PARTNER PHYSICALLY | 449 / 11.0 | 83 / 9.3 | 145 / 12.3 | 156 / 12.3 | 64 / 9.2 | 64 / 20.6 | 143 / 13.8 | 133 / 9.0 | 60 / 9.3 | 42 / 7.9 | 98 / 9.5 | 70 / 10.6 | 59 / 11.3 | 98 / 13.4 | 88 / 16.2 | 28 / 5.9 |
| NO ANSWER | 72 / 1.8 | 18 / 2.0 | 18 / 1.5 | 23 / 1.8 | 8 / 1.1 | 9 / 2.9 | 14 / 1.3 | 28 / 1.9 | 8 / 1.2 | 4 / .8 | 13 / 1.3 | 9 / 1.4 | 5 / 1.0 | 16 / 2.2 | 8 / 1.5 | 10 / 2.1 |
| SIGMA | 4091 / 100.6 | 894 / 100.5 | 1184 / 100.5 | 1280 / 100.7 | 702 / 100.6 | 312 / 100.4 | 1042 / 100.4 | 1483 / 100.7 | 646 / 100.4 | 535 / 100.4 | 1034 / 100.6 | 662 / 100.7 | 527 / 100.9 | 731 / 100.2 | 547 / 100.6 | 472 / 100.0 |

Q. 25 WHAT IS THE MOST UNPLEASANT ASPECT OF SEX FOR YOU?

TABLE 25

| | TOTAL | MARITAL STATUS | | | | AGE | | | | RACE | | |
|---|---|---|---|---|---|---|---|---|---|---|---|---|
| | | MARR'D LIVING WITH WIFE | NEVER MARR'D LIVING W/O PARTNR | LIVING WITH PARTNR MARR'D UN- | DIVRCE OR WIDOWD LIVING ALONE | 18-29 | 30-39 | 40-54 | 55-65 | WHITE | BLACK | OTHER |
| TOTAL RESPONDENTS | 4066 100.0 | 2639 100.0 | 763 100.0 | 280 100.0 | 383 100.0 | 1547 100.0 | 927 100.0 | 1143 100.0 | 432 100.0 | 3559 100.0 | 240 100.0 | 138 100.0 |
| ENGAGING IN FOREPLAY | 146 3.6 | 102 3.9 | 21 2.8 | 10 3.6 | 13 3.4 | 53 3.4 | 22 2.4 | 39 3.4 | 30 6.9 | 114 3.2 | 18 7.5 | 5 3.6 |
| HAVING AN UNRESPONSIVE WOMAN | 2377 58.5 | 1595 60.4 | 421 55.2 | 150 53.6 | 211 55.1 | 888 57.4 | 582 62.8 | 659 57.7 | 242 56.0 | 2146 60.3 | 108 45.0 | 61 44.2 |
| ODORS AND DISCHARGE | 1001 24.6 | 623 23.6 | 173 22.7 | 83 29.6 | 122 31.9 | 354 22.9 | 223 24.1 | 325 28.4 | 95 22.0 | 853 24.0 | 73 30.4 | 41 29.7 |
| WOMAN MAKING DEMANDS | 237 5.8 | 162 6.1 | 37 4.8 | 17 6.1 | 21 5.5 | 83 5.4 | 46 5.0 | 75 6.6 | 31 7.2 | 191 5.4 | 15 6.3 | 20 14.5 |
| FEELING GUILTY | 246 6.1 | 109 4.1 | 95 12.5 | 18 6.4 | 24 6.3 | 146 9.4 | 33 3.6 | 40 3.5 | 27 6.3 | 203 5.7 | 25 10.4 | 14 10.1 |
| NO ANSWER | 134 3.3 | 95 3.6 | 28 3.7 | 5 1.8 | 5 1.3 | 42 2.7 | 33 3.6 | 37 3.2 | 19 4.4 | 114 3.2 | 6 2.5 | 2 1.4 |
| SIGMA | 4141 101.9 | 2686 101.7 | 775 101.7 | 283 101.1 | 396 103.5 | 1566 101.2 | 939 101.5 | 1175 102.8 | 444 102.8 | 3621 101.8 | 245 102.1 | 143 103.5 |

Q. 25 WHAT IS THE MOST UNPLEASANT ASPECT OF SEX FOR YOU?

TABLE 25

| | TOTAL | INCOME | | | | EDUCATION | | | | | OCCUPATION | | | | | |
| --- | --- | --- | --- | --- | --- | --- | --- | --- | --- | --- | --- | --- | --- | --- | --- | --- |
| | | UNDER $10000 | $10-14999 | $15-24999 | $25000 & OVER | LESS THAN H.S. GRAD | HIGH SCHL GRAD | SOME COLLEGE | COLLEGE GRAD | SOME/COMPL POST GRAD GRAD | PROFESSION | MANAGERIAL | OTHER WHITE COLLR | BLUE COLLR | RET'D/UNEMP/OTHER | STUDENT |
| TOTAL RESPONDENTS | 4066 100.0 | 889 100.0 | 1178 100.0 | 1271 100.0 | 698 100.0 | 311 100.0 | 1038 100.0 | 1472 100.0 | 643 100.0 | 533 100.0 | 1028 100.0 | 658 100.0 | 523 100.0 | 729 100.0 | 544 100.0 | 472 100.0 |
| ENGAGING IN FOREPLAY | 146 3.6 | 44 4.9 | 46 3.9 | 41 3.2 | 12 1.7 | 20 6.4 | 49 4.7 | 43 2.9 | 20 3.1 | 10 1.9 | 34 3.3 | 18 2.7 | 25 4.8 | 23 3.2 | 33 6.1 | 10 2.1 |
| HAVING AN UNRESPONSIVE WOMAN | 2377 58.5 | 508 57.1 | 643 54.6 | 783 61.6 | 431 61.7 | 138 44.4 | 579 55.8 | 884 60.1 | 399 62.1 | 346 64.9 | 596 58.0 | 406 61.7 | 306 58.5 | 426 58.4 | 293 53.9 | 282 59.7 |
| ODORS AND DISCHARGE | 1001 24.6 | 193 21.7 | 303 25.7 | 317 24.9 | 181 25.9 | 95 30.5 | 262 25.2 | 355 24.1 | 153 23.8 | 117 22.0 | 281 27.3 | 158 24.0 | 123 23.5 | 179 24.6 | 128 23.5 | 108 22.9 |
| WOMAN MAKING DEMANDS | 237 5.8 | 52 5.8 | 83 7.0 | 63 5.0 | 37 5.3 | 26 8.4 | 67 6.5 | 77 5.2 | 31 4.8 | 30 5.6 | 44 4.3 | 39 5.9 | 36 6.9 | 48 6.6 | 42 7.7 | 24 5.1 |
| FEELING GUILTY | 246 6.1 | 82 9.2 | 82 7.0 | 57 4.5 | 24 3.4 | 21 6.8 | 64 6.2 | 100 6.8 | 38 5.9 | 19 3.6 | 53 5.2 | 24 3.6 | 25 4.8 | 50 6.9 | 34 6.3 | 53 11.2 |
| NO ANSWER | 134 3.3 | 24 2.7 | 39 3.3 | 39 3.1 | 27 3.9 | 18 5.8 | 35 3.4 | 42 2.9 | 13 2.0 | 16 3.0 | 38 3.7 | 22 3.3 | 15 2.9 | 21 2.9 | 22 4.0 | 6 1.3 |
| SIGMA | 4141 101.9 | 903 101.4 | 1196 101.5 | 1300 102.3 | 712 101.9 | 318 102.3 | 1056 101.8 | 1501 102.0 | 654 101.7 | 538 101.0 | 1046 101.8 | 667 101.2 | 530 101.4 | 747 102.6 | 552 101.5 | 483 102.3 |

Q. 26 WHAT IS YOUR ATTITUDE TOWARDS CHEATING ON YOUR WIFE OR STEADY GIRL FRIEND?

TABLE 26

| | TOTAL | MARITAL STATUS | | | | AGE | | | | RACE | | |
|---|---|---|---|---|---|---|---|---|---|---|---|---|
| | | MARR'D LIVING WITH WIFE | NEVER MARR'D LIVING W/O PARTNR MARR'D | LIVING WITH PARTNR UN-MARR'D | DIVRCE OR WIDOWD LIVING ALONE | 18-29 | 30-39 | 40-54 | 55-65 | WHITE | BLACK | OTHER |
| TOTAL RESPONDENTS | 4066 100.0 | 2639 100.0 | 763 100.0 | 280 100.0 | 383 100.0 | 1547 100.0 | 927 100.0 | 1143 100.0 | 432 100.0 | 3559 100.0 | 240 100.0 | 138 100.0 |
| WOULD NEVER BECOME INVOLVED WITH ANYONE ELSE | 1366 33.6 | 1004 38.0 | 205 26.9 | 54 19.3 | 103 26.9 | 463 29.9 | 291 31.4 | 404 35.3 | 204 47.2 | 1244 35.0 | 52 21.7 | 31 22.5 |
| WOULD CHEAT ONLY IF AWAY FROM PARTNER FOR LONG PERIOD | 530 13.0 | 354 13.4 | 93 12.2 | 34 12.1 | 49 12.8 | 195 12.6 | 107 11.5 | 168 14.7 | 58 13.4 | 461 13.0 | 39 16.3 | 17 12.3 |
| WOULD CHEAT ONLY IF I FELL IN LOVE | 285 7.0 | 167 6.3 | 70 9.2 | 15 5.4 | 33 8.6 | 113 7.3 | 55 5.9 | 83 7.3 | 32 7.4 | 231 6.5 | 14 5.8 | 22 15.9 |
| WOULD CHEAT ONLY IF AFFAIR WAS BRIEF AND CASUAL | 727 17.9 | 451 17.1 | 154 20.2 | 59 21.1 | 63 16.4 | 318 20.6 | 172 18.6 | 187 16.4 | 47 10.9 | 641 18.0 | 41 17.1 | 26 18.8 |
| WOULD CHEAT ONLY IF RELATIONSHIP WITH REGULAR PARTNER WAS BAD | 701 17.2 | 421 16.0 | 123 16.1 | 62 22.1 | 95 24.8 | 268 17.3 | 178 19.2 | 201 17.6 | 52 12.0 | 622 17.5 | 43 17.9 | 16 11.6 |
| WOULD CHEAT TO HAVE DIFFERENT SEXUAL PARTNERS REGARDLESS OF WIFE OR GIRL FRIEND | 474 11.7 | 252 9.5 | 112 14.7 | 57 20.4 | 52 13.6 | 203 13.1 | 129 13.9 | 104 9.1 | 37 8.6 | 387 10.9 | 50 20.8 | 24 17.4 |
| NO ANSWER | 63 1.5 | 37 1.4 | 18 2.4 | 2 .7 | 6 1.6 | 23 1.5 | 12 1.3 | 19 1.7 | 6 1.4 | 44 1.2 | 5 2.1 | 4 2.9 |
| SIGMA | 4146 101.9 | 2686 101.7 | 775 101.7 | 283 101.1 | 401 104.7 | 1583 102.3 | 944 101.8 | 1166 102.1 | 436 100.9 | 3630 102.1 | 244 101.7 | 140 101.4 |

TABLE 26

Q. 26 WHAT IS YOUR ATTITUDE TOWARDS CHEATING ON YOUR WIFE OR STEADY GIRL FRIEND?

| | TOTAL | INCOME | | | | EDUCATION | | | | | OCCUPATION | | | | | |
| --- | --- | --- | --- | --- | --- | --- | --- | --- | --- | --- | --- | --- | --- | --- | --- | --- |
| | | UNDER $10000 | $10-14999 | $15-24999 | $25000 & OVER | LESS THAN H.S. GRAD | HIGH SCHL GRAD. | SOME COL-LEGE | COL-LEGE GRAD | SOME/ COMPL POST GRAD. | PRO-FES-SION. | MANA-GER-IAL | OTHER WHITE COLLR | BLUE COLLR | RET'D, UNEMP. OTHER | STU-DENT |
| TOTAL RESPONDENTS | 4066 100.0 | 889 100.0 | 1178 100.0 | 1271 100.0 | 698 100.0 | 311 100.0 | 1038 100.0 | 1472 100.0 | 643 100.0 | 533 100.0 | 1028 100.0 | 658 100.0 | 523 100.0 | 729 100.0 | 544 100.0 | 472 100.0 |
| WOULD NEVER BECOME INVOLVED WITH ANYONE ELSE | 1366 33.6 | 276 31.0 | 415 35.2 | 421 33.1 | 246 35.2 | 106 34.1 | 382 36.8 | 460 31.3 | 203 31.6 | 190 35.6 | 343 33.4 | 225 34.2 | 184 35.2 | 251 34.4 | 204 37.5 | 122 25.8 |
| WOULD CHEAT ONLY IF AWAY FROM PARTNER FOR LONG PERIOD | 530 13.0 | 140 15.7 | 138 11.7 | 161 12.7 | 89 12.8 | 49 15.8 | 155 14.9 | 171 11.6 | 84 13.1 | 64 12.0 | 132 12.8 | 81 12.3 | 73 14.0 | 94 12.9 | 75 13.8 | 64 13.6 |
| WOULD CHEAT ONLY IF I FELL IN LOVE | 285 7.0 | 60 6.7 | 80 6.8 | 96 7.6 | 45 6.4 | 14 4.5 | 62 6.0 | 109 7.4 | 53 8.2 | 38 7.1 | 64 6.2 | 46 7.0 | 41 7.8 | 44 6.0 | 34 6.3 | 47 10.0 |
| WOULD CHEAT ONLY IF AFFAIR WAS BRIEF AND CASUAL | 727 17.9 | 169 19.0 | 196 16.6 | 239 18.8 | 118 16.9 | 47 15.1 | 139 13.4 | 293 19.9 | 123 19.1 | 114 21.4 | 196 19.1 | 120 18.2 | 93 17.8 | 119 16.3 | 67 12.3 | 113 23.9 |
| WOULD CHEAT ONLY IF RELATIONSHIP WITH REGULAR PARTNER WAS BAD | 701 17.2 | 145 16.3 | 208 17.7 | 225 17.7 | 119 17.0 | 46 14.8 | 177 17.1 | 272 18.5 | 107 16.6 | 91 17.1 | 170 16.5 | 122 18.5 | 77 14.7 | 134 18.4 | 94 17.3 | 83 17.6 |
| WOULD CHEAT TO HAVE DIFFERENT SEXUAL PARTNERS REGARDLESS OF WIFE OR GIRL FRIEND | 474 11.7 | 113 12.7 | 132 11.2 | 137 10.8 | 87 12.5 | 47 15.1 | 118 11.4 | 177 12.0 | 74 11.5 | 50 9.4 | 131 12.7 | 62 9.4 | 57 10.9 | 84 11.5 | 70 12.9 | 54 11.4 |
| NO ANSWER | 63 1.5 | 10 1.1 | 24 2.0 | 23 1.8 | 3 .4 | 9 2.9 | 15 1.4 | 22 1.5 | 6 .9 | 4 .8 | 14 1.4 | 8 1.2 | 8 1.5 | 17 2.3 | 5 .9 | 3 .6 |
| SIGMA | 4146 101.9 | 913 102.5 | 1193 101.2 | 1302 102.5 | 707 101.2 | 318 102.3 | 1048 101.0 | 1504 102.2 | 650 101.0 | 551 103.4 | 1050 102.1 | 664 100.8 | 533 101.9 | 743 101.8 | 549 101.0 | 486 102.9 |

Q. 27 HAVE YOU EVER CHEATED ON YOUR WIFE OR STEADY GIRL FRIEND?

TABLE 27

| | TOTAL | MARITAL STATUS | | | | AGE | | | | RACE | | |
|---|---|---|---|---|---|---|---|---|---|---|---|---|
| | | MARR'D LIVING WITH WIFE | NEVER MARR'D LIVING W/O PARTNR | LIVING WITH PARTNR UN-MARR'D | DIVRCE OR WIDOWD LIVING ALONE | 18-29 | 30-39 | 40-54 | 55-65 | WHITE | BLACK | OTHER |
| TOTAL RESPONDENTS | 4066 100.0 | 2639 100.0 | 763 100.0 | 280 100.0 | 383 100.0 | 1547 100.0 | 927 100.0 | 1143 100.0 | 432 100.0 | 3559 100.0 | 240 100.0 | 138 100.0 |
| NO | 2011 49.5 | 1482 56.2 | 295 38.7 | 89 31.8 | 145 37.9 | 716 46.3 | 453 48.9 | 562 49.2 | 272 63.0 | 1827 51.3 | 64 26.7 | 59 42.8 |
| YES, WITH PARTNER'S KNOWLEDGE AND CONSENT | 222 5.5 | 101 3.8 | 58 7.6 | 27 9.6 | 36 9.4 | 116 7.5 | 44 4.7 | 49 4.3 | 13 3.0 | 191 5.4 | 17 7.1 | 12 8.7 |
| YES, WITH ONE OR TWO OTHERS | 1160 28.5 | 687 26.0 | 247 32.4 | 97 34.6 | 128 33.4 | 446 28.8 | 267 28.8 | 343 30.0 | 101 23.4 | 1000 28.1 | 95 39.6 | 33 23.9 |
| YES, WITH MANY DIFFERENT WOMEN | 528 13.0 | 332 12.6 | 83 10.9 | 52 18.6 | 61 15.9 | 175 11.3 | 143 15.4 | 167 14.6 | 41 9.5 | 434 12.2 | 54 22.5 | 20 14.5 |
| NEVER HAD A WIFE OR STEADY GIRL FRIEND | 113 2.8 | 17 .6 | 73 9.6 | 12 4.3 | 11 2.9 | 84 5.4 | 11 1.2 | 12 1.0 | 6 1.4 | 91 2.6 | 7 2.9 | 11 8.0 |
| NO ANSWER | 46 1.1 | 28 1.1 | 10 1.3 | 3 1.1 | 5 1.3 | 16 1.0 | 11 1.2 | 13 1.1 | 2 .5 | 30 .8 | 3 1.3 | 3 2.2 |
| SIGMA | 4080 100.4 | 2647 100.3 | 766 100.5 | 280 100.0 | 386 100.8 | 1553 100.3 | 929 100.2 | 1146 100.2 | 435 100.8 | 3573 100.4 | 240 100.1 | 138 100.1 |

Q. 27 HAVE YOU EVER CHEATED ON YOUR WIFE OR STEADY GIRL FRIEND?

TABLE 27

| | TOTAL | INCOME | | | | EDUCATION | | | | | OCCUPATION | | | | | |
| --- | --- | --- | --- | --- | --- | --- | --- | --- | --- | --- | --- | --- | --- | --- | --- | --- |
| | | UNDER $10000 | $10-14999 | $15-24999 | $25000 & OVER | LESS THAN H.S. GRAD | HIGH SCHL GRAD. | SOME COLLEGE | COLLEGE GRAD GRAD. | SOME/COMPL POST GRAD. | PRO-FES-SION. | MANA-GER-IAL | OTHER WHITE COLLR | BLUE COLLR | RET'D, UNEMP, OTHER | STU-DENT |
| TOTAL RESPONDENTS | 4066 100.0 | 889 100.0 | 1178 100.0 | 1271 100.0 | 698 100.0 | 311 100.0 | 1038 100.0 | 1472 100.0 | 643 100.0 | 533 100.0 | 1028 100.0 | 658 100.0 | 523 100.0 | 729 100.0 | 544 100.0 | 472 100.0 |
| NO | 2011 49.5 | 408 45.9 | 600 50.9 | 644 50.7 | 346 49.6 | 144 46.3 | 542 52.2 | 689 46.8 | 316 49.1 | 286 53.7 | 507 49.3 | 337 51.2 | 273 52.2 | 374 51.3 | 263 48.3 | 209 44.3 |
| YES, WITH PARTNER'S KNOWLEDGE AND CONSENT | 222 5.5 | 67 7.5 | 65 5.5 | 52 4.1 | 37 5.3 | 12 3.9 | 43 4.1 | 86 5.8 | 48 7.5 | 32 6.0 | 63 6.1 | 29 4.4 | 17 3.3 | 24 3.3 | 33 6.1 | 47 10.0 |
| YES, WITH ONE OR TWO OTHERS | 1160 28.5 | 246 27.7 | 337 28.6 | 367 28.9 | 205 29.4 | 93 29.9 | 297 28.6 | 435 29.6 | 174 27.1 | 145 27.2 | 273 26.6 | 192 29.2 | 156 29.8 | 214 29.4 | 156 28.7 | 139 29.4 |
| YES, WITH MANY DIFFERENT WOMEN | 528 13.0 | 106 11.9 | 150 12.7 | 174 13.7 | 92 13.2 | 49 15.8 | 123 11.8 | 200 13.6 | 88 13.7 | 59 11.1 | 156 15.2 | 83 12.6 | 61 11.7 | 98 13.4 | 68 12.5 | 47 10.0 |
| NEVER HAD A WIFE OR STEADY GIRL FRIEND | 113 2.8 | 57 6.4 | 23 2.0 | 21 1.7 | 12 1.7 | 7 2.3 | 23 2.2 | 58 3.9 | 13 2.0 | 11 2.1 | 19 1.8 | 9 1.4 | 11 2.1 | 15 2.1 | 22 4.0 | 31 6.6 |
| NO ANSWER | 46 1.1 | 10 1.1 | 11 .9 | 14 1.1 | 6 .9 | 7 2.3 | 13 1.3 | 11 .7 | 5 .8 | 2 .4 | 13 1.3 | 9 1.4 | 6 1.1 | 5 .7 | 4 .7 | 2 .4 |
| SIGMA | 4080 100.4 | 894 100.5 | 1186 100.6 | 1272 100.2 | 698 100.1 | 312 100.5 | 1041 100.2 | 1479 100.4 | 644 100.2 | 535 100.5 | 1031 100.3 | 659 100.2 | 524 100.2 | 730 100.2 | 546 100.3 | 475 100.7 |

Q. 28 WHAT WOULD BE MOST LIKELY TO TEMPT YOU TO CHEAT?

TABLE 28

| | TOTAL | MARITAL STATUS | | | | AGE | | | | RACE | | |
|---|---|---|---|---|---|---|---|---|---|---|---|---|
| | | MARR'D LIVING WITH WIFE | NEVER MARR'D LIVING W/O PARTNR | LIVING WITH PARTNR UN-MARR'D | DIVRCE WIDOWD OR LIVING ALONE | 18-29 | 30-39 | 40-54 | 55-65 | WHITE | BLACK | OTHER |
| TOTAL RESPONDENTS | 4066 100.0 | 2639 100.0 | 763 100.0 | 280 100.0 | 383 100.0 | 1547 100.0 | 927 100.0 | 1143 100.0 | 432 100.0 | 3559 100.0 | 240 100.0 | 138 100.0 |
| POOR SEX AT HOME | 1086 26.7 | 830 31.5 | 108 14.2 | 50 17.9 | 98 25.6 | 293 18.9 | 269 29.0 | 385 33.7 | 134 31.0 | 950 26.7 | 71 29.6 | 26 18.8 |
| FIGHTING AT HOME | 748 18.4 | 503 19.1 | 107 14.0 | 56 20.0 | 82 21.4 | 274 17.7 | 200 21.6 | 209 18.3 | 63 14.6 | 664 18.7 | 32 13.3 | 24 17.4 |
| EXCEPTIONALLY ATTRACTIVE WOMAN | 1008 24.8 | 549 20.8 | 265 34.7 | 92 32.9 | 101 26.4 | 517 33.4 | 221 23.8 | 208 18.2 | 61 14.1 | 884 24.8 | 63 26.3 | 36 26.1 |
| AVAILABLE WOMAN AT WORK | 334 8.2 | 205 7.8 | 77 10.1 | 23 8.2 | 29 7.6 | 127 8.2 | 74 8.0 | 105 9.2 | 27 6.3 | 281 7.9 | 27 11.3 | 13 9.4 |
| A WOMAN WHO UNDER-STANDS ME BETTER | 438 10.8 | 209 7.9 | 143 18.7 | 33 11.8 | 53 13.8 | 231 14.9 | 79 8.5 | 94 8.2 | 31 7.2 | 367 10.3 | 43 17.9 | 20 14.5 |
| WOULD NOT BE TEMPTED | 629 15.5 | 464 17.6 | 87 11.4 | 28 10.0 | 50 13.1 | 187 12.1 | 126 13.6 | 186 16.3 | 127 29.4 | 568 16.0 | 23 9.6 | 24 17.4 |
| NO ANSWER | 90 2.2 | 52 2.0 | 21 2.8 | 9 3.2 | 8 2.1 | 33 2.1 | 19 2.0 | 27 2.4 | 8 1.9 | 70 2.0 | 6 2.5 | 3 2.2 |
| SIGMA | 4333 106.6 | 2812 106.7 | 808 105.9 | 291 104.0 | 421 110.0 | 1662 107.3 | 988 106.5 | 1214 106.3 | 451 104.5 | 3784 106.4 | 265 110.5 | 146 105.8 |

TABLE 28

Q. 28 WHAT WOULD BE MOST LIKELY TO TEMPT YOU TO CHEAT?

| | TOTAL | INCOME | | | | EDUCATION | | | | | OCCUPATION | | | | | |
| --- | --- | --- | --- | --- | --- | --- | --- | --- | --- | --- | --- | --- | --- | --- | --- | --- |
| | | UNDER $10000 | $10-14999 | $15-24999 | $25000 & OVER | LESS THAN H.S. GRAD | HIGH SCHL GRAD. | SOME COL-LEGE | COL-LEGE GRAD | SOME/ COMPL POST GRAD. | PRO-FES-SION. | MANA-GER-IAL | OTHER WHITE COLLR | BLUE COLLR | RET'D/ UNEMP, OTHER | STU-DENT |
| TOTAL RESPONDENTS | 4066 100.0 | 889 100.0 | 1178 100.0 | 1271 100.0 | 698 100.0 | 311 100.0 | 1038 100.0 | 1472 100.0 | 643 100.0 | 533 100.0 | 1028 100.0 | 658 100.0 | 523 100.0 | 729 100.0 | 544 100.0 | 472 100.0 |
| POOR SEX AT HOME | 1086 26.7 | 173 19.5 | 321 27.2 | 386 30.4 | 201 28.8 | 87 28.0 | 317 30.5 | 366 24.9 | 152 23.6 | 138 25.9 | 291 28.3 | 192 29.2 | 153 29.3 | 215 29.5 | 141 25.9 | 67 14.2 |
| FIGHTING AT HOME | 748 18.4 | 164 18.4 | 196 16.6 | 249 19.6 | 134 19.2 | 64 20.6 | 175 16.9 | 256 17.4 | 116 18.0 | 113 21.2 | 191 18.6 | 143 21.7 | 106 20.3 | 132 18.1 | 83 15.3 | 68 14.4 |
| EXCEPTIONALLY ATTRACTIVE WOMAN | 1008 24.8 | 261 29.4 | 274 23.3 | 304 23.9 | 163 23.4 | 71 22.8 | 204 19.7 | 414 28.1 | 170 26.4 | 133 25.0 | 259 25.2 | 152 23.1 | 109 20.8 | 150 20.6 | 125 23.0 | 188 39.8 |
| AVAILABLE WOMAN AT WORK | 334 8.2 | 79 8.9 | 104 8.8 | 87 6.8 | 60 8.6 | 28 9.0 | 90 8.7 | 123 8.4 | 53 8.2 | 33 6.2 | 80 7.8 | 47 7.1 | 48 9.2 | 60 8.2 | 50 9.2 | 39 8.3 |
| A WOMAN WHO UNDER-STANDS ME BETTER | 438 10.8 | 134 15.1 | 120 10.2 | 115 9.0 | 61 8.7 | 32 10.3 | 99 9.5 | 181 12.3 | 72 11.2 | 46 8.6 | 98 9.5 | 53 8.1 | 46 8.8 | 83 11.4 | 61 11.2 | 79 16.7 |
| WOULD NOT BE TEMPTED | 629 15.5 | 125 14.1 | 201 17.1 | 188 14.8 | 113 16.2 | 58 18.6 | 177 17.1 | 205 13.9 | 102 15.9 | 82 15.4 | 146 14.2 | 96 14.6 | 79 15.1 | 122 16.7 | 115 21.1 | 55 11.7 |
| NO ANSWER | 90 2.2 | 20 2.2 | 26 2.2 | 26 2.0 | 14 2.0 | 7 2.3 | 25 2.4 | 26 1.8 | 12 1.9 | 12 2.3 | 25 2.4 | 15 2.3 | 10 1.9 | 15 2.1 | 11 2.0 | 6 1.3 |
| SIGMA | 4333 106.6 | 956 107.6 | 1242 105.4 | 1355 106.5 | 746 106.9 | 347 111.6 | 1087 104.8 | 1571 106.8 | 677 105.2 | 557 104.6 | 1090 106.0 | 698 106.1 | 551 105.4 | 777 106.6 | 586 107.7 | 502 106.4 |

Q. 29 HOW DO YOU FEEL ABOUT BEING IN LOVE?

TABLE 29

| | TOTAL | MARITAL STATUS | | | | AGE | | | | RACE | | |
|---|---|---|---|---|---|---|---|---|---|---|---|---|
| | | MARR'D LIVING WITH WIFE | NEVER MARR'D LIVING W/O PARTNR | LIVING WITH UN-MARR'D PARTNR | DIVRCE OR WIDOWD LIVING ALONE | 18-29 | 30-39 | 40-54 | 55-65 | WHITE | BLACK | OTHER |
| TOTAL RESPONDENTS | 4066 100.0 | 2639 100.0 | 763 100.0 | 280 100.0 | 383 100.0 | 1547 100.0 | 927 100.0 | 1143 100.0 | 432 100.0 | 3559 100.0 | 240 100.0 | 138 100.0 |
| IT'S THE MOST IMPORTANT THING IN LIFE | 1563 38.4 | 1067 40.4 | 290 38.0 | 92 32.9 | 113 29.5 | 644 41.6 | 321 34.6 | 408 35.7 | 184 42.6 | 1397 39.3 | 75 31.3 | 43 31.2 |
| IT'S GOOD, BUT ONE CAN LIVE A FULL LIFE WITHOUT IT | 1024 25.2 | 642 24.3 | 194 25.4 | 72 25.7 | 116 30.3 | 372 24.0 | 273 29.4 | 292 25.5 | 85 19.7 | 898 25.2 | 63 26.3 | 35 25.4 |
| IF YOU'RE IN LOVE SEX IS BETTER | 876 21.5 | 560 21.2 | 155 20.3 | 64 22.9 | 97 25.3 | 311 20.1 | 201 21.7 | 271 23.7 | 89 20.6 | 785 22.1 | 49 20.4 | 21 15.2 |
| LOVE IS NECESSARY FOR GOOD SEX | 362 8.9 | 246 9.3 | 68 8.9 | 23 8.2 | 25 6.5 | 127 8.2 | 75 8.1 | 109 9.5 | 48 11.1 | 304 8.5 | 29 12.1 | 16 11.6 |
| SEX IS BETTER WITHOUT LOVE TO COMPLICATE IT | 136 3.3 | 78 3.0 | 29 3.8 | 12 4.3 | 17 4.4 | 57 3.7 | 27 2.9 | 35 3.1 | 17 3.9 | 101 2.8 | 16 6.7 | 14 10.1 |
| LOVE IS AN OLD-FASHIONED IDEA | 122 3.0 | 63 2.4 | 27 3.5 | 12 4.3 | 20 5.2 | 47 3.0 | 28 3.0 | 32 2.8 | 15 3.5 | 98 2.8 | 12 5.0 | 8 5.8 |
| NO ANSWER | 60 1.5 | 34 1.3 | 13 1.7 | 7 2.5 | 6 1.6 | 22 1.4 | 18 1.9 | 14 1.2 | 3 .7 | 44 1.2 | 1 .4 | 3 2.2 |
| SIGMA | 4143 101.8 | 2690 101.9 | 776 101.6 | 282 100.8 | 394 102.8 | 1580 102.0 | 943 101.6 | 1161 101.5 | 441 102.1 | 3627 101.9 | 245 102.2 | 140 101.5 |

TABLE 29

Q. 29 HOW DO YOU FEEL ABOUT BEING IN LOVE?

| | TOTAL | INCOME | | | | EDUCATION | | | | | OCCUPATION | | | | | |
| --- | --- | --- | --- | --- | --- | --- | --- | --- | --- | --- | --- | --- | --- | --- | --- | --- |
| | | UNDER $10000 | $10-14999 | $15-24999 | $25000 & OVER | LESS THAN H.S. GRAD | HIGH SCHL GRAD | SOME COLLEGE | COLLEGE GRAD | SOME/COMPL POST GRAD | PROFESSION. | MANAGERIAL | OTHER WHITE COLLR | BLUE COLLR | RET'D, UNEMP, OTHER | STUDENT |
| TOTAL RESPONDENTS | 4066 100.0 | 889 100.0 | 1178 100.0 | 1271 100.0 | 698 100.0 | 311 100.0 | 1038 100.0 | 1472 100.0 | 643 100.0 | 533 100.0 | 1028 100.0 | 658 100.0 | 523 100.0 | 729 100.0 | 544 100.0 | 472 100.0 |
| IT'S THE MOST IMPORTANT THING IN LIFE | 1563 38.4 | 348 39.1 | 470 39.9 | 477 37.5 | 257 36.8 | 116 37.3 | 408 39.3 | 573 38.9 | 250 38.9 | 184 34.5 | 409 39.8 | 247 37.5 | 206 39.4 | 280 38.4 | 199 36.6 | 176 37.3 |
| IT'S GOOD, BUT ONE CAN LIVE A FULL LIFE WITHOUT IT | 1024 25.2 | 224 25.2 | 297 25.2 | 331 26.0 | 168 24.1 | 69 22.2 | 258 24.9 | 368 25.0 | 171 26.6 | 144 27.0 | 248 24.1 | 160 24.3 | 145 27.7 | 185 25.4 | 148 27.2 | 114 24.2 |
| IF YOU'RE IN LOVE SEX IS BETTER | 876 21.5 | 175 19.7 | 241 20.5 | 288 22.7 | 164 23.5 | 75 24.1 | 189 18.2 | 338 23.0 | 132 20.5 | 129 24.2 | 227 22.1 | 155 23.6 | 104 19.9 | 149 20.4 | 103 18.9 | 111 23.5 |
| LOVE IS NECESSARY FOR GOOD SEX | 362 8.9 | 92 10.3 | 88 7.5 | 109 8.6 | 69 9.9 | 18 5.8 | 112 10.8 | 110 7.5 | 60 9.3 | 53 9.9 | 92 8.9 | 57 8.7 | 42 8.0 | 68 9.3 | 46 8.5 | 47 10.0 |
| SEX IS BETTER WITHOUT LOVE TO COMPLICATE IT | 136 3.3 | 31 3.5 | 39 3.3 | 42 3.3 | 24 3.4 | 15 4.8 | 30 2.9 | 54 3.7 | 16 2.5 | 17 3.2 | 37 3.6 | 21 3.2 | 12 2.3 | 19 2.6 | 21 3.9 | 19 4.0 |
| LOVE IS AN OLD-FASHIONED IDEA | 122 3.0 | 30 3.4 | 42 3.6 | 35 2.8 | 15 2.1 | 15 4.8 | 36 3.5 | 40 2.7 | 20 3.1 | 11 2.1 | 20 1.9 | 16 2.4 | 19 3.6 | 29 4.0 | 22 4.0 | 14 3.0 |
| NO ANSWER | 60 1.5 | 8 .9 | 17 1.4 | 19 1.5 | 12 1.7 | 5 1.6 | 17 1.6 | 17 1.2 | 5 .8 | 10 1.9 | 17 1.7 | 13 2.0 | 5 1.0 | 7 1.0 | 8 1.5 | 4 .8 |
| SIGMA | 4143 101.8 | 908 102.1 | 1194 101.4 | 1301 102.4 | 709 101.5 | 313 100.6 | 1050 101.2 | 1500 102.0 | 654 101.7 | 548 102.8 | 1050 102.1 | 669 101.7 | 533 101.9 | 737 101.1 | 547 100.6 | 485 102.8 |

TABLE 30

Q. 30 WHAT SORT OF SEXUAL EXPERIENCE WOULD YOU PREFER A WIFE TO HAVE HAD PRIOR TO MARRIAGE?

| | TOTAL | MARITAL STATUS | | | | AGE | | | | RACE | | |
|---|---|---|---|---|---|---|---|---|---|---|---|---|
| | | MARR'D LIVING WITH WIFE | NEVER MARR'D LIVING W/O PARTNR | MARR'D LIVING WITH UN-MARR'D PARTNR | DIVRCE OR WIDOWD LIVING ALONE | 18-29 | 30-39 | 40-54 | 55-65 | WHITE | BLACK | OTHER |
| TOTAL RESPONDENTS | 4066 100.0 | 2639 100.0 | 763 100.0 | 280 100.0 | 383 100.0 | 1547 100.0 | 927 100.0 | 1143 100.0 | 432 100.0 | 3559 100.0 | 240 100.0 | 138 100.0 |
| NO OTHER MAN EXCEPT YOURSELF | 1301 32.0 | 1005 38.1 | 185 24.2 | 40 14.3 | 71 18.5 | 388 25.1 | 251 27.1 | 436 38.1 | 220 50.9 | 1122 31.5 | 71 29.6 | 53 38.4 |
| ONE OR A FEW MEN SHE REALLY LOVED | 833 20.5 | 496 18.8 | 183 24.0 | 72 25.7 | 82 21.4 | 343 22.2 | 214 23.1 | 220 19.2 | 51 11.8 | 752 21.1 | 48 20.0 | 20 14.5 |
| A FEW CASUAL AFFAIRS | 466 11.5 | 276 10.5 | 102 13.4 | 44 15.7 | 44 11.5 | 197 12.7 | 101 10.9 | 137 12.0 | 30 6.9 | 398 11.2 | 42 17.5 | 12 8.7 |
| MANY MEN | 89 2.2 | 51 1.9 | 19 2.5 | 9 3.2 | 10 2.6 | 39 2.5 | 16 1.7 | 25 2.2 | 8 1.9 | 69 1.9 | 6 2.5 | 7 5.1 |
| IT WOULD NOT MATTER | 1364 33.5 | 801 30.4 | 272 35.6 | 116 41.4 | 174 45.4 | 582 37.6 | 344 37.1 | 319 27.9 | 118 27.3 | 1218 34.2 | 72 30.0 | 44 31.9 |
| NO ANSWER | 40 1.0 | 25 .9 | 9 1.2 | 2 .7 | 4 1.0 | 9 .6 | 8 .9 | 13 1.1 | 7 1.6 | 25 .7 | 2 .8 | 3 2.2 |
| SIGMA | 4093 100.7 | 2654 100.6 | 770 100.9 | 283 101.0 | 385 100.4 | 1558 100.7 | 934 100.8 | 1150 100.5 | 434 100.4 | 3584 100.6 | 241 100.4 | 139 100.8 |

Q. 30 WHAT SORT OF SEXUAL EXPERIENCE WOULD YOU PREFER A WIFE TO HAVE HAD PRIOR TO MARRIAGE?  TABLE 30

| | TOTAL | INCOME | | | | EDUCATION | | | | | OCCUPATION | | | | | |
|---|---|---|---|---|---|---|---|---|---|---|---|---|---|---|---|---|
| | | UNDER $10000 | $10-14999 | $15-24999 | $25000 & OVER | LESS THAN H.S. GRAD | HIGH SCHL GRAD. | SOME COL-LEGE | COL-LEGE GRAD | SOME/ COMPL POST GRAD. | PRO-FES-SION. | MANA-GER-IAL | OTHER WHITE COLLR | BLUE COLLR | RET'D, UNEMP, OTHER | STU-DENT |
| TOTAL RESPONDENTS | 4066 100.0 | 889 100.0 | 1178 100.0 | 1271 100.0 | 698 100.0 | 311 100.0 | 1038 100.0 | 1472 100.0 | 643 100.0 | 533 100.0 | 1028 100.0 | 658 100.0 | 523 100.0 | 729 100.0 | 544 100.0 | 472 100.0 |
| NO OTHER MAN EXCEPT YOURSELF | 1301 32.0 | 264 29.7 | 385 32.7 | 412 32.4 | 230 33.0 | 130 41.8 | 408 39.3 | 417 28.3 | 174 27.1 | 146 27.4 | 322 31.3 | 202 30.7 | 184 35.2 | 252 34.6 | 192 35.3 | 126 26.7 |
| ONE OR A FEW MEN SHE REALLY LOVED | 833 20.5 | 178 20.0 | 244 20.7 | 255 20.1 | 151 21.6 | 56 18.0 | 167 16.1 | 293 19.9 | 167 26.0 | 138 25.9 | 226 22.0 | 147 22.3 | 112 21.4 | 136 18.7 | 89 16.4 | 99 21.0 |
| A FEW CASUAL AFFAIRS | 466 11.5 | 101 11.4 | 129 11.0 | 150 11.8 | 83 11.9 | 31 10.0 | 115 11.1 | 184 12.5 | 70 10.9 | 58 10.9 | 110 10.7 | 86 13.1 | 50 9.6 | 75 10.3 | 72 13.2 | 60 12.7 |
| MANY MEN | 89 2.2 | 14 1.6 | 37 3.1 | 22 1.7 | 15 2.1 | 8 2.6 | 26 2.5 | 32 2.2 | 10 1.6 | 12 2.3 | 23 2.2 | 9 1.4 | 13 2.5 | 18 2.5 | 14 2.6 | 11 2.3 |
| IT WOULD NOT MATTER | 1364 33.5 | 332 37.3 | 379 32.2 | 430 33.8 | 216 30.9 | 88 28.3 | 310 29.9 | 545 37.0 | 222 34.5 | 179 33.6 | 344 33.5 | 209 31.8 | 161 30.8 | 246 33.7 | 179 32.9 | 177 37.5 |
| NO ANSWER | 40 1.0 | 7 .8 | 12 1.0 | 12 .9 | 5 .7 | 1 .3 | 16 1.5 | 11 .7 | 3 .5 | 3 .6 | 7 .7 | 8 1.2 | 6 1.1 | 9 1.2 | 1 .2 | 1 .2 |
| SIGMA | 4093 100.7 | 896 100.8 | 1186 100.7 | 1281 100.7 | 700 100.2 | 314 101.0 | 1042 100.4 | 1482 100.6 | 646 100.6 | 536 100.7 | 1032 100.4 | 661 100.5 | 526 100.6 | 736 101.0 | 547 100.6 | 474 100.4 |

Q. 31 WHAT PERCENT OF THE TIME DOES THE WOMAN YOU'RE HAVING SEX WITH HAVE AN ORGASM EITHER BEFORE OR AFTER SEXUAL INTERCOURSE?

TABLE 31

| | TOTAL | MARITAL STATUS | | | | AGE | | | | RACE | | |
|---|---|---|---|---|---|---|---|---|---|---|---|---|
| | | MARR'D LIVING WITH WIFE | NEVER MARR'D LIVING W/O PARTNR | LIVING WITH PARTNR UN-MARR'D | DIVRCE OR WIDOWD LIVING ALONE | 18 TO 29 | 30-39 | 40-54 | 55-65 | WHITE | BLACK | OTHER |
| TOTAL RESPONDENTS | 4066 100.0 | 2639 100.0 | 763 100.0 | 280 100.0 | 383 100.0 | 1547 100.0 | 927 100.0 | 1143 100.0 | 432 100.0 | 3559 100.0 | 240 100.0 | 138 100.0 |
| 0 TO 9% | 541 13.3 | 399 15.1 | 75 9.8 | 28 10.0 | 39 10.2 | 156 10.1 | 129 13.9 | 190 16.6 | 65 15.0 | 494 13.9 | 13 5.4 | 13 9.4 |
| 10 TO 19% | 280 6.9 | 180 6.8 | 54 7.1 | 22 7.9 | 24 6.3 | 114 7.4 | 59 6.4 | 66 5.8 | 40 9.3 | 252 7.1 | 18 7.5 | 4 2.9 |
| 20 TO 29% | 222 5.5 | 144 5.5 | 47 6.2 | 13 4.6 | 18 4.7 | 84 5.4 | 59 6.4 | 58 5.1 | 20 4.6 | 191 5.4 | 16 6.7 | 8 5.8 |
| 30 TO 39% | 246 6.1 | 158 6.0 | 52 6.8 | 19 6.8 | 17 4.4 | 109 7.0 | 51 5.5 | 67 5.9 | 19 4.4 | 210 5.9 | 22 9.2 | 8 5.8 |
| 40 TO 49% | 217 5.3 | 142 5.4 | 43 5.6 | 12 4.3 | 20 5.2 | 81 5.2 | 38 4.1 | 75 6.6 | 23 5.3 | 191 5.4 | 12 5.0 | 7 5.1 |
| 50 TO 59% | 397 9.8 | 248 9.4 | 76 10.0 | 26 9.3 | 47 12.3 | 163 10.5 | 84 9.1 | 109 9.5 | 40 9.3 | 352 9.9 | 25 10.4 | 11 8.0 |
| 60 TO 69% | 231 5.7 | 147 5.6 | 52 6.8 | 13 4.6 | 19 5.0 | 94 6.1 | 47 5.1 | 66 5.8 | 23 5.3 | 201 5.6 | 15 6.3 | 9 6.5 |
| 70 TO 79% | 278 6.8 | 174 6.6 | 52 6.8 | 25 8.9 | 27 7.0 | 116 7.5 | 64 6.9 | 79 6.9 | 19 4.4 | 238 6.7 | 14 5.8 | 11 8.0 |
| 80 TO 89% | 250 6.1 | 166 6.3 | 38 5.0 | 25 8.9 | 21 5.5 | 87 5.6 | 71 7.7 | 69 6.0 | 22 5.1 | 220 6.2 | 12 5.0 | 13 9.4 |
| 90% OR MORE | 707 17.4 | 473 17.9 | 101 13.2 | 56 20.0 | 76 19.8 | 263 17.0 | 190 20.5 | 191 16.7 | 60 13.9 | 623 17.5 | 41 17.1 | 23 16.7 |
| I'M NOT SURE WHEN SHE HAS AN ORGASM | 609 15.0 | 355 13.5 | 153 20.1 | 38 13.6 | 63 16.4 | 254 16.4 | 122 13.2 | 147 12.9 | 81 18.8 | 510 14.3 | 52 21.7 | 29 21.0 |
| NO ANSWER | 88 2.2 | 53 2.0 | 20 2.6 | 3 1.1 | 12 3.1 | 26 1.7 | 13 1.4 | 26 2.3 | 20 4.6 | 77 2.2 | 2 1.4 | 2 1.4 |
| SIGMA | 4066 100.1 | 2639 100.1 | 763 100.0 | 280 100.0 | 383 99.9 | 1547 99.9 | 927 100.2 | 1143 100.1 | 432 100.0 | 3559 100.1 | 240 100.1 | 138 100.0 |

Q. 31 WHAT PERCENT OF THE TIME DOES THE WOMAN YOU'RE HAVING SEX WITH HAVE AN ORGASM EITHER BEFORE OR AFTER SEXUAL INTERCOURSE?

TABLE 31

| | TOTAL | INCOME | | | | EDUCATION | | | | | OCCUPATION | | | | | |
| --- | --- | --- | --- | --- | --- | --- | --- | --- | --- | --- | --- | --- | --- | --- | --- | --- |
| | | UNDER $10000 | $10-14999 | $15-24999 | $25000 & OVER | LESS THAN H.S. GRAD. | HIGH SCHL GRAD. | SOME COLLEGE | COLLEGE GRAD. | SOME/ COMPL POST GRAD. | PRO-FESSION. | MANA-GER-IAL | OTHER WHITE COLLR | BLUE COLLR | RET'D, UNEMP, OTHER | STU-DENT |
| TOTAL RESPONDENTS | 4066 100.0 | 889 100.0 | 1178 100.0 | 1271 100.0 | 698 100.0 | 311 100.0 | 1038 100.0 | 1472 100.0 | 643 100.0 | 533 100.0 | 1028 100.0 | 658 100.0 | 523 100.0 | 729 100.0 | 544 100.0 | 472 100.0 |
| 0 TO 9% | 541 13.3 | 103 11.6 | 144 12.2 | 184 14.5 | 107 15.3 | 54 17.4 | 127 12.2 | 185 12.6 | 82 12.8 | 87 16.3 | 145 14.1 | 87 13.2 | 77 14.7 | 98 13.4 | 77 14.2 | 45 9.5 |
| 10 TO 19% | 280 6.9 | 56 6.3 | 92 7.8 | 91 7.2 | 39 5.6 | 27 8.7 | 74 7.1 | 93 6.3 | 46 7.2 | 37 6.9 | 78 7.6 | 44 6.7 | 42 8.0 | 48 6.6 | 35 6.4 | 28 5.9 |
| 20 TO 29% | 222 5.5 | 45 5.1 | 58 4.9 | 70 5.5 | 46 6.6 | 20 6.4 | 58 5.6 | 82 5.6 | 30 4.7 | 32 6.0 | 53 5.2 | 41 6.2 | 30 5.7 | 42 5.8 | 30 5.5 | 23 4.9 |
| 30 TO 39% | 246 6.1 | 46 5.2 | 79 6.7 | 69 5.4 | 52 7.4 | 11 3.5 | 53 5.1 | 90 6.1 | 50 7.8 | 35 6.6 | 59 5.7 | 50 7.6 | 35 6.7 | 32 4.4 | 33 6.1 | 31 6.6 |
| 40 TO 49% | 217 5.3 | 40 4.5 | 61 5.2 | 73 5.7 | 43 6.2 | 11 3.5 | 59 5.7 | 86 5.8 | 34 5.3 | 21 3.9 | 45 4.4 | 37 5.6 | 28 5.4 | 48 6.6 | 22 4.0 | 33 7.0 |
| 50 TO 59% | 397 9.8 | 92 10.3 | 107 9.1 | 136 10.7 | 60 8.6 | 21 6.8 | 113 10.9 | 149 10.1 | 55 8.6 | 49 9.2 | 106 10.3 | 62 9.4 | 46 8.8 | 79 10.8 | 55 10.1 | 42 8.9 |
| 60 TO 69% | 231 5.7 | 56 6.3 | 82 7.0 | 59 4.6 | 34 4.9 | 23 7.4 | 52 5.0 | 85 5.8 | 40 6.2 | 31 5.8 | 48 4.7 | 43 6.5 | 34 6.5 | 44 6.0 | 31 5.7 | 28 5.9 |
| 70 TO 79% | 278 6.8 | 65 7.3 | 85 7.2 | 89 7.0 | 39 5.6 | 15 4.8 | 82 7.9 | 103 7.0 | 44 6.8 | 31 5.8 | 84 8.2 | 45 6.8 | 41 7.8 | 43 5.9 | 27 5.0 | 27 5.7 |
| 80 TO 89% | 250 6.1 | 43 4.8 | 81 6.9 | 93 7.3 | 31 4.4 | 13 4.2 | 70 6.7 | 79 5.4 | 48 7.5 | 39 7.3 | 62 6.0 | 44 6.7 | 37 7.1 | 50 6.9 | 24 4.4 | 27 5.7 |
| 90% OR MORE | 707 17.4 | 131 14.7 | 186 15.8 | 222 17.5 | 164 23.5 | 54 17.4 | 160 15.4 | 278 18.9 | 110 17.1 | 90 16.9 | 208 20.2 | 122 18.5 | 75 14.3 | 120 16.5 | 96 17.6 | 61 12.9 |
| I'M NOT SURE WHEN SHE HAS AN ORGASM | 609 15.0 | 193 21.7 | 178 15.1 | 157 12.4 | 73 10.5 | 53 17.0 | 169 16.3 | 215 14.6 | 94 14.6 | 67 12.6 | 118 11.5 | 69 10.5 | 64 12.2 | 115 15.8 | 106 19.5 | 119 25.2 |
| NO ANSWER | 88 2.2 | 19 2.1 | 25 2.1 | 28 2.2 | 10 1.4 | 9 2.9 | 21 2.0 | 27 1.8 | 10 1.6 | 14 2.6 | 22 2.1 | 14 2.1 | 14 2.7 | 10 1.4 | 8 1.5 | 8 1.7 |
| SIGMA | 4066 100.1 | 889 99.9 | 1178 100.0 | 1271 100.0 | 698 100.0 | 311 100.0 | 1038 99.9 | 1472 100.2 | 643 100.2 | 533 99.9 | 1028 100.0 | 658 99.8 | 523 99.9 | 729 100.1 | 544 100.0 | 472 99.9 |

TABLE 32

Q. 32 HOW DO YOU FEEL ABOUT HAVING SEX WITH OLDER WOMEN?

| | TOTAL | MARITAL STATUS | | | | AGE | | | | RACE | | |
|---|---|---|---|---|---|---|---|---|---|---|---|---|
| | | MARR'D LIVING WITH WIFE | NEVER MARR'D LIVING W/O PARTNR | LIVING WITH PARTNR UN-MARR'D | DIVRCE OR WIDOWD LIVING ALONE | 18-29 | 30-39 | 40-54 | 55-65 | WHITE | BLACK | OTHER |
| TOTAL RESPONDENTS | 4066 100.0 | 2639 100.0 | 763 100.0 | 280 100.0 | 383 100.0 | 1547 100.0 | 927 100.0 | 1143 100.0 | 432 100.0 | 3559 100.0 | 240 100.0 | 138 100.0 |
| THE WOMAN MUST BE MY AGE OR YOUNGER | 668 16.4 | 522 19.8 | 69 9.0 | 30 10.7 | 47 12.3 | 139 9.0 | 118 12.7 | 257 22.5 | 152 35.2 | 586 16.5 | 38 15.8 | 21 15.2 |
| THE WOMAN COULD BE 5 YEARS OLDER, NOT MORE | 663 16.3 | 410 15.5 | 160 21.0 | 41 14.6 | 52 13.6 | 261 16.9 | 143 15.4 | 207 18.1 | 49 11.3 | 573 16.1 | 49 20.4 | 19 13.8 |
| THE WOMAN COULD BE 10 YEARS OLDER, NOT MORE | 458 11.3 | 275 10.4 | 112 14.7 | 30 10.7 | 41 10.7 | 220 14.2 | 122 13.2 | 102 8.9 | 13 3.0 | 409 11.5 | 24 10.0 | 16 11.6 |
| AGE DOESN'T MATTER, BUT SHE MUST NOT LOOK OLDER | 521 12.8 | 329 12.5 | 99 13.0 | 38 13.6 | 55 14.4 | 198 12.8 | 124 13.4 | 155 13.6 | 44 10.2 | 453 12.7 | 31 12.9 | 21 15.2 |
| AGE DOES NOT MATTER AT ALL | 1555 38.2 | 972 36.8 | 284 37.2 | 119 42.5 | 179 46.7 | 645 41.7 | 383 41.3 | 381 33.3 | 143 33.1 | 1379 38.7 | 86 35.8 | 53 38.4 |
| PREFER AN OLDER WOMAN | 143 3.5 | 77 2.9 | 35 4.6 | 19 6.8 | 12 3.1 | 74 4.8 | 23 2.5 | 26 2.3 | 19 4.4 | 114 3.2 | 15 6.3 | 8 5.8 |
| NO ANSWER | 88 2.2 | 72 2.7 | 11 1.4 | 3 1.1 | 2 .5 | 22 1.4 | 23 2.5 | 21 1.8 | 13 3.0 | 68 1.9 | 3 1.3 | 1 .7 |
| SIGMA | 4096 100.7 | 2657 100.6 | 770 100.9 | 280 100.0 | 388 101.3 | 1559 100.8 | 936 101.0 | 1149 100.5 | 433 100.2 | 3582 100.6 | 246 102.5 | 139 100.7 |

Q. 32 HOW DO YOU FEEL ABOUT HAVING SEX WITH OLDER WOMEN?

TABLE 32

| | TOTAL | INCOME | | | | EDUCATION | | | | | OCCUPATION | | | | | |
| --- | --- | --- | --- | --- | --- | --- | --- | --- | --- | --- | --- | --- | --- | --- | --- | --- |
| | | UNDER $10000 | $10-14999 | $15-24999 | $25000 & OVER | LESS THAN H.S. GRAD | HIGH SCHL GRAD | SOME COLLEGE | COLLEGE GRAD | SOME/ COMPL POST GRAD | PRO-FESSION. | MANA-GER-IAL | OTHER WHITE COLLR | BLUE COLLR | RET'D, UNEMP OTHER | STU-DENT |
| TOTAL RESPONDENTS | 4066 100.0 | 889 100.0 | 1178 100.0 | 1271 100.0 | 698 100.0 | 311 100.0 | 1038 100.0 | 1472 100.0 | 643 100.0 | 533 100.0 | 1028 100.0 | 658 100.0 | 523 100.0 | 729 100.0 | 544 100.0 | 472 100.0 |
| THE WOMAN MUST BE MY AGE OR YOUNGER | 668 16.4 | 125 14.1 | 208 17.7 | 219 17.2 | 113 16.2 | 74 23.8 | 219 21.1 | 186 12.6 | 102 15.9 | 78 14.6 | 151 14.7 | 126 19.1 | 92 17.6 | 121 16.6 | 111 20.4 | 51 10.8 |
| THE WOMAN COULD BE 5 YEARS OLDER, NOT MORE | 663 16.3 | 158 17.8 | 189 16.0 | 186 14.6 | 125 17.9 | 56 18.0 | 161 15.5 | 238 16.2 | 114 17.7 | 84 15.8 | 154 15.0 | 110 16.7 | 90 17.2 | 132 18.1 | 79 14.5 | 80 16.9 |
| THE WOMAN COULD BE 10 YEARS OLDER, NOT MORE | 458 11.3 | 110 12.4 | 104 8.8 | 153 12.0 | 89 12.8 | 27 8.7 | 94 9.1 | 179 12.2 | 73 11.4 | 80 15.0 | 136 13.2 | 67 10.2 | 59 11.3 | 72 9.9 | 42 7.7 | 70 14.8 |
| AGE DOESN'T MATTER, BUT SHE MUST NOT LOOK OLDER | 521 12.8 | 109 12.3 | 158 13.4 | 167 13.1 | 85 12.2 | 37 11.9 | 137 13.2 | 216 14.7 | 77 12.0 | 50 9.4 | 138 13.4 | 82 12.5 | 55 10.5 | 107 14.7 | 62 11.4 | 67 14.2 |
| AGE DOES NOT MATTER AT ALL | 1555 38.2 | 343 38.6 | 449 38.1 | 493 38.8 | 261 37.4 | 98 31.5 | 374 36.0 | 590 40.1 | 255 39.7 | 215 40.3 | 402 39.1 | 244 37.1 | 205 39.2 | 270 37.0 | 212 39.0 | 184 39.0 |
| PREFER AN OLDER WOMAN | 143 3.5 | 34 3.8 | 51 4.3 | 35 2.8 | 22 3.2 | 24 7.7 | 32 3.1 | 45 3.1 | 21 3.3 | 19 3.6 | 36 3.5 | 16 2.4 | 16 3.1 | 20 2.7 | 34 6.3 | 17 3.6 |
| NO ANSWER | 88 2.2 | 16 1.8 | 22 1.9 | 26 2.0 | 14 2.0 | 3 1.0 | 23 2.2 | 25 1.7 | 8 1.2 | 10 1.9 | 20 1.9 | 17 2.6 | 9 1.7 | 10 1.4 | 9 1.7 | 6 1.3 |
| SIGMA | 4096 100.7 | 895 100.8 | 1181 100.2 | 1279 100.5 | 709 101.7 | 319 102.6 | 1040 100.2 | 1479 100.6 | 650 101.2 | 536 100.6 | 1037 100.8 | 662 100.6 | 526 100.6 | 732 100.4 | 549 101.0 | 475 100.6 |

TABLE 33

Q. 33 HOW DO YOU FEEL ABOUT TODAY'S WOMEN?

| | TOTAL | MARITAL STATUS | | | | AGE | | | | RACE | | |
|---|---|---|---|---|---|---|---|---|---|---|---|---|
| | | MARR'D LIVING WITH WIFE | NEVER MARR'D LIVING W/O PARTNR | LIVING WITH PARTNR UN-MARR'D | DIVRCE OR WIDOWD LIVING ALONE | 18-29 | 30-39 | 40-54 | 55-65 | WHITE | BLACK | OTHER |
| TOTAL RESPONDENTS | 4066 100.0 | 2639 100.0 | 763 100.0 | 280 100.0 | 383 100.0 | 1547 100.0 | 927 100.0 | 1143 100.0 | 432 100.0 | 3559 100.0 | 240 100.0 | 138 100.0 |
| THEY ARE TOO INDEPENDENT | 948 23.3 | 648 24.6 | 153 20.1 | 56 20.0 | 91 23.8 | 288 18.6 | 241 26.0 | 303 26.5 | 113 26.2 | 807 22.7 | 68 28.3 | 36 26.1 |
| THEY ARE MORE INTELLIGENT THAN EVER | 738 18.2 | 492 18.6 | 131 17.2 | 57 20.4 | 58 15.1 | 300 19.4 | 177 19.1 | 191 16.7 | 69 16.0 | 660 18.5 | 31 12.9 | 34 24.6 |
| THEY EXPECT TOO MUCH FROM MEN | 465 11.4 | 284 10.8 | 89 11.7 | 36 12.9 | 56 14.6 | 182 11.8 | 84 9.1 | 144 12.6 | 53 12.3 | 399 11.2 | 44 18.3 | 13 9.4 |
| THEY ARE BETTER COMPANY | 913 22.5 | 556 21.1 | 197 25.8 | 62 22.1 | 98 25.6 | 380 24.6 | 204 22.0 | 246 21.5 | 81 18.8 | 823 23.1 | 41 17.1 | 21 15.2 |
| THEY'VE BECOME MORE LOVING AND GIVING | 688 16.9 | 411 15.6 | 156 20.4 | 55 19.6 | 65 17.0 | 310 20.0 | 157 16.9 | 174 15.2 | 46 10.6 | 604 17.0 | 44 18.3 | 24 17.4 |
| THEY ARE TOO PROMISCUOUS ("FAST") | 335 8.2 | 222 8.4 | 62 8.1 | 17 6.1 | 34 8.9 | 113 7.3 | 66 7.1 | 96 8.4 | 60 13.9 | 288 8.1 | 25 10.4 | 14 10.1 |
| NO ANSWER | 130 3.2 | 92 3.5 | 19 2.5 | 9 3.2 | 10 2.6 | 41 2.7 | 31 3.3 | 32 2.8 | 17 3.9 | 103 2.9 | 6 2.5 | 2 1.4 |
| SIGMA | 4217 103.7 | 2705 102.6 | 807 105.8 | 292 104.3 | 412 107.6 | 1614 104.4 | 960 103.5 | 1186 103.7 | 439 101.7 | 3684 103.5 | 259 107.8 | 144 104.2 |

TABLE 33

**Q. 33 HOW DO YOU FEEL ABOUT TODAY'S WOMEN?**

| | TOTAL | INCOME | | | | EDUCATION | | | | | OCCUPATION | | | | | |
|---|---|---|---|---|---|---|---|---|---|---|---|---|---|---|---|---|
| | | UNDER $10000 | $10-14999 | $15-24999 | $25000 & OVER | LESS THAN H.S. GRAD | HIGH SCHL GRAD. | SOME COL-LEGE | COL-LEGE GRAD | SOME/COMPL POST GRAD. | PRO-FES-SION. | MANA-GER-IAL | OTHER WHITE COLLR | BLUE COLLR | RET'D, UNEMP, OTHER | STU-DENT |
| TOTAL RESPONDENTS | 4066 100.0 | 889 100.0 | 1178 100.0 | 1271 100.0 | 698 100.0 | 311 100.0 | 1038 100.0 | 1472 100.0 | 643 100.0 | 533 100.0 | 1028 100.0 | 658 100.0 | 523 100.0 | 729 100.0 | 544 100.0 | 472 100.0 |
| THEY ARE TOO INDEPENDENT | 948 23.3 | 211 23.7 | 312 26.5 | 291 22.9 | 128 18.3 | 90 28.9 | 308 29.7 | 322 21.9 | 121 18.8 | 88 16.5 | 231 22.5 | 141 21.4 | 132 25.2 | 199 27.3 | 156 28.7 | 72 15.3 |
| THEY ARE MORE INTELLIGENT THAN EVER | 738 18.2 | 143 16.1 | 220 18.7 | 244 19.2 | 128 18.3 | 49 15.8 | 149 14.4 | 295 20.0 | 137 21.3 | 97 18.2 | 179 17.4 | 128 19.5 | 106 20.3 | 122 16.7 | 83 15.3 | 94 19.9 |
| THEY EXPECT TOO MUCH FROM MEN | 465 11.4 | 125 14.1 | 124 10.5 | 141 11.1 | 72 10.0 | 61 19.6 | 131 12.6 | 166 11.3 | 55 8.6 | 47 8.8 | 106 10.3 | 71 10.8 | 53 10.1 | 91 12.5 | 74 13.6 | 54 11.4 |
| THEY ARE BETTER COMPANY | 913 22.5 | 210 23.6 | 231 19.6 | 273 21.5 | 196 28.1 | 48 15.4 | 180 17.3 | 331 22.5 | 169 26.3 | 175 32.8 | 240 23.3 | 153 23.3 | 103 19.7 | 149 20.4 | 102 18.8 | 129 27.3 |
| THEY'VE BECOME MORE LOVING AND GIVING | 688 16.9 | 153 17.2 | 200 17.0 | 216 17.0 | 115 16.5 | 43 13.8 | 187 18.0 | 276 18.8 | 106 16.5 | 67 12.6 | 187 18.2 | 103 15.7 | 78 14.9 | 127 17.4 | 77 14.2 | 91 19.3 |
| THEY ARE TOO PROMISCUOUS ("FAST") | 335 8.2 | 72 8.1 | 102 8.7 | 100 7.9 | 60 8.6 | 27 8.7 | 95 9.2 | 116 7.9 | 48 7.5 | 48 9.0 | 79 7.7 | 62 9.4 | 44 8.4 | 52 7.1 | 59 10.8 | 33 7.0 |
| NO ANSWER | 130 3.2 | 22 2.5 | 30 2.5 | 45 3.5 | 22 3.2 | 4 1.3 | 23 2.2 | 46 3.1 | 19 3.0 | 22 4.1 | 29 2.8 | 18 2.7 | 21 4.0 | 14 1.9 | 13 2.4 | 13 2.8 |
| SIGMA | 4217 103.7 | 936 105.3 | 1219 103.5 | 1310 103.1 | 719 103.0 | 322 103.5 | 1073 103.4 | 1552 105.5 | 655 102.0 | 544 102.0 | 1051 102.2 | 676 102.8 | 537 102.6 | 754 103.3 | 564 103.8 | 486 103.0 |

TABLE 34

Q. 34 HOW WOULD YOU FEEL WHEN A LOVE AFFAIR ENDS?

| | TOTAL | MARITAL STATUS | | | | AGE | | | | RACE | | |
|---|---|---|---|---|---|---|---|---|---|---|---|---|
| | | MARR'D LIVING WITH WIFE | NEVER MARR'D LIVING W/D PARTNR | MARR'D LIVING WITH PARTNR UN-MARR'D | DIVRCE OR WIDOWD LIVING ALONE | 18-29 | 30-39 | 40-54 | 55-65 | WHITE | BLACK | OTHER |
| TOTAL RESPONDENTS | 4066 100.0 | 2639 100.0 | 763 100.0 | 280 100.0 | 383 100.0 | 1547 100.0 | 927 100.0 | 1143 100.0 | 432 100.0 | 3559 100.0 | 240 100.0 | 138 100.0 |
| A LITTLE SAD, BUT ADJUST EASILY | 1515 37.3 | 1025 38.8 | 252 33.0 | 95 33.9 | 142 37.1 | 524 33.9 | 378 40.8 | 449 30.3 | 162 37.5 | 1315 36.9 | 92 38.3 | 54 39.1 |
| QUITE HURT, BUT QUICKLY SEEK A NEW WOMAN | 806 19.8 | 500 18.9 | 157 20.6 | 64 22.9 | 85 22.2 | 331 21.4 | 196 21.1 | 202 17.7 | 77 17.8 | 704 19.8 | 62 25.8 | 21 15.2 |
| QUITE HURT, AVOID WOMEN FOR A WHILE | 876 21.5 | 517 19.6 | 217 28.4 | 55 19.6 | 87 22.7 | 394 25.5 | 171 18.4 | 221 19.3 | 85 19.7 | 799 22.5 | 39 16.3 | 24 17.4 |
| INDIFFERENT | 386 9.5 | 260 9.9 | 68 8.9 | 28 10.0 | 30 7.8 | 146 9.4 | 79 8.5 | 112 9.8 | 48 11.1 | 314 8.8 | 32 13.3 | 25 18.1 |
| SO DEPRESSED MY WORK SUFFERS | 245 6.0 | 139 5.3 | 45 5.9 | 28 10.0 | 33 8.6 | 93 6.0 | 51 5.5 | 78 6.8 | 22 5.1 | 229 6.4 | 7 2.9 | 3 2.2 |
| CLOSE TO A MENTAL BREAKDOWN | 92 2.3 | 59 2.2 | 12 1.6 | 11 3.9 | 10 2.6 | 36 2.3 | 18 1.9 | 27 2.4 | 11 2.5 | 68 1.9 | 9 3.8 | 13 9.4 |
| NO ANSWER | 187 4.6 | 153 5.8 | 24 3.1 | 5 1.8 | 5 1.3 | 46 3.0 | 39 4.2 | 63 5.5 | 30 6.9 | 164 4.6 | 4 1.7 | |
| SIGMA | 4107 101.0 | 2653 100.5 | 775 101.5 | 286 102.1 | 392 102.3 | 1570 101.5 | 932 100.4 | 1152 100.8 | 435 100.6 | 3593 100.9 | 245 102.1 | 140 101.4 |

TABLE 34

Q. 34 HOW WOULD YOU FEEL WHEN A LOVE AFFAIR ENDS?

| | TOTAL | INCOME | | | | EDUCATION | | | | | | OCCUPATION | | | | |
|---|---|---|---|---|---|---|---|---|---|---|---|---|---|---|---|---|
| | | UNDER $10000 | $10-14999 | $15-24999 | $25000 & OVER | LESS THAN H.S. GRAD | HIGH SCHL GRAD | SOME COL-LEGE | COL-LEGE GRAD | SOME/COMPL POST GRAD | PRO-FES-SION. | MANA-GER-IAL | OTHER WHITE COLLR | BLUE COLLR | RET'D, UNEMP, OTHER | STU-DENT |
| TOTAL RESPONDENTS | 4066 100.0 | 889 100.0 | 1178 100.0 | 1271 100.0 | 698 100.0 | 311 100.0 | 1038 100.0 | 1472 100.0 | 643 100.0 | 533 100.0 | 1028 100.0 | 658 100.0 | 523 100.0 | 729 100.0 | 544 100.0 | 472 100.0 |
| A LITTLE SAD, BUT ADJUST EASILY | 1515 37.3 | 343 38.6 | 421 35.7 | 474 37.3 | 269 38.5 | 126 40.5 | 422 40.7 | 514 34.9 | 240 37.3 | 195 36.6 | 413 40.2 | 251 38.1 | 181 34.6 | 265 36.4 | 208 38.2 | 162 34.3 |
| QUITE HURT, BUT QUICKLY SEEK A NEW WOMAN | 806 19.8 | 161 18.1 | 245 20.8 | 259 20.4 | 139 19.9 | 57 18.3 | 196 18.9 | 315 21.4 | 126 19.6 | 104 19.5 | 188 18.3 | 129 19.6 | 107 20.5 | 167 22.9 | 103 18.9 | 101 21.4 |
| QUITE HURT, AVOID WOMEN FOR A WHILE | 876 21.5 | 209 23.5 | 269 22.8 | 250 19.7 | 144 20.6 | 55 17.7 | 203 19.6 | 331 22.5 | 150 23.3 | 121 22.7 | 208 20.2 | 142 21.6 | 125 23.9 | 141 19.3 | 109 20.0 | 117 24.8 |
| INDIFFERENT | 386 9.5 | 98 11.0 | 107 9.1 | 117 9.2 | 59 8.5 | 24 7.7 | 112 10.8 | 142 9.6 | 64 10.0 | 38 7.1 | 88 8.6 | 57 8.7 | 52 9.9 | 75 10.3 | 54 9.9 | 50 10.6 |
| SO DEPRESSED MY WORK SUFFERS | 245 6.0 | 47 5.3 | 70 5.9 | 81 6.4 | 47 6.7 | 21 6.8 | 46 4.4 | 97 6.6 | 40 6.2 | 36 6.8 | 67 6.5 | 38 5.8 | 31 5.9 | 39 5.3 | 34 6.3 | 30 6.4 |
| CLOSE TO A MENTAL BREAKDOWN | 92 2.3 | 27 3.0 | 24 2.0 | 28 2.2 | 13 1.9 | 16 5.1 | 14 1.3 | 36 2.4 | 14 2.2 | 11 2.1 | 22 2.1 | 9 1.4 | 7 1.3 | 21 2.9 | 23 4.2 | 8 1.7 |
| NO ANSWER | 187 4.6 | 20 2.2 | 51 4.3 | 70 5.5 | 35 5.0 | 16 5.1 | 53 5.1 | 57 3.9 | 13 2.0 | 31 5.8 | 51 5.0 | 38 5.8 | 23 4.4 | 28 3.8 | 20 3.7 | 9 1.9 |
| SIGMA | 4107 101.0 | 905 101.7 | 1187 100.6 | 1275 100.7 | 706 101.1 | 315 101.2 | 1046 100.8 | 1492 101.3 | 647 100.6 | 536 100.6 | 1037 100.9 | 664 101.0 | 526 100.5 | 736 100.9 | 551 101.2 | 477 101.1 |

Q. 35 IN WHAT SECTION OF THE UNITED STATES DO YOU LIVE?

TABLE 35

| | TOTAL | MARITAL STATUS | | | | AGE | | | | RACE | | |
|---|---|---|---|---|---|---|---|---|---|---|---|---|
| | | MARR'D LIVING WITH WIFE | NEVER MARR'D LIVING W/O PARTNR | LIVING WITH UN-MARR'D PARTNR | DIVRCE OR WIDOWD LIVING ALONE | 18-29 | 30-39 | 40-54 | 55-65 | WHITE | BLACK | OTHER |
| TOTAL RESPONDENTS | 4066 100.0 | 2639 100.0 | 763 100.0 | 280 100.0 | 383 100.0 | 1547 100.0 | 927 100.0 | 1143 100.0 | 432 100.0 | 3559 100.0 | 240 100.0 | 138 100.0 |
| NORTHEAST | 1330 32.7 | 844 32.0 | 275 36.0 | 85 30.4 | 125 32.6 | 528 34.1 | 288 31.1 | 366 32.0 | 146 33.8 | 1195 33.6 | 65 27.1 | 29 21.0 |
| NORTH CENTRAL | 1025 25.2 | 640 24.3 | 228 29.9 | 70 25.0 | 87 22.7 | 418 27.0 | 224 24.2 | 278 24.3 | 103 23.8 | 923 25.9 | 46 19.2 | 24 17.4 |
| SOUTH | 812 20.0 | 548 20.8 | 131 17.2 | 52 18.6 | 81 21.1 | 306 19.8 | 190 20.5 | 237 20.7 | 77 17.8 | 676 19.0 | 77 32.1 | 37 26.8 |
| WEST | 837 20.6 | 570 21.6 | 116 15.2 | 67 23.9 | 84 21.9 | 278 18.0 | 213 23.0 | 247 21.6 | 99 22.9 | 730 20.5 | 47 19.6 | 47 34.1 |
| NO ANSWER | 62 1.5 | 37 1.4 | 13 1.7 | 6 2.1 | 6 1.6 | 17 1.1 | 12 1.3 | 15 1.3 | 7 1.6 | 35 1.0 | 5 2.1 | 1 .7 |
| SIGMA | 4066 100.0 | 2639 100.1 | 763 100.0 | 280 100.0 | 383 99.9 | 1547 100.0 | 927 100.1 | 1143 99.9 | 432 99.9 | 3559 100.0 | 240 100.1 | 138 100.0 |

Q. 35 IN WHAT SECTION OF THE UNITED STATES DO YOU LIVE?

TABLE 35

| | TOTAL | INCOME | | | | EDUCATION | | | | | OCCUPATION | | | | | |
| --- | --- | --- | --- | --- | --- | --- | --- | --- | --- | --- | --- | --- | --- | --- | --- | --- |
| | | UNDER $10000 | $10-14999 | $15-24999 | $25000 & OVER | LESS THAN H.S. GRAD | HIGH SCHL GRAD. | SOME COL-LEGE | COL-LEGE GRAD | SOME/ COMPL POST GRAD. | PRO-FES-SION.IAL | MANA-GER-IAL | OTHER WHITE COLLR | BLUE COLLR | RET'D, UNEMP, OTHER | STU-DENT |
| TOTAL RESPONDENTS | 4066 100.0 | 889 100.0 | 1178 100.0 | 1271 100.0 | 698 100.0 | 311 100.0 | 1038 100.0 | 1472 100.0 | 643 100.0 | 533 100.0 | 1028 100.0 | 658 100.0 | 523 100.0 | 729 100.0 | 544 100.0 | 472 100.0 |
| NORTHEAST | 1330 32.7 | 249 28.0 | 365 31.0 | 412 32.4 | 295 42.3 | 100 32.2 | 330 31.8 | 451 30.6 | 236 36.7 | 197 37.0 | 355 34.5 | 239 36.3 | 166 31.7 | 221 30.3 | 159 29.2 | 156 33.1 |
| NORTH CENTRAL | 1025 25.2 | 218 24.5 | 279 23.7 | 342 26.9 | 178 25.5 | 78 25.1 | 225 21.7 | 423 28.7 | 163 25.3 | 126 23.6 | 266 25.9 | 161 24.5 | 131 25.0 | 168 23.0 | 117 21.5 | 153 32.4 |
| SOUTH | 812 20.0 | 223 25.1 | 234 19.9 | 256 20.1 | 97 13.9 | 70 22.5 | 240 23.1 | 287 19.5 | 109 17.0 | 95 17.8 | 189 18.4 | 128 19.5 | 107 20.5 | 161 22.1 | 109 20.0 | 106 22.5 |
| WEST | 837 20.6 | 193 21.7 | 281 23.9 | 242 19.0 | 121 17.3 | 60 19.3 | 225 21.7 | 299 20.3 | 127 19.8 | 112 21.0 | 202 19.6 | 118 17.9 | 115 22.0 | 170 23.3 | 157 28.9 | 56 11.9 |
| NO ANSWER | 62 1.5 | 6 .7 | 19 1.6 | 19 1.5 | 7 1.0 | 3 1.0 | 18 1.7 | 12 .8 | 8 1.2 | 3 .6 | 16 1.6 | 12 1.8 | 4 .8 | 9 1.2 | 2 .4 | 1 .2 |
| SIGMA | 4066 100.0 | 889 100.0 | 1178 99.9 | 1271 99.9 | 698 100.0 | 311 100.1 | 1038 100.0 | 1472 99.9 | 643 100.0 | 533 100.0 | 1028 100.0 | 658 100.0 | 523 100.0 | 729 99.9 | 544 100.0 | 472 100.1 |

TABLE 36

Q. 36 WHAT IS YOUR AGE?

| | TOTAL | MARR'D LIVING WITH WIFE | NEVER MARR'D LIVING W/O PARTNR | LIVING WITH PARTNR UN-MARR'D MARR'D | DIVRCE OR WIDOWD LIVING ALONE | AGE 18-29 | AGE 30-39 | AGE 40-54 | AGE 55-65 | RACE WHITE | RACE BLACK | RACE OTHER |
|---|---|---|---|---|---|---|---|---|---|---|---|---|
| TOTAL RESPONDENTS | 4066 100.0 | 2639 100.0 | 763 100.0 | 280 100.0 | 383 100.0 | 1547 100.0 | 927 100.0 | 1143 100.0 | 432 100.0 | 3559 100.0 | 240 100.0 | 138 100.0 |
| 18 TO 19 | 258 6.3 | 44 1.7 | 182 23.9 | 15 5.4 | 17 4.4 | 258 16.7 | | | | 234 6.6 | 16 6.7 | 7 5.1 |
| 20 TO 29 | 1289 31.7 | 512 19.4 | 483 63.3 | 156 55.7 | 137 35.8 | 1289 83.3 | | | | 1144 32.1 | 77 32.1 | 49 35.5 |
| 30 TO 39 | 927 22.8 | 726 27.5 | 55 7.2 | 53 18.9 | 93 24.3 | | 927 100.0 | | | 818 23.0 | 52 21.7 | 36 26.1 |
| 40 TO 44 | 323 7.9 | 270 10.2 | 9 1.2 | 13 4.6 | 31 8.1 | | | 323 28.3 | | 283 8.0 | 23 9.6 | 7 5.1 |
| 45 TO 54 | 820 20.2 | 696 26.4 | 19 2.5 | 26 9.3 | 79 20.6 | | | 820 71.7 | | 709 19.9 | 48 20.0 | 22 15.9 |
| 55 TO 64 | 361 8.9 | 320 12.1 | 9 1.2 | 11 3.9 | 21 5.5 | | | | 361 83.6 | 311 8.7 | 17 7.1 | 11 8.0 |
| 65 | 71 1.7 | 61 2.3 | 1 .1 | 4 1.4 | 5 1.3 | | | | 71 16.4 | 56 1.6 | 6 2.5 | 5 3.6 |
| NO ANSWER | 17 .4 | 10 .4 | 5 .7 | 2 .7 | | | | | | 4 .1 | 1 .4 | 1 .7 |
| SIGMA | 4066 99.9 | 2639 100.0 | 763 100.1 | 280 99.9 | 383 100.0 | 1547 100.0 | 927 100.0 | 1143 100.0 | 432 100.0 | 3559 100.0 | 240 100.1 | 138 100.0 |

TABLE 36

# Q. 36 WHAT IS YOUR AGE?

| | TOTAL | INCOME UNDER $10000 | $10-14999 | $15-24999 | $25000 & OVER | EDUC. LESS THAN H.S. GRAD | HIGH SCHL GRAD. | SOME COL-LEGE | COL-LEGE GRAD | SOME/COMPL POST GRAD. | OCC. PRO-FES-SION. | MANA-GER-IAL | OTHER WHITE COLLR | BLUE COLLR | RET'D, UNEMP, OTHER | STU-DENT |
|---|---|---|---|---|---|---|---|---|---|---|---|---|---|---|---|---|
| TOTAL RESPONDENTS | 4066 100.0 | 889 100.0 | 1178 100.0 | 1271 100.0 | 698 100.0 | 311 100.0 | 1038 100.0 | 1472 100.0 | 643 100.0 | 533 100.0 | 1028 100.0 | 658 100.0 | 523 100.0 | 729 100.0 | 544 100.0 | 472 100.0 |
| 18 TO 19 | 258 6.3 | 125 14.1 | 38 3.2 | 50 3.9 | 39 5.6 | 31 10.0 | 71 6.8 | 132 9.0 | 12 1.9 | 8 1.5 | 25 2.4 | 14 2.1 | 20 3.8 | 30 4.1 | 44 8.1 | 105 22.2 |
| 20 TO 29 | 1289 31.7 | 489 55.0 | 410 34.8 | 270 21.2 | 113 16.2 | 44 14.1 | 238 22.9 | 579 39.3 | 273 42.5 | 136 25.5 | 284 27.6 | 145 22.0 | 137 26.2 | 210 28.8 | 163 30.0 | 312 66.1 |
| 30 TO 39 | 927 22.8 | 102 11.5 | 256 21.7 | 380 29.9 | 187 26.8 | 46 14.8 | 222 21.4 | 305 20.7 | 142 22.1 | 199 37.3 | 323 31.4 | 173 26.3 | 124 23.7 | 168 23.0 | 88 16.2 | 33 7.0 |
| 40 TO 44 | 323 7.9 | 21 2.4 | 86 7.3 | 138 10.9 | 78 11.2 | 30 9.6 | 89 8.6 | 108 7.3 | 42 6.5 | 52 9.8 | 100 9.7 | 70 10.6 | 51 9.8 | 64 8.8 | 27 5.0 | 5 1.1 |
| 45 TO 54 | 820 20.2 | 84 9.4 | 241 20.5 | 301 23.7 | 191 27.4 | 87 28.0 | 256 24.7 | 237 16.1 | 138 21.5 | 92 17.3 | 218 21.2 | 183 27.8 | 124 23.7 | 176 24.1 | 95 17.5 | 14 3.0 |
| 55 TO 64 | 361 8.9 | 48 5.4 | 120 10.2 | 110 8.7 | 82 11.7 | 55 17.7 | 135 13.0 | 92 6.3 | 29 4.5 | 39 7.3 | 66 6.4 | 68 10.3 | 58 11.1 | 72 9.9 | 87 16.0 | 1 .2 |
| 65 | 71 1.7 | 18 2.0 | 26 2.2 | 20 1.6 | 7 1.0 | 17 5.5 | 24 2.3 | 17 1.2 | 6 .9 | 7 1.3 | 11 1.1 | 3 .5 | 8 1.5 | 8 1.1 | 39 7.2 | 1 .2 |
| NO ANSWER | 17 .4 | 2 .2 | 1 .1 | 2 .2 | 1 .1 | 1 .3 | 3 .3 | 2 .1 | 1 .2 | | 1 .1 | 2 .3 | 1 .2 | 1 .1 | 1 .2 | 1 .2 |
| SIGMA | 4066 99.9 | 889 100.0 | 1178 100.0 | 1271 100.1 | 698 100.0 | 311 100.0 | 1038 100.0 | 1472 100.0 | 643 100.1 | 533 100.0 | 1028 99.9 | 658 99.9 | 523 100.0 | 729 99.9 | 544 100.2 | 472 100.0 |

Q. 37 WHAT IS YOUR RACIAL BACKGROUND?

TABLE 37

| | TOTAL | MARITAL STATUS | | | | AGE | | | | RACE | | |
|---|---|---|---|---|---|---|---|---|---|---|---|---|
| | | MARR'D LIVING WITH WIFE | NEVER MARR'D LIVING W/O PARTNR | LIVING WITH UN-PARTNR MARR'D | DIVRCE OR WIDOWD LIVING ALONE | 18-29 | 30-39 | 40-54 | 55-65 | WHITE | BLACK | OTHER |
| TOTAL RESPONDENTS | 4066 100.0 | 2639 100.0 | 763 100.0 | 280 100.0 | 383 100.0 | 1547 100.0 | 927 100.0 | 1143 100.0 | 432 100.0 | 3559 100.0 | 240 100.0 | 138 100.0 |
| WHITE | 3559 87.5 | 2313 87.6 | 670 87.8 | 245 87.5 | 330 86.2 | 1378 89.1 | 818 88.2 | 992 86.8 | 367 85.0 | 3559 100.0 | | |
| BLACK | 240 5.9 | 156 5.9 | 42 5.5 | 15 5.4 | 27 7.0 | 93 6.0 | 52 5.6 | 71 6.2 | 23 5.3 | | 240 100.0 | |
| OTHER | 138 3.4 | 84 3.2 | 28 3.7 | 14 5.0 | 12 3.1 | 56 3.6 | 36 3.9 | 29 2.5 | 16 3.7 | | | 138 100.0 |
| NO ANSWER | 129 3.2 | 86 3.3 | 23 3.0 | 6 2.1 | 14 3.7 | 20 1.3 | 21 2.3 | 51 4.5 | 26 6.0 | | | |
| SIGMA | 4066 100.0 | 2639 100.0 | 763 100.0 | 280 100.0 | 383 100.0 | 1547 100.0 | 927 100.0 | 1143 100.0 | 432 100.0 | 3559 100.0 | 240 100.0 | 138 100.0 |

Q. 37 WHAT IS YOUR RACIAL BACKGROUND?

TABLE 37

| | TOTAL | INCOME | | | | EDUCATION | | | | | OCCUPATION | | | | | |
|---|---|---|---|---|---|---|---|---|---|---|---|---|---|---|---|---|
| | | UNDER $10000 | $10-14999 | $15-24999 | $25000 & OVER | LESS THAN H.S. GRAD | HIGH SCHL GRAD | SOME COL-LEGE | COL-LEGE GRAD GRAD. | SOME/ COMPL POST GRAD. | PRO-FES-SION. | MANA-GER-IAL | OTHER WHITE COLLR | WHITE BLUE COLLR | RET'D, UNEMP, OTHER | STU-DENT |
| TOTAL RESPONDENTS | 4066 100.0 | 889 100.0 | 1178 100.0 | 1271 100.0 | 698 100.0 | 311 100.0 | 1038 100.0 | 1472 100.0 | 643 100.0 | 533 100.0 | 1028 100.0 | 658 100.0 | 523 100.0 | 729 100.0 | 544 100.0 | 472 100.0 |
| WHITE | 3559 87.5 | 713 80.2 | 1025 87.0 | 1159 91.2 | 645 92.4 | 253 81.4 | 880 84.8 | 1323 89.9 | 577 89.7 | 488 91.6 | 939 91.3 | 602 91.5 | 469 89.7 | 616 84.5 | 445 81.8 | 406 86.0 |
| BLACK | 240 5.9 | 92 10.3 | 80 6.8 | 44 3.5 | 22 3.2 | 31 10.0 | 81 7.8 | 77 5.2 | 30 4.7 | 15 2.8 | 43 4.2 | 24 3.6 | 17 3.3 | 60 8.2 | 60 11.0 | 30 6.4 |
| OTHER | 138 3.4 | 63 7.1 | 36 3.1 | 24 1.9 | 15 2.1 | 14 4.5 | 34 3.3 | 41 2.8 | 23 3.6 | 22 4.1 | 20 1.9 | 12 1.8 | 16 3.1 | 28 3.8 | 23 4.2 | 33 7.0 |
| NO ANSWER | 129 3.2 | 21 2.4 | 37 3.1 | 44 3.5 | 16 2.3 | 13 4.2 | 43 4.1 | 31 2.1 | 13 2.0 | 8 1.5 | 26 2.5 | 20 3.0 | 21 4.0 | 25 3.4 | 16 2.9 | 3 .6 |
| SIGMA | 4066 100.0 | 889 100.0 | 1178 100.0 | 1271 100.1 | 698 100.0 | 311 100.1 | 1038 100.0 | 1472 100.0 | 643 100.0 | 533 100.0 | 1028 99.9 | 658 99.9 | 523 100.1 | 729 99.9 | 544 99.9 | 472 100.0 |

TABLE 38

Q. 38 WHAT IS YOUR TOTAL AMOUNT OF SCHOOLING?

| | TOTAL | MARITAL STATUS | | | | AGE | | | | RACE | | |
|---|---|---|---|---|---|---|---|---|---|---|---|---|
| | | MARR'D LIVING WITH WIFE | NEVER MARR'D LIVING W/O PARTNR | LIVING WITH UN-MARR'D PARTNR | DIVRCE OR WIDOWD LIVING ALONE | 18-29 | 30-39 | 40-54 | 55-65 | WHITE | BLACK | OTHER |
| TOTAL RESPONDENTS | 4066 100.0 | 2639 100.0 | 763 100.0 | 280 100.0 | 383 100.0 | 1547 100.0 | 927 100.0 | 1143 100.0 | 432 100.0 | 3559 100.0 | 240 100.0 | 138 100.0 |
| LESS THAN GRAMMAR SCHOOL GRADUATE | 31 .8 | 23 .9 | 7 .9 | | 1 .3 | 12 .8 | 2 .2 | 4 .3 | 12 2.8 | 23 .6 | 4 1.7 | 3 2.2 |
| GRAMMAR SCHOOL GRADUATE | 42 1.0 | 31 1.2 | 3 .4 | 3 1.1 | 5 1.3 | 8 .5 | 4 .4 | 16 1.4 | 14 3.2 | 34 1.0 | 3 1.3 | 3 2.2 |
| LESS THAN HIGH SCHOOL GRADUATE | 238 5.9 | 171 6.5 | 25 3.3 | 14 5.0 | 28 7.3 | 55 3.6 | 40 4.3 | 97 8.5 | 46 10.6 | 196 5.5 | 24 10.0 | 8 5.8 |
| HIGH SCHOOL GRADUATE | 1038 25.5 | 743 28.2 | 118 15.5 | 76 27.1 | 100 26.1 | 309 20.0 | 222 23.9 | 345 30.2 | 159 36.8 | 880 24.7 | 81 33.8 | 34 24.6 |
| SOME COLLEGE | 1472 36.2 | 835 31.6 | 394 51.6 | 108 38.6 | 135 35.2 | 711 46.0 | 305 32.9 | 345 30.2 | 109 25.2 | 1323 37.2 | 77 32.1 | 41 29.7 |
| COLLEGE GRADUATE | 643 15.8 | 406 15.4 | 134 17.6 | 46 16.4 | 57 14.9 | 285 18.4 | 142 15.3 | 180 15.7 | 35 8.1 | 577 16.2 | 30 12.5 | 23 16.7 |
| SOME POST GRADUATE | 244 6.0 | 171 6.5 | 33 4.3 | 16 5.7 | 24 6.3 | 85 5.5 | 70 7.6 | 65 5.7 | 24 5.6 | 225 6.3 | 8 3.3 | 9 6.5 |
| POST GRADUATE DEGREE(S) | 289 7.1 | 215 8.1 | 33 4.3 | 15 5.4 | 26 6.8 | 59 3.8 | 129 13.9 | 79 6.9 | 22 5.1 | 263 7.4 | 7 2.9 | 13 9.4 |
| NO ANSWER | 69 1.7 | 44 1.7 | 16 2.1 | 2 .7 | 7 1.8 | 23 1.5 | 13 1.4 | 12 1.0 | 11 2.5 | 38 1.1 | 6 2.5 | 4 2.9 |
| SIGMA | 4066 100.0 | 2639 100.1 | 763 100.0 | 280 100.0 | 383 100.0 | 1547 100.1 | 927 99.9 | 1143 99.9 | 432 99.9 | 3559 100.0 | 240 100.1 | 138 100.0 |

Q. 38 WHAT IS YOUR TOTAL AMOUNT OF SCHOOLING?　　　　　　　　　　TABLE 38

| | TOTAL | INCOME UNDER $10000 | INCOME $10-14999 | INCOME $15-24999 | INCOME $25000 & OVER | EDU LESS THAN H.S. GRAD. | EDU HIGH SCHL GRAD. | EDU SOME COLLEGE | EDU COLLEGE GRAD GRAD. | EDU SOME/COMPL POST GRAD. | OCC PRO-FESSION. | OCC MANA-GERIAL | OCC OTHER WHITE COLLR | OCC BLUE COLLR | OCC RET'D, UNEMP, OTHER | OCC STU-DENT |
|---|---|---|---|---|---|---|---|---|---|---|---|---|---|---|---|---|
| TOTAL RESPONDENTS | 4066 / 100.0 | 889 / 100.0 | 1178 / 100.0 | 1271 / 100.0 | 698 / 100.0 | 311 / 100.0 | 1038 / 100.0 | 1472 / 100.0 | 643 / 100.0 | 533 / 100.0 | 1028 / 100.0 | 658 / 100.0 | 523 / 100.0 | 729 / 100.0 | 544 / 100.0 | 472 / 100.0 |
| LESS THAN GRAMMAR SCHOOL GRADUATE | 31 / .8 | 20 / 2.2 | 5 / .4 | 5 / .4 | 1 / .1 | 31 / 10.0 | | | | | 6 / .6 | 2 / .3 | 2 / .4 | 2 / .3 | 16 / 2.9 | 2 / .4 |
| GRAMMAR SCHOOL GRADUATE | 42 / 1.0 | 17 / 1.9 | 15 / 1.3 | 6 / .5 | 4 / .6 | 42 / 13.5 | | | | | 11 / 1.1 | 4 / .6 | 3 / .6 | 8 / 1.1 | 14 / 2.6 | |
| LESS THAN HIGH SCHOOL GRADUATE | 238 / 5.9 | 77 / 8.7 | 94 / 8.0 | 50 / 3.9 | 16 / 2.3 | 238 / 76.5 | | | | | 35 / 3.4 | 29 / 4.4 | 17 / 3.3 | 75 / 10.3 | 71 / 13.1 | 6 / 1.3 |
| HIGH SCHOOL GRADUATE | 1038 / 25.5 | 243 / 27.3 | 394 / 33.4 | 316 / 24.9 | 82 / 11.7 | | 1038 / 100.0 | | | | 166 / 16.1 | 115 / 17.5 | 162 / 31.0 | 349 / 47.9 | 206 / 37.9 | 22 / 4.7 |
| SOME COLLEGE | 1472 / 36.2 | 345 / 38.8 | 419 / 35.6 | 494 / 38.9 | 205 / 29.4 | | | 1472 / 100.0 | | | 268 / 26.1 | 246 / 37.4 | 211 / 40.3 | 240 / 32.9 | 152 / 27.9 | 307 / 65.0 |
| COLLEGE GRADUATE | 643 / 15.8 | 118 / 13.3 | 151 / 12.8 | 207 / 16.3 | 163 / 23.4 | | | | 643 / 100.0 | | 210 / 20.4 | 160 / 24.3 | 86 / 16.4 | 36 / 4.9 | 59 / 10.8 | 81 / 17.2 |
| SOME POST GRADUATE | 244 / 6.0 | 33 / 3.7 | 47 / 4.0 | 87 / 6.8 | 76 / 10.9 | | | | | 244 / 45.8 | 112 / 10.9 | 57 / 8.7 | 20 / 3.8 | 5 / .7 | 13 / 2.4 | 32 / 6.8 |
| POST GRADUATE DEGREE(S) | 289 / 7.1 | 25 / 2.8 | 33 / 2.8 | 92 / 7.2 | 139 / 19.9 | | | | | 289 / 54.2 | 201 / 19.6 | 37 / 5.6 | 15 / 2.9 | 5 / .7 | 9 / 1.7 | 20 / 4.2 |
| NO ANSWER | 69 / 1.7 | 11 / 1.2 | 20 / 1.7 | 14 / 1.1 | 12 / 1.7 | | | | | | 19 / 1.8 | 8 / 1.2 | 7 / 1.3 | 9 / 1.2 | 4 / .7 | 2 / .4 |
| SIGMA | 4066 / 100.0 | 889 / 99.9 | 1178 / 100.0 | 1271 / 100.0 | 698 / 100.0 | 311 / 100.0 | 1038 / 100.0 | 1472 / 100.0 | 643 / 100.0 | 533 / 100.0 | 1028 / 100.0 | 658 / 100.0 | 523 / 100.0 | 729 / 100.0 | 544 / 100.0 | 472 / 100.0 |

Q. 39 WHAT WAS THE APPROXIMATE TOTAL INCOME OF YOUR HOUSEHOLD BEFORE TAXES IN 1976?

TABLE 39

| | TOTAL | MARITAL STATUS | | | | AGE | | | | RACE | | |
|---|---|---|---|---|---|---|---|---|---|---|---|---|
| | | MARR'D LIVING WITH WIFE | NEVER MARR'D LIVING W/O PARTNR | LIVING WITH PARTNR UN-MARR'D | DIVRCE OR WIDOWD LIVING ALONE | 18-29 | 30-39 | 40-54 | 55-65 | WHITE | BLACK | OTHER |
| TOTAL RESPONDENTS | 4066 100.0 | 2639 100.0 | 763 100.0 | 280 100.0 | 383 100.0 | 1547 100.0 | 927 100.0 | 1143 100.0 | 432 100.0 | 3559 100.0 | 240 100.0 | 138 100.0 |
| UNDER $8,000 | 541 13.3 | 159 6.0 | 249 32.6 | 57 20.4 | 76 19.8 | 421 27.2 | 46 5.0 | 40 3.5 | 33 7.6 | 442 12.4 | 46 19.2 | 42 30.4 |
| $8,000 TO $9,999 | 348 8.6 | 177 6.7 | 93 12.2 | 43 15.4 | 35 9.1 | 193 12.5 | 56 6.0 | 65 5.7 | 33 7.6 | 271 7.6 | 46 19.2 | 21 15.2 |
| $10,000 TO $14,999 | 1178 29.0 | 779 29.5 | 174 22.8 | 98 35.0 | 127 33.2 | 448 29.0 | 256 27.6 | 327 28.6 | 146 33.8 | 1025 28.8 | 80 33.3 | 36 26.1 |
| $15,000 TO $24,999 | 1271 31.3 | 984 37.3 | 137 18.0 | 56 20.0 | 94 24.5 | 320 20.7 | 380 41.0 | 439 38.4 | 130 30.1 | 1159 32.6 | 44 18.3 | 24 17.4 |
| $25,000 AND OVER | 698 17.2 | 526 19.9 | 98 12.8 | 25 8.9 | 48 12.5 | 152 9.8 | 187 20.2 | 269 23.5 | 89 20.6 | 645 18.1 | 22 9.2 | 15 10.9 |
| NO ANSWER | 30 .7 | 14 .5 | 12 1.6 | 1 .4 | 3 .8 | 13 .8 | 2 .2 | 3 .3 | 1 .2 | 17 .5 | 2 .8 | 2 .8 |
| SIGMA | 4066 100.1 | 2639 99.9 | 763 100.0 | 280 100.1 | 383 99.9 | 1547 100.0 | 927 100.0 | 1143 100.0 | 432 99.9 | 3559 100.0 | 240 100.0 | 138 100.0 |

Q. 39 WHAT WAS THE APPROXIMATE TOTAL INCOME OF YOUR HOUSEHOLD BEFORE TAXES IN 1976?

TABLE 39

| | TOTAL | INCOME | | | | EDUCATION | | | | | OCCUPATION | | | | | |
|---|---|---|---|---|---|---|---|---|---|---|---|---|---|---|---|---|
| | | UNDER $10000 | $10-14999 | $15-24999 | $25000 & OVER | LESS THAN H.S. GRAD | HIGH SCHL GRAD | SOME COL-LEGE | COL-LEGE GRAD | SOME/COMPL POST GRAD GRAD | PRO-FES-SION. | MANA-GER-IAL | OTHER WHITE COLLR | BLUE COLLR | RET'D, UNEMP, OTHER | STU-DENT |
| TOTAL RESPONDENTS | 4066 100.0 | 889 100.0 | 1178 100.0 | 1271 100.0 | 698 100.0 | 311 100.0 | 1038 100.9 | 1472 100.0 | 643 100.0 | 533 100.0 | 1028 100.0 | 658 100.0 | 523 100.0 | 729 100.0 | 544 100.0 | 472 100.0 |
| UNDER $8,000 | 541 13.3 | 541 60.9 | | | | 69 22.2 | 111 10.7 | 239 16.2 | 76 11.8 | 42 7.9 | 63 6.1 | 15 2.3 | 21 4.0 | 56 7.7 | 125 23.0 | 242 51.3 |
| $8,000 TO $9,999 | 348 8.6 | 348 39.1 | | | | 45 14.5 | 132 12.7 | 106 7.2 | 42 6.5 | 16 3.0 | 46 4.5 | 25 3.8 | 48 9.2 | 80 11.0 | 93 17.1 | 46 9.7 |
| $10,000 TO $14,999 | 1178 29.0 | | 1178 100.0 | | | 114 36.7 | 394 38.0 | 419 28.5 | 151 23.5 | 80 15.0 | 240 23.3 | 166 25.2 | 180 34.4 | 323 44.3 | 172 31.6 | 74 15.7 |
| $15,000 TO $24,999 | 1271 31.3 | | | 1271 100.0 | | 61 19.6 | 316 30.4 | 494 33.6 | 207 32.2 | 179 33.6 | 369 35.9 | 274 41.6 | 204 39.0 | 231 31.7 | 107 19.7 | 59 12.5 |
| $25,000 AND OVER | 698 17.2 | | | | 698 100.0 | 21 6.8 | 92 7.9 | 205 13.9 | 163 25.3 | 215 40.3 | 306 29.8 | 176 26.7 | 69 13.2 | 38 5.2 | 43 7.9 | 49 10.4 |
| NO ANSWER | 30 .7 | | | | | 1 .3 | 3 .3 | 9 .6 | 4 .6 | 1 .2 | 4 .4 | 2 .3 | 1 .2 | 1 .1 | 4 .7 | 2 .4 |
| SIGMA | 4066 100.1 | 889 100.0 | 1178 100.0 | 1271 100.0 | 698 100.0 | 311 100.1 | 1038 100.0 | 1472 100.0 | 643 99.9 | 533 100.0 | 1028 100.0 | 658 99.9 | 523 100.0 | 729 100.0 | 544 100.0 | 472 100.0 |

TABLE 40

Q. 40 WHAT TYPE OF JOB DO YOU CURRENTLY HOLD?

| | TOTAL | MARITAL STATUS | | | | AGE | | | | RACE | | |
|---|---|---|---|---|---|---|---|---|---|---|---|---|
| | | MARR'D LIVING WITH WIFE | NEVER MARR'D LIVING W/O PARTNR | LIVING WITH PARTNR UN-MARR'D | DIVRCE OR WIDOWD LIVING ALONE | 18-29 | 30-39 | 40-54 | 55-65 | WHITE | BLACK | OTHER |
| TOTAL RESPONDENTS | 4066 100.0 | 2639 100.0 | 763 100.0 | 280 100.0 | 383 100.0 | 1547 100.0 | 927 100.0 | 1143 100.0 | 432 100.0 | 3559 100.0 | 240 100.0 | 138 100.0 |
| PROFESSIONAL | 1028 25.3 | 750 28.4 | 130 17.0 | 61 21.8 | 87 22.7 | 309 20.0 | 323 34.8 | 318 27.8 | 77 17.8 | 939 26.4 | 43 17.9 | 20 14.5 |
| MANAGERIAL | 658 16.2 | 509 19.3 | 55 7.2 | 43 15.4 | 51 13.3 | 159 10.3 | 173 18.7 | 253 22.1 | 71 16.4 | 602 16.9 | 24 10.0 | 12 8.7 |
| OTHER WHITE COLLAR | 523 12.9 | 364 13.8 | 78 10.2 | 34 12.1 | 47 12.3 | 157 10.1 | 124 13.4 | 175 15.3 | 66 15.3 | 469 13.2 | 17 7.1 | 16 11.6 |
| BLUE COLLAR | 729 17.9 | 519 19.7 | 106 13.9 | 49 17.5 | 55 14.4 | 240 15.5 | 168 18.1 | 240 21.0 | 80 18.5 | 616 17.3 | 60 25.0 | 28 20.3 |
| RETIRED | 125 3.1 | 95 3.6 | 3 .4 | 10 3.6 | 17 4.4 | 8 .5 | 2 .2 | 22 1.9 | 92 21.3 | 101 2.8 | 8 3.3 | 6 4.3 |
| UNEMPLOYED | 142 3.5 | 68 2.6 | 37 4.8 | 13 4.6 | 24 6.3 | 77 5.0 | 24 2.6 | 27 2.4 | 14 3.2 | 114 3.2 | 20 8.3 | 5 3.6 |
| STUDENT | 472 11.6 | 107 4.1 | 266 34.9 | 41 14.6 | 57 14.9 | 417 27.0 | 33 3.6 | 19 1.7 | 2 .5 | 406 11.4 | 30 12.5 | 33 23.9 |
| OTHER | 277 6.8 | 178 6.7 | 45 5.9 | 20 7.1 | 34 8.9 | 122 7.9 | 62 6.7 | 73 6.4 | 20 4.6 | 230 6.5 | 32 13.3 | 12 8.7 |
| NO ANSWER | 112 2.8 | 49 1.9 | 43 5.6 | 9 3.2 | 11 2.9 | 58 3.7 | 18 1.9 | 16 1.4 | 10 2.3 | 82 2.3 | 6 2.5 | 6 4.3 |
| SIGMA | 4066 100.1 | 2639 100.1 | 763 99.9 | 280 99.9 | 383 100.1 | 1547 100.0 | 927 100.0 | 1143 100.0 | 432 99.9 | 3559 100.0 | 240 99.9 | 138 99.9 |

TABLE 40

# Q. 40 WHAT TYPE OF JOB DO YOU CURRENTLY HOLD?

| | TOTAL | INCOME UNDER $10000 | $10-14999 | $15-24999 | $25000 & OVER | LESS THAN H.S. GRAD | HIGH SCHL GRAD | SOME COLLEGE | COLLEGE GRAD | SOME/COMPL POST GRAD | PRO-FESSIONAL | MANAGERIAL | OTHER WHITE COLLR | BLUE COLLR | RET'D, UNEMP, OTHER | STUDENT |
|---|---|---|---|---|---|---|---|---|---|---|---|---|---|---|---|---|
| | | | | | | | | | | | | | | | | |
| TOTAL RESPONDENTS | 4066 100.0 | 889 100.0 | 1178 100.0 | 1271 100.0 | 698 100.0 | 311 100.0 | 1038 100.0 | 1472 100.0 | 643 100.0 | 533 100.0 | 1028 100.0 | 658 100.0 | 523 100.0 | 729 100.0 | 544 100.0 | 472 100.0 |
| PROFESSIONAL | 1028 25.3 | 109 12.3 | 240 20.4 | 369 29.0 | 306 43.8 | 52 16.7 | 166 16.0 | 268 18.2 | 210 32.7 | 313 58.7 | 1028 100.0 | | | | | |
| MANAGERIAL | 658 16.2 | 40 4.5 | 166 14.1 | 274 21.6 | 176 25.2 | 35 11.3 | 115 11.1 | 246 16.7 | 160 24.9 | 94 17.6 | | 658 100.0 | | | | |
| OTHER WHITE COLLAR | 523 12.9 | 69 7.8 | 180 15.3 | 204 16.1 | 69 9.9 | 22 7.1 | 162 15.6 | 211 14.3 | 86 13.4 | 35 6.6 | | | 523 100.0 | | | |
| BLUE COLLAR | 729 17.9 | 136 15.3 | 323 27.4 | 231 18.2 | 38 5.4 | 85 27.3 | 349 33.6 | 240 16.3 | 36 5.6 | 10 1.9 | | | | 729 100.0 | | |
| RETIRED | 125 3.1 | 41 4.6 | 49 4.2 | 23 1.8 | 12 1.7 | 36 11.6 | 48 4.6 | 26 1.8 | 10 1.6 | 5 .9 | | | | | 125 23.0 | |
| UNEMPLOYED | 142 3.5 | 76 8.5 | 35 3.0 | 20 1.6 | 9 1.3 | 27 8.7 | 44 4.2 | 43 2.9 | 21 3.3 | 5 .9 | | | | | 142 26.1 | |
| STUDENT | 472 11.6 | 288 32.4 | 74 6.3 | 59 4.6 | 49 7.0 | 8 2.6 | 22 2.1 | 307 20.9 | 81 12.6 | 52 9.8 | | | | | | 472 100.0 |
| OTHER | 277 6.8 | 101 11.4 | 88 7.5 | 64 5.0 | 22 3.2 | 38 12.2 | 114 11.0 | 83 5.6 | 28 4.4 | 12 2.3 | | | | | 277 50.9 | |
| NO ANSWER | 112 2.8 | 29 3.3 | 23 2.0 | 27 2.1 | 17 2.4 | 8 2.6 | 18 1.7 | 48 3.3 | 11 1.7 | 7 1.3 | | | | | | |
| SIGMA | 4066 100.1 | 889 100.1 | 1178 100.2 | 1271 100.0 | 698 99.9 | 311 100.1 | 1038 99.9 | 1472 100.0 | 643 100.2 | 533 100.0 | 1028 100.0 | 658 100.0 | 523 100.0 | 729 100.0 | 544 100.0 | 472 100.0 |

INCOME — EDUCATION — OCCUPATION

# Index